Redress for Victims of Crimes Under International Law

Ilaria Bottigliero

Redress for Victims of Crimes Under International Law

2004

Springer-Science+Business Media, B.V.

A C.I.P. Catalogue record for this book is available from the Library of Congress.

Printed on acid-free paper.

ISBN 978-90-04-13884-1 ISBN 978-94-017-6027-0 (eBook)
DOI 10.1007/978-94-017-6027-0

Originally published by Koninklijke Brill NV, Leiden, The Netherlands in 2004
Softcover reprint of the hardcover 1st edition 2004

To my dear Lyal, with all my love and admiration

TABLE OF CONTENTS

Acknowledgements xiii
Table of Treaties, Draft Conventions and Declarations xv
Table of International Cases xix
Table of Domestic Cases xxiii
Table of Domestic Legislation xxv

CHAPTER I Introduction 1
1. A Word about Key Terms and Concepts 4
a. 'Redress' 4
b. 'Victims' 6
c. 'Crimes under International Law' 7
2. Structure of the Book 11

CHAPTER II Origins of the Victims' Right to Redress: The Historical Swing from Restoration to Retribution and Back to Restoration 13
1. Legal Justice and Victims' Redress in Pre-Roman Civilizations and in Some of the Main Religious Traditions 14
2. Victims' Redress in Roman Law 18
3. The Shift to Retribution During the Middle Ages 23
4. Back to Restoration: The Right to Redress in Two Contemporary Examples 25
a. Reparations for Crime Victims in Europe and the European Convention on the Compensation of Victims of Violent Crimes 25
b. Redress in Native North American Indian Justice Systems: A Holistic Approach 32
5. From Retributive Justice to Restorative Justice: A Necessary Passage? 34

CHAPTER III The Victims' Right to Redress as Exercised in Domestic Fora 39

1. Strengths and Weaknesses of Domestic Jurisdiction over Crimes under International Law 40
   - a. A Reading of the Passive Personality Principle in the Light of the *Pinochet Case* 42
   - b. Can Victims Rely on Universal Jurisdiction? 46
   - c. The Example of the US Alien Tort Claims Act (ATCA) 52
   - d. Class Actions under the ATCA 57
     - *i.* *The Marcos Litigation* 58
     - *ii.* *The Karadzic Case* 60
   - e. Domestic Litigation under the ATCA and the Torture Victim Protection Act (TVPA): Is This an Effective Forum for Obtaining Victims' Redress? 62
2. Recognition and Enforcement of Foreign Judgments on Crimes under International Law: A Challenge for the Future 66
   - a. The Brussels and Lugano Conventions 67
   - b. Prospects for the Application of the Preliminary Draft Convention on Jurisdiction and Foreign Judgments in Civil and Commercial Matters (The Draft Hague Convention) 68
3. The Way Ahead 77

CHAPTER IV State-Based Reparations 79

1. State Responsibility and Inter-State Reparations: The Traditional Framework 79
2. Individual Victims as Direct Beneficiaries of State Reparations 82
3. Individual Redress Based on State Responsibility: The Unique Example of the UN Compensation Commission and Compensation Fund for Claims Against Iraq 89

4. The Role of the State in Providing Quasi-Judicial and Non-Judicial Symbolic Redress 95
a. Redress in a Broader Framework: Truth Commissions and Truth-finding Mechanisms . 103
i. *Argentina* 104
ii. *Chile* 105
iii. *El Salvador* 106
iv. *South Africa* 107
b. Is it Sufficient to Learn the Truth? 109

CHAPTER V Evolution of the Victims' Right to Redress through International Human Rights Law, Jurisprudence and Standards 111
1. Universal Human Rights Treaties: An Indirect Approach to Reparations 112
a. Redress for Violations of the International Covenant on Civil and Political Rights in the Practice of the United Nations Human Rights Committee 113
i. *The Duty to Investigate the Violation* . 116
ii. *The Duty to Prosecute and Punish those Responsible* 118
iii. *The Incompatibility between Amnesty Laws and the Right to a Remedy* 120
b. Redress in the Convention against Torture and Other Cruel, Inhuman or Degrading Treatment or Punishment 123
c. Redress in Other Human Rights Instruments . . 125
2. Regional Human Rights Standards 128
a. Africa 128
b. The Americas 133
i. *The Legal Basis for the Victims' Right to Redress in the American Convention* 136
ii. *The Extent of the Victims' Right to Redress* 139
iii. *The Execution of Judicial Awards* 144

c. Europe ... 146
i. The Extent of the Right to a Remedy under Article 13 of the European Convention ... 147
ii. 'Just Satisfaction' under Article 41 of the European Convention: A 'Safety Net' for Victims ... 152
d. Asian National Standards ... 159
i. 'Asian Values' ... 160
ii. Domestic Implementation of the Victims' Right to Redress in Asia: The Example of India ... 165
3. UN Standards ... 167
a. The Durban Declaration and Programme of Action ... 172
b. The Contribution of Special Rapporteurs and Independent Experts of the UN Commission on Human Rights ... 179
i. The van Boven 'Basic Principles and Guidelines' ... 179
ii. The Bassiouni Revised 'Principles and Guidelines' ... 180
iii. Further Action on Redress of the UN Commission on Human Rights and Sub-Commission on the Promotion and Protection of Human Rights ... 182
c. UN Sponsored *Ad Hoc* Redress Mechanisms ... 185
4. The Contribution of *Ad Hoc* Judicial Human Rights Bodies: The Case of the Human Rights Chamber for Bosnia and Herzegovina ... 185
5. Summing Up ... 190

CHAPTER VI Victims' Redress in International Criminal Law: Current Mechanisms and Future Prospects ... 193
1. The Victims' Right to Reparation in the International Criminal Tribunals for the Former Yugoslavia and for Rwanda ... 196
a. The Tribunals' Restitution Scheme ... 196
b. The Tribunals' Indirect Approach to Compensation ... 200

c. Implementing ICTY and ICTR Redress Provisions: The Denial of a Right or Simply Too Difficult a Task? 202
i. *The Response of the ICTY to the Question of Victims' Redress* 205
ii. *The Response of the ICTR to the Question of Victims' Redress* 207
d. What Role for the Victims Aside From Being Witnesses? 209
e. Enjoying the Right to Redress in the ICTY and ICTR: A Lost Cause for Victims? 211
2. The Role of Victims and Their Right to Redress in the International Criminal Court 212
a. The Three Pillars of the ICC Reparation Regime 215
i. *Ensuring Effective Victims' Participation in the ICC: A Question of Procedure* 215
ii. *ICC Reparation Mechanisms and the Establishment of a Trust Fund* 222
iii. *The Role and Functions of the Victims and Witnesses Unit* 233
b. The Principle of Complementarity *vis-à-vis* Victims' Redress: What Happens If Domestic Courts Are Unable or Unwilling to Provide Redress? 235
c. Implementation and Support Provisions of the ICC Reparation Regime 238
d. ICC Reparation Awards in Practice: Where International Law Meets Private Law 239
3. The 'Value Added' of the ICC 242

CHAPTER VII Towards a Comprehensive Redress Regime for Victims of Crimes under International Law 249

Bibliography 255
Index 295

ACKNOWLEDGMENTS

This book is a revised version of my Doctorate thesis which I completed at the Graduate Institute of International Studies, Geneva, Switzerland. I wish to express my deep gratitude to Professors Andrew Clapham and Vera Gowlland for their guidance, insight and encouragement over the years in supervising my work. I wish to thank Professor Georges Abi-Saab, Honorary Professor at the Graduate Institute, for his constant support. Many thanks go also to Professor Peter Malanczuk of the City University of Hong Kong for his helpful comments on State responsibility. Professor Theo van Boven of the University of Maastricht has provided me with valuable advice on the final draft, and I wish to thank him for having agreed to act as External Examiner at my Doctorate defence. I am immensely grateful to my husband, Professor Lyal S. Sunga of the University of Hong Kong, who followed this project with love and care from its very first draft to its final version and shared his expertise and precious foresight with wonderful generosity. He has been and continues to be a source of great inspiration for me. Finally, I wish to thank my parents Enzo and Marcella for their constant and loving support, my sister Francesca and little Chiara, who brought joy and happiness to our lives.

I have tried to take into account all relevant facts and events that occurred prior to November 2003. Responsibility for any shortcomings in the book remains solely mine.

Ilaria Bottigliero
November 2003
Hong Kong, China

TABLE OF TREATIES, DRAFT CONVENTIONS AND DECLARATIONS

1864 Convention for the Amelioration of the Condition of the Wounded in Armies in the Field . . . 193

1872 Draft Convention for the Establishment of an International Judicial Body Suitable for the Prevention and Punishment of Violations of the Geneva Convention . . . 194

1907 Convention Relative to the Creation of an International Prize Court (Hague Convention No. XII) . . . 83

1907 Convention Respecting the Laws and Customs of War on Land (Hague Convention No. IV) . . . 82

1919 Treaty of Versailles . . . 84

1922 Convention for the Protection of Minorities . . . 84

1925 Protocol for the Prohibition of the Use in War of Asphyxiating, Poisonous or Other Gases, and of Bacteriological Methods of Warfare . . . 2, 85

1935 Harvard Research Draft Convention on Jurisdiction with Respect to Crime . . . 41

1945 London Agreement Concerning the Prosecution and Trial of the Major War Criminals of the Axis Powers . . . 7, 195

1948 American Declaration of Rights and Duties of Man . . . 134

1948 UN Convention on the Prevention and Punishment of the Crime of Genocide . . . 8, 9, 41, 52, 186, 195

1948 Universal Declaration of Human Rights . . . 112, 134, 161, 165, 167

1949 Geneva Conventions . . . 8, 9, 41, 48, 52, 61, 82, 186, 197

1950 European Convention for the Protection of Human Rights and Fundamental Freedoms . . . 30, 146, 147, 152, 154, 158, 186

1951 Convention Relating to the Status of Refugees . . . 187

1951 San Francisco Peace Treaty . . . 2, 86, 102

1957 Convention on the Nationality of Married Women . . . 187

1957 Treaty of Rome Establishing the European Economic Community (EEC) . . . 27

1961 Convention on the Reduction of Statelessness . . . 187

1963 UN Declaration on the Elimination of All Forms of Racial Discrimination . . . 127

1963 Vienna Convention on Consular Relations . . . 81, 87

1965 International Convention on the Elimination of All Forms of Racial Discrimination 127, 128, 187
1966 International Covenant on Civil and Political Rights 113-123, 146, 167, 187, 206
1966 International Covenant on Economic, Social and Cultural Rights 125, 187
1966 Optional Protocol to the International Covenant on Civil and Political Rights 115, 187
1966 Protocol to the Convention Relating to the Status of Refugees . 187
1968 Brussels Convention 67, 68
1968 Convention on the Non-Applicability of Statutory Limitations to War Crimes and Crimes against Humanity 173
1969 American Convention on Human Rights 120, 134-145
1970 Hague Convention for the Suppression of Unlawful Seizure of Aircraft 48, 51
1973 International Convention on the Suppression and Punishment of the Crime of Apartheid 48, 128
1974 European Convention on the Non-Applicability of Statutory Limitations to Crimes against Humanity and War Crimes 173
1975 UN Declaration on the Protection of all Persons from Being Subjected to Torture and Other Cruel, Inhuman or Degrading Treatment or Punishment 169
1977 Protocol I Additional to the four Geneva Conventions of 12 August 1949 and Relating to the Protection of Victims of International Armed Conflicts (Additional Protocol I) 82, 186
1977 Protocol Additional to the Geneva Conventions of 12 August 1949 and Relating to the Protection of Victims of Non-International Armed Conflicts (Additional Protocol II) 8, 186, 197
1978 UN Declaration on Race and Racial Prejudice 128, 169
1979 International Convention Against the Taking of Hostages 51
1979 UN Convention on the Elimination of All Forms of Discrimination against Women 187
1981 African [Banjul] Charter on Human and People's Rights 129, 130, 132
1983 European Convention on the Compensation of Victims of Violent Crimes 25, 26, 28, 30

1984 UN Convention against Torture and Other Cruel, Inhuman or Degrading Treatment or Punishment 9, 46, 48, 49, 51, 59, 123, 124, 149, 187
1985 Inter-American Convention to Prevent and Punish Torture 135
1985 UN Declaration of Basic Principles of Justice for Victims of Crime and Abuse of Power 6, 89, 168, 169, 172, 181, 228
1985 UN Standard Minimum Rules for the Administration of Juvenile Justice (Beijing Rules) 169
1987 European Convention on the Prevention of Torture and Inhuman or Degrading Treatment or Punishment 187
1988 Body of Principles for the Protection of All Persons under Any Form of Detention or Imprisonment 169
1988 Convention against Illicit Traffic in Narcotic Drugs and Psychotropic Substances 48
1988 Lugano Convention 67, 68
1989 Convention on the Rights of the Child 125, 187
1989 ILO Convention No. 169 Concerning Indigenous and Tribal Peoples in Independent Countries 126
1989 Principles on the Effective Prevention and Investigation of Extra-legal, Arbitrary and Summary Executions 169, 170
1990 Charter of Paris for a New Europe 146
1990 International Convention on the Protection of the Rights of All Migrant Workers and Members of Their Families 126, 187
1991 Mexico Agreements 106
1992 European Charter for Regional or Minority Languages 187
1992 Principles Relating to the Status and Functioning of National Institutions for Protection and Promotion of Human Rights (Paris Principles) 162
1992 UN Declaration on the Protection of All Persons from Enforced Disappearance 170
1993 Bangkok Declaration 163
1993 Declaration on the Elimination of Violence against Women . . . 170
1994 Framework Convention for the Protection of National Minorities 187
1994 Inter-American Convention on the Forced Disappearance of Persons 136
1994 Protocol No. 11 to the Convention for the Protection of Human Rights and Fundamental Freedoms, Restructuring the Control Machinery Established Thereby 152, 153

1995 Convention on the Safety of United Nations and Associated Personnel 75
1995 Peace Agreement for Bosnia and Herzegovina (Dayton Peace Agreement) 185, 186
1996 ILC Draft Code of Crimes against the Peace and Security of Mankind 7, 8
1998 Declaration on the Right and Responsibility of Individuals, Groups and Organs of Society to Promote and Protect Universally Recognized Human Rights and Fundamental Freedoms 170
1998 Protocol to the Charter on Human and People's Rights, Establishing the African Court on Human Rights 132, 133
1998 Statute of the International Criminal Court 4, 7-10, 37, 73, 74, 159, 165, 195, 196, 204-206, 211-215, 217, 218, 220, 221, 223-230, 232-234, 236-238, 240-242
1999 Preliminary Draft Convention on Jurisdiction and Foreign Judgments in Civil and Commercial Matters 11, 68, 69, 71-77
2001 Durban Declaration and Programme of Action . 172, 173, 177, 178

TABLE OF INTERNATIONAL CASES

Akdivar Case, 1996 152
Aksoy v. *Turkey*, 1996 .... 149, 152
Al-Adsani v. *the United Kingdom*, 2001 .... 57, 88, 148
Aloeboetoe et al. Case, 1993 .... 137, 138, 143, 144
Arrest Warrant Case, 2002 49
Aydin v. *Turkey*, 1997 150
Barcelona Traction Case, 1970 80
Blake Case, 1999 .... 138, 143, 144
Blaskic Case, 1996 210
Caballero-Delgado and Santana Case, 1997 .... 142, 144
Çakici v. *Turkey*, 1999 .... 151, 157
Case Concerning the Vienna Convention on Consular Relations (La Grand Case), 2001 87
Castillo Páez Case, 1998 142
Chorzów Factory Case, 1928 .... 80, 81
Costello-Roberts v. *the United Kingdom*, 1991 155
Cutting Case, 1886 42
Damjanovic v. *the Federation of Bosnia and Herzegovina*, 1998 188
Delalic et al. Case, 1997 210
Donnelly Case, 1973 151
El Amparo Case, 1996 .... 143, 144
Forty Mothers v. *Sweden*, 1977 155
Frederiksen and Others v. *Denmark*, 1998 149
Garrido and Baigorria Case, 1998 142
Godínez Cruz Case, 1989 137
Greece v. *the United Kingdom Case*, 1958-1959 151
Handyside v. *the United Kingdom Case*, 1974 151
Hazar and Acik v. *Turkey*, 1992 152
Ian Cowan v. *Le Tresor Public*, 1989 27
Ireland v. *the United Kingdom*, 1978 154
Islamic Community in BiH v. *Republika Srpska*, 1999 188
Ivcher Bronstein Case, 2001 134
I'm Alone Case, 1933-1935 81
Jankovic v. *Republika Srpska*, 1998 188
Klass and others v. *Germany*, 1974 .... 148, 154
Kurt v. *Turkey*, 1998 150

Leander Case, 1987 148
Loayza Tamayo Case, 1998 . . . . 142, 143
Lotus Case, 1927 . . . . 41, 47
Mahmut Kaya v. *Turkey*, 2000 158
Martini Case, 1930 80
Mavrommatis Palestine Concession Case, 1924 . . . . 79, 92
Mentes v. *Turkey*, 1997 149
Neira Alegría Case, 1996 142
Nottebohm Case, 1955 92
Nuremberg Trials, 1946 . . . . 7, 195
Open Door and Dublin Well Woman v. *Ireland*, 1992 154
Palmagero Gold Fields Case, 1931 80
Paniagua Morales et al. Case, 1998 141
Papamichalopoulos and others v. *Greece*, 1995 156
Paraguay v. *US Case*, 1998 80
Poropat and others, 1997 188
Prosecutor v. *Aleksovski*, 1999 203
Prosecutor v. *Anto Furundzija*, 1998 150
Prosecutor v. *Dusko Tadic*, 1995 . . . . 197, 210
Prosecutor v. *Jean-Bosco Barayagwiza*, 1999 62
Prosecutor v. *Jean-Paul Akayesu*, 1996 210
Prosecutor v. *Théoneste Bagosora*, 1996 203
Prulj v. *the Federation of Bosnia and Herzegovina*, 1998 188
Rainbow Warrior Case, 1986 81
Ringeisen Case, 1972 155
Russian Indemnity Case, 1912 80
Salman v. *Turkey*, 2000 . . . . 150, 151, 155, 157
Selmouni v. *France*, 1999 150
Spanish Zones of Morocco Claims, 1925 80
Suárez Rosero Case, 1999 143
Sygounis, Kotsis and 'Union of Police Officers' v. *Greece*, 1994 149
Tanli v. *Turkey*, 2001 150
Tanrikulu v. *Turkey*, 1999 151
Temple Case, 1962 80
Tokyo Trials, 1946 . . . . 7, 195
Trujillo Oroza Case, 2000 . . . . 141, 142
United States Diplomatic and Consular Staff in Tehran Case, 1980 81
Vagrancy Case, 1972 155
Velásquez Rodriguez Case, 1989 . . . . 137, 138, 140, 141, 142, 145
Villagrán Morales et al. Case ('Street Children' Case), 1999 . . . . 140, 141

Vilvarajah and Others v. *the United Kingdom,* 1991 147
Yarrow P.L.C. and Others v. *the United Kingdom*, 1983 149
Yasa v. *Turkey*, 1998 151

TABLE OF DOMESTIC CASES

Aguamina Corporation Case, 1997 59
Argentine Republic v. *Amerada Hess Shipping Corporation*, 1989 56
Arvinder Singh Bagga v. *State of Uttar Pradesh*, 1995 166
Attorney-General of the Government of Israel v. *Eichmann*, 1961 . . . 51, 52
Bishan Das v. *State of Punjab*, 1961 166
Cabiri v. *Assasie-Gyimah*, 1996 62
Chiranjit Kaur v. *Union of India*, 1994 166
D.K. Basu v. *State of West Bengal*, 1997 167
Demjanjuk v. *Petrovsky*, 1985 52
Doe v. *Karadzic*, 1994 . . . . 60, 61
Fédération Nationale des Déportés et Internés Résistants et Patriotes et al. v. *Barbie*, 1985 52
Filártiga v. *Peña-Irala*, 1980 . . . . 54-56, 58, 61, 63, 69
Forti and another v. *Suarez-Mason*, 1987 . . . . 58, 64
In re Estate of Ferdinand E. Marcos Litigation, 1992-1995 . 58-60, 64, 249
In Re G., 1997 . . . . 52, 69
Kadic v. *Karadzic*, 1995 . . . . 54, 60-62, 69
Kochunni v. *State of Madras*, 1959 165
Lafontant v. *Aristide*, 1994 57
M.C. Mehta v. *Union of India*, 1987 167
Mushikiwabo v. *Barayagwiza*, 1996 . . . . 62, 64, 69
Nilabati Behere v. *State of Orissa*, 1993 166
Padmini v. *State of T. N.*, 1993 167
Paul (et al.) v. *Avril*, 1993 . . . . 58, 64
Peoples Union for Democratic Rights v. *Police Commissioner*, 1989 . . 166
Public Prosecutor v. *Djajic*, 1997 52
Rudul Shah v. *State of Bihar*, 1983 167
Saheli v. *C.P.*, 1990 167
Siderman de Blake v. *Republic of Argentina*, 1992 56
Tata Iron & Steel Co. v. *Sarkar*, 1961 165
Tel-Oren v. *Libyan Arab Republic Case*, 1984 . . . . 55, 56
The Pinochet Case, 1998 . . . . 42-46, 49, 249
The Queen v. *Clotworthy*, 1998 35
Todd v. *Panjaitan*, 1994 . . . . 58, 64
US v. *Yunis*, 1988 43
X et al v. *the State*, 1995 85

TABLE OF DOMESTIC LEGISLATION

Acts No. 23.852 and 24.043 of Argentina, 1990 104
Amnesty Decree Law of Chile, 1978 120
Assyrian Code, c. 1450-1250 BC 15
Australian International Criminal Court (Consequential Amendments) Act, 2002 243
Austrian Act for the Grant of Assistance to Victims of Crime, 1972 27
Austrian General Civil Code, 1811 29
Austrian Government Liability Act, 1949 29
Austrian Penal Code, 1975 29
Belgium Victims Assistance Act and Compensation Scheme for Victims of Violent Crimes, 1985 .... 27, 30
Canada's Crimes Against Humanity and War Crimes Act, 2000 .. 243, 244
Code of Hammurabi, 1750 BC 15-17
Colombian Law No. 288, 1996 122
Danish Compensation from the State for Victims of Crimes (Consolidation) Act, 1985 .... 27, 31
Danish Damages Liability Act, 1984 30
Dutch Bill on International Crimes (Rules Concerning Serious Violations of International Humanitarian Law), 2002 243
Dutch Criminal Injuries Compensation Fund Act, 1975 31
Finnish Criminal Injuries Compensation Act, 1973 .... 27, 30
French General Compensation Scheme, 1990 31
French *Loi No. 2002-268 relative à la Coopération avec la Cour Pénale Internationale*, 2002 243
German Act to Introduce The Code Of Crimes Against International Law, 2002 243
German Civil Code, 1896 29
German Final Federal Compensation Law (BEG), 1965 97
German Victim's Compensation Act, 1976 .... 29, 31
Greek Civil Code, 1946 30
Hittite Laws, c. 1600-717 BC 15
Irish Scheme of Compensation for Personal Injuries Criminally Inflicted, 1974 .... 30, 31
Israeli Nazi and Nazi Collaborators (Punishment) Law, 1951 52

Italian Civil Code, 1942 30
Law 19.123 of Chile, 1992 105
Law of the XII Tables, 451-450 BC 19-21
Norwegian Act on Implementation of the Rome Statute, 2001 243
Norwegian Scheme on Compensation from the State for Personal
Injury Caused by a Criminal Act, 1976 31
Ordinance No. 120 of the French Commander, 1947 96
Peruvian Law No. 23.506, 1985 122
Portuguese Civil Code, 1966 29
Portuguese Law No. 423/91 on Protection of Victims
of Violent Crimes, 1991 . . . . 30, 31
Slovenian Law on Nomination of Judges
to International Tribunals/Courts 243
South Africa International Criminal Court Bill 243
Spanish *Ley Organica del Poder Judicial*, 1985 43
Swedish Criminal Injuries Compensation Act, 1978 31
Swiss Federal Law on Cooperation with the ICC 243
UK Extradition Act, 1989 . . . . 43, 44
UK International Criminal Court Act, 2001 . . . . 243, 244
UK Magistrates' Courts (International Criminal Court) Rules, 2001 . . . 243
UK Military Government Law No. 59, 1949 96
UK Offences Against the Person Act, 1861 44
US Alien Tort Claims Act, 1789 . . . . 52-58, 60-65, 77, 98
US Anti-Terrorism and Effective Death Penalty Act, 1996 57
US Civil Liberties Act, 1988 97
US Foreign Sovereign Immunities Act, 1976 . . . . 56-58, 61, 62
US General Federal-Question Jurisdictional Statute, 1998 60
US Military Government Law No. 59, 1947 96
US Omnibus Diplomatic Security and Anti-terrorism Act, 1986 43
US Torture Victim Protection Act (TVPA), 1991 . 53, 54, 56, 60, 62, 63, 65

CHAPTER I

Introduction

Redress for crime victims forms a basic principle of justice. From ancient tribal customs to the law of the main religious traditions, from Roman Law through the Middle Ages to the present, most of the world's legal systems have recognized the basic principle that victims of criminal offenses should receive some form of redress. Paradoxically, however, victims of ordinary crimes such as theft, robbery, assault or murder have always had a much easier time obtaining redress in one form or another than victims of the more severe crimes such as genocide, war crimes or crimes against humanity. Only in exceptional cases have victims of extremely severe violations of human dignity received fair, adequate and prompt reparation for their suffering.

Why have victims of the worst crimes received 'second class' treatment or no justice at all? As we know, victims of ordinary crimes can access established means for redress. However, for crimes and violations on a grand scale, such as those perpetrated during war, involving large numbers of victims, the situation is more complicated: the greatest crimes pose the greatest challenge in terms of redress. To take a few examples, consider the 'comfort women' of South East Asia asking for an apology from the Government of Japan, or the attempts of Bangladeshi women to obtain an apology from Pakistan for the mass rape suffered during the Liberation War of 1971. These are not the only cases. Victims of apartheid in South Africa still have not received proper compensation or rehabilitation, despite the operation of the Truth and Reconciliation Commission. Victims of the genocide in Rwanda have been mainly left uncompensated. The quest for redress of families and victims of violent political repression, massacres and disappearances during Mexico's 'Dirty War' in the 1960s and 1970s has been left unanswered. Consider also the refusal of the Australian Government to acknowledge responsibility or to offer an apology for the forcible abduction of Aboriginal children for 'assimilation' into white families. Finally, consider the emblematic case of 180 Chinese plaintiffs seeking compensation in Japanese courts for the atrocities of 'Germ Warfare Unit 731', which spread disease in several Chinese provinces and conducted terrible human experiments with chemical and bacteriological materials during World War II. In this case, the Japanese

Government even acknowledged that it violated the 1925 Geneva Protocol,[1] but it has refused to pay compensation, arguing that all compensation issues had been settled by the 1951 San Francisco Peace Treaty.[2]

Although these kinds of crimes are of universal concern, redress for victims is not universally guaranteed in practice. Victims' redress is often uneven, depending on which system victims are trying to access, their country of origin and the effectiveness of inter-State enforcement procedures, not to mention extra-legal considerations, such as the political climate in post-conflict reparation settlements or the need to find proper funds for victims' compensation. One of the main obstacles to reparation has been that war crimes, crimes against humanity, genocide and other similar crimes committed on a large scale typically are perpetrated in the context of highly unstable political situations which often involve the breakdown of regional or international peace and security and the collapse of key State institutions responsible for law enforcement and the rule of law. In most of these cases, domestic avenues for redress have been blocked or have proven ineffective. Where victims' reparations issues have been eventually addressed, they have been dealt with in the context of peace settlements, national reconciliation programmes or peace-building efforts, but they have often been subordinated or even sacrificed to political or strategic considerations. Worse, victims' reparations have sometimes been bargained away completely in peace negotiations or postponed indefinitely. A further complicating factor has been that massive crimes often involve large numbers of victims, which has made effective redress particularly difficult, often requiring *ad hoc* solutions that extend beyond simple monetary compensation. As a result, the access of victims to redress has been very inconsistent and highly unpredictable. Victims have been generally left on the periphery of domestic and international political agenda.

On the crest of major advances in international criminal law, the international community has begun to acknowledge that, just as crimes of serious concern to the international community as a whole cannot be considered ordinary crimes, victims of these crimes cannot be considered ordinary victims. Over the last decade or so, the international community has shown renewed interest in victims' issues at various levels. Civil society, governments, non-governmental organizations (NGOs), inter-governmental

---

1 Protocol for the Prohibition of the Use in War of Asphyxiating, Poisonous or Other Gases, and of Bacteriological Methods of Warfare, *adopted* on 17 June 1925, *entered into force* on 8 February 1928.

2 Treaty of Peace with Japan, *signed* at San Francisco on 8 September 1951, *entered into force* on 28 April 1952.

organizations and other actors have increasingly recognized the centrality of victims' redress in the global search for peace and justice, particularly where major crimes of concern to the international community are involved, and that victims' redress for egregious crimes can no longer be ignored.

Despite the renewed interest of the international community in victims' issues and the emergence of coherent redress principles in law and practice, in many cases, victims of massive crimes still have been unable to obtain adequate redress. Why has this been so? Perhaps one of the main weaknesses of victims' redress at present is that currently available mechanisms at domestic, regional and universal levels remain very fragmented: they form a 'patchwork' rather than a system and they lack institutional cohesiveness and universality in scope. Even where reparation provisions could be applied, such as in the International Criminal Tribunal for the former Yugoslavia (ICTY) or in the International Criminal Tribunal for Rwanda (ICTR),[3] there has not been sufficient political will on the part of the relevant institutions to make these provisions work fully.

We therefore have to consider whether the international community could develop more adequate avenues for victims' redress. Accordingly, the present work examines the historical origins of the principle of victims' redress, its evolution, its application in the current frameworks of domestic law, regional and universal human rights regimes, humanitarian law, State responsibility, United Nations (UN) practice and international criminal law. Finally, this study reflects on some possible ways in which the international community could better address the question of victims' redress. It is argued that to develop more effective redress for victims of major crimes, the international community must move beyond the fragmented approach we now have, towards a more comprehensive redress regime - a regime which encompasses domestic, regional and universal solutions and applies coherent redress principles on a non-discriminatory basis to provide all victims of crimes under international law with fair, adequate and prompt redress.

---

[3] Statute of the International Tribunal for the Prosecution of Persons Responsible for Serious Violations of International Humanitarian Law Committed in the Territory of the Former Yugoslavia Since 1991, *approved* by Security Council resolution 827 (1993), *adopted* on 25 May 1993; and Statute of the International Criminal Tribunal for the Prosecution of Persons Responsible for Genocide and Other Serious Violations of International Humanitarian Law Committed in the Territory of Rwanda and Rwandan Citizens Responsible for Genocide and Other Such Violations Committed in the Territory of Neighbouring States, between 1 January 1994 and 31 December 1994, *decided* by Security Council resolution 955 of 8 November 1994.

More specifically, this enquiry first traces, examines and analyzes common principles and primary elements of victims' redress for crimes under international law, currently emerging from the development of UN human rights standards and international and domestic law and practice. It explores avenues for the implementation of the victims' right to seek and obtain redress in light of recent developments in international criminal law, particularly in the context of the new International Criminal Court (ICC).[4] From the angles of State responsibility, individual responsibility, human rights regimes and domestic fora, it is argued that the question of victims' redress for massive or systematic crimes must reach beyond the context of the relationship between perpetrator and victim, and that the way towards a more comprehensive redress regime must involve the active participation of the international community at large, including civil society and victims' groups, human rights NGOs, Governments, and intergovernmental organizations.

1. A Word about Key Terms and Concepts

At this juncture, it is useful to introduce some terms and concepts key to the present work to clarify its scope and direction, in particular the terms 'redress', 'victims' and 'crimes under international law', which carry various meanings and continue to develop over time.

a. 'Redress'

For the purpose of the present study, we shall use the term 'redress' as an umbrella term to encompass broadly redress-related concepts as they are employed in various legal regimes dealing with the question. While the term 'reparation' is the more regularly used term of legal content, the present study adopts the term 'redress' as one that extends conceptually beyond narrowly defined notions of remedy, compensation, restitution, recovery, rehabilitation, apologies, etc., without prejudice to the use of these narrower terms in more specific senses.

---

[4] Statute of the International Criminal Court, *adopted in Rome in a non-recorded vote*, 120 *in favour*, 7 *against* and 21 *abstaining*, on 17 July 1998 (A/CONF.183/9), hereinafter referred to as 'ICC Statute' or 'Rome Statute'. As of 31 October 2003, the Rome Statute had been signed by 139 States and ratified by 92 States.

The term 'redress' has a fairly broad meaning. Black's Law Dictionary[5] defines 'redress' as: "[s]atisfaction for an injury or damages sustained ... [d]amages or equitable relief" and then mentions the terms 'recovery' and 'restitution' as synonyms. When we turn to 'recovery', this term is defined as:

> In its most extensive sense, the restoration or vindication of a right existing in a person, by the formal judgment or decree of a competent court, at his instance and suit, or the obtaining, by such judgment, of some right or property which has been taken or withheld from him.

and 'restitution' as an:

> Act of restoring; restoration; restoration of anything to its rightful owner; the act of making good or giving equivalent for any loss, damage or injury; and indemnification. ... Restoration of status quo and [an] amount which would put plaintiff in as good a position as he would have been if no contract had been made and restores to plaintiff value of what he parted with in performing contract. ... In torts, restitution is essentially the measure of damages.

The related concept of '*restitutio in integrum*' typical of the civil law is defined as:

> Restoration or restitution to the previous condition. This was effected by the praetor on equitable grounds, at the prayer of an injured party, by rescinding or annulling a contract or transaction valid by the strict law, or annulling a change in the legal condition produced by an omission, and restoring the parties to their previous situation or legal relations. The restoration of a cause to its first state, on petition of the party who was cast, in order to have a second hearing.

Finally, Black's Law Dictionary defines the term 'remedy' as:

> the means by which a right is enforced or the violation of a right is prevented, redressed, or compensated ... [or] any remedial right to which an aggrieved party is entitled with or without resort to a tribunal.

---

5 Black's Law Dictionary, Fifth Edition (1979).

and 'reparation' as "payment of any injury; redress for a wrong done. Payment made by one country to another for damages during war". The term 'reparation' is often used to encompass restitution, compensation and rehabilitation.

b. 'Victims'

The term 'victim' is also used in a great variety of senses. In a legal sense, 'victim' refers broadly to a person (or perhaps a group of persons or even an organization) who has been the object of a crime or tort.

Defining 'victims of crimes under international law' can be problematic. Like the usage of the term 'redress' discussed above, the term 'victim' carries various connotations which depend upon the legal context in which it is used. For example, the UN Declaration of Basic Principles of Justice for Victims of Crime and Abuse of Power[6] defines 'victims of abuse of power' as:

> persons who, individually or collectively, have suffered harm, including physical or mental injury, emotional suffering, economic loss or substantial impairment of their fundamental rights, through acts or omissions that do not yet constitute violations of national criminal laws but of internationally recognized norms relating to human rights.[7]

As we shall see, in the 'Basic Principles and Guidelines on the Right to a Remedy and Reparation for Victims of Violations of International Human Rights and Humanitarian Law'[8] the UN Special Rapporteur and also the Independent Expert on the Right to Restitution, Compensation and Rehabilitation for Victims of Grave Violations of Human Rights and Fundamental

---

6 UN Declaration of Basic Principles of Justice for Victims of Crime and Abuse of Power, *adopted* by UN General Assembly (UNGA) resolution 40/34 of 29 November 1985.

7 Also, the Declaration defines 'victims of crime' as "persons who, individually or collectively, have suffered harm, including physical or mental injury, emotional suffering, economic loss or substantial impairment of their fundamental rights, through acts or omissions that are in violation of criminal law operative within Member States, including those laws proscribing criminal abuse of power".

8 Annex to 'The Right to Restitution, Compensation and Rehabilitation for Victims of Grave Violations of Human Rights and Fundamental Freedoms', Final Report of the Independent Expert M. Cherif Bassiouni, submitted in accordance with Commission resolution 1999/33, UN Doc. E/CN.4/2000/62 of 18 January 2000.

Freedoms have developed similar definitions of 'victim' of human rights and humanitarian law violations, which include dependants, members of the immediate family or household and persons who have suffered physical, mental or economic harm in assisting the victim or preventing the occurrence of further violations. The definitions elaborated in the context of the UN Declaration and Basic Principles and Guidelines provide a general indication as to whom may be considered a victim according to various situational contexts. By adopting expanded notions of victim which may include 'next-of-kin', descendants and ascendants, 'indirect victims' or 'potential victims' as well as juridical persons such as non-governmental and international organizations, as in the reparation regime of the ICC Statute 1998, these definitions also fall more closely in line with recent doctrine and jurisprudence.

c. 'Crimes under International Law'

The third cluster of terms and concepts of importance to the present study involves 'crimes under international law' - massive crimes for which victims always have had the most difficult time in obtaining redress. The concept of 'crimes under international law' has evolved over a long period of time. In early customary international law particularly heinous acts, such as the slaughter of innocent civilians, rape, pillage and certain means and methods of warfare, were considered so serious as to be recognized as crimes regardless of where or by whom they were perpetrated, and in that sense, they were considered to be crimes of universal concern and hence 'crimes under international law'. In addition to war crimes, the Congress of Vienna, held in 1815, outlawed piracy and slave-trading as crimes under international law. Following the end of World War II, the International Military Tribunals at Nuremberg and Tokyo[9] put the spotlight on 'crimes against peace' (today basically termed the 'crime of aggression'), 'war crimes' and 'crimes against humanity'. In 1947, the UN General Assembly entrusted the International Law Commission (ILC) with the task of codifying the Nuremberg Principles and elaborating an international criminal code and court.[10] Over the next fifty years, the ILC put forward several versions of its Draft Code of Crimes against the Peace and Security of Mankind reflecting the current state of general

---

9 International Military Tribunal at Nuremberg, *established* pursuant to the Nuremberg Charter annexed to the London Agreement of 8 August 1945; and International Military Tribunal for the Far East, *established* on 9 January 1946 in Tokyo.

10 UNGA resolution 177(II) of 21 November 1947.

recognition as to the kinds of acts that the international community considered to qualify as 'crimes under international law'. In its 1996 version, the Draft Code of Crimes against the Peace and Security of Mankind listed the following crimes: aggression, genocide, crimes against humanity, crimes against UN and associated personnel and war crimes.[11]

In 1948, the UN General Assembly adopted the Genocide Convention[12] which established genocide as a 'crime under international law'. In 1949, the four Geneva Conventions[13] included for the first time provisions imposing individual criminal responsibility for certain particularly serious violations referred to as 'grave breaches of the Geneva Conventions', and thereby established that these violations constituted 'crimes under international law' as well.

With the UN Security Council's establishment of the ICTY and ICTR in 1993 and 1994 respectively, the field of 'international criminal law' has assumed a more important role. Notably, the UN Security Council decided to vest in the ICTY and ICTR competence only over crimes recognized to be well-established in customary international law. With respect to the ICTY these were: grave breaches of the Geneva Conventions 1949; violations of the laws or customs of war; genocide; and crimes against humanity. With respect to the ICTR these were: genocide; crimes against humanity; and violations of Article 3 common to the Geneva Conventions 1949 and of Additional Protocol II.[14]

Today, crimes under international law have been largely codified in the Rome Statute of the ICC 1998 - a landmark development in international criminal law. Under the Rome Statute, the ICC exercises jurisdiction over individuals accused of having committed war crimes, genocide, crimes against humanity and eventually the crime of aggression.[15] The general categories of

---

11 *See* UN Doc. A/CN.4/L.532 of 8 July 1996.

12 Convention on the Prevention and Punishment of the Crime of Genocide, *adopted unanimously* on 9 December 1948, *entered into force* on 12 January 1951. UNGA resolution 96(I) of 1947 declared genocide to be a crime under international law and entrusted the Economic and Social Council (ECOSOC) to "undertake the necessary studies, with a view to drawing up a draft convention on the crime of genocide".

13 Geneva Conventions, *adopted* on 12 August 1949, *entered into force* on 21 October 1950.

14 Protocol Additional to the Geneva Conventions of 12 August 1949 and relating to the Protection of Victims of Non-International Armed Conflicts (Protocol II), *adopted* on 8 June 1977.

15 According to Article 5(2) of the Rome Statute, the ICC will exercise jurisdiction over the crime of aggression only once "a provision is adopted in accordance with articles 121 and 123 defining the crime and setting out the conditions

genocide, war crimes and crimes against humanity cover a multiplicity of criminal acts. For example, the following acts amount to crimes against humanity under Article 7 of the Rome Statute, when committed "as part of a widespread or systematic attack directed against any civilian population, with knowledge of the attack": murder; extermination; enslavement, including human trafficking, in particular of women and children; deportation or forcible transfer of population; imprisonment or other severe deprivation of physical liberty in violation of fundamental rules of international law; torture, irrespective of whether it was committed by a person with a connection to the State, or for a particular purpose, such as, for example, obtaining a confession (as covered in the UN Torture Convention 1984);[16] rape, sexual slavery, enforced prostitution, forced pregnancy, enforced sterilization, or any other form of sexual violence of comparable gravity; persecution against any identifiable group or collectivity on political, racial, national, ethnic, cultural, religious, gender, or other grounds that are universally recognized as impermissible under international law; enforced disappearance of persons; apartheid; and other inhumane acts of a similar character intentionally causing great suffering, or serious injury to body or to mental or physical health.

Under Article 8 on war crimes, the ICC has jurisdiction over grave breaches of the Geneva Conventions 1949; other serious violations of the laws and customs applicable in international armed conflict; serious violations of Article 3 common to the four Geneva Conventions applicable in time of non-international armed conflicts; and other serious violations of the laws and customs applicable in non-international armed conflict. For example, it is a war crime to conscript or enlist children under the age of fifteen into armed forces, or to use them to participate actively in hostilities. Attacks intentionally directed against UN personnel, crimes of sexual violence and widespread, long-term and severe damage to the natural environment also constitute war crimes under Article 8 of the Rome Statute. As for the crime of genocide, the Rome Statute incorporates *verbatim* the definition of the Genocide Convention 1948.

At present, the Rome Statute represents the most up-to-date expression of the international community's understanding as to which crimes under international law give rise to individual responsibility for the purposes of international prosecution and punishment, based on well-established interna-

---

under which the Court shall exercise jurisdiction with respect to this crime".

16 UN Convention against Torture and Other Cruel, Inhuman or Degrading Treatment or Punishment (hereinafter referred to as the 'Torture Convention'), *adopted and opened for signature, ratification and accession* by UNGA resolution 39/46 of 10 December 1984, *entered into force* on 26 June 1987.

tional law and standards.[17] However, it must be noted that the material scope of the Rome Statute's definitions of crimes is narrower than those found in general international law,[18] and that nothing prevents States from adopting or developing wider definitions of crimes under international law in their domestic legislation, particularly as regards victims' redress. This may apply, for example, to the case of torture which some commentators consider to be an 'international crime under customary law' even where perpetrated in time of peace as a single act, rather then in a systematic manner or on a widespread basis.[19]

To sum up, the term 'crimes under international law' includes any act for which international law prescribes individual criminal responsibility and ultimately:

---

[17] On the long debate over the inclusion in the Rome Statute of only those crimes widely accepted by the international community at large, *see generally* Herman von Hebel and Darryl Robinson, "Crimes within the Jurisdiction of the Court", in Roy S. Lee (ed.), *The International Criminal Court: The Making of the Rome Statute, Issues, Negotiations, Results*, Kluwer Law International (1999), pp. 79-126. *See also* M. Cherif Bassiouni, *The Statute of the International Criminal Court: A Documentary History*, Transnational Publishers (1998).

[18] On this point, *see* Lyal S. Sunga, "The Crimes within the Jurisdiction of the International Criminal Court (Part II, Articles 5-10)", *European Journal of Crime, Criminal Law and Criminal Justice*, Vol. 6/4 (1998) at 378, arguing that "the Rome Statute foresees a narrower range than either that reflected in general international law, or indeed, that proposed at various stages in the work of the International Law Commission". Sunga remarks that acts such as the threat of aggression, intervention, colonial domination, the recruitment, use, financing or training of mercenaries, international terrorism or the illicit international traffic in narcotic drugs do not figure in the Rome Statute, although certain of these crimes "even claim a relatively high level of support from the international community at large and remain well anchored in established norms extant in treaty law, and to a lesser degree, international custom".

[19] *See* Antonio Cassese, *International Law*, Oxford University Press (2001) at 254. Even the ICC, in its determinations, can apply "applicable treaties and the principles and rules on international law, including the established principles of the international law of armed conflict" in addition to the Statute, Elements of Crimes and Rules of Procedure and Evidence. *See* Article 21(1)(b) of the Rome Statute. For the sake of completeness, one must mention also that a number of multilateral conventions address certain crimes of concern to the international community, such as hijacking, unlawful acts against civil aviation, maritime navigation and fixed platforms at sea (oil rigs for example), crimes against internationally protected persons, hostage-taking, terrorist bombings, the counterfeiting of monetary currency, damage of submarine cables, the international traffic in obscene publications and mercenarism.

> whether particular acts are considered to constitute crimes under international law, or even potential threats to international peace and security depends upon the extent of State recognition to this effect.[20]

The precise scope of 'crimes under international law' will undoubtedly continue to evolve through jurisprudence of the ICC and *ad hoc* international criminal tribunals, human rights judicial and quasi-judicial mechanisms, regional human rights systems, and domestic law and practice. The inevitable ambiguities and imperfections in the definition and scope of specific norms prohibiting crimes under international law, mean that there will also remain a certain lack of clarity as to the precise scope of redress. This does not mean, however, that the whole field of legal norms and standards on redress either does not exist, or should not be explored, until the scope of 'crimes under international law' is defined entirely, perfectly and conclusively, since such an approach would be inherently unrealistic.

2. Structure of the Book

This study is structured in seven chapters. Chapter II places the origins of the law and practice on redress for victims of crime in historical perspective and highlights the tension between restorative justice and retributive justice. Chapter III evaluates domestic implementation mechanisms and discusses the question of the enforcement of judgments abroad, in light of the draft Hague Convention on Jurisdiction and Foreign Judgments in Civil and Commercial Matters 1999. Chapter IV focuses on the question of redress in the context of State responsibility, State-based reparation mechanisms and compensation schemes. Chapter V analyzes the contribution of international human rights law and jurisprudence as well as UN standards to current notions of redress for victims of crimes under international law. Chapter VI examines the law on redress as expressed and codified in international criminal law, with a special focus on the reparation regime of the ICC. Chapter VII identifies the key elements in norms and implementation reviewed in the earlier chapters which point the way towards a more comprehensive redress regime for victims of crimes under international law.

---

[20] *See* Lyal S. Sunga, *The Emerging System of International Criminal Law: Developments in Codification and Implementation*, Kluwer Law International (1997) at 4-5.

CHAPTER II

Origins of the Victims' Right to Redress: The Historical Swing from Restoration to Retribution and Back to Restoration

To appreciate why, historically, victims of crimes under international law have encountered great difficulty in obtaining their basic right to reparation, it is valuable to trace the origins and evolution of this right in different legal traditions. Although most of the world's legal and cultural traditions have long embraced the basic principle of victims' redress, the rise of retributive approaches gradually eroded the central position victims had enjoyed in early tribal societies, and this often hindered the development of adequate reparation mechanisms, frustrating the victims' right to redress and hopes for rehabilitation. Generally, current systems of justice administration at both domestic and international levels remain firmly anchored to retributive principles and their primary focus is fixed almost exclusively on the prosecution and punishment of the perpetrator, rather than on the rehabilitation of the victim. In the specific case of crimes under international law, the mainly retributive character of justice administration systems can still be considered to be one of the structural obstacles preventing the full enjoyment of the victims' right to redress.

Over the last decade or so, however, the international community increasingly integrated fundamental elements of reparative and restorative justice within established legal procedures, thus redirecting its focus more to individual victims. This Chapter traces the historical swing in law and practice from restoration to retribution, and back to restoration. It is argued that the international community seems to be increasingly recognizing that the right to adequate and fair redress for crime victims should combine in a more harmonious fashion both restorative and retributive elements of justice, especially where victims of human rights violations of a massive character are involved.

1. Legal Justice and Victims' Redress in Pre-Roman Civilizations and in Some of the Main Religious Traditions

In early communities - including tribal societies - compensation for crime victims was seen more as a way of settling private disputes directly between the offender and the victim than as an element of 'punishment' for a breach of a legal obligation in the retributive sense.[1] Early social systems commonly considered compensation by the offender to the victim as a way to deal with the desire of victims to be vindicated for the harm suffered. This form of satisfaction could minimize the risk that victims would take the law into their own hands. The principle of compensation as applied privately within early communities was refined and developed normatively alongside the development of the rule of law within organized State systems. To suppress the desire of victims to seek revenge on a private basis, over the centuries, most legal systems developed mechanisms aimed at channelling the victim's anger and enabling crime victims to benefit from some form of redress, based on the principle that whoever suffers injury or damage caused by an unlawful action has the right to 'vindicate' the damage suffered.

Alongside the 'practical' need for societies to provide for victims' remedies to prevent revenge-related violence, philosophers and legal thinkers have elaborated theories for the attribution of remedies, mainly by trying to define the essential elements of justice and how the law should reflect these principles. This process has not been an easy one however, particularly because of difficulties in coming to a widely acceptable definition of justice. In this sense, as Snyder remarks:

> ... it has been easier to recognize injustice than it has been to define justice. Partially, this is due to the fact that justice has frequently been equated with some species of absolute truth.[2]

Consequently, instead of seeking a definition of justice many societies have preferred to recognize injustice in particular concrete instances and to provide for a remedy in each case. While an injustice would be seen as a breach of

---

[1] However, some exceptionally serious crimes were not considered to give rise to monetarily assessable damages and they could be redeemed only by the death of the wrongdoer.

[2] R. Neil Snyder, "Natural Law and Equity", in Ralph A. Newman (ed.), *Equity in the World's Legal Systems: A Comparative Study*, Etablissement Emile Bruylant, Brussels, Belgium (1973) at 34.

Divine Law, the determination of a remedy would be left to human judgment. In the Egyptian civilization, for example, the idea of justice was personified by Ma'at, the Goddess of Justice. However, in their legal determinations, judges would follow the written law and exercise their prerogative to fill in gaps and establish remedies wherever needed.[3] Early Mesopotamian civilizations also contemplated the concept of liability for damages among their basic rules. Principles of restitution and compensation were enshrined in the Code of Hammurabi (c. 1750 BC), in the Assyrian Code (c. 1450-1250 BC) and in Hittite Laws (c. 1600-717 BC). In particular, the latter related a number of offences against life to the payment of specific compensation in gold or silver. The application of the compensatory system in Hittite law went so far that, in case of murder, instead of punishing the offender with death - which was a common punishment for offenses against life and property in all contemporary societies - the offender could instead 'substitute' the murdered person with a person of equivalent social value.[4]

The Code of Hammurabi[5] expressed the principle of compensation as follows:

> If any one steal cattle or sheep, or an ass, or a pig or a goat, if it belong to a god or to the court, the thief shall pay thirtyfold therefor; if they belonged to a freed man of the king he shall pay tenfold; if the thief has nothing with which to pay he shall be put to death.[6]

The Code of Hammurabi also enshrined the principle of retaliation in the form of an 'eye for an eye and a tooth for a tooth', and in the following variations:

> If a man put out the eye of another man, his eye shall be put out. If he break another man's bone, his bone shall be broken. If he put out the eye of a freed man, or break the bone of a freed man, he shall pay one gold mina. If he put out the eye of a man's slave, or break the bone of a man's slave, he shall pay one-half of its value. If a man knock out the teeth of his equal, his teeth shall be knocked out. If he

---

3 *Ibid.* at 35.

4 *See* Leroy S. Rouner (ed.), *Human Rights and the World's Religions*, University of Notre Dame Press, Notre Dame, Indiana (1988) at 17.

5 The Code of Hammurabi, translated by L. W. King, The Avalon Project at the Yale Law School, http://www.yale.edu/lawweb/avalon/hamframe.htm.

6 *Ibid.* at para. 8.

> knock out the teeth of a freed man, he shall pay one-third of a gold mina.[7]

Paragraphs 23 and 24 of the Code provided for an early form of victim's compensation by the community in cases of an unknown offender - a concept which is still being developed in most modern societies. The Code stated:

> If the robber is not caught, then shall he who was robbed claim under oath the amount of his loss; then shall the community, ... on whose ground and territory and in whose domain it was compensate him for the goods stolen. If persons are stolen, then shall the community ... pay one mina of silver to their relatives.[8]

In case of assault against a person, the amount of compensation to be paid by the offender according to the Code of Hammurabi would vary according to the rank of the victim,[9] the intention behind the offender's behaviour and the damage suffered by the victim.[10]

Notably, the Code of Hammurabi embodies a number of compensation provisions which address offences committed against women, including the following:

> If a man strike a free-born woman so that she lose her unborn child, he shall pay ten shekels for her loss. If the woman die, his daughter shall be put to death. If a woman of the free class lose her child by a blow, he shall pay five shekels in money. If this woman die, he shall pay half a mina. If he strike the maid-servant of a man, and she

---

7 *Ibid.* at paras. 196-201.

8 *Ibid.* at paras. 23-24.

9 Compensation could range from "sixty blows with an ox-whip in public" where an offender assaulted a man of a higher rank (para. 202) to the payment of one gold mina if a free-born man struck "the body of another free-born man of equal rank" (para. 203), to the payment of ten shekels in money in the case of a freed man having struck the body of another freed man (para. 204), to more severe sanctions, such as in the case of a slave of a freed man assaulting a freed man, for which the Code of Hammurabi provided for the ear of the slave to be cut off (para. 205).

10 Paras. 206 to 208 of the Code of Hammurabi provide that: "if during a quarrel one man strike another and wound him, then he shall swear, 'I did not injure him wittingly', and pay the physicians"; and that: "if the man die of his wound, he shall swear similarly, and if he (the deceased) was a free-born man, he shall pay half a mina in money", and instead "if he was a freed man, he shall pay one-third of a mina".

> lose her child, he shall pay two shekels in money. If this maid-servant die, he shall pay one-third of a mina.[11]

In the Holy Scriptures of the Jewish tradition, the legitimacy of blood revenge is a well-established principle and the idea of justice is strictly related to retribution and punishment, rather than to reparation and compensation. In the Old Testament, Jahweh says that: "whoever sheds the blood of man, by man shall his blood be shed, for in the image of God was man created",[12] and "you shall not take a ransom for the life of a murderer who is guilty of death, but he shall surely be put to death".[13] As Fishbane explains:

> In biblical law there is no correlation between persons and property, no commensurable exchange between human worth and economic value .... Thus, in ancient Israel intentional murder is punishable by death, there being no substitution. ... For at the core of the biblical system is the perception that the person is of absolute and inviolable worth: created in the divine image.[14]

However, in the case of a dispute, the Old Testament also commands that both parties shall come before God and whomever God convicts must make twofold restitution to the other.[15]

The doctrine of absolute retribution expressed in the Old Testament was revolutionised through the teachings of Jesus as reflected in the New Testament and enshrined in the principle "love your enemy and requite evil with good". In Christianity, the focus of justice shifts from punishment for evil conduct to reward for good actions. Jesus opposed the Jewish concept of

---

11 *Ibid.* at paras. 209-214. It is also interesting to note that the Code of Hammurabi provided for compensation for those who suffered injuries caused by a physician. In this case, redress to the victim would vary from monetary compensation (as provided for in paras. 215, 216 and 217) to more extreme sanctions such as in the case when: "... a physician make a large incision with the operating knife, and kill him, or open a tumour with the operating knife, and cut out the eye, his hands shall be cut off" (para. 218).

12 Genesis 9:6.

13 Numbers 35:31. The only exceptions allowing for the payment of compensation to the victims' family would be a non-intentional homicide or a homicide not committed personally, such as, for example, in the case of a person killed by an animal or property of another person. Exodus 21:28-30.

14 Michael Fishbane, "The Image of the Human and the Rights of the Individual in Jewish Tradition", in Rouner (ed.), *supra* note 4 at 18.

15 Exodus 22:9.

justice as retribution and instead argued that one should not pass judgment on others so that one may not have judgment passed upon himself or herself.[16] In this sense, justice can be found only in God and "the justice of the believer is not his or her own justice; it's 'alien justice', *justitia aliena*".[17] The relationship between God and the human being is an essential element also in the teachings of Islam, where the rights of individuals and the obligations towards Allah are strictly interconnected.

2. Victims' Redress in Roman Law

In general, the Roman legal system followed a strictly positivist approach: it was the legal norm that determined a moral standard and not vice-versa. In other words, Roman Law would provide for the protection and implementation of a given right, not because of its intrinsic moral value which had to be protected in order to honour justice, but simply because the legislator provided for a remedy in case of a breach of such right. Contrary to Natural Law theories, which considered remedies purely as a means to achieve justice, Roman Law viewed remedies themselves as the final aim of the administration of justice. As a result of this positivist approach, Roman Law has always accorded remedies to victims of a wrongful action a fundamental place in the justice system. As Stein notes:

> ... the Roman lawyers did not think in terms of rights but rather in terms of remedies. Their discussions centre round such questions as: is there an action, or a defence, in this situation and what is its scope?[18]

Consequently, the Roman legal system provided for a rather strict system of reparation and compensation according to various typical situations, sometimes leaving very little room for equitable considerations or judicial discretion, at

---

16 Matthew 7:1.

17 Trutz Rendtorff, "Christian Concepts of the Responsible Self", in Rouner (ed.), *supra* note 4 at 39.

18 Peter Stein, "Equitable Principles in Roman Law", in Newman (ed.), *supra* note 2 at 78.

least in the early stages of its development.[19] Roman Law remains influential in most civil law systems.

The focus on remedies in Roman Law dates back at least to the early Roman Law of the XII Tables (*Lex XII Tabularum*), enacted around the mid-fifth century BC (451-450 BC) by a Commission of ten men (*Decemviri*). The XII Tables codified for the first time customary principles of social conduct within the community, especially with respect to the relationship between patricians and plebeians. The Law of the XII Tables was binding for both groups, and magistrates were charged with its impartial enforcement. The XII Tables merit attention because they shape the contours of subsequent Roman Law, and hence, also civil law legal systems in general. As Cicero wrote in *De Oratore*:

> Though all the world exclaims against me, I will say what I think: that single little book of the Twelve Tables, if anyone look to the fountains and sources of laws, seems to me, assuredly, to surpass the libraries of all the philosophers, both in weight of authority, and in plenitude of utility.[20]

In the Law of the XII Tables, the exercise of sanctions attached to certain offences was left to a type of customarily regulated private justice, instead of being treated under public law procedures, to satisfy the drive of the victim for revenge and to fulfill the need for private reparation. This particular character of early Roman Law is typical of what Kelsen describes as 'primitive legal orders', characterized by only two stages:

> the development of the general norm through custom, and its application by the subject whose interests, protected by this norm, have been violated. This subject is authorized by the legal order to react against the violator of the law with the sanction provided by it. Primitive law is characterized by the technique of self-help. Blood revenge is a typical example: the subject himself whose interests have been violated, and not a special organ, must determine whether or not

---

19 *See* B. F. Brown, "Equity in the Law of the United States of America", in Newman (ed.), *supra* note 2 at 214-215. For a critical analysis of how the doctrine of equitable principles has mitigated only partially the strictly positive approach of countries influenced by Roman legal tradition *see* Newman, *ibid.* at 589-599.

20 Marcus Tullius Ciceronis (Cicero), *De Oratore*, Book I, 44, Loeb Classical Library, Translated by E.W. Sutton & H. Rackham, Harvard University Press, Cambridge (1996).

> a delict has been committed. The subject himself must fulfill the sanction; it is not decreed by an individual norm, enacted and executed by an organ different from the injured. The primitive law of self-help is characterized by the fact that the general norm is applied directly to the concrete instance without an individual norm.[21]

As long as the *delictum* did not pose a threat to public order, the early Law of the XII Tables granted victims the liberty to find and capture the offender and to provide evidence of his or her guilt. This custom, which was also typical of pre-Roman societies, included the execution by the victim of sanctions related to a *furtum manifestum* (a theft in which the thief was found *cum res furtiva*, meaning with the stolen goods), or to personal aggression of more or less serious nature, classified under the rubric of *iniuria*, but also to offences of less serious calibre such as *furtum nec manifestum* (a theft in which the thief was not found *in flagrante delicto*) and related offences.[22]

Perhaps to avoid instances of abuse of justice by the victim, the XII Tables later introduced a strict system of mandatory monetary compensation for certain types of offences. This system was based on the concept of objective responsibility for the damage caused, meaning that compensation had to be paid whether or not the offence was intentional. For example, violent acts of a less serious nature could entail the payment of twenty-five 'as'[23] to the victims, while the compensation to be paid for more serious offences such as an *os fractum* (broken bone) was assessed at one hundred and fifty to three hundred 'as'. For one offence at least, the *membrum ruptum* (literally broken limb, but generally used to indicate any injury other than a broken bone), the XII Tables provided for the *lex talionis* according to the principle that: *ni cum eo pacit, talio esto*.[24] The power of sanction exercised by the victim could

---

21 Hans Kelsen, *What is Justice? Justice, Law, and Politics in the Mirror of Science*, Collected Essays by Hans Kelsen, University of California Press, Berkeley and Los Angeles (1957) at 246, arguing that the 'steps' which characterize legal orders over time tend to increase.

22 *See* Arlette Lebigre, *Quelques Aspects de la Responsabilité Pénale en Droit Romain Classique*, Presses Universitaires de France, Paris (1967) at 66-70.

23 A bronze coin of low value.

24 Table VIII provided that: "If a person has maimed another's limb, let there be retaliation in kind (*lex talionis*), unless he agrees to make compensation with him". For further discussion, *see* Lebigre, *supra* note 22, *see also* Bruno Schmidlin and Carlo Augusto Cannata, *Droit Privé Romain: Obligations - Successions - Procédure*, Vol. II, Payot, Lausanne (1991) at 171.

extend even to the killing of offenders found guilty of *furtum nocturnum* (night theft), or of those offenders that *se telo defendit*, meaning that they fought against being captured. However, in the latter case (killing of an offender fighting against being captured), the law established a judicial procedure of verification by a magistrate (*endoploratio*) and witness corroboration of the evidence.[25] Finally, in case of complicity in the *delictum*, the victim could bring a legal action and claim full compensation from any of the alleged perpetrators, according to the principle of double or multiple compensation.[26]

The compensation system set up by the Roman Law of the XII Tables is similar in many ways to the treatment of crimes in pre-Roman societies, where the immediate reparation of an offence was considered an absolute priority to be dealt with according to a rigid set of compensation provisions. As in pre-Roman civilizations, the Law of the XII Tables left little room to consider the circumstances surrounding the delict, or for any legal distinctions based on factors such as *dolus* or *culpa*, and it thus risked victims abusing their power.

The fixed-sum compensation system typical of the Law of the XII Tables was entirely revised following the introduction of Praetorial Law around the end of the second century BC, when the State began to play a more active role in the prosecution and punishment of a number of serious offences. For example, the State, in addition to the victim, could trigger a criminal action for offences that undermined the public order or threatened the fundamental interests of the community.[27] As for the determination of compensation, Praetorial Law introduced a new kind of legal action (*actio iniuriarum*) which provided for the determination not only of material damages, but also of moral damages. In addition, the Praetor himself could determine a monetary sum to be payed as equitable compensation to victims on a case-by-case basis, according to the principle *quantum iudici bonum et aequum videbitur*.[28] All available remedies were listed in a Praetorial edict and were applied according to the *ius honorarium*, a body of law to aid, supplement or correct civil law. This was done by "offering more convenient remedies to persons who already held rights of action at civil law" or by "granting remedies to persons who did

---

25 *See* Lebigre, *supra* note 22 at 67-68.

26 *See* Schmidlin and Cannata, *supra* note 24 at 170.

27 These offences were known as *perduellio*. On the origins and development of the *perduellio*, *see* Lebigre, *supra* note 22 at 98-103.

28 *See* Schmidlin and Cannata, *supra* note 24 at 171.

not have rights of action at civil law".[29] Remedies would include defences to actions brought by others (for example in case of a transaction completed under fraud or duress), the possibility of obtaining *restitutio in integrum*, and in certain cases, direct action for damages for fraud or duress (*actio doli*). However, the Praetor could issue an order for restitution only with *causa cognita*, meaning that he would have to acquire personal knowledge of the circumstances which led to the allegations put forward by the complainant, with the aim of verifying the truth of such allegations[30] - an approach which has strongly influenced current legal procedure in most civil law systems. Importantly, the case-by-case focus of Praetorial Law not only highlighted the role of the judge in the administration of justice, but contributed strongly to the consolidation of the principle of equity in matters relating to redress.

The *Lex Aquilia de damno* (Aquilian Law) further developed the concept of responsibility as well as its corollary theory of reparation and strongly influenced the evolution of legal theories on compensation. Adopted by plebiscite in 286 BC, the Aquilian law of responsibility radically shifted the focus from the retribution of the offender as a form of moral satisfaction for the victim - as in the old *lex talionis* - to the determination and reparation of the objective damage caused by the illicit action (*damnum iniuria datum*), thus weakening the link between punishment and remedy. As Winiger explains:

> ... the *ratio legis* of Aquilian Law was primarily to redress the economic damage suffered by the injured owner, even if, in certain instances, jurists had mentioned the punitive character of Aquilian Law.[31]

The structure of Aquilian responsibility rested on the cause / effect relationship between damage suffered by a person or an object, and a delict committed either intentionally (*dolus*) or with negligence (*culpa*). Whenever a direct causal link between delict and damage suffered could be established (*damnum corpore corpori datum*), the offender would be subject to a given

---

29 *See* Stein, quoting the functions of the *ius honorarium* as expressed by the Roman jurist Papinian, *supra* note 18 at 76-77.

30 *Ibid.* at 77.

31 Bénédict Winiger, *La Responsabilité Aquilienne Romaine: Damnum Iniuria Datum*, Helbing & Lichtenhahn, Bâle et Francfort-sur-le-Main (1997) at 33. My translation. The original passage in French reads as follows: "... la *ratio legis* de la *Lex Aquilia* était principalement de remplacer au proprietaire lésé le dommage économique subi, même si, dans certains fragments, les juristes mentionnèrent le caractère punitif de la *Lex Aquilia*".

sanction aimed at restoring the *status quo ante*, which would normally include the payment of compensation for the material damage encountered by the victim or by the victims' legitimate heirs and successors (*tantum aes domino [ero] dare damnas esto*). Conversely, without manifest and calculable damage, there could be no *iniuria*, and logically, there could be no responsibility.

3. The Shift to Retribution During the Middle Ages

The principle of victims' redress and its methods of implementation have evolved throughout the centuries within the changing political and legal context and the development of civil society. Matters relating to compensation formerly addressed within the private sphere, became part of State-controlled procedures, following the establishment of centralized systems. For example, as Zedner notes,[32] in twelfth-century England under the Kingdoms of Henry I and Henry II, compensation law and practice were highly influenced by the gradual shift in the balance within the system of justice administration, from a decentralized system to a highly centralized, State-controlled system of public prosecution, from which the victim was gradually alienated. The award of compensation directly to crime victims decreased radically with the emergence of the notion of 'crimes against the King's peace' - a concept derived from Roman Praetorial Law - according to which crimes of a particularly serious nature ought to be considered as offenses not only against the victim, but also against the King and the community.[33] Consequently, compensation would no longer be paid to individual victims - at least not exclusively - but to the King instead, generally in the form of a fine or *bot*.[34] Starting from the early Middle

---

32 For a most useful analysis of the law and practice related to issues of compensation for crime victims in early and modern England, *see* Lucia Zedner, "England", in Albin Eser and Susanne Walther (eds.), *Reparation in Criminal Law: International Perspectives*, Ed. Iuscrim, Max-Planck Inst. Für Ausländisches und International Strafrecht (1996), Vol. 1 at 109-227.

33 The notion of the King's peace influenced compensation systems in all of northern Europe. Tapio Lappi-Seppala explains the role of 'King's peace' in northern countries in "Finland", in Eser and Walther (eds.), *ibid.* at 322-323.

34 *See Victims of Crime*, Report No. 6 of the Community Law Reform Committee of the Australian Capital Territory, June 1993, at http://actg.canberra.edu.au/actag/Reports/CLRC.R6.Report6c2.html. Black's Law Dictionary, Fifth Edition (1979) defines *bot* or *bote* as a term of old English law indicating a recompense or compensation, or a profit or advantage. It was also used with the meaning of reparation or amends for any damage done. Similarly, a *man-bot* was the payment of compensation for slaying a victim. A *wer* was a pecuniary compensation set up for an

Ages, in addition to the payment of a *bot* to the victim, the offender would also have to pay a *wite*, a penalty to the King or the landlord who convened the court and helped bring about a reconciliation between the victim and offender. In the course of the twelfth century, the *wite* was gradually increased at the expense of the *bot*, until finally the *bot* was completely eliminated and the victim was left without compensation.[35]

As a result of the process of centralization, which brought the system of justice administration under stricter State control, the interests of victims were increasingly disregarded. This tendency became further pronounced with the wave of retributivism that swept the 1700s, which focussed mainly on the punishment of offenders, rather than the welfare of victims. In addition, retributivism brought about a massive proliferation in domestic criminal codes of offenses punishable by the mandatory use of the death penalty, further marginalizing individual victims and their efforts to receive redress. It was not until the end of the eighteenth century and the mitigation of pure retributive theories that victims could again play a more or less active role in the administration of justice in general and in criminal proceedings in particular.[36]

The renewed vitality of victims' participation in the administration of justice resulted also in the restoration of a fairer social balance between victims and perpetrators - a balance that had been upset by the excessive threat and use of capital punishment. However, victims were often powerful and wealthy persons compared to offenders, and the fate of offenders often depended upon whether victims were willing to show mercy to wrongdoers. Also, victims had the authority to decide whether or not to institute criminal proceedings against the alleged offender - proceedings which in many cases could result in the death penalty.[37] On the other side, offenders could appeal to the victims for mercy to escape the death sentence - a circumstance which accentuated disparities among classes within the justice system.

---

injury, or the value of a victim's life, which depended upon the rank of the victim in society. In case of serious offences such as homicide, the offender would have to pay a *wergild*, partly to the Crown for the loss of the subject, partly to the lord whose vassal the victim was, partly to the party inured or his or her next-of-kin.

35 *Victims of Crime, ibid.*

36 *See* Zedner, *supra* note 32.

37 On the historical development and social interactions of the death penalty *see* *Capital Punishment*, UN publication, Sales no. 62.IV.2, as reproduced in E. Lawson, *Encyclopedia of Human Rights*, Second Ed., Taylor & Francis (1996). This study was prepared by M. Ancel, following UNGA resolution 1936 [XIV] requesting ECOSOC to initiate a study on capital punishment.

4. Back to Restoration: The Right to Redress in Two Contemporary Examples

Although still reflecting retributive theories, many modern legal systems grant victims some role in the legal process. New streams of restorative legal doctrine are expanding and refining the theory of redress, and are breathing new life into the classic debate between retributionists, on the one hand, and proponents of rehabilitative justice, on the other.[38] Since the 1960s, the field of victimology has highlighted a number of issues related to crime victims, such as their relationship with offenders, their role in society and their rehabilitation. Also, in many instances, victims themselves have become more organized and have fought for recognition and effective implementation of their rights.

The following two case studies exemplify the modern trend across various legal traditions to go beyond purely retributive justice schemes, to incorporate restorative elements aimed at granting crime victims a more central role in justice administration and to provide for better mechanisms to support their search for redress. On the one hand, European countries have set up rather complex and refined legislation, mainly focussed on the payment of monetary compensation for injuries suffered and on the restitution of unlawfully taken property, through judicial proceedings. On the other hand, the Native North American Indian legal treatment of victims takes a completely different approach to redress within a more restorative, community-oriented perspective. Although these represent divergent implementation mechanisms, both legal traditions reveal a clear convergence and unity in purpose as they attempt to reach beyond the simple punishment of the offender and to incorporate restorative elements in their treatment of crime victims.

a. Reparations for Crime Victims in Europe and the European Convention on the Compensation of Victims of Violent Crimes

The principle of reparation from the offender to the victim in case of criminal offense is well established in all European countries. On the wave of the renewed interest in victims' rights at both the domestic and international levels over the last twenty years, many European States have encouraged

---

[38] For a concise overview of social and legal theories on punishment, *see* Nigel Walker, *Why Punish? Theories of punishment reassessed*, Oxford University Press (1991).

initiatives aimed at improving the treatment of victims within domestic legal systems to balance ongoing efforts for the development of more humane and enlightened policies concerning the treatment of offenders.

In 1975, the Council of Europe's Committee on Crime Problems established a Select Committee to draw up common principles governing the compensation of crime victims, with particular reference to compensation from public funds where the offender is unable to provide compensation to the victim. In 1981, the Committee further established a Select Committee of Experts charged with the study of matters concerning 'The Victim and Criminal and Social Policy'. On the basis of the work of the Select Committee, and encouraged by the introduction of domestic legislation on victims' compensation in a number of European States, in 1983 the Committee of Ministers of the EEC adopted the European Convention on the Compensation of Victims of Violent Crimes.[39] Although the Convention addresses intentional crimes committed in the domestic context, its principles and guidelines reflect current regional standards on redress as they are applied in domestic legislation. These standards may be of particular relevance for victims of crimes under international law, especially where cases are prosecuted in domestic courts.

As a result of the establishment of the Convention, European countries seem to have reached a certain degree of consolidation with respect to basic redress principles within domestic legislation relating to compensation for crime victims. Most European legislation provides victims of crime with an enforceable right to receive compensation from the offender. Judicial practice however, seems to show that the effective implementation of the victims' right to redress is not always an easy task. Access to justice at the domestic level is often complicated and in many countries judicial procedures may be overly long and expensive. In addition, often the offender's identity cannot be discovered, or he or she cannot be apprehended. In other cases, the offender is unwilling or unable to provide financial compensation to the victim. The situation is further complicated by the fact that domestic legislation and jurisprudence in European countries continue to suffer from certain inconsis-

---

39 European Convention on the Compensation of Victims of Violent Crimes, *adopted* by the Committee of Ministers in June 1983, *opened for signature* on 24 November 1983, *entered into force* on 1 February 1988. European Treaty Series No. 116, 1983. For a study on the impact of the Convention on the human rights system in Europe, *see* Giancarlo Scalese, "Un nuovo passo verso l'ampliamento del catalogo dei diritti umani: la Convenzione europea sul risarcimento delle vittime di crimini violenti", *Comunità Internazionale*, Vol. 51, No. 3 (1996), pp. 554-580.

tencies with respect to a number of fundamental issues, such as the right of victims to institute proceedings against the State for compensation (*locus standi*). On this matter, while the territoriality principle of *locus delictus* seems well established, the question of the nationality of the plaintiff claiming compensation from the State under domestic compensation schemes remains controversial.[40]

The Preamble of the Convention invokes the principles of 'equity and social solidarity' as motivations for the award of compensation.[41] At the implementation level, the idea of 'social solidarity' enshrined in the Conven-

---

[40] According to the law and practice of certain European countries, a victim of a criminal offence may be eligible for State compensation only if he or she is a national or permanent resident of the State in which territory the crime was committed. This is the case in Austria, for example, where according to the Crime Victims Compensation Act 1972, only Austrian citizens and citizens of member States of the 'European Economic Area' (under certain conditions) may be granted assistance payments. Similarly, in Belgium, Article 31 of the Victims Compensation Act 1985, provides for compensation exclusively to victims of Belgian nationality or to those who have been authorised to "enter, reside or establish" in the Kingdom. Finnish compensation law provides also for the nationality or permanent residence requirement. On this matter, it has been argued that the nationality requirement may result in a breach of the Treaty Establishing the European Economic Community 1957, which in Article 7 expressly prohibits any discrimination among citizens of the community. *See* Treaty of Rome Establishing the European Economic Community (EEC), *adopted* on 25 March 1957, *entered into force* on 1 January 1958. In particular, when seized with the question of nationality the European Court of Justice ruled that discrimination among EU citizens on grounds of nationality was indeed a breach of the EEC Treaty. *See Ian Cowan* v. *Le Tresor Public*, Case 186/87 of 2 February 1989, European Court Rep. 1989 at 195, in which a British tourist suffered injuries in French territory and was denied access to State compensation under French law on the grounds that he did not fulfill the requirement of nationality. In that case, the ECJ ruled that French law was in breach of Article 7 of the Rome Treaty. French legislation on compensation matters has been amended subsequently.

[41] Domestically, legislation concerning State compensation for victims often expressly recognizes 'principles of humanity and justice' and 'social solidarity'. *See e.g.* the Austrian Act for the Grant of Assistance to Victims of Crime, *entered into force* on 1 September 1972, the Finnish Criminal Injuries Compensation Act 1973, *entered into force* on 1 March 1974, and the Danish Compensation from the State for Victims of Crimes (Consolidation) Act of 1985 (Act No. 470 of 1 November 1985), all discussed in detail in Desmond Greer (ed.), *Compensating Crimes Victims - A European Survey*, ed. Iuscrim, Max-Planck Inst. Für Ausländisches und International Strafrecht (1996).

tion is translated into an obligation for the signatories to take the necessary steps to give effect to the principles of the Convention. This includes States introducing schemes for victims' compensation where violent crimes were committed in their territory, in particular where the offender has not been identified or is without sufficient resources. In addition, the Preamble of the Convention makes special reference to the need to "establish minimum provisions" for victims' compensation, although Article 4 provides for the setting of both a minimum threshold and an upper limit for compensation.

Perhaps one of the main innovations of the European Convention is the introduction of the principle of subsidiary State compensation among the Convention's 'Basic Principles'.[42] According to the principle of subsidiary compensation, Article 2 provides that a State shall contribute to compensation for victims of intentional crimes of violence "when compensation is not fully available from other sources", and that compensation shall be awarded "even if the offender cannot be prosecuted or punished". The principle of territorial competence (*lex locus delictus*) as expressed in Article 3 also figures among the Convention's basic principles. In this respect, a State where the crime was committed must pay compensation to victims who are either nationals of the State parties to the Convention, or nationals of any member States of the Council of Europe who are at the same time permanent residents of the State bound to pay compensation.

Following the adoption of the European Convention on Compensation, a number of States have introduced domestic legislation on victims' compensation in an effort to meet the Convention's minimum requirements. Indeed, even States which have neither signed nor ratified the Convention appear to have adapted their legislation concerning victims and victims' compensation in order to provide fair access to legal proceedings and to ensure the effective right to redress.

In this context, it is interesting to note that many European States seem to operate according to a number of common principles relating to various aspects of compensation for victims of criminal offences. Such principles provide a useful framework for compensation practices at both domestic and international levels and may be summarized as follows:

- **Nature of redress**: To achieve full reparation (*restitutio in integrum*) and, as much as possible, the restoration of the *status quo ante*, judiciaries in European countries seem to resort mainly to monetary compensation covering both 'positive loss' (*quantum mihi abest*) and

---

42 The Convention's Basic Principles are expressed in Articles 1 to 11.

'loss of profit' (*quantum lucrari potui*). Occasionally, and depending on the specific case, restitution in kind has also been awarded.

- **Extent of redress**: European legal systems operate mainly on the principle according to which liability to pay damages to crime victims arises from an injury or loss resulting from an intentional or negligent unlawful action.[43] It is commonly recognized that compensation should be 'fair', 'just' and 'equitable' and should restore the victim as much as possible to his or her position prior to the wrongful act. While compensation for material injuries is relatively easy to assess, the extent of redress for moral injuries remains more a matter of judicial discretion.
- **Redress for material and moral damages**: Traditionally, compensation was awarded only where there was a sufficiently direct cause / effect relationship between a criminal act and a material injury suffered by the victim. However, legislation in most European countries provides also for compensation for moral damages, especially in cases of sexual offences and where the criminal act has caused 'pain and suffering'.[44]

---

43 However, certain State-sponsored victim compensation programmes require a higher standard of liability and restrict the award of compensation only to victims of actions which are both unlawful and intentional. In Germany, for example, on the one hand Article 823(1) of the Civil Code states that: "any person who wilfully or negligently injures the life, body, health, freedom, property or other right of another unlawfully, must compensate him for any damage arising therefrom". On the other hand, the Victim's Compensation Act 1976 establishes, among other conditions, that State compensation should be awarded exclusively to victims who prove that the criminal act causing injuries was not only unlawful but also intentional. For a review of German legislation on this matter, *see* Michael Kaiser and Michael Kilchling, "Germany", in Greer (ed.), *supra* note 41 at 255-297. *Similarly*, Article 1 of Portuguese Law No. 423/91 on Protection of Victims of Violent Crimes 1991, provides for State compensation only for "serious personal injury resulting from an intentionally violent act", while under the Portuguese Civil Code, both intentional and negligent unlawful actions give rise to liability for the payment of damages.

44 *See e.g.* Article 1329 of 'Das Allgemeine Burgerliche Gesetzbuch', the General Civil Code of Austria, and Article 312 of the Austrian Penal Code. In addition, Articles 1325 *et seq.* of the Austrian Civil Code provide for compensation for damages for pain and suffering resulting from the hardship arising from the injury. In case of offenses pertaining to human rights, however, all the above mentioned provisions must be read in the light of the Government Liability Act 1949, according to which agents of the Government are liable for personal injury or damage to property only in case of "unlawful and culpable conduct". *See* Wolfgang Raschka, "National Reports on Crime

- **Victim's participation in the proceedings**: Generally, individual crime victims are allowed to file compensation claims either in civil or criminal proceedings, where they enjoy the same procedural rights and status as the plaintiff. In order for a victim to be eligible for compensation in a criminal proceeding, he or she must become a civil party (*partie civile*) to the criminal proceedings against the offender.[45] This means that a judge of the criminal trial may award compensation to the victim exclusively if the victim participates in the criminal proceedings and makes a specific claim for redress, either in the form of compensation or in other forms.
- **State compensation**: A number of European countries have adopted legislation providing for State-funded financial support to victims of violent crimes as a subsidiary means of compensation, in line with the principle of social solidarity enshrined in the European Convention on the Compensation of Victims of Violent Crimes 1983.[46] However,

---

Victim Compensation in Various Member States of the Council of Europe: Austria", in Greer (ed.), *supra* note 41 at 15-66. *See further, inter alia*, Article 3 of the Danish Damages Liability Act 1984, which contains a similar provision on the award of damages for pain and suffering resulting from the injury; Article 5 of the Finnish Criminal Injuries Compensation Act 1973; Articles 299 and 932 of the Greek Civil Code; Article 2059 of the Italian Civil Code. However, *see* the Irish General Scheme of Compensation for Personal Injuries Criminally Inflicted 1974, *amended* in 1986, and Portuguese Law No. 423/91 on Protection of Victims of Violent Crimes of 30 October 1991, both specifically excluding the payment of compensation for non-pecuniary loss, to reduce the high costs of providing full redress.

45 However, in the United Kingdom as in other common law countries, there is no *partie civile* system and victims have no formal standing in the criminal proceedings. As for the status of victims in legal systems allowing them to participate in the criminal proceeding, legislation often guarantees victims the right to be informed and provides for a duty of the authorities to respect the victim's personal sphere - a duty that derives directly from Articles 6 and 8 of the European Convention on Human Rights 1950. *See e.g.* Article 10(3) of the Danish Victim Compensation Act 1985, Article 47(a) of the Austrian Code of Criminal Procedure (StPO) and the 'Guidelines for the Public Prosecutor and the Police' (Vaillant Guidelines) *adopted* by The Netherlands in February 1986.

46 *See e.g.* the Victims Assistance Act and Compensation Scheme for Victims of Violent Crimes 1985, *adopted* in Belgium to better cover gaps in victims' compensation for criminal matters. The Victims Assistance Act also establishes a Compensation Fund partially supported by the budget of the Ministry of Justice and provides for a fixed-sum obligatory 'solidarity contribution' to be paid by all convicted offenders. Similarly, Denmark enacted in 1976 a Compensation Act from the State for Victims of Crimes,

even countries which have adopted this kind of legislation are still far from having recognized a general enforceable right of victims to receive compensation directly from the State in addition to, or instead of, from the offender. In other words, the State seems to provide compensation to victims not on the basis of having incurred legal responsibility for failing to have prevented certain criminal acts, but purely as a form of social support for victims in general.[47] In addition, the award of State compensation is usually restricted to cases of violent crime where the victim has suffered personal injuries.

- **Payment for damages**: According to the trend in European legislation, damages to victims of criminal offenses are paid by:
  - a. the offender as part of a sentence or provisional remedy imposed upon him or her, or as a result of a judicial order; or
  - b. the State, through subsidiary systems of victims' compensation, under which a victim may file a claim for compensation directly before the State.

---

later amended by the 1985 Consolidation Act and by Act No. 366 of 18 May 1994. Under French law, the State provides for compensation for crime victims under a General Compensation Scheme, *enacted* in the Law of 6 July 1990, *entered into force* on 1 January 1991, and for victims of terrorism according to a special 1986 compensation scheme, amended by the Law of 6 July 1990. *See also* the German Victim Compensation Act, *promulgated* on 11 May 1976, *entered into force* on 16 May 1976, *amended* in 1985 and the War Victims Maintenance Act; the Dutch State Compensation Scheme set out in the Criminal Injuries Compensation Fund Act 1975; the Norwegian scheme on 'Compensation from the State for Personal Injury Caused by a Criminal Act' 1976, also establishing a Compensation Tribunal for Victims of Violence; Portuguese Law No. 423/91 on Protection of Victims of Violent Crimes of 30 October 1991; and the Swedish Criminal Injuries Compensation Act of 1978, *amended* in 1994. As concerns common law legislation, Ireland adopted in 1974 (backdated to 1972) a 'Scheme of Compensation for Personal Injuries Criminally Inflicted' establishing a special Criminal Injuries Compensation Tribunal which awards compensation on an *ex gratia* basis. The UK has long experience in State compensation, which dates back to 1964 for Great Britain and to 1968 for Northern Ireland. For a review of British law on compensation *see* David Miers, *State Compensation for Criminal Injuries*, London, Blackstone Press (1997). One may consider, however, the absence of any general legislation on compensation from the State in countries such as Italy (except for victims of organized criminal associations and terrorism).

47 The relevant Finnish legislation however, guarantees victims a legal right to compensation enforceable against the State. The amount of the compensation award remains at the discretion of the State.

Generally, State compensation has been intended mainly to provide a complementary means of redress. In practice however, victims seem to rely primarily on State compensation: reparation from the offender often proves practically impossible to obtain or, in many instances, is unsatisfactory to the victims.

- **Recipients of compensation**: *In primis*, the victim benefits from compensation where he or she survives the offense. Where the victim is deceased, his or her rights extend generally to the spouse and the victim's descendants and ascendants. However, several laws provide for compensation to be granted exclusively in favour of the individual victim who has personally suffered injuries caused by the criminal act, in which case the rights of the victim do not pass to his or her relatives.[48]

b. Redress in Native North American Indian Justice Systems: A Holistic Approach

Native North American Indian justice systems present some interesting alternatives to retributive theories. In contrast to Western justice systems, which tend to separate the offender from the victim and to focus on the punishment of the offender, rather than on the rehabilitation of the victim, Native North American Indian justice systems are generally based on a more holistic approach which explores the offender / victim relationship from a broader perspective. In many Native North American Indian philosophies, justice is expressed as a circle:

> ... that connects everyone involved with a problem or conflict on a continuum, with everyone focussed on the same centre. The centre of the circle represents the underlying issues that need to be resolved to attain peace and harmony for the individuals and the community.[49]

In the 'circle of justice' the focus is on the victim and the need to heal and renew his or her physical, emotional, mental and spiritual well-being through restoration and reparation. In this process, the offender is also encouraged to regain dignity and trust within the community through dialogue with the victim

---

48 This is the case in Finnish law. *See* Lappi-Seppala, *supra* note 33 at 374-375.

49 *Indigenous Systems and Tribal Society*, paper by A. Pecos Melton, President of the American Indian Development Associates, http://www.opj.usdoj.gob/nij/rest-just/ch1/indigenous.htm.

aimed at "making amends through apology, asking forgiveness, making restitution".[50] Recently, the United States and Canada have granted indigenous peoples a certain measure of autonomy in the administration of justice according to their original indigenous tribal systems.[51] In general, tribes exercise territorial jurisdiction over lands and people in their territories, as well as jurisdiction *ratione materiae* over criminal, juvenile and civil matters. Disputes are settled in various fora, which range from the more traditional family and community fora (family gatherings or talking circles with the help of facilitators and tribal officials); to traditional courts incorporating modern judicial practices into traditional community fora; to quasi-modern courts based on the Anglo-American legal model; to tribal courts reflecting modern legal systems.[52] The applicable law typically encompasses tribal customs, traditions and practices, written codes, procedural codes and guidelines.

The victim plays a central role in the restorative / reparative Native North American Indian justice systems. The offender, or his or her family, is expected to confront the victim and the victim's family, to explain his or her behaviour, to recognize responsibility for it, to accept accountability, and to make amends and express remorse for the wrongdoing. With the help of the community, of trained facilitators and tribal mediators, the victim receives support to help understand the motives behind the wrongful act, which can be the first step towards personal healing, and possibly, forgiveness. Offenders are encouraged to ask for forgiveness from the victim and family, although forgiveness from the victim is not always considered an essential or necessary element of many Native North American Indian justice processes. As for the offender, he or she must perform restorative and reparative acts aimed at the restoration of the *status quo ante*, and full compliance is required for any given

---

50 *Ibid.*

51 A flourishing literature is growing in the field of traditional Native justice systems, relating to alternative methods of healing and dispute resolution. *See*, *inter alia*, Ross Green, *Justice in Aboriginal Communities: Sentencing Alternatives*, Purich Publishing, Saskatoon, Saskatchewan, Canada (1998); Robert Ross, "Aboriginal Community Healing in Action: the Hollow Water", *Justice as Healing: A Newsletter on Aboriginal Concepts of Justice*, Native Law Centre at the University of Saskatchewan (Spring 1995); Larissa Behrendt, *Aboriginal Dispute Resolution: A Step Towards Self-Determination and Community Autonomy*, Australia: Federation Press (1995); Robert Yazzie, "The Navajo Response to Crime", *Justice as Healing: A Newsletter on Aboriginal Concepts of Justice* Vol. 3, No. 2 (Summer 1998); Bria Huculak, "From the Power to Punish to the Power to Heal", *Justice as Healing: A Newsletter on Aboriginal Concepts of Justice* (Fall 1995).

52 *Indigenous Systems and Tribal Society*, *supra* note 49.

sanction. As in Western systems, Native North American Indian justice systems also use sanctions to appease the victims' desire for revenge. These may range from public ridicule and shame for less serious wrongs to temporary or permanent banishment from the tribe or withdrawal of 'citizenship' rights for more serious crimes.[53]

In a way, the Native North American Indian 'circle of justice' is the antithesis of the compartmentalised approach of Western systems of justice administration in which, following the criminal act, the State forces offender and victim to become adversaries whose interests are expected to diverge and never meet. For centuries, the separation of offender and victim has been used to avoid private revenge, which is arguably a risk to be taken into account, especially in the immediate aftermath of the criminal offence. Over the longer term however, this may not be the best way to provide redress for victims or to restore harmony in the community, as discussed below.

5. From Retributive Justice to Restorative Justice: A Necessary Passage?

With a few exceptions, such as Native North American Indian traditions, most justice systems of the past and present find their roots in retributive philosophies and focus mainly on the punishment of the criminal offender rather than on the rehabilitation of the victim.[54] The punishment inflicted on the offender is considered not only as a necessary retribution and a deterrent for potential perpetrators, but is intended also to satisfy the desire for revenge of the victim which - it is assumed - is an intrinsic and undeniable instinct. In many Western legal systems following the common law tradition,

---

[53] On the elements, theory and practice of the Native American Indian traditional justice system, *see generally* the following articles published in *Justice as Healing: A Newsletter on Aboriginal Concepts of Justice*: James J. R. Guest, "Aboriginal Legal Theory and Restorative Justice", Vol. 3, No. 4 (Winter 1998); Michael R. Peterson, "Developing a Restorative Justice Programme", Vol. 5, No. 3 (Fall 2000); Robert Yazzie, "Healing as Justice: the American Experience" (Spring 1995); and Neil R. Schriml, "State, the Community and Restorative Justice", Vol. 1, No. 1 (Spring 1996).

[54] As George P. Fletcher argues in "The Place of Victims in the Theory of Retribution", *Buffalo Criminal Law Review*, No. 3 (1999) at 1, "remarkably, the theory of criminal law has developed without paying much attention to the place of victims in the analysis of responsibility or in the rationale for punishment. ... In the last several decades we have witnessed notable strides toward attending to the rights and interests of crime victims, but these concerns have yet to intrude upon the discussion of the central issues of wrongdoing, blame, and punishment".

the justice process triggered by a criminal act terminates with the punishment of the offender, and reparation to victims is not usually contemplated as a part of the punishment. Claims for reparation are normally filed separately in civil courts once the criminal proceedings have established the responsibility of the offender.

Although some legal systems have been increasingly experimenting with forms of reconciliation between victim and offender, at present, redress for victims remains mainly in the form of monetary compensation awarded in a court of law, paid either by the offender directly or with the participation of the State. Arguably, the money victims may receive as compensation for the damage suffered may provide considerable and necessary support, especially when the victim has lost his or her earning ability because of the offence. However, money can rarely restore the *status quo ante*: certainly it is not a central element of the victim's healing process, and arguably, it should form only a part of victims' redress.

Nevertheless, the feasibility or even the desirability of a justice system based primarily on restorative purposes remains to be seen, especially in case of crimes under international law where the punishment of the offender and the fight against impunity are essential elements in the achievement of international criminal justice. The critical question is whether victims and society in general would benefit more from such an approach, as compared, for example, to simple compensation mechanisms set up within retributive legal systems.

In practice, some contradictions may arise in the attempt to complement or substitute elements of restorative justice in a system strongly based on retribution. This is well illustrated in *The Queen* v. *Clotworthy*,[55] in which, following a series of meetings parallel to the trial proceedings with a restorative justice facilitator, the victim offered forgiveness to the offender who showed a willingness to repair the damage he had caused. In particular, the victim came to the conclusion that imprisonment of the offender would be a wasteful and inappropriate way to resolve the matter. As a consequence, the victim and the offender reached an agreement which was subsequently endorsed by the District Court. The Court imposed a suspended sentence of two years' imprisonment and ordered reparation of NZ$15,000 to cover the cost of cosmetic plastic surgery for the victim. The offender was also required to serve two hundred hours of community service.

---

55 *The Queen* v. *Clotworthy*, Appeal Court of New Zealand 114/98, Wellington, 1998. In this case, the offender, Mr. Clotworthy, stabbed the victim in the back and slashed him in the face during a robbery, leaving him severely injured and partially disfigured, and causing a resurgence of the victim's pre-existing epileptic condition.

The Crown appealed however, arguing that a suspended sentence of two years was not appropriate, despite the victim's submissions arguing that imprisonment would achieve nothing for the offender or himself. The Appeal Court commended the victim for having forgiven the offender and for having found a constructive compromise. However, it reversed the District Court decision, by arguing that:

> a wider dimension must come into the sentencing exercise than simply the position as between victim and offender. The public interest in consistency, integrity of the criminal justice system and deterrence of others are factors of major importance.

The Appeal Court held that the offer of reparation did not justify a suspension of the sentence, and consequently imposed a sentence of three years' imprisonment (instead of the usual sentence of five or six years in similar cases) and reduced the reparation award to NZ$5,000, on the basis that the offender, having to serve a prison term, would not be able to work and pay the previously awarded NZ$15,000. In its concluding arguments, the Appeal Court stated that the judgment was not intended to express a general opposition to the concept of restorative justice, but that:

> [restorative justice] policies must ... be balanced against other sentencing policies, particularly ... those ... dealing with cases of serious violence. Which aspect should predominate will depend on an assessment of where the balance should lie in the individual case. Even if the balance is found, as in this case, to lie in favour of [other sentencing] policies, the restorative aspects can have, as here a significant impact on the length of the term of imprisonment which the Court is directed to impose. They find their place in the ultimate outcome in that way.[56]

Despite the potential contradictions of introducing restorative elements in retributive justice systems and the need to find a balance on a case-by-case

---

[56] *Ibid.* For further reflection on the impact of this case on the theory of restorative justice *see* Charles Barton, "Empowerment and Retribution in Criminal Justice", in Heather Strang and John Braithwaite (eds.), *Restorative Justice: Philosophy to Practice*, Ashgate Dartmouth, Sidney (2000) in which the author argues that restorative practices and retributive justice can coexist and that the strength of restorative justice lies in the empowerment of both the victim and the offender and not in the rejection of punishment and retribution.

basis, with regard to crimes under international law, which typically involve a large number of victims, it would seem worthwhile to follow a complementary approach between retributive procedures and restorative justice, one in which the purely retributive function performed by punitive sanctions is complemented by restorative elements such as apologies, rehabilitation and reconciliation.[57] This tendency has been endorsed by a large number of States in the context of the Rome Statute of the International Criminal Court, which, as discussed in Chapter VI, is based on a compromise approach bringing tighter focus on the victims of genocide, crimes against humanity and war crimes, while preserving the essential retributive function of international criminal justice. Ultimately, in the fight against crimes of such magnitude that threaten the foundations of society, a balance must be found between the need to punish perpetrators and the necessity to rehabilitate victims, with a final aim of reconciliation, reparation, forgiveness, apology and restoration of the social environment injured by the atrocities committed. As Kelsen explains in this memorable passage:

> The same holds true with respect to the principle which probably is most often presented as the essence of justice: like for like, that is, good for good and evil for evil, the principle of retribution. This principle is meaningless unless the answer to the question, what is good and what is evil, is presupposed as self-evident. But the answer to this question is not at all self-evident, since the ideas of good and evil are very different among different peoples and at different times. The principle of retribution expresses only the specific technique of the positive law, which reacts against the evil of the delict with the evil of the sanction. Hence, any positive legal order corresponds to this principle. The question of justice, however, is the question of whether a positive legal order, attaching to the evil of the delict the evil of the sanction, is just, whether that which the lawmaker considers as an evil to society is indeed a behaviour against which society should justly react, and whether the sanction with which society actually reacts is appropriate. To this question, which is the very question of the justice of the law, the principle of retribution is no answer at all. So far as retribution means like for like, it is one of

---

57 For a very useful study on restorative justice, *see generally* H. Strang and J. Braithwaite (eds.), *ibid.,* in which the contributors present a number of interesting arguments proposing restorative justice as a viable alternative to retributive justice, explore various interesting mechanisms for its implementation at the domestic level and examine the various attitudes of different countries towards the incorporation of restorative principles in their respective justice systems.

> the many varieties of the principle of equality, which, too, is presented as the essence of justice.[58]

Certainly, there is no easy answer to this dilemma. Its solution remains, ultimately, a question of moral choice and perhaps politics, rather than a matter of pure legal procedure.

---

[58] Kelsen, *supra* note 21 at 13-14. This extract was originally part of a farewell lecture by Kelsen at the University of California, Berkeley, dated 27 May 1952.

CHAPTER III

The Victims' Right to Redress as Exercised in Domestic Fora

Traditionally, the right to redress for crime victims has been exercised at the domestic level in the context of regular criminal law enforcement. Even within the human rights treaty regime, enforcement of victims' right to redress is normally delegated to domestic courts, as discussed in Chapter V. In practice, however, the access of victims and survivors of genocide, crimes against humanity, war crimes or other crimes under international law, to effective domestic avenues for redress has not always been easy. Most of the time, the nature of these crimes is such that many victims and survivors are involved, and domestic legal systems often do not have the capacity to deal with a great number of reparation claimants. Also, one of the main difficulties has been that frequently the victim's own country of nationality has been involved in the violations and it may be unwilling to guarantee victims either fair access to justice or equitable redress. In other cases, domestic judicial systems may be simply unable to provide victims with compensation or with proper access to justice, such as in the case of Rwanda, where some 80% of judges and lawyers were killed during the 1994 genocide. The option of victims accessing foreign courts for the purpose of redress remains an exception rather than the rule and is subject to a number of serious shortcomings, as discussed below.

Still, because reparation procedures at the international level remain at a formative stage, or may be highly contingent upon political considerations, victims of crimes under international law often have little option but to seek redress at the domestic level. Under growing pressure from organized victims' groups, more and more reparation claims against individual perpetrators for crimes under international law are being filed before domestic courts and dealt with mainly according to domestic standards, either in criminal proceedings (directly or through the *partie civile* procedure typical of civil law systems), or in tort. In particular, victims seem to be relying increasingly on civil actions to obtain compensation, even in cases that would normally fall under criminal jurisdiction, such as genocide, crimes against humanity or war crimes.[1]

The following discussion shows that victims' access to domestic fora in cases of crimes under international law has produced uneven results in terms of redress. It is argued that the very idea of compensating victims of fundamental violations of international law according to purely domestic principles, criteria and proceedings is not only flawed in theory, but difficult to implement in practice for a number of reasons explored below. Indeed, the uneven results in terms of victims' attempts to access domestic fora for redress emphasize the need for a clearly defined and coherent international regime on this matter. The present section therefore highlights strengths and weaknesses in the domestic implementation of the victims' right to redress for crimes under international law and discusses ways in which international instruments can provide guidance in the domestic enforcement of reparation.

1. Strengths and Weaknesses of Domestic Jurisdiction over Crimes under International Law

In current practice, the exercise of domestic jurisdiction and the eventual award of reparations for crimes under international law are performed on the basis of internationally recognized grounds of jurisdiction and are regulated by domestic law as well as international agreements among States.[2]

---

1 For the purposes of compensation, civil actions have the advantage of not only targeting directly the civil liability of a defendant, but also of requiring less action by the State prosecutorial authorities. Paradoxically, this circumstance may favour victims, since States, often for political reasons, might be reluctant to prosecute high-profile individuals suspected of serious human rights violations.

2 More generally, the commitment of States to prosecute and punish perpetrators of crimes under international law reflects the principle *aut dedere aut judicare*, according to which States may either prosecute or extradite suspects of crimes under international law found in their territory. There is much discussion on the status of the principle *aut dedere aut judicare* in international law. For an argument in favour of the customary application of this principle to all international offenses, *see* M. Cherif Bassiouni and Edward Wise, *Aut Dedere Aut Judicare: The Duty to Extradite or Prosecute in International Law*, Martinus Nijhoff (1995) at 21. *See a contrario* Lyal S. Sunga, *The Emerging System of International Criminal Law: Developments in Codification and Implementation*, Kluwer Law International (1997) at 254-255, arguing that the obligation either to extradite or to prosecute has not been established firmly and that it is doubtful that such principle reflects a mandatory obligation of international customary law. In this sense, *see also* Geoff Gilbert, *Aspects of Extradition Law*,

Traditionally, States have exclusive jurisdiction over individuals and property to the limits of their territorial sovereignty and on vessels under their flags in territory *res communis omnium*. Therefore, according to the territoriality principle, the courts of a State where a crime was committed may exercise jurisdiction over such crime. In the case of criminal offences however, a State may claim jurisdiction also on other grounds.[3] In particular,

---

Martinus Nijhoff (1991) at 157, also arguing that the principle *aut dedere aut judicare* applies only when "expressly formulated in multilateral conventions on international criminal law". On the application of this principle to the crime of genocide, *see* William Schabas, *Genocide in International Law*, Cambridge University Press (2000) at 404 - 405, who remarks that the Genocide Convention "stops short of imposing any general duty to try or extradite ... comparable to that found in the 1949 Geneva Conventions for grave breaches". However, Schabas further notes that during the drafting of the Genocide Convention, a UN Secretariat memo indicated that States Parties would be compelled "pursuant to the convention and to 'general principles of law', to punish genocidal acts committed on [their] territory" or to grant extradition to the State where the crime was committed.

[3] In the *Lotus Case* 1927, the Permanent Court of International Justice clarified some aspects related to the exclusive use of the principle of territoriality. In its judgment, the PCIJ opined that: "the territoriality of criminal law ... is not an absolute principle of international law and by no means coincides with territorial sovereignty"; and that all, or nearly all, systems of law extend their jurisdiction to offences committed outside the territory of the State. PCIJ Reports, Series A, No.10. On grounds for jurisdiction *see* the Harvard Research Draft Convention on Jurisdiction with Respect to Crime 1935, *American Journal of International Law*, Vol. 29, No. 443 Supp. (1935). In Chapter XIV of *Principles of Public International Law*, Fourth Ed., Clarendon Press (1990), Ian Brownlie argues that, even though a number of English and American judicial decisions suggest that the territorial principle is exclusive, State practice has not followed this view. He further explains that States have often acted on the basis of the so-called 'objective territorial principle', according to which "jurisdiction is founded when any essential constituent element of a crime is consummated on state territory". M. N. Shaw takes a similar view in *International Law*, Fourth Ed., Cambridge University Press (1997) at 462, where he specifies that, "although jurisdiction is primarily and predominantly territorial, it is not inevitably and exclusively so and states are free to consent to arrangements whereby jurisdiction is exercised outside the national territory and whereby jurisdiction by other states is exercised within the national territory". On grounds for the exercise of jurisdiction for crimes under international law *see also* Rüdiger Wolfrum, "The Decentralized Prosecution of International Offences Through National Courts", *Israel Yearbook on Human Rights*, Vol. 24, pp. 183-199; Covey T. Oliver, "The Jurisdiction (Competence) of States", in Mohammed Bedjaoui (ed.), *International Law: Achievements and Prospects*, Martinus Nijhoff (1991) at 307-325; and Sunga, *supra* note 2 at 249-250.

States may also exercise jurisdiction on the basis of the nationality of the offender, in which case domestic courts may claim jurisdiction over extra-territorial acts if such acts allegedly have been committed by a national (or in certain cases even a resident) of the State in question; according to the 'protective principle' which operates where a State's national interest or security have been threatened or injured by the offence;[4] following the doctrine of universal jurisdiction discussed more fully below; and according to the 'passive personality principle', which is based on the nationality of the person injured and allows domestic courts to exercise jurisdiction over aliens for criminal actions committed abroad against their own nationals. The following discussion critically evaluates the more recent use of the passive personality and universality principles as means of special importance for victims of crimes under international law to gain access and obtain redress in domestic fora.

a. A Reading of the Passive Personality Principle in the Light of the *Pinochet Case*

The passive personality principle has rarely been invoked by States, many of which consider its use controversial under international law.[5] Historically, powerful States such as the US and the UK have strongly opposed any exercise of jurisdiction based on grounds of passive personality, perhaps fearing that it would expose their own nationals to legal proceedings abroad if other countries acted reciprocally.[6] More recently, however, a number of

---

[4] On the use of the 'protective principle' *see generally* Iain Cameron, *The Protective Principle of International Criminal Jurisdiction*, Dartmouth Publishing Company, Aldershot (1994).

[5] The *Cutting Case* of 1886 represents one of the few examples of the use of the passive personality principle. In this case, a Mexican court invoked the passive personality principle in exercising jurisdiction over Mr. Cutting, an American citizen. The Mexican court arrested Cutting while in Mexican territory and convicted him for having published in a Texas newspaper a defamatory statement concerning a Mexican citizen, which is considered a criminal offence under Mexican law. This episode caused diplomatic protest from the United States. However, the outcome of the case was inconclusive because the injured party withdrew the charges. John Bassett Moore, *Digest of International Law*, Vol. II, Washington, D.C., Government Printing Office (1906) at 228-242.

[6] In his textbook *International Law*, *supra* note 3 at 467-468, Shaw discusses this issue and presents as an example of US opposition to the passive personality principle the protests advanced by the US against Greece on the service of summonses by Greek Consuls in the US on US nationals involved in accidents with Greek nationals

States, including the US and other persistent objectors to the passive personality principle, seem to have begun recognizing the value of this principle when applied in certain instances, such as the prosecution of suspects for transboundary terrorism and crimes under international law.[7]

In this context, it is interesting to recall that the *Pinochet Case* was initiated on the basis of the passive personality principle. In fact, the first provisional arrest warrant against Pinochet was issued on 16 October 1998 by Mr. Nicholas Evans, a Metropolitan Magistrate, at the request of Spanish Judge Garzon's extradition order pursuant to section 8(1)(b) of the UK Extradition Act 1989, and on the basis of allegations concerning the murder of Spanish citizens in Chile.[8] Spanish courts claimed jurisdiction over the case on the basis of a 1985 law inspired by the passive personality principle. The *Ley Organica del Poder Judicial* grants Spanish courts jurisdiction over crimes committed by Spanish or foreign citizens outside Spain when such crimes qualify, under Spanish law, as genocide, terrorism or any other crime which, according to international treaties or conventions, must be prosecuted in Spain.

---

on US territory in the 1970s. The author also remarks that in 1986, following the *Achille Lauro* incident, the US adopted the Omnibus Diplomatic Security and Anti-terrorism Act, which inserts into the Criminal Code provisions establishing jurisdiction on grounds of passive personality in cases such as homicide and physical violence. However, the 1986 US Anti-Terrorism Act seems to grant jurisdiction to US courts over suspects of terrorist acts against US nationals only if such acts are committed as part of a terrorist plan aimed at the US itself - a situation that seems to fall more within the meaning of the 'protective principle' rather than being an example of the application of the 'passive personality' principle. On this point *see also* Gilbert, *supra* note 2 at 45.

7 *See US* v. *Yunis (no. 2)*, 681 F. Supp 896 (1988) D. Ct. Columbia, in which a US Court acted on the basis of both universal jurisdiction and the passive personality principle. The Court pointed out that, although the US had historically opposed the passive personality principle, in recent years, the US and the international community at large have accepted the principle in relation to the prosecution and punishment of acts of terrorism and crimes under international law.

8 The extradition order sustained that there was evidence that Pinochet: "between 11 September 1973 and 31 December 1983 within the jurisdiction of the fifth Central Magistrate of the National Court of Madrid did murder Spanish citizens in Chile within the jurisdiction of the Government of Spain". *See* Opinion of the Lords of Appeal for Judgment in the Cause *Regina* v. *Bartle and the Commissioner of Police for the Metropolis and Others (Appellants) EX Parte Pinochet (Respondent) (on appeal from a Divisional Court of the Queen's Bench Division), Regina* v. *Evans and Another and the Commissioner of Police for the Metropolis and Others (Appellants) EX Parte Pinochet (Respondent) (on appeal from a Divisional Court of the Queen's Bench Division)* of 25 November 1998.

Following the first request of the Spanish courts however, the Divisional Court of the Queen's Bench Division in England stated that the arrest warrant was *prima facie* bad for lack of double criminality, and held that the criminal offences alleged in the Spanish extradition request were not subject to extradition according to the UK Extradition Act.[9] Therefore, the condition of reciprocity could not be fulfilled. Specifically, the refusal concerned the fact that, contrary to Spanish law, the murder of a British national by a non-British national on foreign territory would not constitute an offence for which the UK could claim extraterritorial jurisdiction.[10] In addition, it was also found that section 2(3)(a) of the Extradition Act was not satisfied, and that it was not sufficient that the victims were citizens of Spain, since for the Act to apply the accused also had to be a citizen of Spain.

On 23 October 1998, however, Pinochet was arrested again on the basis of a new warrant issued one day earlier by Metropolitan Magistrate Ronald Bartle, following a new application of the Spanish Government based on evidence that Pinochet was accused of offences such as conspiracy to commit torture, conspiracy to commit murder and the crime of hostage-taking. A few days later, on 3 November 1998, Spanish courts requested the extradition of Pinochet for breaches of Spanish law relating to genocide, torture and terrorism, committed mainly in Chile, but also outside Chile. This time, the request for extradition was based on grounds of both the passive personality and universal jurisdiction principles. As the Judges of the *Audiencia National* in Plenary Session ruled:

> Spain is competent to judge the events by virtue of the principle of universal prosecution for certain crimes - a category of international law - established by our internal legislation. It also has a legitimate interest in the exercise of such jurisdiction because more than 50

---

9 *The Matter of an Application for a Writ of Habeas Corpus ad Subjicendum. Re: Augusto Pinochet Duarte*, The High Court of Justice, Queen's Bench Division, Divisional Court, 28 October 1998, 38 ILM (1999) at 68. However, prior to this refusal, Pinochet was arrested at a London Clinic on 16 October 1998 pursuant to the provisional arrest order.

10 Section 9 of the Offences Against the Person Act 1861, allows UK courts to try a defendant for murder outside the territory of the UK only where the defendant is a UK national.

> nationals were killed or disappeared in Chile, victims of the repression reported in the proceedings.[11]

In this second case, the Home Secretary issued an order to proceed with the extradition proceedings, except for the charge of genocide, and stated that all other charges in the second extradition request amounted to extraditable crimes and were not of a political character. Later, the decision to issue the second warrant was quashed pending an appeal to the House of Lords, and Pinochet was released from custody on bail. Eventually, in further proceedings the House of Lords reversed the Divisional Court judgment which granted immunity to Pinochet on the ground that the alleged violations were official acts performed in the exercise of his functions as Head of State.

It is unnecessary, for the purpose of this discussion, to examine in detail the reasons why the House of Lords finally decided to proceed with the extradition proceedings.[12] More important is to highlight that both the first and the second extradition orders against Pinochet by the Spanish court, which eventually led to his arrest, were based on the passive personality principle, combined, in the second order, with universal jurisdiction. Although the House of Lords eventually decided to authorize further proceedings mainly on the principle of universal jurisdiction, rather than on passive personality, it is interesting to note that passive personality played a subsidiary role in the Spanish request for Pinochet's extradition. It is interesting also that the Spanish request for jurisdiction on the ground of passive personality failed mainly because the content *ratione materiae* of the extradition request (acts of murder committed abroad) did not meet the standards of the UK law on extradition. For the sake of argument, if the first Spanish provisional warrant for arrest had been based initially on allegations of torture, rather than of murder of Spanish nationals in Chile, even without any mention of universal jurisdiction, it is questionable whether the UK courts would have refused it as they did, since under UK law, torture is a crime regardless as to where the

---

11 Ruling of the *Audiencia National* in Plenary of 30 October 1998, reasoning released on 5 November 1998. In *Auto de la Sala de lo Penal de la Audiencia Nacional confirmando la jurisdicción de España para conocer de los crímenes de genocidio y terrorismo cometidos durante la dictadura chilena,* http://www.derechos.org/nizkor/chile/juicio/audi.html. Translation of the House of Lords, Opinion of the Lords of Appeal for Judgment, *supra* note 8.

12 For a good discussion of the issues raised in the *Pinochet Case, see* Andrea Bianchi, "Immunity versus Human Rights: the Pinochet Case", *European Journal of International Law,* Vol. 10, No. 2 (1999).

offence was committed. The question seems pertinent also in light of the fact that Articles 5 and 7 of the Torture Convention create not only an obligation for member States either to prosecute or extradite suspects of torture, but also leave it to the discretion of the State to establish jurisdiction where the victim is a national of that State.

For these reasons, should attempts be made to apply this principle in similar cases in the future, other countries might accept it as a valid ground for the exercise of jurisdiction, according to the content and extent of their domestic jurisdiction on the subject matter.[13] It seems possible that the growing pressure by victims on State institutions for the enforcement of their right to redress may encourage domestic courts to assert jurisdiction on the passive personality ground in respect of crimes under international law, based upon a legitimate interest in the protection of national victims. Paradoxically, in certain instances, States may be willing to agree more on the legitimacy of a jurisdictional ground based on victims' claims (such as the passive personality principle) rather than to act according to the principle of universal jurisdiction, for reasons discussed below. However, to date, States appear rather reluctant to exercise jurisdiction exclusively according to the passive personality principle, in the absence of other grounds for jurisdiction. Therefore, its validity as a means of achieving adequate victims' redress remains to be seen.

b. Can Victims Rely on Universal Jurisdiction?

As mentioned above, perpetrators of crimes under international law such as genocide, crimes against humanity and war crimes can be prosecuted by domestic courts on the basis of universal jurisdiction. According to the doctrine of universal jurisdiction, any State is authorized to exercise its jurisdiction over offenders accused of having committed particularly serious breaches of international law, regardless of the territory in which the offence was committed (*locus delicti*), the nationality of the offender or the person injured, and regardless of any national interests which might have been injured

---

13 Following the decision of the UK Home Secretary not to extradite Pinochet, a Belgian judge issued a number of requests asking for further evaluation of Pinochet's health conditions and permission to access his medical files. These were not taken into consideration by UK courts, however.

by the offence.[14] In such cases, it is the particularly serious nature of the offences and the threat they pose to the international community as a whole which forms the basis for the exercise of jurisdiction by any State having custody over suspects.

The principle of universality of jurisdiction over persons alleged to have committed serious crimes under the *jus gentium*, such as war crimes or piracy, dates back to the early fourteenth century.[15] In the last two centuries, the doctrine of universal jurisdiction has developed particularly in relation to the need to punish slave-trading and piracy on the high seas or in *terra nullius* or *res communis omnium*.[16] Some commentators have argued that the exercise of universal jurisdiction for crimes under international law can be justified, by analogy with piracy, because war crimes, crimes against humanity and genocide generally occur in chaotic situations beyond any legal control, such as war zones.[17] However, in his 1927 dissenting opinion on piracy in the *Lotus Case,* Judge Moore invoked the doctrine of universal jurisdiction on a different basis, namely on the principle that any nation may capture and punish an 'enemy of all mankind' in the interest of all. According to this well accepted opinion, the grounds for jurisdiction are based simply on the particular seriousness of the offence, which makes it a concern for the whole international community.[18]

---

14 For a comprehensive treatment of the exercise of State jurisdiction according to the principle of universality *see* Marc Henzelin, *Le Principe de L'universalité en Droit Pénal International: Droit et Obligation pour les États de Poursuivre et Juger Selon le Principle de l'Universalité,* Helbing & Lichtenhahn, Genève (2000).

15 *See* Maurice Hugh Keen, *The Laws of War in the Late Middle Ages* (1965). For further reading, *see* Lyal S. Sunga, *Individual Responsibility in International Law for Serious Human Rights Violations*, Martinus Nijhoff (1992).

16 *See* Brownlie, *supra* note 3 at 304-305.

17 *See* Rena H. Reiss, "The Extradition of John Demjanjuk: War Crimes, Universality Jurisdiction, and the Political Offense Doctrine", *Cornell International Law Journal*, Vol. 20, No. 2 (1987) at 303-304. Together with universal jurisdiction, some commentators introduce the separate notion of 'vicarious administration of justice' as a ground for jurisdiction creating an obligation for States to either prosecute or extradite suspects of particularly serious crimes such as terrorism, should the State of jurisdiction be unable or unwilling to prosecute. *See* Wolfrum, *supra* note 3 at 185.

18 This approach is generally accepted by most commentators. *See*, among others, Bernhard Graefrath, "Universal Criminal Jurisdiction and an International Criminal Court", *European Journal of International Law*, Vol. 1, Nos. 1-2 (1990) at 86; Oliver, *supra* note 3 at 317-320; Bassiouni and Wise, *supra* note 2. *See also* Oscar Schachter, discussing the many controversial issues that may arise in connection with

Universal jurisdiction is a politically sensitive issue that has divided commentators and engaged States in lengthy discussion on international standards for the prosecution and punishment of crimes under international law. Following the events of the Second World War, States have increasingly considered that certain serious violations of international law - primarily war crimes, but also crimes against humanity, genocide, international terrorism, slavery and apartheid - pose a threat to international peace and security and that perpetrators must therefore be effectively prosecuted through all possible means, including universal jurisdiction. With this aim, States have adopted a number of international instruments for the prevention and punishment of crimes under international law which embody provisions relating to extradition agreements, the principle of *aut dedere aut judicare* or, in some cases, the principle of universal jurisdiction.[19]

---

the use of universal jurisdiction by States, *International Law in Theory and Practice*, Martinus Nijhoff (1991) at 267-270.

[19] The 'grave breaches' system of the Geneva Conventions 1949, for example, contains the obligation for States to "search for persons alleged to have committed or to have ordered to be committed" grave breaches of the Conventions and to prosecute them regardless of their nationality or hand them over for trial to another contracting party. Among instruments providing for universal jurisdiction or for the duty of States to prosecute or extradite can be mentioned: the Convention against Illicit Traffic in Narcotic Drugs and Psychotropic Substances 1988; the Hague Convention for the Suppression of Unlawful Seizure of Aircraft 1970; the Convention on the Suppression and Punishment of the Crime of Apartheid 1973; the UN Torture Convention 1984. For an analysis of these and other international instruments *see* Bassiouni and Wise, *supra* note 2. The negotiation and drafting of the Torture Convention 1984, represent a good example of the debate among States over the use of the territoriality principle *versus* universal jurisdiction. Within this forum, it became clear that perpetrators of torture could not be punished by their own State of nationality, under the protection of which they were committing the offence. Considering the scarce use of extradition procedures in torture cases, a wide application of the principle of universal jurisdiction seemed to be the most acceptable solution for the more effective repression and punishment of torture. As Maxim Tardu recalls however, the insertion of a strong provision on universal jurisdiction in the Convention "was opposed for a long time by an odd collection of states - the Eastern European countries, China, several Third World States, and even a few Western governments, such as the United Kingdom and Australia". Maxim E. Tardu, "The United Nations Convention against Torture and Other Cruel and Inhuman or Degrading Treatment or Punishment", *Nordic Journal of International Law*, Vol. 56, No. 4 (1987) at 314. Sceptical States were mainly concerned about the possibility of procedural abuses and felt that the traditional rule of territorial jurisdiction for criminal matters should have been protected and maintained even in extreme cases

However, apart from treaty obligations, there has been little consensus among States on the customary status of a legal obligation to prosecute and punish those responsible for crimes under international law purely on grounds of universal jurisdiction. In the *Pinochet Case,* Lord Slynn of Hadley argued that:

> It does not seem to me that it has been shown that there is any State practice or general consensus let alone a widely supported convention that all crimes against international law should be justiciable in National Courts on the basis of the universality of jurisdiction.[20]

The International Court of Justice decision in the *Arrest Warrant Case*[21] also indicates a lack of clear consensus on the use of universal

---

such as torture. As a result, Articles 5 to 7 of the Torture Convention on universal jurisdiction are rather weak.

20 *See* the *Pinochet Case*, *supra* note 8.

21 *Arrest Warrant of 11 April 2000: Democratic Republic of the Congo* v. *Belgium*, ICJ Judgment of 14 February 2002. In this case, the ICJ was called upon to decide whether an 'arrest warrant issued by Belgian courts against Mr. Abdulaye Yerodia Ndombasi, then Foreign Minister of the Democratic Republic of the Congo, would constitute a violation of the principle of immunity from criminal jurisdiction under international law. The ICJ found that the warrant of arrest issued by Belgian courts constituted a violation of the principle of immunity from criminal jurisdiction and the inviolability which the incumbent Minister for Foreign Affairs of the Democratic Republic of the Congo enjoyed under international law. However, the ICJ made clear that "immunity from jurisdiction enjoyed by incumbent Ministers for Foreign Affairs does not mean that they enjoy impunity in respect of any crimes they might have committed, irrespective of their gravity". In this sense, immunity from jurisdiction may be applicable for a certain period of time and does not necessarily exonerate the person to whom it applies from all criminal responsibility. Accordingly, the Court explained that even sitting members of government, including foreign ministers, may be "tried in their own countries, where the State which they represent or have represented decides to waive that immunity"; they may be tried in other States "after ceasing to hold the office of Minister for Foreign Affairs"; and, most of all, they may be "subject to criminal proceedings before certain international criminal courts, where they have jurisdiction". The formula used by the ICJ Judges leaves untouched the option of trying individuals under immunity before competent international criminal courts. However, the judgment effectively halted a number of pending domestic proceedings for the prosecution and punishment of suspects of crimes under international law, including the proceedings instituted under Belgian law against Israeli Prime Minister Ariel Sharon, accused of having played a role in the massacre of civilians in the Palestinian refugee

jurisdiction as a valid ground to prosecute crimes under international law where the alleged offender is not in custody. On the one hand, Judge Guillaume in his separate opinion expressed the view that:

> a State normally has jurisdiction over an offence committed abroad only if the offender, or at the very least the victim, has the nationality of that State, or if the crime threatens its internal or external security. Additionally, [States] may exercise jurisdiction in cases of piracy and in the situation of subsidiary universal jurisdiction provided for by various conventions if the offender is present on their territory. But apart from these cases, international law does not accept universal jurisdiction; still less does it accept universal jurisdiction *in absentia*.[22]

On the other hand, Judges Higgins, Kooijmans and Buergenthal put forward a more progressive view on the exercise of jurisdiction purely on grounds of universality over persons alleged to have committed crimes under international law - which seems to reflect more accurately the current status of the law on this matter. Judges Higgins, Kooijmans and Buergenthal found it 'undeniable' that: "there is no established practice in which States exercise universal jurisdiction properly so called".[23] Based on a review of national legislation on this matter, the three Judges came to the conclusion that:

> virtually all national legislation envisages links of some sort to the forum State; and no case law exists in which pure universal jurisdiction has formed the basis of jurisdiction.[24]

However, the Judges also found that despite the absence of practice for the exercise of universal jurisdiction:

---

camps of Sabra and Shatila, Lebanon, in 1982. On 26 June 2002, a Belgian Appeal Court declared the case against Mr. Sharon inadmissible by ruling that a case could not proceed against a person who is not found on Belgian territory. The Court's decision was taken even though 1993 Belgian law establishes universal jurisdiction for war crimes. Palestinian survivors of the massacre indicated that they would appeal to the Supreme Court.

22 Separate opinion of Judge Guillaume, *ibid.*

23 Joint separate opinion of Judges Higgins, Kooijmans and Buergenthal, at para. 45.

24 *Ibid.*

> there is equally nothing in this case law which evidences an *opinio juris* on the illegality of such a jurisdiction. In short, national legislation and case law - that is, State practice - is neutral as to the exercise of universal jurisdiction.[25]

Judges Higgins, Kooijmans and Buergenthal further developed their position on the current status of universal jurisdiction and, more generally, on the role of the international community in the fight against impunity, as follows:

> There are moreover, certain indications that a universal criminal jurisdiction for certain international crimes is clearly not regarded as unlawful. ... The international consensus that the perpetrators of international crimes should not go unpunished is being advanced by a flexible strategy, in which newly-established international criminal tribunals, treaty obligations and national courts all have their part to play.[26]

In terms of practical application, only a few examples can be mentioned in which the universality principle has been applied to instances of crimes under international law in the absence of other grounds for jurisdiction. Even in the well known *Eichmann Case* of 1961 - which is often considered a milestone in the application of universal jurisdiction - Israel claimed jurisdiction on the basis of the universality, protective and passive personality principles.[27] More recently, however, a number of European countries have

---

[25] *Ibid.*

[26] *Ibid.* at para. 51. In this context, the Judges cited relevant treaty provisions which do not exclude other grounds of jurisdiction that may be exercised on a voluntary basis, including Article 4(3) of the Hague Convention for the Suppression of Unlawful Seizure of Aircraft 1970; Article 5(3) of the Torture Convention 1984; and Article 5(3) of the International Convention Against the Taking of Hostages 1979. To conclude, Judges Higgins, Kooijmans and Buergenthal indicated that, in the absence of a prohibitive rule and in light of the growing international consensus on the need to punish crimes under international law, the warrant for the arrest of Mr. Yerodia did not as such violate international law.

[27] *Attorney-General of the Government of Israel* v. *Eichmann*, D. Ct. Jerusalem (1961) 36 ILR 5 at paras. 30-40. In this case, Eichmann, a German national accused of having committed war crimes and crimes against humanity during the Nazi regime (as Head of the Jewish Office of the German Gestapo and administrator in charge of the 'final solution'), was forcibly kidnapped in Argentina and abducted to Israel without the knowledge of the Argentinian Government. Brought before Israeli courts, he had to

asserted jurisdiction for war crimes in cases where there was no direct link of territory or nationality between the country and the defendants. In *Public Prosecutor* v. *Djajic*,[28] Germany claimed domestic jurisdiction against a Bosnian-Serb accused of war crimes on the basis of the duty to prosecute or extradite persons responsible for grave breaches of the Geneva Conventions. Similarly, in the case of *In Re G.*[29] the Military Court of Switzerland exercised jurisdiction against a Bosnian-Serb accused of having committed war crimes, on grounds of universal jurisdiction and temporary presence of the defendant in Swiss territory. However, apart from a few examples, there has not developed an established practice on the exercise of jurisdiction on the basis of universality alone. Therefore, at least for the moment, the domestic prosecution and punishment of suspects of crimes under international law purely on grounds of universal jurisdiction seem to hold little promise for victims seeking redress.

c. The Example of the US Alien Tort Claims Act (ATCA)

Currently, the municipal enforcement of the right to reparation for crimes under international law on the basis of domestic legislation remains the most accessible way for victims to obtain redress. As discussed below, this does not mean that domestic legislation is necessarily the most appropriate way for victims of genocide, war crimes or crimes against humanity to obtain redress. Often, victims have to resort to litigation in tort law to obtain satisfaction, notwithstanding that this procedure does not always encompass all aspects of a crime under international law. For example, the procedural aspects of domestic law tailored to a specific judicial system of a given country may conflict with the transboundary character of crimes under international law. In certain instances, however, recourse to domestic legislation by international

---

stand trial under the 1951 Israeli Nazi and Nazi Collaborators (Punishment) Law on the basis of universal jurisdiction for war crimes, crimes against the Jewish people (a criminal offence drafted along the lines of the 1948 Genocide Convention) and crimes against humanity. Eichmann was found guilty and sentenced to death, and his appeal to the Supreme Court of Israel was dismissed. On some of the controversial aspects of this case, *see* the lengthy discussion in Sunga, *supra* note 2 at 263-268. For further jurisprudence, *see also Fédération Nationale des Déportés et Internés Résistants et Patriotes et al.* v. *Barbie*, 78 ILR 125 (1985), a trial held under French jurisdiction in the court of Lyon; and *Demjanjuk* v. *Petrovsky*, 776 F.2d 571, 584 (6th Cir. 1985), a trial held in US courts.

28 Supreme Court of Bavaria, 3rd Strafsenat, Case No. 20/96 of 23 May 1997.

29 Military Tribunal Division 1, Lausanne, 18 April 1997.

crime victims has yielded some remarkable results. It is therefore valuable to analyze some of the more relevant domestic laws providing remedies for victims of crimes under international law, the effectiveness of such remedies, as well as advantages and disadvantages of domestic enforcement of international criminal law. The current discussion will focus in particular on the US Alien Tort Claim Act and its jurisprudence.

The US Alien Tort Claims Act (ATCA)[30] - an Act of the US Congress dated 1789 - has been used by US federal District Courts to litigate claims involving human rights violations.[31] Under the ATCA, federal District Courts may exercise jurisdiction to provide for a remedy in tort to aliens who have been victims of violations of the law of nations, including certain fundamental violations of human rights, such as torture. In order to bring a claim under the ATCA, the following fundamental conditions must be fulfilled:

1) the applicant must be an alien;
2) the suit must be a civil action for a tort only;
3) the tort must be committed in violation of the laws of nations or a treaty of the United States.[32]

In practice, however, the application of jurisdiction under the ATCA has not been as simple as it might appear. In addition to the fulfilment of the above-mentioned necessary conditions, which themselves are not without complications, there are further legal and procedural hurdles that limit victims' access to the ATCA.

First, in order to act under the ATCA, the plaintiffs must have exhausted remedies available in the country where the offences were committed.[33] Second, the court in question must have personal jurisdiction

---

30 Alien Tort Act, 28 U.S.C. §1350 (1994).

31 For a comprehensive overview and analysis of human rights cases litigated under the ATCA, *see* Beth Stephens and Michael Ratner, *International Human Rights Litigation in US Courts*, Transnational Publishers, Irvington-on-Hudson, New York (1996).

32 Section 1350 of the ATCA provides that: "The district courts shall have original jurisdiction of any civil action by an alien for a tort only, committed in violation of the law of nations or a treaty of the United States".

33 The principle of exhaustion of local remedies of the ATCA is also contained in section 2(b) of the Torture Victim Protection Act (TVPA) which provides that: "A court shall decline to hear a claim under this section if the claimant has not exhausted adequate and available remedies in the place in which the conduct giving rise to the claim occurred". Torture Victim Protection Act 1991, Pub. L. No. 102-256, 106 Stat.

over the defendant, meaning that the defendant must bring himself or herself within the territorial jurisdiction of the court.[34] Similarly, even if the court exercises jurisdiction and awards the payment of compensation to the victim, the financial judgment will be recoverable only where the defendant's assets are subject to the jurisdiction of the court.[35] These particular clauses are likely to create substantial difficulties both for the exercise of jurisdiction and for the actual recovery of damages on the part of the victims. In fact, even if the defendant happens to come within the territorial jurisdiction of the court at the moment of notification of the charges against him or her, the defendant may simply collect his or her assets, leave the country and refuse to be present at the trial. In such circumstances, even if the case is likely to be won against the defendant because of non-appearance before the court, the judgment against him or her will not be recoverable because the assets will have been transferred outside the court's jurisdiction. As a matter of fact, in *Filártiga* v. *Peña-Irala*,[36] the award of over US$10 million for damages, including punitive

---

73 (1992) codified in 28 U.S.C. § 1350 (1994). The TVPA was enacted in 1992 by the US Congress in an effort to facilitate the access to justice in US courts by torture victims. According to the TVPA, any individual of any foreign nation who, "under actual or apparent authority, or under color of law" subjects another individual to torture or extrajudicial killing, is liable to pay damages in a civil action to the victim, the victim's legal representative or his or her legitimate claimant.

34 This clause found application in the Karadzic case. The first claims against Karadzic were handed to him in February 1993 in the lobby of the Hotel Intercontinental in Manhattan, New York, on the occasion of his participation in a UN meeting. However, Karadzic later contested the circumstances of putative service. Similarly, the second claims for the appeal were served to Karadzic through alternate means of service, by way of a member of his State Department security detail, outside the Russian Embassy in Manhattan. *Kadic* v. *Karadzic*, 70 F. 3d 232 (2nd Cir. 1995).

35 Also, there may be complications in obtaining evidence from abroad, having to do with the divergent approach of US civil procedure as compared to the procedure of other countries. On this matter, *see* Stephens and Ratner, *supra* note 31 at 186-187, pointing out that many countries are reluctant to accept US discovery orders or to accept the examination of evidence and witnesses on their territory by foreign parties.

36 *Filártiga* v. *Peña-Irala*, 630 F.2d 876 (2nd Cir. 1980). In this case the plaintiffs, two Paraguayan nationals (father and daughter) brought civil proceedings for damages in a US federal District Court against Americo Norberto Peña-Irala, a Paraguayan chief of police accused of having wrongfully caused the death of their son and brother, Joelito Filártiga, through torture in Paraguay in 1976. Both the plaintiffs and the defendant were in US territory at the moment of the civil law suit. At first, the District Court ruled that it did not have jurisdiction to hear the case. However, the US Court of Appeals reversed the District Court judgment by invoking the ATCA and ruled

damages, by the Federal District Court in its final judgment could never be recovered because the defendant's assets were located outside US jurisdiction.[37] In such circumstances, the only possible option for the plaintiff was to try to have the US judgment enforced in the country where the assets of the defendants were located or where the defendant was located. The effectiveness of this approach depends, however, upon the relevant international agreements between the countries in question and, more generally, upon the countries' willingness to cooperate in legal matters.

Third, the application *ratione temporis* of the ATCA can create disadvantages for plaintiffs. Although the ATCA does not explicitly establish any time limitation for bringing suit, claims under the ATCA have been largely treated as analogous to tort actions against the State, which are subject to statutory limitations of one or two years. This short time limitation can hinder the access of foreigners to the US justice system, particularly where they are not familiar with the system. However, in certain extreme cases some courts have applied the statutory limitation of the US Torture Victim Protection Act, which extends the time for bringing a civil law suit to ten years from the moment the alleged wrong occurred.

---

that the District Court did have jurisdiction under such Act to hear the case. The *Filártiga* case holds special importance in the field of human rights litigation, because this was the first time the family of a victim of human rights violations brought a claim in US courts under the ATCA and was awarded damages. As Stephens and Ratner point out: "*Filártiga* cases also reflect an emerging international law concept of the right to a remedy, which holds that all victims of human rights abuses have a right both to receive compensation for their injuries and to hold those responsible accountable for their crimes", *supra* note 31 at 2. Contrary to the *Filártiga* v. *Peña-Irala* decision, in the *Tel-Oren* v. *Libyan Arab Republic Case*, 726 F.2d 774, 824 (D.C.Cir. 1984), a US Court dismissed a claim for damages under the ATCA against members of the Palestinian Liberation Organization (PLO), resulting from an attack on a tourist bus in Israel, on the basis that the PLO did not represent a State as intended under US or international law, but rather an organization, and there was no sufficient connection between the criminal action and a State to give rise to international responsibility. Accordingly, the Court did not seize jurisdiction. This decision has created some ambiguity in US practice concerning the attribution of individual responsibility for human rights violations under international law.

37 577 F. Supp. 860 (E.D.N.Y. 1984). On this point and on the extent of the reach of the *Filártiga* v. *Peña-Irala* decision, *see* Louis Henkin, "International Human Rights Standards in National Law: The Jurisprudence of the United States", in Benedetto Conforti and Francesco Francioni (eds.), *Enforcing International Human Rights in Domestic Courts*, Kluwer Law International (1997).

Fourth, considerations of *forum non conveniens* can limit the exercise of jurisdiction under the ATCA. The defendant can argue that, in his or her particular case, ends of justice would be better served if action were brought and tried in another forum.[38] To make trial proceedings more expeditious and inexpensive, it is important that the court has relatively easy access to sources of proof, such as witnesses and the premises where the offence took place. In claims under the ATCA, circumstances such as the foreign nationality of the plaintiffs or the fact that the torts in question were mainly committed outside the territorial jurisdiction of the District Court can diminish the chances that the court will seize jurisdiction over the case.

Finally, the application *ratione personae* of the ATCA is also subject to important limitations. These derive mainly from the Foreign Sovereign Immunities Act[39] which, *inter alia*, prohibits the exercise of jurisdiction by US courts over a foreign State or foreign State official without the previous consent of the State under consideration, according to the principle *par in parem non habet jurisdictionem*.[40] This particular limitation poses a serious obstacle to the exercise of jurisdiction under the ATCA in case of crimes under international law where the perpetrator was a government agent or public official, such as a military commander, soldier or police officer.[41] To

---

38 However, to date, US courts have never dismissed a case under the ATCA on the basis of the *forum non conveniens* principle.

39 Foreign Sovereign Immunities Act (FSIA) 1976, 28 U.S.C. § 1330, 1602-11 (1994).

40 Stephens and Ratner, *supra* note 31 at 22, point out that "several attempts to expand the *Filártiga* holding to suits against foreign governments have met with little success", due to the concurrent application of the FSIA. Among the failed attempts, the authors mention the *Tel-Oren* case; the *Argentine Republic* v. *Amerada Hess Shipping Corporation* case, in which the US Supreme Court held that the ATCA does not provide an exception to the limitations imposed by the FSIA for suits against foreign governments, 488 U.S. 429 (1989); and the *Siderman de Blake* v. *Republic of Argentina* case, confirming the ban of the FSIA on suits against foreign governments, 965 F. 2nd 699 (9th Cir. 1992).

41 This restriction becomes even heavier in the light of the fact that, while normally the ATCA could be applied to both non-State defendants and State or State agent defendants, in case of torture only State agent defendants can be considered, in conformity with the TVPA. Under the TVPA, US courts can provide torture victims with a remedy irrespective of the nationality of the plaintiff. As in the ATCA, the defendant must be under US jurisdiction, and a judgment awarding compensation can be executed exclusively if the defendant's assets are within US jurisdiction. However, *see* the discussion below concerning the manner in which the Karadzic decision

complicate matters further, US courts have usually read the Act narrowly, and have consistently rejected the argument that State immunity does not apply to agents of States which are parties to human rights treaties, and that by entering such international agreements States have waived their immunities from jurisdiction.[42]

Against this background, one wonders whether, in the case of crimes under international law, this restrictive approach towards immunity conflicts with the well accepted principle that individual responsibility for these kinds of crimes attaches to the perpetrator regardless of the rank or official position of the suspect, as well as the operation of the related principle *aut dedere aut judicare*. Overall, as the issue of immunity shows, the application of the ATCA may not be the most appropriate tool for the litigation of cases involving criminal offences under international law.

d. Class Actions under the ATCA

As mentioned above, crimes under international law often involve large numbers of victims who may share the same cause of action against the same suspects. For this reason, class actions are often considered a particularly appropriate way to obtain redress, because of their capacity to involve and reunite a large number of individuals who have suffered the same or a similar fate. It is therefore important to examine strengths and weaknesses of class

---

expanded the scope of application of the ATCA in case of serious human rights violations. On the question of immunity for acts of State, *see* Pasquale De Sena, "Immunity of State Organs and Defence of Superior Orders as an Obstacle to the Domestic Enforcement of International Human Rights", in Conforti and Francioni (eds.), *supra* note 37 at 367-403.

42 In *Lafontant* v. *Aristide*, 844 F. Supp. 128 (E.D.N.Y. 1994), US courts dismissed a claim for summary execution against the President of Haiti on grounds of immunity for the Head of State. However, the immunity restriction does not apply if the tort is committed within US territory or if it concerns terrorist acts against US citizens. Also, the FSIA was amended in 1996 to include an exception to immunity under section 221 of the Anti-Terrorism and Effective Death Penalty Act of 1996. The immunity applies to claims for damages for personal injury or death caused by an act of torture, extrajudicial killing, aircraft sabotage or hostage-taking, against a State designated by the Secretary of State as a sponsor of terrorism, where the claimant or victim was a national of the US at the time the act occurred. On the implications of State immunity for civil claims *see* the judgment of the European Court of Human Rights in the case of *Al-Adsani* v. *the United Kingdom*, Application no. 35763/97, 21 November 2001.

action claims in domestic courts, as exemplified in the following two cases brought under the ATCA.

i. The Marcos Litigation

Following the *Filártiga* v. *Peña-Irala* decision, a number of US courts took up claims concerning serious human rights violations, filed both by individual victims and by multiple victims organized in class actions.[43] The Marcos litigation is perhaps one of the more interesting examples of class action and inter-State cooperation on redress on the basis of both domestic and international law. In 1994, some ten thousand Filipinos filed a class action suit under the ATCA against Ferdinand Marcos for massive human rights violations.[44] The claimants were mainly leftist activists or members of militant groups linked to a guerrilla movement, who alleged torture, extrajudicial detention and killings committed during the Marcos regime. As a result of the

---

43 *See, inter alia, Forti and another* v. *Suarez-Mason*, District Court, Northern District, California 672 F. Supp. (1987, 1988), and *Paul (et al.)* v. *Avril*, District Court of Florida 812 F. Supp. (14 January 1993). In both cases, concerning acts of torture committed by government officers, the District Court rejected the defendant's argument based on immunity of State agents under the Foreign Sovereign Immunities Act. In *Forti and another* v. *Suarez-Mason,* No. C-97-2058, Northern District California, 20 April 1990, the Court finally awarded the plaintiffs compensatory and punitive damages for torture, disappearance, prolonged arbitrary detention and summary execution. In *Paul* v. *Avril*, 901 F. Supp. 330, Southern District Florida, 1994, the Court awarded the six victims US$41 million in damages for torture, cruel, inhuman or degrading treatment and arbitrary detention committed by the former Haitian dictator Prosper Avril. *See also Todd* v. *Panjaitan*, No. 92-122255, 1994 WL 827111, D. Mass. 26 October 1994, in which the District Court of Massachusetts awarded the mother of a victim of a massacre in East Timor US$14 million as a result of a suit against an Indonesian General involved in the human rights violations campaign.

44 To be valid, class actions under the ATCA must follow certain additional requirements. First, the plaintiffs cannot be above a certain number, since the US Federal Rules of Civil Procedure require that the number of plaintiffs has to be such as to make it practicable to join all the parties during trial; second, the plaintiffs must share the same type of claims and defences and they must be adequately represented by the party bringing the suit; third, the case must share questions of law and / or fact common to the entire class; and fourth, it must be proven that an eventual judgment awarded to a single plaintiff would not deplete the defendant's assets and therefore damage other plaintiffs who may file legal suits against the same defendant for the same claim in the future.

victims' claim, in the case *Estate of Ferdinand E. Marcos Litigation*,[45] a US court in the District of Hawaii held the estate of the defendant responsible for the alleged violations committed during the Marcos presidency. The jury awarded almost US$1.2 billion in exemplary (punitive) damages and US$766 million in compensatory damages. However, a considerable part of Marcos' assets (some US$450 million) was secured in Swiss banks that initially had refused to release the funds.[46] Swiss courts supported the banks' decision not to release Marcos' assets, but did not provide for any alternative means allowing victims' redress, frustrating the order of the US court. The case was then brought before the Federal Supreme Court of Switzerland, which reversed the judgment of the lower court and argued that Switzerland, as a party to the Torture Convention 1984, was obliged to ensure that:

> the victim of an act of torture obtains redress and has an enforceable right to fair and adequate compensation, including the means for as full rehabilitation as possible.[47]

On 10 December 1997, the Swiss Federal Court ordered the transfer of Marcos' assets to an escrow fund in Manila, on the condition that the Philippine Government set up compensation procedures for human rights victims from the assets in the fund.[48] Negotiations have been conducted on an ongoing basis since that time between the Government and the National Democratic Front, a communist rebel group which has been acting on behalf of most of the victims, with the aim of settling the claims as part of a proposed peace settlement between the two parties. However, at the time of writing, no victim had yet received any compensation, and victims were seeking to enforce this

---

45 *In re Estate of Ferdinand E. Marcos Litigation*, 978 F.2d 493 (9th Cir. 1992), *In re Estate of Marcos*, 25 F.3d 1467, 1994 W.L. 262053 (9th Cir., 16 June 1994), *In re Estate of Ferdinand E. Marcos Litigation*, D. Hawaii 1994, aff'd (9th Cir., 16 June 1994), *In re Estate of Ferdinand E. Marcos Litigation*, D.C. No. MDL 840 (D. Hawaii 3 February 1995), *appeal docketed*, No. 95-15770 (9th Cir., 5 May 1995).

46 Credit Suisse in Zurich and Swiss Bank Corporation in Geneva.

47 Article 14 of the Torture Convention, cited in Arrêt du Tribunal Federal 123 II 595 *Auszug aus dem Urteil der I. öffentlichrechtlichen Abteilung i.S. BAP gegen Aguamina Corporation* of 10 December 1997, in "Tribunal Federal Suisse", http://www.eurospider.ch.

48 *Ibid.*

and other judgments involving Marcos' funds in the domestic courts of the Philippines.[49]

ii. The Karadzic Case

In 1994, a class action suit filed by two groups of plaintiffs against Serbian national Radovan Karadzic, former Bosnian Serb leader, resulted in one of the more innovative domestic judgments in civil actions for crimes under international law. On 19 November 1994, in *Doe* v. *Karadzic* the US District Court for the Southern District of New York dismissed for lack of jurisdiction *ratione materiae* the suit filed by two individuals representing two groups of plaintiffs against Radovan Karadzic.[50] However, on 13 October 1995, in *Kadic* v. *Karadzic* the US Court of Appeals for the Second Circuit reversed this ruling and remanded the case for further proceedings, holding that:

> ... subject matter jurisdiction exists, that Karadzic may be found liable for genocide, war crimes, and crimes against humanity in his

---

[49] In July 2003, the Supreme Court of the Philippines ruled that Marcos' funds belonged rightfully to the nation. So far, the only funds that have been tracked down amount to some US$700 million. During the dictatorship however, it is estimated that the Marcoses had accumulated some US$5-10 billion. The funds are currently sitting in an escrow account in the Philippine National Bank and remain practically untraceable, as they were initially distributed among many foreign bank accounts. Two months following the Supreme Court judgment however, in September 2003, Judge Manuel Real of the US district court of Hawaii issued a global injunction barring banks from transferring the Marcos funds to the Philippines. Judge Real argued that the Philippine Supreme Court had not proved that the money had been unlawfully acquired and that the Court had ignored the claims of victims of the Marcos regime. The judgment also suggests that the best way to ensure victims adequate and fair compensation on a non-discriminatory basis would be through the establishment of an international tribunal to settle compensation matters relating to Marcos' funds. This judgment was issued as a result of a class action filed in the courts of Hawaii by some 10,000 victims of Marcos' rule. The President of the Philippines, Gloria Macapagal-Arroyo, expressed her view that the ruling was invalid because it interfered with the sovereignty of the Philippines. *See* the South China Morning Post of 3 October 2003.

[50] *Doe* v. *Karadzic*, 866 F. Supp. 734 (S.D.N.Y. 1994). The plaintiffs based their claims on the ATCA, the TVPA, the General Federal-Question Jurisdictional Statute, 28 U.S.C. §1331 (1998), and on principles of supplemental jurisdiction, 28 U.S.C. § 1367 (Supp. V, 1993). The plaintiffs sought compensatory damages, punitive damages, attorney's fees and injunctive relief for personal injuries suffered as a result of "genocidal acts, torture, extrajudicial killing, and other violations of the law of nations".

> private capacity and for other violations in his capacity as a state actor, and that he is not immune from service of process.[51]

This judgment marks a major step in the interpretation and application of the ATCA to crimes under international law and is to be welcomed.[52] First of all, the judgment reaffirms that the scope *ratione materiae* of the ATCA may cover crimes under international law such as genocide, war crimes and crimes against humanity.[53] Second, the judgment affirmed that Karadzic may be held responsible for crimes committed both in his private capacity and as a State actor.[54] This *dictum* specifically counters the District Court judgment which had held that "acts committed by non-State actors do not violate the law of nations". Third, contrary to the decision of the lower court, the appeal judgment made clear that the defendant would not be considered immune from service of process. When the question of immunity from jurisdiction for Heads of State was raised in *Doe v. Karadzic,* the District Judge noted that "the Court might be deprived of jurisdiction if the Executive Branch were to recognize Karadzic as the Head of State of a friendly nation". The District Judge further recognized that this consideration was not dispositive, but that he believed that it would "militate against this Court exercising jurisdiction".[55] Against this background, the denial of immunity from service of process to Karadzic represents a significant move forward in litigation procedure under the ATCA. It bypasses the limitation imposed by the Foreign Sovereign Immunities Act, which would otherwise grant immunity from jurisdiction to State agents in the

---

51 Jon O. Newman, Chief Judge, in *Kadic* v. *Karadzic*, 70 F. 3d 232 (2nd Cir. 1995).

52 For a commentary on the Karadzic case and its relation to the ATCA, *see*, among others, Alan Frederick Enslen, "*Filartiga*'s Offspring: The Second Circuit Significantly Expands the Scope of the Alien Tort Claim Act with Its Decision in *Kadic* v. *Karadzic*", *Alabama Law Review*, Vol. 48, No. 2, Winter 1997; Eric Johnson, "*Kadic* v. *Karadzic* and *Doe I and II* v. *Karadzic*: The Latest Stage in Alien Tort Act Jurisprudence", *German Yearbook of International Law*, Vol. 39 (1996); and Jordan J. Paust, "Suing Karadzic", *Leiden Journal of International Law*, Vol. 10 (1997).

53 The Court specifically mentioned violations of common Article 3 of the Geneva Conventions 1949, among the acts which can trigger jurisdiction under the ATCA. *Kadic* v. *Karadzic*, 70 F. 3rd at 242-243.

54 To support this argument, the Court of Appeals cited, among a number of other relevant documents, the Third Restatement of the Foreign Relations law of the United States (1986) which expressly provides for individual responsibility for offenses against international law such as piracy, war crimes and genocide.

55 Opinion and Order of the District Judge, *Doe* v. *Karadzic*, 866 F. Supp. at 738.

exercise of their functions. Also, based on the Karadzic case, victims may be able to seek redress in civil courts even against individuals who still hold government positions, pending criminal prosecutions which may be blocked by sovereign immunities.

The *Kadic* v. *Karadzic* judgment paved the way for subsequent cases involving litigation over crimes under international law under the ATCA.[56] However, many questions remain as regards the practical consequences of the Karadzic precedent for the victims' right to redress. At least in the short term, the concrete outcome of this judgment for the victims is likely to be very limited. The victims of Karadzic's atrocities have won a nominal victory - arguably a form of redress - but in terms of monetary compensation, restitution of stolen properties or rehabilitation for the physical and moral injuries suffered, the victims still face formidable challenges in actually getting satisfaction, owing mainly to the difficulty in enforcing the judgment and recovering assets.

e. Domestic Litigation under the ATCA and the TVPA: Is This an Effective Forum for Obtaining Victims' Redress?

Lawyers, judges, NGOs, victims, human rights activists and many others, have spent immense energy litigating individual claims and class

---

[56] Following the *Kadic* v. *Karadzic* case, the US District Court for the Southern District of New York reached similar conclusions in at least two other cases brought under the subject matter jurisdiction, *inter alia,* of the ATCA. In the first case, *Mushikiwabo* v. *Barayagwiza*, No. 94, Civ. 3627 (JSM), 1996 WL 164496 (S.D.N.Y. 9 April 1996), the Court allowed the claims of the plaintiff against Mr. Barayagwiza, a leader of a political party at the time of the genocide in Rwanda, accused of having committed acts of genocide and torture. Interestingly, as in the Karadzic case, the defendant was served with Court proceedings during a visit to the UN in New York. Barayagwiza was indicted by the ICTR and his trial resulted in a controversial series of events which raised serious issues of fair trial and the rights of the accused within the practice of the ICTR. *See Prosecutor* v. *Jean-Bosco Barayagwiza,* ICTR Appeals Chamber Decision of 3 November 1999. On this case, *see* Lyal S. Sunga, "Full Respect for the Rights of Suspect, Accused and Convict: from Nuremberg and Tokyo to the ICC", in Henzelin et al. (eds.), *Le Droit Pénal à l'Épreuve de l'Internationalisation,* University of Geneva (2002). In the case of *Cabiri* v. *Assasie-Gyimah,* 921 F. Supp. 1189 (S.D.N.Y. 1996), the District Court dismissed the motion of the defendant, a former employee of the Ghanaian government alleged of torture, by arguing that an official acting beyond the scope of his authority cannot be shielded by the immunity principle provided for in the Foreign Sovereign Immunities Act.

actions filed under the ATCA and the TVPA. As discussed, over the years, US courts have awarded enormous compensatory and punitive damages against the defendants, thus providing the victims with an exceptional 'nominal victory' - a cheque for the amount of several million dollars ready to be cashed. These, however, usually remain 'nominal victories'. On this point, commentators have argued that:

> a victory which results in a statement about the human rights record of the individual defendant or his government, or in the definition of a new or revised norm of international law, is just as important as monetary compensation.[57]

Yet, in cases of crimes under international law, one wonders whether a 'nominal victory' may be accepted as a satisfactory form of redress, especially considering that the primary objective of the law of tort is precisely to 'adjust the losses' and to "afford compensation for injuries sustained by one person as the result of the conduct of another".[58] While "statements about the human rights record of the individual defendant or his government", or "definitions of a new or revised norm of international law", are valuable elements of State practice on human rights standards as expressed in US domestic jurisprudential interpretation, which should be considered additional and complementary to victims' compensation, the ultimate test on the effectiveness of the US domestic civil litigation system under the ATCA and TVPA must be based on actual results in terms of compensation of the plaintiff at the expense of the tortfeasor. To date, the status of recovery of awards in some of the main cases concerning serious human rights violations litigated under the ATCA and TVPA stands as follows:

- ***Filártiga* v. *Peña-Irala.*** Total damages awarded in 1984 (compensatory and punitive, plus litigation expenses): US$10,385,364. The complainants have not been successful in enforcing the judgment in Paraguay. Apparently, the assets are located abroad.

---

57 Stephens and Ratner, *supra* note 31 at 236.

58 Cecil A. Wright and Allen M. Linden, *Canadian Tort Law: Cases, Notes & Materials*, Seventh Ed., Butterworths, Toronto (1980) at 1-1. Although civil actions under tort law may have different fallouts (moral retribution, deterrence, compensation, appeasement), it is generally agreed that "the immediate object of tort actions is to compensate the plaintiff at the expense of the tortfeasor", *see* Glanville Williams, "The Aims of the Law of Tort", *Current Legal Problems*, Vol. 137 (1951), reproduced in *ibid.* at 1-15.

- ***Forti and another* v. *Suarez-Mason.*** Total damages awarded in 1990 (compensatory and punitive): US$8 million. The claimants retrieved only US$400 from General Suarez-Mason through a local bank account in which the General's wife was receiving a monthly check.
- ***Martinez-Baca* v. *Suarez-Mason.*** Total damages awarded in 1988 (compensatory, punitive, loss of income with interest): US$21,170,699. The complainants have been unable to enforce the judgment.
- ***Quiros de Rapaport et al.* v. *Suarez-Mason.*** Total damages awarded in 1989 (compensatory and punitive): US$60 million. The complainants have been unable to enforce the judgment.
- ***In re Estate of Marcos Litigation.*** Damages awarded in 1995 class action: compensatory US$776 million; punitive US$1.2 billion. The money has remained in the hands of the Philippines Government, pending agreement for distribution to victims, who are currently trying to enforce the judgment in the Philippines' courts.
- ***Abebe-Jiri* v. *Negewo.*** Total damages awarded in 1993 and 1996 (compensatory and punitive): US$1.5 million, but the complainants have not received any money.
- ***Paul (et al.)* v. *Avril.*** Total damages awarded in 1994 to six victims (compensatory and punitive): US$41 million. The claimants have been trying to locate assets to collect their award.
- ***Xuncax* v. *Gramajo.*** Total damages awarded in 1995 to ten victims and survivors (compensatory and punitive): US$45.5 million. The claimants have been trying to locate assets to collect their award.
- ***Todd* v. *Panjaitan.*** Total damages awarded in 1994 (compensatory and punitive): US$14 million. The complainants have not succeeded in enforcing the judgment.
- ***Mushikiwabo* v. *Barayagwiza*:** Total damages awarded in 1996: over US$105 million. The complainants have not succeeded in enforcing the judgment.

To conclude this part of the discussion, civil actions under the ATCA can play a significant and symbolic role in the enforcement of international law through domestic courts, especially in the absence of an effective system of victims' redress at the international level. Civil domestic litigation puts the spotlight on the victims, it may help stir the debate on human rights issues and it sends a clear signal that perpetrators of crimes under international law are not immune from compensation claims in the territory of the US.[59] Also, domestic litigation of human rights cases in US courts serves to reflect State practice on a number of delicate human rights questions (from disappearances to torture, summary executions, arbitrary detention, rape, forced impregnation and forced pregnancy, and many others) and may trigger further action on redress at the inter-State or international level.

As recent practice in US courts shows, cases involving crimes under international law can be successfully brought before US courts, despite numerous procedural challenges. When it comes to actually obtaining redress however, the 'success' of a system cannot be measured strictly on the 'technical perfection' of a judicial proceeding culminating in the award of monumental damages to victims. As a matter of fact, in the vast majority of cases litigated under the ATCA and TVPA the victims have not been able to recover a single cent of their award. Inevitably, this creates a wide gap between the awarding of millions of dollars to victims of serious human rights violations as a matter of formal judgment, and the far from perfect state of actual execution of the judgment which has left victims mainly without compensation. Although it may be argued that compensation is only one of the objectives of tort law, the chronic failure to recover compensation as awarded under the ATCA and TVPA risks disconnecting completely the judicial system from the victims. One has to wonder whether this kind of litigation truly serves the ends of justice or whether justice is instead becoming a display of legal skills, of little practical benefit for the victims. Unless and until States engage in concerted efforts to fill the gap between justice administration and the needs of victims, and establish strong cooperation in inter-State judicial assistance matters, it will be very difficult to conclude that civil litigation under the ATCA and TVPA provides victims with effective redress, other than redress of a purely symbolic kind.

---

59 It is interesting to know that in February 2002 the families of the victims of the September 11 attack on the World Trade Centre filed a class action lawsuit in a federal court in Washington on behalf of all those killed, against Osama bin Laden, al Qaeda, the Taliban and another 138 individuals, organizations and businesses that the U.S. State Department identified as sponsoring or financing terrorist activity. The plaintiffs also listed the Islamic Emirate of Afghanistan, Iraq and Iran, among the conspirators as having provided material support to the terrorists. The plaintiffs sought US$1 billion in compensatory damages and over US$100 billion in punitive damages, in an effort to ensure that the alleged offenders are "financially unable to ever commit such acts again". *See* www.cnn.com, 19 February 2002.

2. Recognition and Enforcement of Foreign Judgments on Crimes under International Law: A Challenge for the Future

Despite new avenues for victims' redress opening up in connection with the administration of international criminal justice, explored in Chapter VI below, and, at the same time, a growing number of victims' claims under domestic jurisdiction, at present, effective implementation of the victims' right to redress depends mainly upon two factors: first, the extent to which international law has been incorporated into the domestic legislation of a country, or more precisely, the extent to which a country has established legislative and judicial implementation procedures for redress;[60] and second, the establishment of effective transboundary mechanisms for criminal law implementation, especially in matters concerning the award of reparation by foreign States and the recognition of reparation decisions by foreign courts.

While the courts of a given country proceed with the investigation and prosecution of cases involving crimes under international law, defendants normally have numerous opportunities to 'relocate' their assets, and sometimes themselves as well, to foreign jurisdictions to avoid the effect of a possible judgment against them. Unfortunately, at present the recognition and enforcement of foreign judgments abroad remain at the same time one of the more important elements and perhaps the weakest point in the domestic implementation of redress. The practice of domestic courts tends to show that, even in the presence of a judgment awarding compensation, restitution or other forms of redress, the probability that individual victims will actually gain access to the perpetrator's assets is small. This is partly due to the fact that a great number of victims' claims for compensation are filed in tort law, rather than being processed in criminal trials. Unlike in criminal proceedings, civil courts do not have the power to arrest the defendant and, even where the defendant is found liable, he or she often would have ample chance to leave the jurisdiction of the court and to remove from such jurisdiction assets targetable for compensation purposes, before interlocutory injunctions to freeze them could be put in place. In the absence of the offender and of his or her assets

---

[60] On this matter, Bianchi argues that despite the poor record of domestic prosecution of crimes under international law following the end of World War II, the recent enactment of a number of domestic statutes expressly allowing the exercise of jurisdiction over international crimes, and war crimes in particular, favours 'increased activism' of domestic courts in this field. *See* Andrea Bianchi, "Immunity versus Human Rights: the Pinochet Case", *European Journal of International Law*, Vol. 10, No. 2 (1999).

from the jurisdiction, victims normally have little practical alternative but to try to have the judgment enforced in the jurisdiction where the offender and the related assets may be located. Some of these problems may be less marked in civil law systems, which have the advantage of incorporating the civil element in a criminal trial through the *partie civile*, as discussed earlier in Chapter II.[61]

In light of the above, cooperation among States in the enforcement of foreign judgments remains an essential condition for the full enjoyment of the victims' right to redress. Frequently, the enforcement of foreign judgments concerning crimes under international law is not simply a matter of legal procedure. Perpetrators often enjoy protection either in their own country or in other countries that may not be willing to cooperate. Needless to say, without the assistance of the country in which the perpetrator is located, very little can be done to enforce a judgment awarding victims' redress. In this context, the Brussels Convention 1968,[62] opened for signature to all EU members, and the Lugano Convention 1988,[63] opened for signature to both EU and EFTA members, approach some of these issues with the aim of facilitating the legal steps leading to the enforcement of foreign judgments and reparation decisions reached in the courts of member States. Although limited in their geographical focus, these instruments remain an important tool for cooperation in judicial matters.

a. The Brussels and Lugano Conventions

The Brussels and Lugano Conventions - also known as 'Double Conventions' or 'European Instruments' - have been elaborated by the Hague Conference on Private International Law and are based on a 'double approach' to the exercise of domestic jurisdiction. The Conventions require Member States to exercise jurisdiction and to recognize or enforce foreign judgments where the case in question falls within certain grounds expressly listed in these Conventions. Conversely, the Conventions prohibit member States from the exercise of jurisdiction and from recognizing or enforcing decisions taken by

---

61 In order for a victim to be eligible for compensation in a criminal proceeding, he or she must, himself or herself, constitute a civil party (*partie civile*) against the offender. This means that a judge of the criminal trial may award compensation to the victim only where the victim participates in the criminal proceedings and files a specific claim for redress.

62 Brussels Convention of 27 September 1968, as amended by the 1989 Accession Convention.

63 Lugano Convention of 16 September 1988.

other member States, under certain circumstances. As concerns the victims' access to justice in case of crimes under international law, the Brussels and Lugano Conventions provide that victims can seek reparations under the jurisdiction of a member State only where the defendant is a resident of that State. The *rationale* behind these restrictions (which are also reflected in the domestic criminal legislation of most European States) can be traced to the attempt of European States to avoid abuse of State-funded compensation schemes.

b. Prospects for the Application of the Preliminary Draft Convention on Jurisdiction and Foreign Judgments in Civil and Commercial Matters (The Draft Hague Convention)

Member States of the Hague Conference are currently in the process of finalizing a new convention on jurisdiction matters entitled the Preliminary Draft Convention on Jurisdiction and Foreign Judgments in Civil and Commercial Matters,[64] which is intended to be universal in scope and to replace the somewhat outdated Brussels and Lugano Conventions. Although focussed on civil judgments, the draft Hague Convention could become a fundamental instrument for the enforcement of victims' redress for crimes under international law, if and when it is adopted and it eventually enters into force, especially since reparation claims for these kinds of crimes are mostly filed as civil actions in domestic courts. At the present stage of negotiations, however, the draft Hague Convention also raises a number of concerns on the access of victims of major crimes to domestic jurisdiction for purposes of redress, as we shall see.

The central problem seems to lie in the choice of the forum for the exercise of domestic jurisdiction and in the fact that the draft Hague Convention is solidly based on the principle of 'habitual residence' as codified in Article 3 which provides that the defendant may be sued in the State of his or

---

[64] Hereinafter referred to as the 'draft Hague Convention'. The draft Hague Convention was *adopted* by the Special Commission of the Hague Conference on Private International Law at the end of its fifth meeting on 30 October 1999 and it was later revised in June 2001. At the time of writing, the Permanent Bureau of the Conference was preparing a final text to be presented to a Diplomatic Conference planned for the end of 2003.

her 'habitual residence'.[65] This approach is inherently contrary to the practice of human rights civil actions against persons suspected of having committed crimes under international law, which have been filed mostly on the basis of the transient presence of the defendant in a given State, rather than on his or her place of habitual residence.[66]

While the principle of 'habitual residence' is one of the pillars of the draft Hague Convention, in certain specific cases the Convention allows the exercise of jurisdiction in fora other than the defendant's habitual residence. However, the exceptions to the habitual residence principle are relatively few and are mostly concerned with situations other than human rights litigation. For example, Article 4 allows Contracting States to settle a dispute which has arisen in connection with a particular legal relationship before a court of their choice, upon agreement between the parties. Similarly, Article 6, on contracts, lists as a suitable forum the courts of a State which has a specific connection with the contract under consideration.

Article 8 on individual contracts of employment may be of particular relevance to human rights claims involving corporations, because it would allow an employee to sue his or her employer, not only in the State of habitual residence, but also in the State of the employee's workplace or in the State

---

65 Nygh and Pocar argue in favour of the principle of habitual residence as enshrined in the maxim *actor sequitur forum rei*, as it tends to favour the defendant, "since it is much more difficult to defend oneself in the courts of a foreign country than in a different court of one's own country". *See* commentary to Article 3 in Peter Nygh and Fausto Pocar, *Hague Conference on Private International Law: Report of the Special Commission on the draft Hague Convention*, ftp://hcch.net/doc/jdgmpd11.doc. The report adds that the residency criterion "is undeniably more reliable in a factual sense, as it tends to denote a person's presence over a fairly prolonged period in a certain place, and to assign only an incidental and non-essential role to the intention of remaining there. Nor should it be forgotten that the connecting factor of habitual residence has been consistently used in the Hague Conventions, and there has never been any real difficulty in applying it in practice".

66 *See e.g.*, *Filartiga* v. *Peña Irala*, *Kadic* v. *Karadzic*, *Mushikiwabo* v. *Barayagwiza*, *In Re G.*, which are discussed above. On the dangers of limiting the exercise of domestic jurisdiction for international crimes *see* "Proposals of the Hague Conference and their Effect on Efforts to Enforce International Human Rights Through Adjudication", paper submitted by P. R. Dubinsky of New York Law School on behalf of the International Association of Democratic Lawyers, November 1998, Work. Doc. No. 17 of the Hague Conference on Private International Law, Special Commission on international jurisdiction and the effects of foreign judgments in civil and commercial matters.

where the business is located. Similarly, draft Article 9 provides that the plaintiff may bring an action against the defendant in the courts of a State in which "a branch, agency or any other establishment of the defendant is situated", provided that the case relates directly to the activities of the branch. Both provisions may find application, for example, in cases where the plaintiff alleges that his or her contract was terminated because of discrimination on the basis of colour, race, religion, sexual orientation, etc.

Finally, States have been debating also a provision under Article 10 which would provide the plaintiff with the choice to bring an action in tort or delict in the courts of a State where the act or omission that caused injury occurred, or in the place where the injury caused by such act or omission has arisen. However, the Special Commission of the Hague Conference regarded this provision as too burdensome for the defendant, since he or she may have to deal with any injury which could have arisen in any State as a consequence of his or her act or omission - a situation which the person responsible for the act or omission could not reasonably control.[67] Therefore, draft Article 10 introduces the concept of predictability and foresees that the possibility of suing the defendant in the State where the injuries arose becomes void where the defendant could establish that he or she "could not reasonably have foreseen that the act or omission could result in an injury of the same nature in that State". Accordingly, should the defendant be able to prove that he or she could not have 'reasonably foreseen' that the injury may have arisen in the plaintiff's State, the plaintiff would be left with no option but to bring the claim for tort or delict in the courts of the State where the act or omission occurred, which is often the court of the defendant. In case of domestic human rights litigation, this prospect may limit significantly the possibilities of victims to access justice mechanisms. As Amnesty International has noted, it is normally very difficult for victims to bring an action against perpetrators of serious human rights violations in the country in which the violations occurred, because the offenders are often in a position of power and they can effectively prevent victims from accessing justice or hinder the conduct of a regular trial.[68]

Articles 12 and 13 on exclusive jurisdiction and provisional and protective measures, along the lines of Article 10, tend to confirm the concern of the drafters to avoid as much as possible the exercise of extraterritorial jurisdiction by member States, especially where compensation and restitution

---

67 Nygh and Pocar, *supra* note 65.

68 *Multilateral Instruments - Justice for Victims: Ensuring Effective Enforcement Abroad of Court Decisions Concerning Reparations*, Amnesty International Report, IOR 53/02/99, June 1999.

matters are involved. According to Article 12(1), a State would have exclusive jurisdiction over proceedings concerning immovable property or tenancies of immovable property located in its territory, unless the tenant is habitually resident in a different State. Similarly, Article 13 on provisional and protective measures indicates that the courts of a State having jurisdiction over a case can order provisional or protective measures exclusively in respect of property which is located under the jurisdiction of that State. In the case of a State not having jurisdiction over a particular case, provisional measures may be ordered, provided only that their enforcement is limited to the territory of that State and that their purpose is to protect, on an interim basis, a pending claim on the merits.

In its present formulation, these particular provisions may hinder considerably the possibilities of victims to obtain an award for restitution of property illegally confiscated in a State other than the one where the property is located. This restriction is even more serious in the light of the fact that the recourse to foreign courts is often the only option victims have to exercise their right to redress following, for example, situations of armed conflict, genocide or ethnic cleansing.

As mentioned, the draft Hague Convention has been solidly based on the principle that Contracting States can exercise jurisdiction over the matters covered by the Convention only where there is a substantial connection between the dispute and the State concerned. At the current stage of negotiations, the 'habitual residence' ground for jurisdiction seems to have prevailed over any other ground for the exercise of State jurisdiction under the draft Hague Convention. It must be mentioned that the draft Hague Convention does not preclude the application of rules of jurisdiction based on the national law of Contracting States (Article 17). The application of these rules however, is specifically prohibited in cases where the defendant is a habitual resident of a Contracting State and where there is no 'substantial connection' between the Contracting State seeking to exercise jurisdiction according to its domestic laws and either the circumstances of the dispute or particular elements related to the defendant (Article 18).

In its Report, the Special Commission explained that while the Contracting States are bound by the Convention to implement domestic legislation on grounds of jurisdiction specifically covered by the Convention in Articles 3 to 13:

> they are by no means bound not to retain in their national law other grounds of jurisdiction for the topics covered by the Convention,

> where such jurisdiction is not incompatible with jurisdiction expressly provided in or not forbidden by the Convention itself.[69]

However, where the defendant is a habitual resident of a Contracting State, Article 18 of the draft Hague Convention prohibits Contracting States from exercising jurisdiction solely on any one of the following grounds:[70] the presence or the seizure in that State of property belonging to the defendant;[71] the nationality of the plaintiff or of the defendant; the domicile, residence or presence of the plaintiff in that State; the carrying on of commercial or other activities by the defendant in that State, except where the dispute is directly related to the activities in question; the service of a writ upon the defendant within the territory of that State; the unilateral designation of the forum by the plaintiff; the existence of proceedings in that State for declaration of enforceability or registration, or for the enforcement of a judgment, except where the dispute is directly related to such proceedings; the temporary residence or presence of the defendant in that State; the signing in that State of the contract from which the dispute arises; the location of a subsidiary or other related entity of the defendant in that State; or the existence of a related criminal action in that State.

This means that the factors listed in Article 18 do not suffice individually to establish a 'substantial connection' between the dispute and the Contracting State for the purposes of exercising jurisdiction under the draft Hague Convention. As a consequence, Contracting States wishing to exercise jurisdiction exclusively on these grounds are bound by the Convention to waive jurisdiction.[72]

To avoid the possible shortcomings of Article 18 for human rights civil actions, the Hague Convention drafters are currently considering an exception to Article 18 that would allow claims for serious human rights violations to be

---

69 *See* Nygh and Pocar, *supra* note 65, commentary to Article 17.

70 During the meeting of June 2001, States could not reach a consensus on this provision. As a result, the whole article is now in brackets and it is unclear whether it will be included in the final text. It is important to note that in its commentary to Article 18, the Special Commission explicitly regards the list of prohibited grounds for jurisdiction as a 'series of examples' of factors which do not establish a substantial connection between the dispute and the State, thus indicating the non-exhaustive character of the list. *Ibid.*

71 With the exception of disputes directly related to that property.

72 As for defendants who are habitual residents of a non-Contracting State, Contracting States are not bound by the draft Hague Convention's restrictions on the use of criteria for the exercise of jurisdiction.

brought before the courts of any Contracting State, irrespectively of the prohibitions listed in Article 18.[73] More specifically, States have been looking at ways in which Contracting States would not be considered bound by the 'substantial connection' criteria of the draft Hague Convention in case of civil actions brought before their courts by victims of crimes under international law such as genocide, war crimes or crimes against humanity.

In the negotiations that led to the 2001 version of the draft Hague Convention, States took into account the more recent developments in international criminal law, as reflected in the ICC Statute. The drafters were especially concerned with the principle of complementarity of the ICC, according to which States Parties of the ICC Statute have the primary obligation to prosecute and punish individuals responsible for crimes under the jurisdiction of the Statute, and the ICC would exercise jurisdiction only where States Parties were unwilling or unable to do so. The drafters regarded this obligation as potentially giving rise to a number of civil claims for redress on the part of the victims, either in the course of domestic criminal proceeding or in independent proceedings in civil courts.[74] To address this, draft Article 18(3) which remains bracketed and subject to further debate, has been proposed as follows:

> [Nothing in this article shall prevent a court in a Contracting State from exercising jurisdiction under national law in an action claiming damages in respect of conduct which constitutes -
>
> [a)[75] genocide, a crime against humanity or a war crime]; or]
>
> b) a serious crime under international law, provided that this State has exercised its criminal jurisdiction over that crime in accordance with an international treaty to which it is a Party and that claims for civil compensatory damages for death or

---

[73] On the impact of the draft Hague Convention on domestic human rights litigation and on the negotiations leading to the adoption of draft Article 18, *see* Beth Van Schaack, "In Defense of Civil Redress: The Domestic Enforcement of Human Rights Norms in the Context of the Proposed Hague Judgments Convention", *Harvard International Law Journal*, Vol. 42, No. 1, Winter 2001, pp. 141-199.

[74] *See* Nygh and Pocar, *supra* note 65, commentary to Article 18.

[75] The square brackets appear in the original text, indicating that the particular text within the brackets is under negotiation and may be redrafted.

> serious bodily injuries arising from that crime.
>
> Sub-paragraph b) only applies if the party seeking relief is exposed to a risk of a denial of justice because proceedings in another State are not possible or cannot reasonably be required].[76]

Draft Article 18(3) leaves Contracting States free to apply internationally recognized criteria for the exercise of jurisdiction in the field of international human rights law and international criminal law, including universal jurisdiction, without the restrictions of the draft Hague Convention. During the negotiations, this formula, based on the idea of inserting an 'exception' to Article 18, was preferred to the option of having crimes under international law completely excluded from the coverage of the draft Hague Convention, so that Contracting States exercising jurisdiction over civil claims regarding crimes under international law would still be bound by the draft Convention's provisions on the recognition and enforcement of judgments.[77] This choice has to be welcomed, considering that the recognition and enforcement of reparation judgments for crimes under international law are often the weakest elements in the enjoyment of the victims' right to redress for these kinds of crimes.

In its current formulation, draft Article 18(3) presents two variants. Variant (a) enables Contracting States to exercise jurisdiction under national law for civil claims in respect of acts of genocide, crimes against humanity or war crimes, without further restrictions. During the negotiations, it was proposed to include in Variant (a) a specific reference to the definitions of genocide, crimes against humanity and war crimes as expressed in the ICC Statute, but this proposal was eventually rejected on the basis that the ICC Statute had not yet entered into force at that time.[78] Considering that the Rome Statute entered into force on 1 July 2002, it would be advisable a revision of Variant (a) to include a specific reference to the crimes of genocide, crimes against humanity or war crimes 'as defined in the ICC Statute' in order to avoid unnecessary debate over the interpretation of these well-established definitions.

In addition to Variant (a), Variant (b) proposes that a Contracting State can exercise jurisdiction for civil actions for damages in respect to 'a serious crime under international law' if that State were to exercise its 'criminal' jurisdiction over that crime "in accordance with an international treaty to which

---

76 This provision combines together two variants initially drafted at previous stages in the negotiations.

77 *See* Nygh and Pocar, *supra* note 65, commentary to Article 18.

78 *Ibid.*, Commentary to Article 18 at footnote 16.

it is a Party", and if the claim under consideration was for "civil compensatory damages for death or serious bodily injury". The exercise of jurisdiction over serious crimes under international law under Variant (b) would be possible only where the party seeking relief "is exposed to a risk of a denial of justice because proceedings in another State are not possible or cannot reasonably be required".

It seems that the drafters included this second variant to avoid gaps in the exercise of State jurisdiction for civil claims ensuing from 'serious crimes under international law' other than genocide, crimes against humanity or war crimes, which are already covered in Variant (a). In this sense, Variant (b) could include, for example, crimes such as terrorism; hijacking; the illicit traffic in narcotic drugs; violations of the Convention on the Safety of UN and Associated Personnel 1995[79]; acts of torture, slavery, disappearances or arbitrary detentions not amounting to crimes against humanity; or war crimes not falling within the ICC definition. Some delegations have even proposed to enumerate directly in Article 18 the relevant international instruments to guide domestic courts in the implementation of the provision.[80]

One of the shortcomings of Variant (b) as it stands, however, is that by allowing the exercise of State jurisdiction over serious crimes under international law only where a State acts on the basis of a specific treaty obligation to that effect, Variant (b) basically excludes from the coverage of the Convention judgments on crimes under international law other than those arising from treaty law, for example crimes under international law considered as such under domestic legislation or customary international law, such as piracy, slavery, terrorism, apartheid or colonial domination. In practice, this flaw may be overcome by the fact that many of the 'serious crimes under international law' in Variant (b) fall within the definition of genocide, crimes against humanity or war crimes in Variant (a), which allows for unrestricted exercise of State jurisdiction. However, it would be still important for the exercise of State jurisdiction for 'serious crimes under international law' under Variant (b) to remain unlinked to treaty restrictions, to grant the full protection of the draft Hague Convention to judgments ensuing from civil actions for damages for crimes which are included neither in the rubric of ICC crimes nor in specific

---

79 Convention on the Safety of United Nations and Associated Personnel, *adopted unanimously* on 17 February 1995.

80 *See* Van Schaack, *supra* note 73 at 186-187.

treaty provisions.[81] Also, this would ensure that judgments coming from countries that are not parties to international conventions covering 'serious crimes under international law' can be properly enforced.

Finally, it is recommended that States consider expanding the coverage of Variant (b) to allow the free exercise of State jurisdiction not only over claims for 'civil compensatory damages' resulting from a 'serious crime under international law', but also over claims for damages other than compensation, such as restitution, rehabilitation, satisfaction and guarantees of non-repetition, in line with current international standards on victims' reparation for crimes under international law.[82]

Issues of *forum non conveniens* are dealt with in Article 22, which allows the courts of a State party the possibility, in exceptional circumstances, to suspend proceedings in a case where it is "clearly inappropriate for that court to exercise jurisdiction" and if "a court of another State has jurisdiction and it is clearly more appropriate to resolve the dispute". At the moment, Article 22 does not provide for any exception in case of proceedings involving crimes under international law. In its current formulation, this provision risks placing victims in the difficult situation of having to refer very delicate cases to the courts of a State which may be unable or unwilling to guarantee a fair and impartial trial or to provide sufficient guarantees for the enjoyment of reparations.

As regards the recognition and enforcement of judgments abroad, the draft Hague Convention makes it clear that a judgment based on grounds of jurisdiction provided for in the Convention "shall be recognized or enforced" (Article 25). However, Articles 26 to 28 provide for a long list of exceptions to this general obligation of recognition. These exceptions include, *inter alia*, the lack of jurisdiction on grounds expressed by the Convention, the manifest incompatibility with the 'public policy' of the State addressed, cases of *lis pendens*, and inconsistency of the judgment with a previous judgment rendered by another court. In practice, the draft Hague Convention seems to provide

---

81 Such as, for example, terrorism, the crime of mercenarism, or the use of nuclear weapons. *See* the work of the ILC in the Draft Statute for an International Criminal Court, Report of the ILC on the work of its forty-sixth session, 2 May-22 July 1994.

82 However, should this provision be adopted in the present form, at least its limitations regarding the claim for non-compensatory damages would be balanced by Article 33 on damages, which provides for the recognition of a judgment awarding non-compensatory, including exemplary or punitive, damages, "at least to the extent that similar or comparable damages could have been awarded in the State addressed".

States with more than ample discretionary power to decide these matters on a case-by-case basis. To avoid future misinterpretations in the application of these provisions, and possible damage to the effective exercise of victims' redress, it would have been preferable to limit the option of Article 28 only to judgments resulting from legal processes falling manifestly short of internationally recognized fair trial standards.

To sum up, the system set up by the draft Hague Convention could work either way: it could be a helpful tool in improving procedures for domestic enforcement of redress, or it could be a serious obstacle for victims in their struggle to obtain justice. It is to be hoped that provisions that do not fall in line with the best interest of victims and with current international standards on the prosecution and punishment of suspects of crimes under international law[83] will be duly revised during the ongoing drafting process.

3. The Way Ahead

National jurisdictions are still among the more accessible avenues - although not perfect ones - through which victims of crimes under international law can obtain redress. On the one hand, domestic legal systems often do not have the proper means to address the issue of reparations in the context of crimes under international law. On the other hand, it must be mentioned that, in a few cases, especially under the ATCA, domestic litigation has facilitated out-of-court legal and political settlements providing victims with considerable monetary compensation. This has been the case in the US$1.2 billion settlement between Swiss banks and the families of the victims of the Nazi regime and in the settlement of around US$5 billion between the German

---

83 In this context, one may recall the Principles of International Cooperation in the Detection, Arrest, Extradition and Punishment of Persons Guilty of War Crimes and Crimes against Humanity, *adopted* by UNGA resolution 3074 (XXVIII) of 3 December 1973, in particular, which state that: "(1) War crimes and crimes against humanity, wherever they are committed, shall be subject to investigation and the persons against whom there is evidence that they have committed such crimes shall be subject to tracing, arrest, trial and, if found guilty, to punishment; ... (3) States shall co-operate with each other on a bilateral and multilateral basis with a view to halting and preventing war crimes and crimes against humanity, and shall take the domestic and international measures necessary for that purpose; (4) States shall assist each other in detecting, arresting and bringing to trial persons suspected of having committed such crimes and, if they are found guilty, in punishing them".

Government and German corporations on the one hand and the families of the victims of the Nazi regime on the other.[84]

Ultimately, it seems clear that redress for victims of crimes under international law cannot be achieved through the efforts of each and every single legal system, whether at the domestic, regional or international level. Rather, it will require a concerted effort at all these levels, with a unity in purpose and coherence in standards, that at the same time allows for variety among implementation mechanisms to accommodate the need for various forms of redress. While it is essential that States adopt international instruments facilitating the enforcement of foreign judgments abroad, and integrate in their domestic law minimum standards on victims' redress as elaborated through the UN,[85] at the same time, the international community needs to work towards the establishment of a comprehensive regime at the international level for the effective redress of all victims of crimes under international law.

---

84 On this point, *see* Harvard Law Review Association, "Corporate Liability for Violations of International Human Rights", *Harvard Law Review*, May 2001.

85 The development of UN standards on redress for victims of international crimes will be discussed in Chapter V.

CHAPTER IV

State-Based Reparations

Principles and standards emerging from recent State practice on redress for victims of crimes under international law reflect a clear trend developing in many areas of international law that places victims of massive human rights violations in a more central position. States are reaching beyond the traditional framework of inter-State reparations and increasingly recognizing the question of victims' redress in multilateral efforts at peace-building and the strengthening of justice administration in post-conflict situations.

The following section explores how States have been adopting additional means and methods for redress which extend beyond the inter-State reparation framework, and have been focussing more directly on the victims. It is argued that this trend has been gradually shaping the State's duty to provide reparations for these kinds of violations and has been making it more consistent with recent advances in international law and practice on victims' redress. In turn, certain developments in State-based redress also suggest the emergence of more generalized recognition for the application of standards and principles designed specifically to grant redress to victims of crimes under international law.

1. State Responsibility and Inter-State Reparations: The Traditional Framework

Historically, the international community has dealt with the question of victims' reparation at the inter-State level within the framework of State responsibility and diplomatic protection. As the Permanent Court of International Justice observed already in 1924 in the case of the *Mavrommatis Palestine Concession*,[1] it is a well-established principle of international law that a State is entitled to protect its subjects and to resort to diplomatic action or to international judicial proceedings on behalf of its subjects, wherever they have been injured by another State acting in violation of international law. In

---

1 *Mavrommatis Palestine Concession Case (Jurisdiction)*, Greece *v*. UK (1924), PCIJ Reports, Series A, No. 2 at 12.

such instances, the State and not the individual becomes the sole claimant in the case.

Where large numbers of victims have been involved, such as in the event of a war, victims' reparation claims have been settled mainly by mixed claims commissions or arbitral tribunals usually established through bilateral agreements - often peace agreements - in which the responsible State agrees to pay an amount to the injured State, which in turn can distribute funds to individual victims according to criteria generally agreed on a bilateral basis.[2]

The practice of inter-State reparations rests on a basic principle of international law, according to which a State commits an internationally wrongful act where conduct "consisting of an action or omission is attributable to the State under international law" and where "that conduct constitutes a breach of an international obligation of the State".[3] As a consequence, a State in breach of an international obligation must provide reparation for the injuries caused.[4] In the *Chorzów Factory Case* 1928, the Permanent Court of

---

2 In his article entitled "Compensating Victims of the Crimes of War", *Virginia Journal of International Law*, Vol. 12, No. 3, April 1972, Benjamin Ferencz lists the Agreement signed at Berlin, 10 August 1922, 3 US Treaties 2601, the Mexican Claims Commission of 1898, the Philippine War Damage Commission, concerned primarily with rehabilitation, and the US Foreign Claims Settlement Commission. More recently, one can also mention the Iran-US Claims Tribunal 1981-1983. On the latter, *see generally* Richard B. Lillich and Daniel B. Magraw, (eds.), *The Iran-United States Claims Tribunal: Its Contribution to the Law of State Responsibility*, Transnational Publishers, Ardsley (1998); David D. Caron, "The Nature of the Iran-United States Claims Tribunal and the Evolving Structure of International Dispute Resolution", *American Journal of International Law*, Vol. 84, pp. 104-156; Charles N. Brower and Jason D. Brueschke, *The Iran-United States Claims Tribunal*, Martinus Nijhoff Publishers, The Hague (1998).

3 Article 3 of the ILC Articles on State Responsibility as adopted at the fifty-third session of the ILC (2001), *Official Records of the General Assembly, Fifty-sixth Session, Supplement No. 10* (A/56/10) at Chapter V.

4 This principle has been confirmed consistently in international jurisprudence. *See e.g.* the judgment of Max Huber establishing that the commission of a wrongful act entails a duty of reparation, *Spanish Zones of Morocco Claims* 1925, 2 RIAA 615; the *Palmagero Gold Fields Case* 1931, 5 RIAA at 298; the *Russian Indemnity Case* 1912, 11 RIAA at 431; the *Temple Case,* ICJ Rep. 1962. *See also* the *Barcelona Traction Case* 1970, and *Reparations for Injuries Suffered in the Service of the United Nations*, Advisory Opinion, ICJ Reports 1949 at 184, affirming the link between injury and the duty to make reparations. For an example of *restitutio in integrum*, *see* the *Martini Case* 1930, 2 RIAA 975 at 1002. Among more recent cases *see Provisional Measures* in the *Paraguay* v. *US Case* 1998, 37 ILM, in which Paraguay claimed *restitutio in*

International Justice set out some basic principles on the extent of a State's duty to make reparation in respect of a breach of an international obligation. The Court stated:

> The essential principle contained in the actual notion of an illegal act - a principle which seems to be established by international practice and in particular by the decisions of arbitral tribunals - is that reparation must, as far as possible, wipe out all the consequences of the illegal act and re-establish the situation which would, in all probability, have existed if that act had not been committed. Restitution in kind or, if this is not possible, payment of a sum corresponding to the value which a restitution in kind would bear; the award, if need be, of damages for loss sustained which would not be covered by restitution in kind or payment in place of it - such are the principles which should serve to determine the amount of compensation due for an act contrary to international law.[5]

In the context of war, the Hague Conventions embody the principle of State compensation for violations of laws and customs of war, which forms part

---

integrum against the US for a breach of the Vienna Convention on Consular Relations 1963, but the ICJ left the issue of availability of restitution open. For a comment on this question, *see* Christine Gray, "The Choice between Restitution and Compensation", *European Journal of International Law*, Vol. 10, No. 2 (1999).

5 *Chorzów Factory Case*, 1928 PCIJ Reports, Series A, No. 17, at 47-48. This principle has been endorsed and expanded in a number of other cases brought to the attention of the international community through international adjudication. One may refer, for example, to the *United States Diplomatic and Consular Staff in Tehran Case* 1980, ICJ Reports 3, in which the ICJ held that Iran had to pay reparations to the US; or to the *I'm Alone Case*, Interim and Final Reports of a Joint Commission, 1933 and 1935, 3 RIAA 1609, *American Journal of International Law* Vol. 29, No. 326 (1935), in which the Joint Final Report of the Commissioners recommended a certain amount to be paid as compensation to Canada. Unlike the *Chorzów Factory Case*, in which the Court laid down principles "to determine the amount of compensation" in case of an act contrary to international law, the Court's judgments in the *Tehran Case* and in the *I'm Alone Case* simply affirm the principle that 'reparation' should be made in case of a breach of international law. This principle was also enunciated in the *Rainbow Warrior Case* 1986, 74 ILR, at 241 and 274, an arbitration case between France and New Zealand, in which the Arbitration Tribunal discussed, among other issues, the issue of 'appropriate satisfaction' and recommended the establishment of a fund for compensation as a way to improve the relationship between the parties to the arbitration.

of customary international law. Article 3 of Hague Convention No. IV[6] obliges belligerent parties violating the provisions of the Regulations annexed to the Convention to pay compensation on an inter-State basis, and further provides that a belligerent party is responsible for all acts committed by persons forming part of its armed forces. Article 41 of Hague Convention No. IV also establishes an inter-State duty of compensation for losses caused by individuals who violate the terms of an armistice acting on their own initiative. Also, the four Geneva Conventions 1949 codify some provisions on reparation and compensation, the more important of which refer to the liability of States for grave breaches of the Conventions. Each of the Conventions establishes that no High Contracting Party shall "absolve itself or any other High Contracting Party of any liability incurred by itself or by another High contracting Party" in respect of grave breaches of the Conventions.[7] The Third Geneva Convention provides for the establishment of an inter-State procedure to compensate prisoners of war for injuries or disabilities.[8] In addition, Protocol I borrows the formula of the Hague Convention and establishes that if a Party to the conflict violates the provisions of the Conventions or of Protocol I, it "shall, if the case demands, be liable to pay compensation. It shall be responsible for all acts committed by persons forming part of its armed forces".[9]

2. Individual Victims as Direct Beneficiaries of State Reparations

While the duty of a State to repair the damage caused to another State for a breach of an international obligation is a well-established international law principle, widely codified and supported by consistent State practice, States have long debated the existence of a State obligation to provide *individual* victims with reparations for internationally wrongful acts, especially

---

6 Convention Respecting the Laws and Customs of War on Land, The Hague, 18 October 1907 (Hague Convention No. IV).

7 *See* Article 51 of Geneva Convention I, Article 52 of Geneva Convention II, Article 131 of Geneva Convention III and Article 148 of Geneva Convention IV.

8 According to Article 68 of the Geneva Convention Relative to the Treatment of Prisoners of War of 12 August 1949 (Geneva Convention III): "Any claim by a prisoner of war for compensation in respect of any injury or other disability arising out of work shall be referred to the Power on which he depends, through the Protecting Power".

9 Article 91 of Protocol I Additional to the four Geneva Conventions of 12 August 1949, and Relating to the Protection of Victims of International Armed Conflicts, *adopted* on 8 June 1977.

in the context of serious human rights violations. In particular, whether individuals have *locus standi* to claim compensation for violations of the laws and customs of war, and whether the obligation to provide compensation as expressed in the Hague Law and in Geneva Law is exclusively an inter-State obligation have been questioned.

Historically, the standing of individual victims as direct beneficiaries of State compensation for war damages has been rather weak. Hague Convention No. XII 1907, which has never entered into force, provided for the establishment of an International Prize Court before which individuals could claim property rights against a foreign State.[10] However, the individual could be prevented from instituting proceedings by his or her State of nationality, wherever the State decided to take over the claim instead. Also in 1907, five Central American States (Costa Rica, Guatemala, Nicaragua, Honduras and El Salvador) established the Central American Court of Justice, an international dispute settlement mechanism the jurisdiction of which was open to States, individuals and domestic institutions to bring claims against a State for violations of treaties and conventions or for other cases of an international character. The Central American Court of Justice worked from 1908 to 1918 and ruled on ten cases, five of which involved individuals. However, none of the cases brought by individuals were successful: four cases were dismissed because of non-exhaustion of local remedies and in another case the Judges ruled against the individual. In the Treaty of Versailles 1919, individual nationals of the Allied and Associated Powers could bring cases against Germany only through a Mixed Arbitral Tribunal, the decisions of which

---

[10] Articles 4 and 5 of the Hague Convention. The following passage from a symposium on the Hague Peace Conferences represents well the 'spirit' of the Hague Conferences with respect to the need to protect individual rights and minority rights: "In the Hague Peace Conferences, individuals represented peoples then denied statehood - Armenians, Macedonians, Poles, Finns, the Young Turks - who sought an international platform to assert their aspirations. They appealed for attention to their condition as essential to the cause of peace - a claim that has resonance today as regards, *inter alia*, the inhabitants of Kosovo, the Kurds, the East Timorese, the Saharawi, and the indigenous persons who sent their representatives to Geneva for the drafting of a declaration on their rights". *See* George H. Aldrich and Christine M. Chinkin, "Symposium: the Hague Peace Conferences: A Century of Achievement and Unfinished Work", *The American Journal of International Law*, Vol. 94, No. 90, January 2000 at 98.

would be final, conclusive and binding upon their nationals.[11] Finally, some minority treaties established following World War I guaranteed individual access to redress mechanisms, and, in certain cases, recognized the right of individuals to petition arbitral tribunals for the purpose of obtaining redress from a State.[12]

Domestically, the argument in favour of a State duty of compensation directly towards individuals has not met with much support, at least thus far. A number of judgments on this matter have interpreted the duty to compensate, as expressed in international humanitarian law, purely as an inter-State obligation to be settled within the context of peace treaties, which does not give rise to any subsequent obligation for the State to pay damages to each individual victim of the belligerent State.

---

11 Treaty of Versailles 1919, Article 304(b) of Section VI. Supported by detailed procedural provisions, Section IV of the Treaty of Versailles also provided for the restoration of property, rights and interests to their respective owners, who could receive equitable compensation for the losses incurred during the war.

12 Such as, for example, the Arbitral Tribunal established between Germany and Poland under the Convention for the Protection of Minorities of 15 May 1922, which allowed individual claims against the State of nationality and the foreign State on various issues, including nationality, right of residence, etc. Some commentators have even argued that the international justiciability of human rights made its appearance in the form of the protection of minority rights, although neither individuals nor minorities were considered as subjects of international law. *See* Alfred de Zayas, "The Examination of Individual Complaints by the UN Human Rights Committee under the Optional Protocol to the International Covenant on Civil and Political Rights", in G. Alfredsson, J. Grimheden, B. G. Ramcharan and A. de Zayas (eds.), *International Human Rights Monitoring Mechanisms*, Kluwer Law International (2001). It is interesting to note that the law on the protection of national minorities has always been concerned with victims' redress, including for crimes under international law. In 1993, Mr. Asbjørn Eide, UN Special Rapporteur of the Sub-Commission on the Prevention of Discrimination and Protection of Minorities, recalled that members of minorities have "a right to an effective remedy by the competent national tribunals for acts violating their rights granted by the constitution or law". The Special Rapporteur specifically extended this principle to victims of mass deportation during armed conflict - a well-established crime under international law - and stated that populations which have been forced to flee during ethnic conflict should be entitled to return and "to receive adequate compensation for losses to which they have been subjected". *See* 'Possible Ways and Means of Facilitating the Peaceful and Constructive Solution of Problems Involving Minorities', Report submitted by Mr. Asbjørn Eide, UN Doc. E/CN.4/Sub.2/1993/34/Add.4 of 11 August 1993 at para. 23.

This approach is reflected in a number of recent judgments by Japanese courts which have consistently rejected compensation claims by Chinese nationals for atrocities suffered during the Second World War. On 27 July 1995, the Tokyo District Court concluded as follows:

> neither the general practice nor the conviction (*opinio juris*) that the State has a duty to pay damages to each individual when that State infringes its obligations under international human rights or international humanitarian law can be said to exist.[13]

On 28 June 2002, the Tokyo District Court confirmed this view in a judgment on a war compensation case filed by three survivors of a 1932 massacre of Chinese villagers in Liaoning province by the Japanese Imperial Army, in which an estimated 700 to 3,000 villagers were killed. As Presiding Judge Yoichi Kikuchi argued: "the Government does not have responsibility, because at the time of the incident there was no law regulating the Government's responsibility to compensate damage claims". Therefore, the claim was rejected.[14] More recently, on 27 August 2002, the Tokyo District Court acknowledged for the first time that Japan's 'Germ Warfare Unit 731' killed large numbers of Chinese in violation of the Geneva Protocol 1925, on the orders of the Imperial Army's headquarters, by spreading plague and other diseases in Quzhou and Ningbo in Zhejiang province and Changde in Hunan province between 1941 and 1942. However, the Court rejected claims for compensation for some US$84,000 for each of the 180 Chinese plaintiffs, on the basis that foreign individuals cannot seek compensation from the Japanese Government, because all reparation issues had been settled by the Peace Treaty.[15] The plaintiffs have appealed against the ruling.

---

13 *See X et al* v. *the State*, Tokyo District Court, Judgment of 27 July 1995, *The Japanese Annual of International Law*, Vol. 39 (1996) at 266.

14 *See* the South China Morning Post of 29 June 2002. Some have argued however, in a different context, that in the process of settling victims' compensation claims on an inter-State basis, for example, through the negotiation of a lump sum agreement for the benefit of the victims, the State's action must be fair to the claimants and that if the settlement is not fair, the claimants have a right to press further claims, even if the inter-State compensation agreement expressly precludes this possibility. *See* Jon M. Van Dyke, "The Fundamental Human Right to Prosecution and Compensation", *Denver Journal of International Law and Policy*, Vol. 9, No. 2, Spring 2001 at 85.

15 *See* the South China Morning Post of 28 August 2002. The decision triggered mass demonstrations in China to protest against the verdict. It has been estimated that as many as 300,000 people died as a consequence of Japanese biological warfare during

In a more recent case however, the Tokyo District Court ordered the Government of Japan to pay ¥190 million (some US$1.7 million) in compensation to thirteen victims of recent incidents involving chemical weapons which had been abandoned in China by the Japanese Imperial Army at the end of the Second World War. Presiding Judge Yoshihiro Katayama argued that the Government had wrongfully omitted to provide information about the chemical weapons it had abandoned and that it had failed to assist with their disposal.[16] The Government of Japan has subsequently appealed.

In its 2001 Draft Articles on the Responsibility of States for Internationally Wrongful Acts,[17] the ILC adopted an open position on the question as

---

the Second World War, but compensation was claimed for only 2,100 individuals for whom names and addresses could be provided. There are a number of factors that have made this legal case of special interest. First, the newly installed communist government of China was not part of the peace negotiations which led to the San Francisco Peace Treaty, according to which Japan has been exempted from paying war reparations (*see* Article 14 of the Peace Treaty, at note 58). In 1952, President Chiang Kai-Shek of Taiwan was called to represent all of China and in this capacity he signed a separate peace treaty with Japan which made no mention of reparations. Second, in 1972, on the occasion of the re-establishment of diplomatic relations between Japan and mainland China, Premier Zhou Enlai expressly renounced all rights to war reparations, in exchange for Japan's acceptance of responsibility for the serious damages suffered by the Chinese people during the war. *See* Frank Ching, "Payouts for War Crimes a Moral Duty" in the South China Morning Post of 1 September 2002. Interestingly, Ching remarks that the question of germ warfare never came up during the International Military Trials in Tokyo following the Second World War, because General Shiro Ishii, the Head of Unit 731, and his colleagues, were granted immunity by the US in return for their research findings.

16 Judgment of 29 September 2003, *citation not yet available at the time of writing*. The victims had filed a lawsuit in Japanese courts in 1996, seeking damages for poison gas incidents in 1974 and 1982 and for a shell explosion in 1995, all of which occurred in Heilongjiang province. Each plaintiff was awarded compensation ranging from ¥6.66 million to ¥20 million. *See* the South China Morning Post of 30 September 2003 and 4 October 2003.

17 The ILC Draft Articles, together with accompanying commentaries, were *adopted* on second reading by the International Law Commission at its fifty-third session, 2001 and referred to the General Assembly for consideration. *See* the text of the articles in "Report of the International Law Commission on the work of its Fifty-third session", *Official Records of the General Assembly, Fifty-sixth session, Supplement No. 10*, UN Doc. A/56/10. On the latest ILC Draft Articles *see* James Crawford, *The ILC's Articles on State Responsibility: Introduction, Text, and Commentaries*, Cambridge University Press (2002). During the fifty-third session, the

to whom should be the beneficiary of the State obligation to make reparation in case of an internationally wrongful act. Although the Draft Articles deal only with the obligation of a State to make full reparation either to another State, to several States, or to the international community as a whole, Article 33(2) indicates that the ILC's approach to the question of State responsibility does not prejudice "any rights, arising from the international responsibility of a State, which may accrue directly to any person or entity other than a State". In this sense, the ILC recognizes the possibility of State responsibility arising from breach of a primary obligation owed to a non-State entity, as expressed in the ILC Commentary to Article 33.[18] Thus, the State owes a secondary obligation to provide reparations directly to that particular non-State entity, without the intermediation of a State, provided there are procedures set up to do so. In practice, this scenario may apply to the current human rights framework, where individuals are the direct beneficiaries of State obligations and there are procedures for the implementation of their right to reparation in case of a breach. In addition to the human rights field, the ILC envisages the possibility of having individual rights *vis-à-vis* the State in other areas of law, as indicated in the *La Grand Case* on the interpretation of Article 36 of the Vienna Convention on Consular Relations.[19] Therefore, provided there is a primary obligation towards individuals and procedural mechanisms to invoke State responsibility in case of breach, the door remains open for individuals to seek reparations directly from the State.

This opportunity is especially relevant to the question of compensation for victims of crimes under international law, which reaches beyond the traditional notion of State responsibility and inter-State compensation and must be approached from several points of view, taking into account each of the various legal regimes concerned. Over the years, the individual has increasingly become a direct holder of certain rights and prerogatives, and can no

---

ILC also discussed the question of State responsibility for international crimes as expressed in Article 19 of the ILC's earlier Draft Articles, which put forward a special regime of State responsibility for 'international crimes', namely breaches of an international obligation so essential for the protection of fundamental interests of the international community that they were considered to have been recognized as crimes by the international community as a whole. *See* the 1976 ILC Draft Articles on State Responsibility, UN Doc. A/CN.4/Ser.A/1976/Add.1. The former Article 19 generated fervent debate on the question of State responsibility for international crimes, but eventually, it was deleted from the draft.

18 *See* ILC Commentary on the Draft Articles at 233-235.

19 *See Case Concerning the Vienna Convention on Consular Relations (La Grand Case)*, Germany *v.* US, Merits, Judgment of 27 June 2001.

longer be considered merely as a beneficiary *vis-à-vis* the State under international law. This trend is most evident in the field of human rights, where individual victims enjoy an enforceable right to seek and obtain redress in the treaty-based framework of human rights protection and promotion.[20] In the event of serious human rights violations, human rights jurisprudence at the regional level has consistently indicated that individual victims hold a right to receive reparation *vis-à-vis* the State that includes not only the payment of appropriate monetary compensation by the State to the individual victim, but also the possible performance of other obligations, such as investigation into the violations, prosecution and punishment of those responsible, adoption of legislation to make the violations criminal offenses and amendment of legislation aimed at reducing impunity.[21]

At this stage, the successful access of individual victims to judicial remedies for State compensation outside the parameters of inter-State settlements or treaty-based obligations seems to depend more upon the discretion of each State rather than on the existence of a specific legal duty. Given the rapidly evolving character of the right to redress, however, prospects remain positive for the emergence of a State obligation under general

---

[20] Outside the treaty-based human rights framework, there seem to have been very few cases in which an individual has filed successful reparation claims against a foreign State in a domestic court for an alleged breach of a human rights obligation. On two occasions, *Suleiman Al-Adsani* v. *Kuwait* (Engcas C.A.) (Evans L.J.), March 1996 and *Suleiman Al-Adsani* v. *Kuwait* (Engcas C.A.) (Smith L.J.), November 1996, UK courts dismissed a case of alleged torture on the argument that the plaintiff did not prove the vicarious responsibility or the lack of immunity of Kuwait for the alleged threats of torture. Following the dismissal, the case was then taken to the European Court of Human Rights where the applicant argued that, by dismissing the case, the UK had violated the plaintiff's civil right to lodge a complaint under Article 6(1) and his right to a remedy under Article 13, with respect to the acts of torture he had suffered by the Kuwaiti authorities. Although the case had been declared admissible by the Court, in a judgment of 21 November 2001 the Court held unanimously that there had been no violation of Article 3 on the prohibition of torture and, by nine votes to eight, that there had been no violation of Article 6(1) on the right to access to court. In this case, the Court argued that: "sovereign immunity is a concept of international law, developed out of the principle *par in parem non habet imperium*, by virtue of which one State shall not be subject to the jurisdiction of another State" and that "the grant of sovereign immunity to a State in civil proceedings pursues the legitimate aim of complying with international law to promote comity and good relations between States through the respect of another State's sovereignty". *See Al-Adsani v. the United Kingdom,* ECHR, Judgment of 21 November 2001 at para. 54.

[21] *See further* discussion on this matter in Chapter V below.

international law to provide individual victims of serious human rights violations with an enforceable right to seek and obtain reparations for violations attributable to the State.[22]

3. Individual Redress Based on State Responsibility: The Unique Example of the UN Compensation Commission and Compensation Fund for Claims Against Iraq

Following the defeat of Iraq in 1991 by international coalition forces engaged in 'Operation Desert Storm', the UN Security Council, acting under Chapter VII of the Charter of the United Nations, adopted resolution 687 on 3 April 1991, which determined the conditions of the cease-fire and established

---

[22] Almost ten years ago, Professor Theo van Boven, Special Rapporteur of the UN Sub-Commission on the Prevention of Discrimination and Protection of Minorities, argued that: "the obligations resulting from State responsibility for breaches of international human rights law entail corresponding rights on the part of individual persons and groups of persons who are under the jurisdiction of the offending State and who are victims of those breaches. The principal right these victims are entitled to under international law is the right to effective remedies and just reparations". *See* "Study concerning the right to restitution, compensation and rehabilitation for victims of gross violations of human rights and fundamental freedoms", Final Report submitted by Mr. Theo van Boven, Special Rapporteur, UN Doc. E./CN.4/Sub.2/1993/8 of 2 July 1993 at para. 45. The Committee on the Elimination of Discrimination Against Women also argued that a State may be responsible under international law for private acts if it fails to provide compensation to the victims, as a part of a general duty to prevent unlawful acts and to punish the perpetrators. *See* Recommendation No. 19 on violence against women, adopted by the Committee at its 11th session, held in 1992. In future ICC implementation, it is possible that States will decide to make subsidiary reparations to victims through the Trust Fund following a general duty under international law. In this sense, both the UN Declaration of Basic Principles of Justice for Victims of Crime and Abuse of Power and the Final Report of the UN Independent Expert on 'The Right to Restitution, Compensation and Rehabilitation for Victims of Gross Violations of Human Rights and Fundamental Freedoms' endorse the subsidiary role of the State in compensating victims of crimes when the responsible party is unable or unwilling to meet his or her obligations. *See* in particular Principle 12 of the UN Declaration of Basic Principles of Justice for Victims of Crime and Abuse of Power, *adopted* by UNGA resolution 40/34 of 29 November 1985; and Principle 18, Annex to 'The Right to Restitution, Compensation and Rehabilitation for Victims of Grave Violations of Human Rights and Fundamental Freedoms' Final Report of the Special Rapporteur, Mr. M. Cherif Bassiouni, submitted in accordance with Commission resolution 1999/33, UN Doc. E/CN.4/2000/62 of 18 January 2000.

the responsibility of Iraq for the invasion and occupation of Kuwait. With the same resolution, the Security Council also directed the UN Secretary-General to develop and present to the Security Council recommendations for setting up a compensation fund as well as a commission to administer it. Interestingly, in his report of 2 May 1991, the Secretary-General recommended that the Commission take the form of a 'claims resolution facility' rather than of a court or an arbitral tribunal, with the task of verifying and evaluating the massive number of expected claims and administering the payment of compensation.[23] As a result, on 20 May 1991, the Security Council adopted resolution 692 (1991) establishing a Compensation Fund and the UN Compensation Commission (UNCC)[24] as a subsidiary organ to process claims and to pay monetary compensation for losses incurred during Iraq's invasion and occupation of Kuwait. Accordingly, the UNCC was set up to hear claims for damages resulting from a broad range of unlawful activities, including violations of human rights and humanitarian law.[25]

The UNCC is a unique compensation mechanism, which departs from traditional inter-State reparation frameworks and incorporates innovative elements into its procedure. The role of the Security Council in the establishment of the UNCC, as well as the Commission's way of approaching the issues of State responsibility and individual compensation, raise a number of interesting questions. These have to do mainly with the legitimacy of the UNCC as a reparation mechanism under international law in general, and more

---

23 *See* UN Doc. S/22559.

24 For further information on the UNCC *see* the UNCC website at http://www.unog.ch/uncc/start.htm. In general, *see* John R. Crook, "Current Development: the United Nations Compensation Commission - a New Structure to Enforce State Responsibility", *The American Journal of International Law*, Vol. 87, No. 144, January 1993. *See also* Marco Frigessi di Rattalma and Tullio Treves (eds.), *The United Nations Compensation Commission: A Handbook*, Kluwer Law International (1999). On the human rights issues arising from the Iraqi occupation of Kuwait, *see* Walter Kälin (ed.), *Human Rights in Times of Occupation: The Case of Kuwait*, Law Books in Europe, Berne (1994).

25 In his 1992 report, the UN Special Rapporteur on the Situation of Human Rights in Kuwait under Iraqi Occupation, Mr. Walter Kälin, pointed out a number of widespread, gross and systematic human rights violations he considered attributable to Iraqi occupying forces in Kuwait, including arbitrary and summary executions; torture and cruel, inhuman or degrading treatment; mass arrest, detention and deportation of civilians; disappearances; hostage-taking; and use of civilian as 'human shields'. *See* "Report on the situation of human rights in Kuwait under Iraqi occupation", UN Doc. E/CN.4/1992/26 of 16 January 1992.

specifically with the validity of the UNCC as a precedent for the compensation of individual victims in case of crimes under international law.

The first point relates to the fact that the UNCC is the only compensation system that has ever been established by the Security Council acting under Chapter VII. This particular setting has a double effect: first, as a political body, it gives the UNCC the power to enjoy the full prerogatives derived from Chapter VII authority; and second, it places the issue of victims' compensation squarely within the enforcement framework of the maintenance of international peace and security, thus affirming this issue to be a matter of prime concern for the international community as a whole. However, the fact that the UNCC was created under Chapter VII authority merely as a 'claims resolution facility' to facilitate the settlement of claims against Iraq, and not as an arbitration tribunal or as an adjudicatory body, implies that Iraq has little standing to rebut the claims or to verify their legitimacy under the terms of the settlement. On this and other related points, a number of commentators have criticized the legality of the UNCC as a reparation mechanism under international law.[26]

The second innovation worth noting is the particular approach of the UNCC in terms of State responsibility, diplomatic protection and reparation mechanisms. The UNCC reparation regime, although based on State responsibility for injuries suffered during the Iraqi invasion of Kuwait, departs from the traditional inter-State reparation framework based on the principle of diplomatic protection, and grants individuals a quasi-independent, primary role in accessing the compensation scheme. In the classic law of State responsibility, according to the principle of diplomatic protection there is no obligation for a State in breach of international law to compensate individual victims of a foreign nationality who have suffered damage.[27] Rather, victims can call for the 'protection' of their own State of nationality, which may take up their claims and seek reparation from the State in breach of an international obligation. In this case, the State seeking reparation becomes the only claimant

---

26 *See* Peter Malanczuk, "International Business and New Rules of State Responsibility? - The Law Applied by the United Nations (Security Council) Compensation Commission for Claims Against Iraq", in K. - H. Böckstiegel (ed.), *Perspectives of Air Law, Space Law and International Business Law for the Next Century*, Carl Heymanns Verlag KG (1996), pp. 117-145. *See also* Bernhard Graefrath, "Iraq: Reparations and the Security Council", *Zeitschrift für ausländisches öffentliches Recht und Völkerrecht* (1995) pp. 1-68; Vera Gowlland-Debbas, "Security Council Enforcement Action and Issues of State Responsibility", *International and Comparative Law Quarterly*, No. 43 (1994), pp. 55-98.

27 In fact, this obligation does not even apply to the State's own nationals.

and the eventual distribution to individual victims of the funds received as reparation remains a matter of municipal law at the discretion of the State.[28]

In contrast, under the UNCC regime, compensation is provided not only to injured States, but also to individual victims and corporations, through an innovative procedure. Individual and corporate claims must be presented through the claimants' respective Governments, or in the case of individual victims, through an international organization on behalf of individuals who were not in a position to have their claims filed by a Government. Although Governments make an initial grouping, evaluation and processing of the claims prior to sending them to the UNCC Secretariat, individual and corporate claimants remain the legitimate holders of the reparation claims.[29] The UNCC reparation regime goes even further to provide that Governments can present claims coming not only from their own nationals, but also from individuals who are resident in their territory, thus going beyond the nationality link - a fundamental element in the framework of diplomatic protection.[30]

In terms of procedure, to ensure the proper management of the awards, Governments and international organizations acting on behalf of individual or corporate claimants, are obliged to distribute the award to successful claimants within six months of having received payment from the Commission and to

---

[28] The principle of 'diplomatic protection' is widely recognized in international law and jurisprudence. *See inter alia Mavrommatis Palestine Concession Case (Jurisdiction)*, Greece *v.* UK (1924), PCIJ Reports, Series A, No. 2 and *Administrative Decision No. V*, US v. Germany (1924), Mixed Claims Commission, 7 R.I.A.A. 119.

[29] The reason for this indirect procedure may be traced to the impossibility of the UNCC's dealing with a potentially huge number of individual claims. Since its establishment in 1991, the Commission has received approximately 2.6 million claims seeking compensation in excess of US$300 billion. According to the official data available at the UNCC website http://www.unog.ch/uncc/start.htm "some one hundred Governments have submitted claims for their nationals, corporations and/or themselves. Thirteen offices of the United Nations Development Programme (UNDP), the United Nations High Commissioner for Refugees (UNHCR) and the United Nations Relief and Works Agency for Palestine Refugees in the Near East (UNRWA), have also submitted claims for individuals who were not in a position to have their claims filed by Governments".

[30] *See* the *Nottebohm Case*, Liechtenstein *v.* Guatemala, ICJ Reports 1955. On the departure of the UNCC regime from the traditional framework of diplomatic protection, Malanczuk argues that the Security Council has altered three major requirements of the customary law of diplomatic protection, namely the nationality link, the rule of continuos nationality and the rule of exhaustion of local remedies. *See* Malanczuk, *supra* note 26 at 137.

report to the Commission's Council on this procedure. Contrary to the recommendations of the Special Rapporteur on the situation of human rights in Kuwait under Iraqi Occupation, the UNCC cannot receive claims from Iraqi nationals.

A third innovation in the UNCC's *modus operandi* is the 'priority policy' which relates to individual claims. Acting on humanitarian considerations, individual claims to the UNCC take precedence over governmental and corporate claims.[31] Specifically, the UNCC has prioritized claims according to the following six-category scale:

a. individual displacement claims;[32]

b. individual claims for serious personal injury or where a spouse, child or parent died as a result of Iraq's invasion and occupation of Kuwait;[33]

c. individual claims for damages up to US$100,000 each for various kind of losses, including departure from Kuwait or Iraq, personal injury, mental pain and anguish, loss of personal property, loss of bank accounts, stocks and other securities, loss of income, loss of real property, and individual business losses;[34]

---

31 Individual claims for displacement constituted the vast majority of the claims submitted to the UNCC. They were all settled by 2002.

32 These were claims by individuals who had to depart from Kuwait or Iraq between 2 August 1990 (the date of Iraq's invasion of Kuwait) and 2 March 1991 (the date of the cease-fire). The Governing Council set compensation for successful claims in this category at the fixed sum of US$2,500 for individual claimants and US$5,000 for families. In total, the Governing Council has approved the payment of more than US$3.2 billion in compensation for over 860,000 successful claimants. *See* UNCC website at http://www.unog.ch/uncc/start.htm.

33 Compensation for successful claims in this category was set at US$2,500 for individuals and up to US$10,000 for families. The Commission has received approximately 6,000 claims of this kind, submitted by forty-seven Governments and seven offices of three international organizations, seeking a total of approximately US$21 million in compensation. In December 1995, the Commission concluded the claims processing programme for this category. Payment of US$13,450,000 in compensation was made available from January 1994 to December 1996 for distribution to 3,945 successful claimants. *Ibid.*

34 The Commission received approximately 420,000 claims of this kind, submitted by eighty-five Governments and eight offices of three international organisations, seeking a total of approximately US$9 billion in compensation. In addition, the Central Bank of the Government of Egypt submitted a consolidated claim on behalf of over 800,000 workers in Iraq, for a total of over 1,240,000 individual claims for the non-transfer of remittances by Iraqi banks to beneficiaries in Egypt, with

d. individual claims for damages above US$100,000 each, for losses similar to the ones described in point 'c', and mainly related to the loss of personal and real property, or the loss of income and business-related losses.[35]

e. claims by corporations, other private legal entities and public sector enterprises, including claims for construction or other contract losses; losses from the non-payment for goods or services; losses relating to the destruction or seizure of business assets; loss of profits; and oil sector losses.[36]

f. claims filed by Governments and international organizations for losses incurred in evacuating citizens; providing relief to citizens; damage to diplomatic premises and loss of, and damage to, other government property; and damage to the environment.[37]

Finally, to finance the payment of compensation awards under the UNCC regime, the Security Council established a Compensation Fund for the benefit of the victims, operating on 25% of the revenues of the sales of Iraqi oil in accordance with the United Nations Oil-for-Food Programme. More specifically, Security Council resolution 705 (1991) determines that Iraq's contribution to the Compensation Fund must not exceed 30% of the annual value of Iraq's oil exports. Also, the Fund covers entirely the working costs of the Commission, which means that Iraq has also paid for all of the Commission's work. As for the form of compensation, in line with the report of the Special Rapporteur on the situation of human rights in Kuwait under Iraqi occupation, individual victims have been awarded compensation not only for material damages, but also for moral damages, mental pain and anguish.[38]

---

a value claimed at approximately US$491 million. The Governing Council approved the payment of more than US$4.9 billion to successful claimants, and in June 1999 the Commission concluded the processing of claims. *Ibid.*

35 Under this category, the Commission received approximately 10,500 claims submitted by fifty Governments and eight offices of three international organisations, seeking a total of approximately US$10 billion in compensation.

36 Approximately 5,800 claims were submitted under this category by seventy Governments seeking a total of approximately US$80 billion in compensation.

37 Under this category, the Commission has received approximately 300 claims, submitted by forty-three Governments and six international organisations, seeking a total of approximately US$210 billion in compensation.

38 In his report at para. 260, the Special Rapporteur considered that the award of non-material damages for victims of human rights violations would be in line with recent developments in international law. *See supra* note 25.

The combination of all these elements, together with strong institutional support from the UNCC administration, has placed victims of serious human rights and humanitarian law violations committed during the Iraqi invasion of Kuwait in a unique position to enjoy their right to seek and obtain redress. On a practical level, the UNCC has been able to provide swift compensation to a very large number of individual victims of serious human rights violations - a task other institutions have failed to fulfill thus far.[39] Serious shortcomings however, such as the UNCC's highly political character and the lack of proper defense of Iraq in the reparation proceedings, call into question not only the UNCC's fairness in general, but also its validity as an example for future reparation mechanisms in similar post-war situations.

4. The Role of the State in Providing Quasi-Judicial and Non-Judicial Symbolic Redress

State action in support of victims' redress - irrespective of whether it is based on a purely moral duty or on a legal obligation - is usually fundamental for the victims' full enjoyment of the right to reparation, including the right to know the truth surrounding the harm suffered, and to obtain justice.[40] The magnitude of crimes under international law, as well as the great number of victims they often involve, requires the support of State-based structures to ensure effective redress within the broader framework of restoration, national reconciliation, truth-finding, peace-making and confidence-building. In

---

39 For a critique of claims commissions and compensation tribunals dealing with victims' reparation in modern war situations, *see* Michael J. Matheson, "The Twelfth Waldemar A. Solf Lecture in International Law", *Military Law Review*, Vol. 161, No. 181, September 1999 at 199, pointing out that historically it has been very difficult, if not impossible, for claims commissions and arbitral tribunals to deal with the vast number of victims resulting from war situations. *See also*, in a different context, the failure of the ICTY and ICTR to provide adequate compensation to victims of similar kinds of violations as those under the competence of the UNCC. On this matter and on the UNCC as a feasible system for the civil compensation for wartime damages *see* Rosemary E. Libera, "Divide, Conquer, and Pay: Civil Compensation for Wartime Damages", *Boston College International & Comparative Law Review*, Vol. 24, pp. 291-312.

40 These were the three elements Mr. Joinet's identified as comprising the victims' legal rights. *See* "The Administration of Justice and the Human Rights of Detainees, Question of the Impunity of Perpetrators of Human Rights Violations (Civil and Political)", Final Report prepared by Mr. Joinet pursuant to Sub-Commission decision 1996/119, UN Doc. E/CN.4/Sub.2/1997/20 of 26 June 1997.

particular, it has been increasingly clear that the role and responsibility of States faced with the question of reparation for crimes under international law must go beyond simple monetary compensation. Recent State initiatives on victims' redress for these kinds of crimes point to a shift beyond the traditional concept of inter-State reparation towards the adoption of alternative methods of redress focussing more on individual victims as bearers of specific rights. In this context, many States have taken the first steps towards practical measures for collective as well as individual redress with respect to crimes often committed many years ago.

France, for example, in 1996 formally acknowledged the responsibility of the French Government for crimes against humanity committed during the Vichy regime. In the year 2000, Germany established a joint US-German trust fund for the compensation of victims of slave labour during the Nazi regime, under the pressure of some 55 class actions pending against German firms in US courts.[41] Prior to the establishment of the Joint Fund, the Federal Republic of Germany provided reparation to victims of Nazi persecution through *ad hoc* legislation enacted following the Second World War. German compensation law was initially designed to cover only restitution of property or indemnification for loss of property.[42] Later, its scope was expanded to cover loss of life, including homicide, manslaughter, death in concentration camps, deterioration of health conditions due to emigration or improper living conditions, suicide due to persecution and economic difficulties, damage to limb or health, including mental health, damage to liberty, including military detention, forced stay in concentration camps or in a ghetto, forced labour, compulsory

---

41 Half of the US$4.8 billion compensation fund is financed by some three thousand German companies, many of which forced hundred of thousands of people into slavery and slave labour during the Nazi regime. Under the compensation agreement, some 900,000 victims and their families will receive individual payments of up to around US$8,000. The payment of compensation under the trust fund will bar beneficiaries from taking any further action for compensation, but not from recovering looted artwork. *See* CNN.com of 16 July 2000.

42 Property restitution was implemented on the basis of military legislation of the three Western occupying powers, specifically under US Military Government Law No. 59 of 20 November 1947, UK Military Government Law No. 59 of 12 May 1949 and Ordinance No. 120 of the French Commander of 10 November 1947. *See* Ferencz, *supra* note 2.

exhibition of the Star of David, and damage to professional and economic prospects.[43]

In Brazil, then President Cardozo recently issued a statement on responsibility for serious and systematic human rights violations committed during the military dictatorship in that country between 1964 and 1985. Spain recently conferred the status of ex-servicemen upon the anti-Fascist and International Brigade members fighting for the Republicans during the Spanish Civil War. It is also notable that Pope John Paul II has issued official apologies and recognized the responsibility of the Catholic Church for violations that occurred many centuries ago. In 1988, President Reagan signed the Civil Liberties Act,[44] which offered official apologies for the evacuation, relocation, and internment of some 120,000 Americans of Japanese ancestry in US prison camps during the Second World War. The Civil Liberties Act also offered compensation of US$20,000 to each eligible claimant, to be provided over a period of ten years, and it established a public education fund.[45] However, the compensation question for Japanese-Americans interned in US camps remains open with respect to about 2,000 Latin Americans of Japanese origin who were deported from various Latin American countries and interned in US camps and who were denied compensation under the Civil Liberties Act on the ground that they were not US nationals at the time of internment. In 1998, the Clinton administration approved a settlement to pay compensation of up to US$5,000

---

43 *See* the 1965 Final Federal Compensation Law (*Bundesentschadigungs-schlussgesetz*, or BEG). A number of countries entered into agreements with Germany to compensate individual claimants residing in their territories, under the BEG. Along similar lines, on 23 June 2000 the Czech Republic adopted a law providing for the restitution of property confiscated during the Second World War to Czech Jews and Jewish organizations and for the compensation for owners whose property could not be returned.

44 Civil Liberties Act of 1988, 50 U.S.C. §1989 *et seq.*

45 *See* Sean D. Murphy, "Contemporary Practice of the United States Relating to International Law", *The American Journal of International Law*, Vol. 93, No. 628, July 1999. At 654, the author notes that the first payments were issued in October 1990 and that by February 1999, the US Office of Redress Administration had paid out more than US$1.6 billion to more than 82,250 claimants, representing 99% of potential claimants. For an analysis of the US redress policy to Japanese-Americans under the Civil Liberties Act, *see* Natsu Taylor Saito, "Symbolism Under Siege: Japanese American Redress and the 'Racing' of Arab Americans as 'Terrorists'", *Asian Law Journal*, Vol. 8, No. 1, May 2001.

to claimants who could not benefit from the previous compensation scheme.[46] By February 1999, 145 Latin Americans of Japanese origin had received compensation under the settlement, while some 400 claims were still pending.[47] In the meantime, a number of these persons have also sought compensation against the US Government in civil courts under the ATCA. To take yet another example, after more than 50 years, the US issued a controversial acknowledgment that US soldiers had killed an unconfirmed number of unarmed civilians during the Korean War.[48]

More recently, North Korean leader Kim Jong-il admitted that thirteen Japanese citizens were abducted, of whom nine were killed, by North Korean secret agents during the 1970s and 1980s and he officially apologized to Japanese Prime Minister Junichiro Koizumi during his official visit to North Korea in September 2002.[49] Kim Jong-il also declared that an enquiry had been opened and that those responsible for the 'misguided abductions' had been punished. During the same official visit, the Japanese Prime Minister also offered official apologies and possible economic aid plans in recognition of the Japanese colonial rule over the Korean peninsula from 1910 to 1945, that had

---

46 The U.S. Court of Federal Claims approved the settlement on 25 January 1999. *See* Murphy, *ibid.* at 655.

47 *Ibid.*

48 In the case of US killings in the Korean War, the families of the victims rejected the official 2001 report issued by the Pentagon after 14 months of investigations, which admitted the killing of civilians, including refugees, in July 1950 near No Gun Ri, 200 km south of Seoul, but ruled out any possibility of compensation on the argument that the commanders did not order the shootings. *See* US Department of the Army Inspector General, *No Gun Ri Review*, January 2001. In particular, the victims' families contend that the official US report omitted to take account of 'declassified military documents' recently found in US archives showing clear evidence of command responsibility in the shooting of around 400 South Korean refugees, including women and children. Among these documents is a memo of 27 July 1950 from Maj. Gen. William Kean to subordinates, ordering that, since civilians in No Gun Ri had been directed to evacuate the area and the evacuation had been reported to have been accomplished, "all civilians seen in this area are to be considered as enemy and action taken accordingly". *See* the "Associated Press Special Report: Bridge at No Gun Ri" (2000). Victims' relatives plan to bring the case to the UN Human Rights Committee and they have been seeking an official apology from the US Government as well as compensation.

49 The thirteen Japanese nationals had been kidnapped to train North Korean spies in Japanese language and culture, so that they could eventually infiltrate South Korea using the abductees' identities. *See* the South China Morning Post of 18 September 2002.

"caused tremendous damage and suffering". However, the Prime Minister made it clear that economic aid was not compensation, and that both sides had waived the right to seek compensation for property damaged before and during World War II.[50]

All these steps are of particular significance to the victims' right to redress in light of the fact that often, victims of crimes under international law consider 'satisfaction' in such forms as official apologies,[51] recognition of responsibility on an official basis, acknowledgment of the dignity and suffering of victims, organization of commemorative ceremonies, erection of monuments and declaration of national days of remembrance,[52] as among adequate forms of reparation, together with the prosecution and punishment of individual perpetrators.

Unfortunately, in other cases, victims and survivors of genocide, crimes against humanity, war crimes or other crimes under international law have not been able to enjoy reparation from the State, either in the form of satisfaction or otherwise. This has been partly due to the difficulties States have encountered in trying to elaborate a concept of 'crime of State' and, more importantly, to determine the legal consequences in terms of State responsibility.[53] Furthermore, the unevenness among instances where State reparations for crimes under international law were provided seems to have depended upon factors beyond technical and legal considerations, such as the delay with which States were willing to acknowledge certain responsibilities, whether political

---

50 *See* the South China Morning Post of 14 September 2002.

51 *See generally* Mark Gibney and Erik Roxstrom, "The Status of State Apologies", *Human Rights Quarterly*, Vol. 23, No. 4, November 2001 at 911-939.

52 Under the ILC Draft Articles on State responsibility, satisfaction is a supplementary means of reparation consisting of "an acknowledgement of the breach, an expression of regret, a formal apology or another appropriate modality". In Article 37, States have a duty to provide satisfaction in case it has not been possible to repair the wrong with restitution or compensation.

53 The ILC finally dropped the notion of State crimes from its latest version of the Draft Articles on State responsibility, as discussed above. Chapter III of the new ILC Draft Articles only refers to "serious breaches of obligations under peremptory norms of general international law". However, as far as victims' redress is concerned, the situation may not change much whether we talk of 'crimes of States' or of "serious breaches of obligations under peremptory norms of general international law" as in the latest version of the ILC Draft Articles, as long as it is understood that the 'gravity' or 'seriousness' of these kinds of violations make them different from other breaches of international obligations, especially in terms of the legal consequences that may be involved, including for victims' redress.

conditions were ripe for reconciliation and redress in civil society and the position of redress questions in the agenda of the international community at the time.[54] In this context, victims of the following cases, to mention just a few examples, have been still awaiting proper redress:

- The 'comfort women' of Korea, China, Taiwan, Indonesia and the Philippines, who were forced into sexual slavery by the Japanese Imperial Army during the Second World War.[55] It is estimated that some 200,000 women and girls were forced into sexual slavery and, as a consequence, that they have suffered from serious, long-lasting physical and psychological damage. Those responsible for atrocities of a sexual nature were not prosecuted in the Tokyo Trials following World War II. In December 1991, a number of 'comfort women', mostly from Korea, filed a lawsuit in Tokyo against the Japanese Government, claiming compensation for the damage suffered. The Japanese Government initially denied any involvement of its army in the forced prostitution of women and girls during the Second World War. However, the uncovering of documentary evidence from Japan's Self Defense Agency Library in 1992 pressured the Government into finally admitting the existence of the so-called 'comfort women' and creating the 'Asian Woman's Fund', a private foundation to provide support and financial assistance to the 'comfort women'.[56] However, the former 'comfort women' have refused any private donations and have continued their legal battle to obtain official apologies and compensation from the Japanese Government.[57] So far, all claims have

---

[54] *See generally* Elazar Barkan, *The Guilt of Nations: Restitution and Negotiating Historical Injustices*, Johns Hopkins University Press (2001).

[55] On this question, *see generally* George Hicks, *The Comfort Women*, W. W. Norton & Co., New York (1995). *See also* Watanabe Kazuko, "Militarism, Colonialism, and the Trafficking of Women: 'Comfort Women' Forced into Sexual Labour for Japanese Soldiers", *Bulletin of Concerned Asian Scholars*, Vol. 26, No. 4, October-December 1994.

[56] The Fund has been asking Japanese cabinet ministers to provide donations for the compensation of some 290 'comfort women' from South Korea, the Philippines and Taiwan, who have been offered ¥2 million each. Prime Minister Junichiro Koizumi is expected to give about ¥150,000, while other cabinet ministers were asked to contribute ¥100,000. *See* the South China Morning Post of 26 June 2002.

[57] In 2000, a number of NGOs, human rights activists and scholars gathered in Tokyo to adopt the Charter of the Women's International War Crimes Tribunal 2000 for the Trial of Japanese Military Sexual Slavery, which led to the establishment of the

been rejected by the Tokyo District Court, on the argument that peace treaties have settled all war-related issues.[58]

- Persons subjected to forced labour as Asian and Allied prisoners of war forced to work in Japanese companies during the Second World War. In this case, it is estimated that as many as 700,000 Koreans, 40,000 Chinese, an unknown number of other Asians, and around 70,000 Allied prisoners were forced into slave labour by the Japanese during the war.[59] As of July 2000, there were more than 30 class actions filed in California against Japanese companies, including Mitsubishi, Mitsui and Nippon Steel for, *inter alia*, human rights violations, forced labour, slavery and unjust enrichment. So far, both the Japanese Government and Japanese firms have taken a consistently negative attitude towards compensation and apologies, despite growing political pressure from the US, where a number of congressmen presented the House of Representatives with a bill seeking apologies and compensation to victims. Also, compensation claims filed in Japanese courts have met with little success: most claims were rejected and a few had been settled out of court with little satisfaction for the plaintiffs. As of March 2000, only one South Korean plaintiff had received compensation of¥4.1 million from a Japanese steel company, NKK.[60] Japan has consistently argued that all reparation issues were settled by 1952, when the US seized some US$90 million of Japanese

---

Women's International War Crimes Tribunal - a symbolic people's tribunal with the primary task of "bringing out truths and establishing the legal responsibility of states and individuals involved in sexual violence ... perpetrated by the Japanese Imperial Army in connection with Japan's colonial domination and war of aggression throughout the Asia-Pacific region". *See* the Charter of the Women's International War Crimes Tribunal on Japan's Military Sexual Slavery 2000 at www.iccwomen.org/tokyo/charter.htm.

58 On 29 March 2002 the Tokyo District Court also rejected two lawsuits filed by former 'comfort women' from China who demanded compensation for ¥23 million and public apologies. Again, the Court argued that all reparation matters were settled by a 1972 agreement between Japan and China. *See supra* note 15.

59 *See* The Economist of 8 July 2000.

60 *See* The Economist of 4 March 2000. On the victims' efforts to receive compensation in Japanese courts, *see* Petra Schmidt, "Japan's Wartime Compensation: Forced Labour", *Asia-Pacific Journal on Human Rights and the Law*, Vol. 2 (2000).

assets to compensate prisoners of war, based on Article 14(2) of the San Francisco Peace Treaty 1951.[61]

- Some 200,000 Bangladeshi women raped during the 1971 nine-month Liberation War that marked the secession of Bengali East Pakistan from West Pakistan to become the independent State of Bangladesh. It is estimated that around 200,000 women were forcibly held in army barracks and cantonments across Bangladesh and systematically raped by Pakistani army regulars. In addition, an estimated 300,000 Bengali Muslims were killed. Human rights activists have repeatedly urged the Bangladeshi authorities to request official apologies and compensation from Pakistan, but both current and past Bangladesh Governments have failed so far to raise the matter at the inter-State level. Human rights activist Shaheen Akhtar recalls that following independence, rape victims were officially declared *biranganas*, or national heroines, by the new Government and were offered facilities for medical treatment and rehabilitation.[62] Despite this, rape victims soon became 'outcasts' because of the sexual nature of the violation they had suffered. Akhtar explains that:

> a Government campaign to reunite them with their husbands and families or marry them off failed miserably. Government dowries were handed out to men, and a few hundred rape victims got married only to be deserted by their husbands within months. Even the babies they gave birth to after their harrowing ordeal were branded 'enemies' chil-

---

[61] Article 14(2) of the San Francisco Peace Treaty provides that: "each of the Allied Powers shall have the right to seize, retain, liquidate or otherwise dispose of all property, rights and interests of (a) Japan and Japanese nationals, (b) persons acting for or on behalf of Japan or Japanese nationals, and (c) entities owned or controlled by Japan or Japanese nationals" for the purposes of reparation for 'damage and suffering' caused by Japan during the war. Article 16 of the Peace Treaty also provides that: "as an expression of its desire to indemnify those members of the armed forces of the Allied Powers who suffered undue hardships while prisoners of war of Japan, Japan will transfer its assets and those of its nationals in countries which were neutral during the war, or which were at war with any of the Allied Powers, or, at its option, the equivalent of such assets, to the International Committee of the Red Cross which shall liquidate such assets and distribute the resultant fund to appropriate national agencies, for the benefit of former prisoners of war and their families on such basis as it may determine to be equitable".

[62] *See* interview of 11 March 2002 in the South China Morning Post.

dren', forcing tens of thousands of mothers to give them up for adoption abroad.[63]

- Australian Aborigines forcibly taken away from their families and assimilated into white families between the early 1900s and the mid-1970s under Australia's policy of assimilation of indigenous people, during which time it is estimated that thousands of Aboriginal children where forcibly displaced and assimilated. So far, Australian Prime Minister John Howard has refused to issue any form of apology for the violations, arguing that he is unwilling "to apologize for things my Government and my generation of Australians didn't do", and that an apology on this matter would open the floodgates for expensive reparations his Government was not prepared to provide.[64]

a. Redress in a Broader Framework: Truth Commissions and Truth-finding Mechanisms

As part of comprehensive efforts to build peace and reconciliation, some countries in transition from situations of civil war, violence, dictatorship and massive human rights violations have taken the initiative in establishing truth-finding and redress mechanisms to deal with victims of crimes under international law. Over the past ten years, the Governments of Argentina, Bolivia, Chad, Chile, El Salvador, Ethiopia, Haiti, Honduras, the Philippines, Rwanda, South Africa, Uganda, Uruguay and Zimbabwe, among others, have shifted from pure monetary compensation to broader forms of redress. In addition to compensation plans, Governments have enacted *ad hoc* domestic legislation to prosecute and punish individuals responsible for crimes under international law committed in their territory and to establish truth commissions, fact-finding commissions, commissions of enquiry or similar institutions.[65]

---

63 *Ibid.*

64 *See* International Herald Tribune of 8-9 July 2000.

65 For an excellent comparative study of truth commissions *see* Priscilla B. Hayner, "Fifteen Truth Commissions - 1974 to 1994: A Comparative Study", *Human Rights Quarterly*, Vol. 16, No. 4, November 1994, pp. 597-655. On non-prosecutorial mechanisms for truth-finding in case of gross human rights violations, *see* Steven R. Ratner and Jason S. Abrams, *Accountability for Human Rights Atrocities in International Law: Beyond the Nuremberg Legacy*, Clarendon Press (1997) at 193-204. *See also* Dinah Shelton, *Remedies in International Human Rights Law*, Oxford University Press (1999) at 328-330.

i. Argentina

After seven years of military rule, in December 1983 the new democratically elected President of Argentina, Raúl Alfonsín, created a National Commission on Disappeared Persons[66] to investigate the practice of forced disappearance and to provide information for the purpose of future prosecution. In addition to the Commission, the Government created domestic reparation schemes for victims of unlawful detention during the military regime.[67] The Argentinian reparation scheme did not yield fully satisfactory results in terms of redress, perhaps because of its limited scope of application which focussed mainly on unlawful detention and to a much lesser extent on other widespread and serious human rights violations, such as forced disappearance, torture and abduction committed during the 'Dirty War'.[68] The reparation framework relied primarily on monetary compensation, which in effect diverted the focus from other essential forms of reparation and from establishing truth-finding mechanisms. Moreover, the beneficiaries of State-based compensation were formally banned from seeking other kinds of reparation. Finally, the whole process of truth-finding and judicial determination of responsibility was considerably diluted by the extensive concession of pardons and the adoption of laws granting blanket amnesties, under the Presidencies of Alfonsín and Menem.[69] As a result, domestic courts could

---

66 *Comision Nacional para la Desaparicion de Personas*, also known as the 'Sábato Commission', from the Latin American novelist Ernesto Sábato who was named Chairman or the Commission.

67 For example, Acts No. 23.852 and 24.043 of September 1990 granted an exemption from military service to sons or brothers of disappeared persons, and extended compensation to persons who had been detained as a result of military court decisions, even if they had not filed claims for damages. By 1994, approximately 9,000 requests had been submitted, 5,000 had been processed and 2,000 were being reviewed. Of these, 700 had been rejected. *See* Second Periodic Report of Argentina to the Human Rights Committee, UN Doc. CCPR/C/SR.1389 of 5 April 1994.

68 *See* van Boven final report at paras. 118-121. *See however* Act No. 24.321 of May 1994, providing compensation to relatives of victims of enforced disappearances and to members of human rights NGOs. For an evaluation of the work of Latin American truth commissions *see generally* Jo M. Pasqualucci, "The Whole Truth and Nothing but the Truth: Truth Commissions, Impunity and the Inter-American Human Rights System", *Boston University International Law Journal*, Vol. 21, No. 321, Fall 1994.

69 For some reflections on the use of amnesty in case of crimes under international law *see* Roman Boed, "The Effect of a Domestic Amnesty on the Ability of Foreign States to Prosecute Alleged Perpetrators of Serious Human Rights

process only a small portion of the cases forwarded by the Argentinian Truth Commission concerning human rights violations during the military regimes.[70]

ii. Chile

On 25 April 1990, the new democratically elected president of Chile, Patricio Aylwin, enacted a Supreme Decree establishing a National Commission on Truth and Reconciliation to clarify the truth on serious human rights violations committed during the sixteen-year dictatorship between 11 September 1973 and 11 March 1990. In addition, Law 19.123 of 8 February 1992 established a National Corporation for Reparation and Reconciliation to implement the Commission's recommendations and to determine facts concerning disappearance cases, including the location of the bodies of individuals who had disappeared and were later declared dead. In its report, the Commission recommended symbolic reparation, including the erection of a monument and the building of a remembrance park, but also more practical measures such as the legal and administrative resolution of questions relating to the acknowledgment of the victims' death, compensation in the form of social benefits, health care, education and pension, as well as other measures aimed at preventing future violations, such as the ratification of human rights instruments and the creation of a national human rights commission.[71] One of the Commission's shortcomings was its limited mandate, covering only violations which resulted in the death or disappearance of the victim; violations such as torture for example were not compensated. Also, the Commission did

---

Violations", *Cornell International Law Journal,* Vol. 33, No. 297 (2000). *See also* Kristin Henrard, "The Viability of National Amnesties in View of the Increasing Recognition of Individual Criminal Responsibility in International Law", *Michigan State University - DCL Journal of International Law,* Vol. 8, No. 595, Fall 1999.

70 *See* Ratner and Abrams *supra* note 65 at 147-149, noting that in Argentina, for example, the truth commission established under the Alfonsín Government following the democratic elections of 1993, forwarded to the judicial authorities (both military and civilian) more than 1,000 claims for human rights violations committed during the military junta. However, suspects were charged mainly with common crimes under Argentinean law, since the Argentinean criminal code failed to incorporate properly international crimes and, in particular, crimes against humanity. In addition, the military courts refused to prosecute the junta leaders and eventually the Federal Court of Appeals seized jurisdiction.

71 Report of the Chilean Commission on Truth and Reconciliation, Vol. 2, cited in Pasqualucci, *supra* note 68 at 339. On the Chilean report *see* Mark Ensalaco, "Truth Commissions for Chile and El Salvador: A Report and Assessment", *Human Rights Quarterly,* Vol. 16 (1994) pp. 656-675.

not facilitate efforts to prosecute and punish individuals responsible for the violations. As of 1996, the Commission paid compensation to 4,886 relatives of victims totalling US$80.2 million.[72]

iii. El Salvador

The Commission on the Truth in El Salvador was established in accordance with the 1991 Mexico Agreements and was formally installed on 13 July 1992 under the sponsorship of the United Nations to investigate serious acts of violence that had occurred since 1980, whether of an individual character or as part of a systematic pattern of violence.[73] The Truth Commission in El Salvador was the first of its kind in Latin America established within the context of UN efforts to secure peace throughout the country.

The UN Secretary-General made public the Commission's report[74] on 15 March 1993 amidst a highly tense political climate generated by the fact that the report contained the names of individual officers of the Salvadorian armed forces, civil service and the judiciary, who had been personally involved in human rights violations. The report recommended that these individuals be dismissed from their posts or disqualified from such employment either temporarily or permanently.[75] The Commission's report dedicates ample coverage to victims, including an analysis of the victims' testimony, a list of victims whose identity was not kept confidential, a list of disappeared persons compiled by the UN Working Group on Enforced Disappearances and a call for compensation, based on the principle that: "justice does not stop at punishment; it also demands reparation. The victims and, in most cases, their families, are entitled to moral and material compensation".[76] Given the financial situation

---

72 *See* Michael Reisman, "Compensation for Human Rights Violations", in Albrecht Randelzhofer and Christian Tomuschat (eds.), *State Responsibility and the Individual: Reparation in Instances of Grave Violations of Human Rights*, Kluwer Law International (1999) at 106.

73 For an overview of the UN involvement in El Salvador, *see The United Nations and El Salvador, 1990-1995*, The United Nations Blue Books Series, Vol. IV, UN Department of Public Information, New York (1995).

74 "From Madness to Hope: The 12-Year War in El Salvador", report of the Commission on the Truth for El Salvador, annex to a Letter dated 29 March 1993 from the Secretary-General to the President of the Security Council, UN Doc. S/25500 of 1 April 1993.

75 The report names over forty military officers and eleven members of the Farabundo Marti National Liberation Front as responsible for gross and systematic human rights violations in El Salvador. *Ibid.*

76 *Ibid.* at Part V, Chapter IV.

of the country, the Commission recommended the creation of a special fund as an autonomous body for the material compensation of victims, which would receive contributions from the international community and would be set up under the auspices and coordination of the UN Secretariat.[77] The commission also recommended measures for moral compensation, namely the construction of a national monument to the victims with their names, recognition of the good names of the victims and of the serious crimes for which they suffered, and the institution of a national day of remembrance.

Unfortunately, in 1994 the Independent Expert of the UN Commission on Human Rights noted that the general climate of impunity was causing human rights violations in the country to continue and that:

> the recommendations of the Commission on the Truth have to date not had any practical impact and their partial implementation cannot in general terms be taken as a declaration of intent.[78]

The post-conflict climate of impunity in El Salvador also actively prevented effective implementation of the victims' right to redress. In this context, the Commission remarked that, although pardon can be an essential element of national reconciliation and the reunification of society, the achievement of justice requires punishment for the guilty and adequate compensation for the victims and their families.[79]

iv. *South Africa*

The Truth and Reconciliation Commission of post-apartheid South Africa has played a fundamental role in the country's reconciliation process. However, it provided little support for individual victims in terms of reparation. The Commission began its work in December 1995 through three Committees: the Human Rights Violations Committee, the Reparations and Rehabilitation

---

[77] The Commission also recommended that El Salvador take measure to differentiate between domestic compensation procedures for criminal acts and compensation for victims of human rights violations. *See* Report of the Secretary-General on the implementation of the recommendations of the Commission of the Truth, UN Doc. S/26581 of 14 October 1993.

[78] Report on the situation of human rights in El Salvador prepared by the Independent Expert of the Commission on Human rights, UN Doc. E/CN.4/1994/11 of 3 February 1994.

[79] Report of the Commission on the Truth for El Salvador, Part V (Recommendations) Chapter IV on Steps Towards National Reconciliation, *supra* note 74.

Committee and the Amnesty Committee. While the Human Rights Violations Committee and the Amnesty Committee achieved their goals essentially as planned, the Reparations and Rehabilitation Committee faced enormous obstacles, the first of which was a chronic lack of funds for the compensation of victims. Although the Committee recommended compensatory measures, most victims could not be compensated, even when the amounts of the reparation awards were seemingly insignificant.[80] As a form of reparation, the Committee also recommended that the families of around 22,000 victims receive an annual grant of approximately US$2,800-3,500 over a six-year period. However, by 1998 only around 20,000 victims had received a partial payment of US$300, while funds for the remaining payments were never allocated.[81] In a study on the political climate of South Africa during the operation of the Truth Commission, Wilson remarks on the deep sense of betrayal felt by victims because of the lack of action on the reparation issue. This feeling is well expressed in the following press release by a survivors' group, published in connection with a victims' demonstration on the compensation issue:

> The TRC [Truth and Reconciliation Commission] has compromised our right to justice and to making civil claims. In good faith we came forward and suffered the re-traumatisation of exposing our wounds in public in the understanding that this was necessary in order to be considered for reparations. We now feel that we have been used in a cynical process of political expediency.[82]

In addition, the Commission adopted a policy of full amnesty for those who admitted their responsibility for the apartheid regime in the country - an element that caused even greater frustration for victims.

---

80 *See* Richard A. Wilson, *The Politics of Truth and Reconciliation in South Africa: Legitimizing the Post-Apartheid Regime*, Cambridge University Press (2001) at 22, recounting the situation of women asking for a tombstone for the death of their husbands or sons as a form of reparation - a request the Committee was not able to afford.

81 *Ibid.*

82 Khulumani Support Group press release of 27 October 1999, cited in Wilson, *ibid.*

b. Is it Sufficient to Learn the Truth?

Truth commissions and other fact-finding mechanisms are important restorative elements in victims' redress and, more generally, in the process of reconciliation, peace-building and confidence-building in countries with a history of massive or systematic human rights violations. They also mark a shift toward restorative justice and a more global approach to victims' redress. This must be welcomed. However, they can only play a partial role in victims' redress for crimes under international law. Redress for violations of such magnitude as genocide, crimes against humanity or war crimes cannot be solved adequately by relying exclusively on domestic initiatives, such as the establishment of localized truth commissions or restricted compensation funds, even where they are sponsored by international institutions. Arguably, truth commissions should be only one of the elements of a more integrated response by the international community to the question of redress for victims of crimes under international law, that includes the establishment of mechanisms for the prosecution and punishment of those responsible and an effective trust funds for victims' compensation.

CHAPTER V

Evolution of the Victims' Right to Redress through International Human Rights Law, Jurisprudence and Standards

Principles and standards on victims' redress for crimes under international law have been emerging from various fields of international law. Despite the limitations discussed in the preceding chapters, domestic courts in many countries have been developing jurisprudence that relates interestingly to redress. States have been expanding their range of redress activities beyond the realm of traditional inter-State reparations, and have been applying particular principles and standards to better address issues such as the nature of the crimes, the high number of victims involved, the need to restore peace in civil society, the promotion and protection of human rights, and the maintenance of regional and international peace and security.

A similar trend can be detected in the law and practice of international human rights, where some of the main principles and standards on redress for victims of crimes under international law have been emerging largely through jurisprudence concerning particularly serious human rights violations, such as torture or disappearances. Recent international human rights adjudication on these and other serious human rights violations has introduced greater clarity in the applicability and extent of the victims' right to redress, signalling gradual expansion beyond traditional forms of monetary compensation and domestic legal remedies, to encompass, where appropriate, also the legal responsibility of the State to render justice to victims by punishing the offender or setting up investigative or fact-finding mechanisms.

To appreciate the current status of the victims' right to redress in international human rights law and its main operating principles in relation to crimes under international law, this Chapter explores how redress provisions developed over time in universal and regional human rights instruments, as well as in the relevant soft law. We then evaluate the current practice of various human rights mechanisms for victims' redress as regards serious human rights violations.

1. Universal Human Rights Treaties: An Indirect Approach to Reparations

Many international and regional human rights instruments that have been adopted over the last fifty years or so enshrine the basic principle of victims' redress. However, the right to redress as expressed in these instruments, including the right to receive compensation, is intended to be exercised mostly in the domestic context.[1] This is a rather 'indirect' approach to reparations, and in this sense, the express inclusion of compensation provisions in international human rights instruments and the setting up of international reparation mechanisms such as trust funds for victims, have been the exception rather than the rule.

Article 8 of the Universal Declaration of Human Rights 1948[2] provides for an enforceable right to an effective remedy through the action of competent domestic tribunals, as follows:

> Everyone has the right to an effective remedy by the competent national tribunals for acts violating the fundamental rights granted him by the constitution or by law.

Although the Declaration is a resolution of the United Nations General Assembly, rather than a treaty, and as such, is not legally binding, it remains one of the more influential international human rights instruments and has paved the way for the further development of international human rights treaty law. Indeed, human rights instruments adopted since the Declaration tend to follow the scope of Article 8 of the Declaration and delegate implementation of the 'right to an effective remedy' to domestic judicial systems, rather than

---

1 *See generally* Giorgio Gaja, "New Instruments and Institutions?" in Philip Alston (ed.), *The EU and Human Rights*, Oxford University Press (1999) at 787-790, in which the author argues that adequate judicial and administrative remedies under national laws are not always available for all human rights violations, that they tend to be rather limited for some rights, especially economic and social rights, and that the cost of accessing these remedies is often prohibitive for the victims.

2 Universal Declaration of Human Rights, *adopted* and *proclaimed* by UNGA resolution 217 A (III) of 10 December 1948. On the Universal Declaration of Human Rights *see generally* Gudmundur Alfredsson and Asbjørn Eide (eds.), *The Universal Declaration of Human Rights: A Common Standard of Achievement*, Martinus Nijhoff, The Hague (1999).

providing directly for mechanisms aimed to compensate victims.[3] In this context, while most human rights treaties embody at least the principle of domestic remedies for victims for breaches of treaty obligations, only in a few cases do they expand on this principle to include more specific provisions on reparation in its various possible forms - such as restitution, monetary compensation, rehabilitation, satisfaction and guarantees of non-repetition. This may have been due to the fact that victims' compensation has been traditionally considered a 'secondary right' - a sort of an 'extra' right deriving from a breach of a primary right protected by specific legal provisions. Consequently, the right to redress, as it has evolved around a number of human rights themes of particular concern for the international community, has never really departed from its indirect approach to the question of compensation, as discussed below.

a. Redress for Violations of the International Covenant on Civil and Political Rights in the Practice of the United Nations Human Rights Committee

The International Covenant on Civil and Political Rights (ICCPR) 1966,[4] provides expressly for an individual right to a remedy in case of breaches of the Covenant, irrespective as to their magnitude or seriousness. Under Article 2(3), States Parties have a general obligation to ensure that:

> (a) any person whose rights or freedoms as herein recognized are violated shall have an effective remedy, notwithstanding that the violation has been committed by persons acting in an official capacity;
>
> (b) any person claiming such a remedy shall have his right thereto determined by competent judicial, administrative or legislative authorities, or by any other competent authority

---

3 On this point, Nowak argues that it is a general principle of international law that: "not only the statutory implementation and structuring of international norms of human rights but also the specific protection of the individual against violations of these rights are primarily domestic concerns". Manfred Nowak, *UN Covenant on Civil and Political Rights: CCPR Commentary*, N. P. Engel Publisher, Kehl (1993) at 57.

4 *Adopted and opened for signature, ratification and accession* by UNGA resolution 2200 A (XXI) of 16 December 1966.

provided for by the legal system of the State, and to develop the possibilities of judicial remedy;[5]

(c) the competent authorities shall enforce such remedies when granted.[6]

Over the last twenty-five years or so, the practice of the UN Human Rights Committee[7] on individual 'communications' under the procedure of the

---

5 *See* an interesting account of the history of this provision in Nowak *supra* note 3 at 58-60, who explains that Article 2(3)(b) represents a compromise between the common law tradition that views the right to a remedy as fulfilled only once a formal judicial decision has been issued, and the civil law legal systems, which tend to grant States more freedom with respect to the procedures used to fulfill the victims' right to a remedy. In his Commentary, the author argues that decisions made exclusively by "political and subordinate administrative organs (especially governments) do not constitute an effective remedy within the meaning of para. 3(b)". Consequently, States must accord priority to judicial remedies.

6 The ICCPR provides for a specific right to 'compensation' only in Articles 9(5) referring to victims of unlawful arrest or detention or faulty criminal conviction and in Article 14(6) referring to victims of miscarriage of justice.

7 The UN Human Rights Committee was established by States Parties to the ICCPR on 20 September 1976 in accordance with Article 28 of the Covenant. It is composed of 18 elected independent experts and began its work on 1 January 1977. The Committee convenes publicly three times a year following a one-week session of the Working Group to examine the quinquennial reports of States Parties on the implementation of the rights protected by the Covenant. As Steiner explains: "The Committee's mandate confines its work to matters covered by the ICCPR and its protocols. That work amounts primarily to determining whether and how States are implementing the rights declared in those instruments". He further identifies three main activities of the Human Rights Committee, namely: reviewing State reports and responding to them through 'concluding observations'; issuing General Comments to all States Parties that clarify the Covenant's obligations; and handling communications under the Protocol. *See* Henry J. Steiner, "Individual Claims in a World of Massive Violations: What Role for the Human Rights Committee?" in Philip Alston and James Crawford (eds.), *The Future of UN Human Rights Treaty Monitoring*, Cambridge University Press (2000) at 20-21. With respect to State reports, the Committee seeks to initiate a constructive dialogue with the State Party under scrutiny, following which the Committee adopts concluding observations and makes appropriate suggestions and recommendations. NGOs may submit information on particular situations to the Committee. On the role of NGOs in reporting human rights violations within the UN system, *see* Andrew Clapham, "UN Human Rights Reporting Procedures: An NGO Perspective", in Alston and Crawford (eds.), *ibid.* at 175-198.

Optional Protocol to the ICCPR[8] has clarified considerably the status and components of the victims' rights to seek and obtain redress for ICCPR violations. Although the Committee's mandate does not cover crimes under international law as such or violations other than those listed in the ICCPR,[9] the

---

[8] Under the procedure of the Optional Protocol to the International Covenant on Civil and Political Rights, *adopted and opened for signature, ratification and accession* by UNGA resolution 2200 A (XXI) of 16 December 1966, *entered into force* on 23 March 1976, the Committee also examines written communications by individuals who claim to be victims of a violation by a State Party to the Covenant, provided that all available domestic remedies have been exhausted and that such remedies are effective and expeditious. In case of individual petitions, the Committee meets behind closed doors, issues a final decision on the merits of the case and recommends to the parties adequate remedies for the violations. To date, ninety-five States had become parties to the Optional Protocol. The admissibility of a communication is also subject to other conditions, including that the same matter must not be under examination by other procedures of international investigation or settlement (Article 5). More than ever, the Committee is faced with a growing number of individual cases and limited resources. Despite the fact that the Committee is increasingly focussing its activities on individual complaints rather than State reports, its work with respect to individual communications is still hindered by many difficulties. In his last progress report, the Special Rapporteur on Follow-up to Individual Communications reported information on 161 individual cases coming from 36 States Parties. The Special Rapporteur noted that some 30% of the Committee's recommendations had been implemented. *See* Human Rights Committee Press Release, Seventy-fourth Session, 2 April 2002. On individual complaints *see* Steiner *supra* note 7, arguing that justice in individual cases is an ideal that the Committee cannot reach, mainly because of its limited capacity to follow up cases of gross human rights violations. For a very thorough analysis of the activities of the Committee on individual complaints, *see* Alfred de Zayas, "The Examination of Individual Complaints by the UN Human Rights Committee under the Optional Protocol to the International Covenant on Civil and Political Rights", in G. Alfredsson, J. Grimheden, B. G. Ramcharan and A. de Zayas (eds.), *International Human Rights Monitoring Mechanisms*, Kluwer Law International (2001) at 67-121.

[9] In particular, the UN Human Rights Committee was established to monitor the implementation of the ICCPR by States Parties with respect to individuals within their territories and subject to their jurisdiction. According to Article 2 of the ICCPR, each State Party undertakes to respect and to ensure to "all individuals within its territory and subject to its jurisdiction" the rights recognized in the Covenant. As a result of the ICCPR's scope of application, which extends to all individuals under the jurisdiction of States Parties and not only those within their boundaries, the Human Rights Committee extends its monitoring activities also to territories occupied by States Parties. This has been the case for the Palestinian territories under Israeli occupation. In its Concluding Observations on Israel's 1998 Report to the Human Rights Committee, the

Committee's case-law on individual complaints for the most serious human rights violations under the ICCPR, such as torture and disappearances, has contributed substantially to the gradual expansion and better definition of the victims' right to redress for crimes under international law.[10]

In cases involving serious human rights violations, the Committee has elaborated upon the basic notion of 'remedy' as enshrined in Article 2(3) of the ICCPR and reflected in most human rights instruments, to develop principles and standards that go beyond monetary compensation.[11] In particular, the following components stand out as the pillars of the right to redress for victims of these kinds of violations:

i. The Duty to Investigate the Violation

In *Rodriguez* v. *Uruguay*,[12] a milestone in the development of the right to redress for victims of serious human rights violations, the Committee expressed in clear terms its views on the scope of the right to a remedy and reparation under Article 2(3). In that case, Mr. Hugo Rodriguez, the alleged victim, presented a communication to the Committee alleging a number of human rights violations, including torture and ill-treatment. In response to the

---

Committee expressed deep concern over the fact that "Israel continues to deny its responsibilities to fully apply the Covenant in the occupied territories". The Committe expressed the view that "the Covenant must be held applicable to the occupied territories and those areas of southern Lebanon and West Bekaa where Israel exercises effective control". With specific regard to compensation, the Committee expressed regret over the introduction by the Israeli Government of a draft law which would deny victims compensation "for excesses committed by members of the security forces against Palestinian residents of the occupied territories". *See* Concluding Observations of the Human Rights Committee: Israel, Human Rights Committee, Sixty-third session, UN Doc. CCPR/C/79/Add.93 of 18 August 1998 at paras. 10, 13 and 18.

10 In its views, the Committee uses both the terms 'gross' and 'serious' when referring to violations such as torture and disappearances. *See*, *inter alia*, *Rodriguez* v. *Uruguay*, Comm. No. 322/1988, CCPR/C/51/D/322/1988 of 9 August 1994, and *Zelaya* v. *Nicaragua*, Comm. No. 328/1988, CCPR/C/51/D/328/1988 of 18 August 1994. For the purposes of the present discussion, the words 'gross' and 'serious' are used to refer to violations of similar gravity.

11 On this question, one may wish to consult a very comprehensive analysis by Manfred Nowak, "The Right of Victims of Gross Human Rights Violations to Reparation" in F. Coomans et al. (eds.), *Rendering Justice to the Vulnerable,* Kluwer Law International (2000) at 203-225.

12 *Rodriguez* v. *Uruguay*, *supra* note 10. On the Committee's views on torture *see among others Antonio Vianna Acosta* v. *Uruguay*, Comm. No. 110/1981, and *Tshitenge Muteba* v. *Zaire*, Comm. No. 124/1982.

allegations, Uruguay argued that the communication be ruled inadmissible on the grounds of non-exhaustion of domestic remedies, and explained that:

> victims of torture may file claims for compensation through appropriate judicial or administrative channels; compensation from the State of Uruguay may, for instance, be claimed in the competent administrative Court. The State party notes that many such claims for compensation have been granted, and similar actions are pending before the Courts.[13]

However, the Committee held emphatically that local remedies must be both 'available and effective' and that:

> In the light of the gravity of the allegations, it was the State party's responsibility to carry out investigations ... The absence of such investigation and of a final report constituted a considerable impediment to the pursuit of civil remedies, e.g. for compensation.[14]

In terms of the State's obligation pursuant to Article 2(3), the Committee found that: "the responsibility for investigations falls under the State Party's obligation to grant an effective remedy". It further found that:

> The right to lodge complaints against maltreatment prohibited by [A]rticle 7 must be recognized in the domestic law. Complaints must be investigated promptly and impartially by competent authorities so as to make the remedy effective.

The Committee reached similar conclusions with respect to the scope of the victim's right to a remedy in a number of other important cases involving serious human rights violations. In *Zelaya* v. *Nicaragua*,[15] Mr. Roberto Zelaya Blanco, a Nicaraguan engineer and University professor, was detained for ten years during the Sandinista regime. Together with his brother and sister,[16] he presented a communication against Nicaragua alleging a number of violations of the Covenant, including "torture, pseudo-medical and pharmacological

---

13 *Rodriguez* v. *Uruguay*, *ibid.*

14 *Ibid.*

15 *Zelaya* v. *Nicaragua*, *supra* note 10.

16 At the time of the communication, Mr. Blanco's brother and sister, of Nicaraguan origin, were citizens of the United States and residing in the United States. Mr. Roberto Zelaya Blanco was also a resident of the United States.

experiments, inhuman treatment and death threats while in prison" and violation of the right to an effective remedy.[17] The Committee expressed the view that the victim was entitled to an 'effective remedy' and urged Nicaragua not only to grant 'appropriate compensation' to the victim, but also to launch official investigations into the violations and to ensure that similar violations did not occur in the future.[18]

The Committee took a similar view in *Laureano* v. *Peru,*[19] a case involving the disappearance of a female minor in Peruvian military prisons. In connection with the obligations imposed by Article 2(3) of the Covenant, the Committee urged Peru:

> to open a proper investigation into the disappearance of Ana Rosario Celis Laureano and her fate, to provide for appropriate compensation to the victim and her family, and to bring to justice those responsible for her disappearance, notwithstanding any domestic amnesty legislation to the contrary.[20]

ii. The Duty to Prosecute and Punish those Responsible

The case of *Bautista* v. *Colombia*[21] is also very significant in relation to the evolution of the victim's right to a remedy for serious human rights violations beyond mere compensation. The alleged victim, Ms. Nydia Erika Bautista de Arellana, was a Colombian citizen and activist of the 19 April Movement ('M-19'), who disappeared on 30 August 1987 and whose body was

---

17 The authors of the communication also alleged, *inter alia*, the confiscation of property during the Sandinista regime and asked for its restitution. The Committee could not make a finding on this specific matter, however, because the Covenant does not protect the right of property *per se*. The only way for the Committee to examine the issue would have been to find a link between the alleged confiscation and a discriminatory policy on the part of the regime - a fact that could not be proven because of lack of evidence.

18 *Zelaya* v. *Nicaragua*, *supra* note 10. *See also Irene Bleier Lewenhoff and Rosa Valiño de Bleier* v. *Uruguay*, Comm. No. 30/1978, *Guillermo Ignacio Dermit Barbato and Hugo Haroldo Dermig Barbato* v. *Uruguay*, Comm. No. 84/1981, *John Khemraadi Baboeram et al.* v. *Suriname*, Comm. No. 146/1983 and 148-154/1983.

19 *Laureano* v. *Peru*, Comm. No. 540/1993, CCPR/C/56/D/540/1993 of 16 April 1996. In this communication, the grandfather of the alleged victim contended that the armed forces of Peru were responsible for the disappearance of his granddaughter, Ana Rosario Celis Laureano, aged 16 at the time of the alleged violations.

20 *Ibid.* at para. 10.

21 *Bautista* v. *Colombia*, Comm. No. 563/1993, CCPR/C/55/D/563/1993 of 13 November 1995.

subsequently recovered.[22] In its efforts to obtain redress for the violations suffered, the family of the victim filed a claim for compensation with the Administrative Tribunal of Cundinamarca. In its judgment on the case, the Administrative Tribunal concluded that the Colombian authorities involved in the victim's illegal disappearance and death were fully responsible,[23] and it therefore awarded the equivalent of 1000 grams in gold to both parents, the husband and the son of Nydia Bautista, and the equivalent of 500 grams in gold to her sister. The Tribunal also directed the Ministry of Defence to pay a total of 1,575,888.20 pesos plus interest and inflation-adjustment to Nydia Bautista's son for the moral harm suffered.[24]

However, in his communication to the Committee, the author also alleged 'unacceptable negligence and delays' in the criminal investigations into the violations. He remarked that the case had not been given due consideration, as the competent organs (the human rights units of the Chief Prosecutor's office) were not functioning and even the building supposed to house the human rights units, remained unoccupied.[25] In the light of these facts, the Committee rejected Colombia's view that compensation awarded by the Administrative Tribunal constituted an effective remedy for the family of Nydia Bautista, and observed that:

> purely disciplinary and administrative remedies cannot be deemed to constitute adequate and effective remedies within the meaning of article 2, paragraph 3, of the Covenant, in the event of particularly

---

22 The author of the communication recounts that: "on 12 September 1987, the body of a woman had been found in the municipality of Guayabetal, Cundinamarca, Colombia. The death certificate, which had been drawn up before the body was buried at the cemetery of Guayabetal, indicated that it concerned a 35-year old woman 'wearing a white dress with blue spots and a white hand-bag, blindfolded, the hands tied together, face mutilated'. According to the autopsy, the deceased had been shot in the head". The case was then suspended and the identity of the woman remained unknown until the early 1990s, when Nydia Bautista's family learned about the unidentified woman buried in Guayabetal and pressured the Special Investigations Division of the Attorney-General's Office to exhume the body. On 26 July 1990 Nydia's sister identified the pieces of cloth, bag and an earring and, on 11 September 1990, a detailed report of forensic experts confirmed that the remains were those of Nydia Bautista. *Ibid.*

23 Judgment summarized in *Bautista* v. *Colombia*, *ibid.*

24 *Ibid.*

25 *Ibid.*

> serious violations of human rights, notably in the event of an alleged violation of the right to life.[26]

The Committee reiterated the duty of Colombia to:

> investigate thoroughly alleged violations of human rights, and in particular forced disappearances of persons and violations of the right to life, and to prosecute criminally, try and punish those held responsible for such violations.[27]

Further, the Committee urged Colombia to expedite the criminal proceedings on the case under examination and to ensure that similar events did not occur in the future.

iii. The Incompatibility between Amnesty Laws and the Right to a Remedy

In *Rodriguez* v. *Uruguay*, the Committee expressed its strong reservations on amnesty laws in case of gross human rights violations and declared that such laws were incompatible with the obligation of States to provide victims with a remedy under Article 2(3) of the ICCPR,[28] as follows:

> amnesties for gross violations of human rights and legislation such as Law No. 15.848, *Ley de Caducidad de la Pretensión Punitiva del*

---

26 *Ibid.*

27 However, the Committee made clear that the Covenant "does not provide a right for individuals to require that the State criminally prosecute another person" and cited a number of decisions on this point, including *H.C.M.A.* v. *the Netherlands*, Comm. No. 213/1986 of 30 March 1989, para. 11.6; *S.E.* v. *Argentina*, Comm. No. 275/1988 of 26 March 1990, para. 5.5; and *R.A., V.N. et al.* v. *Argentina* Comm. No. 343-345/1988 of 26 March 1990, para. 5.5.

28 At the regional level, the incompatibility between amnesty laws for gross human rights violations and the victims' right to redress has been strongly asserted by the Inter-American Commission on Human Rights in *Report No. 36/96, Case No. 10.843* of 15 October 1996, in which the Commission decided that the 1978 Amnesty Decree Law of Chile was in breach of Article 25 of the American Convention on Human Rights 1969, because it deprived victims and their families of their "right to effective recourse against the violations of their rights". For a critique of the 1999 amnesty law in Sierra Leone applying, *inter alia*, to those responsible for serious human rights violations committed during the bloody eight-year civil war *see* Jon M. Van Dyke, "The Fundamental Human Right to Prosecution and Compensation", *Denver Journal of International Law and Policy*, Vol. 9, No. 2, Spring 2001 at 79.

> *Estado*, are incompatible with the obligations of the State party under the Covenant. The ... adoption of this law effectively excludes in a number of cases the possibility of investigation into past human rights abuses and thereby prevents the State party from discharging its responsibility to provide effective remedies to the victims of those abuses. ... In adopting this law, the State party has contributed to an atmosphere of impunity which may undermine the democratic order and give rise to further grave human rights violations.[29]

In stressing this incompatibility, the Committee referred to its General Comment No. 20(44) on article 7(d) and referred to the obligation to fully investigate allegations of torture, and the victims' right to an effective remedy:

> Article 7 should be read in conjunction with article 2, paragraph 3 ... Amnesties are generally incompatible with the duty of States to investigate such acts; to guarantee freedom from such acts within their jurisdiction; and to ensure that they do not occur in the future. States may not deprive individuals of the right to an effective remedy, including compensation and such full rehabilitation as may be possible.[30]

In this sense, the Committee held in a number of cases that the adoption of amnesty laws is prejudicial to the conduct of investigations into past human rights abuses. Consequently, the Committee urged Uruguay:

> to take effective measures: (a) to carry out an official investigation into the author's allegations of torture, in order to identify the persons responsible ... and to enable the author to seek civil redress; (b) to grant appropriate compensation to Mr. Rodriguez; and (c) to ensure that similar violations do not occur in the future.

Over its twenty-five years of activity, the Committee has assisted countless victims in their efforts to exercise the right to redress. Although, strictly speaking, the views of the Committee are not legally binding, many States have taken concrete steps to implement the Committee's recommendations on the victims' right to a remedy.[31] On the basis of the Committee's

---

29 *Rodriguez* v. *Uruguay*, *supra* note 10 at para. 12.4.

30 *Ibid.* at para. 12.3.

31 On the degree of State compliance with the Committee's decisions, *see* the view of de Zayas, in G. Alfredsson, J. Grimheden, B. G. Ramcharan and A. de Zayas (eds.), *supra* note 8 at 71, who regards the present situation as 'encouraging' and

views, a number of countries have also reached friendly settlements for compensation with victims who have had their cases examined by the Committee,[32] and others have enacted 'enabling legislation' to provide compensation for victims of ICCPR violations.[33] In many cases however, implementation of the Committee's decision on victims' redress at the domestic level remains an arduous task, especially where States which have been requested to pay monetary compensation have challenged the views and

---

explains how States have taken 'meaningful steps' to comply, including paying compensation to victims. *See however* Markus G. Schmidt, "Follow-up Procedures to Individual Complaints and Periodic State Reporting Mechanisms", *ibid.* at 203 and 207, who argues that only a minority of follow-up replies by States Parties (around 25% - 30%) can be considered satisfactory. In relation to the follow-up on the right to a remedy, the Human Rights Committee has remarked that: "Attempts to categorize follow-up replies are necessarily imprecise. Roughly 30 per cent of the replies received could be considered satisfactory in that they display the State Party's willingness to implement the Committee's [v]iews or to offer the applicant an appropriate remedy. Many replies simply indicate that the victim has failed to file a claim for compensation within statutory deadlines and that no compensation can therefore be paid to the victim". *See* 1999 Report of the Human Rights Committee, UN Doc. A/54/40 at para. 459. For a general discussion on the nature of the Committee's views, *see* Yvonne Klerk, "The Character of the Views of the Human Rights Committee", in F. Coomans et al. (eds.) *supra* note 11 at pp. 149-159.

32 *See*, among other cases, the case of Ecuador, which reached a friendly settlement for compensation with Mr. Villacres Ortega on the basis of the Committee's views on 26 February 1999. In the agreement, Ecuador recognized its international responsibility for having violated articles 7 and 10, paragraph 1, of the ICCPR and agreed to pay Mr. Ortega, within 90 days, US$25,000 for damages. Ecuador also agreed to take civil, penal and administrative action against the perpetrators of the violations and to take the necessary steps to bring them to justice. Ecuador reserved its right to claim back from the perpetrators the amount of damages paid. A similar agreement was concluded with Mr. Garcia Fuenzalida on 16 June 1999. *See* 1999 Report of the Human Rights Committee, UN Doc. A/54/40 at para. 466 and annex IX.

33 These are domestic laws granting legal status to the decisions of international judicial and semi-judicial bodies, including the UN Human Rights Committee. Among countries that have enacted legislation of this kind, Schmidt mentions Peru (Law No. 23.506 of 1985, which unfortunately was rescinded in 1996 by the Fujimori administration); Colombia (Law No. 288 of 1996, which also contains specific compensation provisions for victims whose cases were heard by the Committee and received a positive decision); and Argentina, which has been considering the enactment of similar legislation. *See* Schmidt, *supra* note 31 at 208.

jurisdiction of the Committee or even the existence of a victim's right to redress under international law.[34]

The Human Rights Committee has provided a unique kind of laboratory for the development of the right to a remedy for victims of serious human rights violations, thus contributing enormously to the evolution of this right as it could apply in connection with crimes under international law. As late as 1993, Nowak remarked that general international law imposed no obligation on States as to how they were to implement their international obligations and he argued that the practice of the Human Rights Committee basically confirmed the absence of any obligation to take positive measures in implementing the Covenant at the domestic level, with few exceptions.[35] It is remarkable however, that since Nowak's observation only a decade ago, the relatively consistent practice of the Committee concerning redress for serious violations of the ICCPR, in the context of the right to a remedy, seems to have given rise to a set of relatively clear and precise obligations of conduct on States, including the duty to carry out prompt and impartial investigations, to bring the perpetrators to justice and to pay victims appropriate compensation.

b. Redress in the Convention against Torture and Other Cruel, Inhuman or Degrading Treatment or Punishment

The prohibition against torture is a well-established norm of customary international law. Nevertheless, torture is one of the most frequent human rights violations. Its widespread and systematic occurrence makes torture one of the most common crimes under international law, and one that many States have not so far addressed. To the contrary, the high number of torture victims worldwide indicates that the practice of many States has not fallen in line with the prohibition against torture.

With 128 ratifications, the Torture Convention forms one of the pillars in the codification of the fundamental principle of victims' right to redress for human rights violations. At the same time, the Convention provides for supervisory procedures and alternative compensation solutions. The Torture Convention is one of the few instruments that expressly require States Parties

---

[34] So far, the Committee's practice has been not to interfere with the amount of compensation awarded at the domestic level as a remedy for the victim, unless compensation is 'truly derisory'. *Ibid.* at 207.

[35] However, Nowak detected an early indication of a change and noted that: "there is, however, a certain tendency to promote the direct applicability of the Covenant". Nowak, *supra* note 3 at 53-54.

to take "effective legislative, administrative, judicial or other measures" to prevent torture in their territories (Article 2). The obligation to enact preventive domestic legislation is supported by further provisions requiring concerned States Parties to examine available information on torture cases, to make a preliminary inquiry into the facts and either to prosecute or extradite those suspected of torture found in their territory (Article 6) - an obligation which has been challenged many times before international supervisory mechanisms, both judicial and quasi-judicial, particularly in relation to violations of the right to redress and compensation. Quite advanced for its time, the Torture Convention also obliges each State Party to ensure that a "prompt and impartial investigation" is conducted "wherever there is reasonable ground to believe that an act of torture has been committed in any territory under its jurisdiction" (Article 12). As discussed above, this requirement is becoming a fundamental element of the right to redress for victims of crimes under international law, including widespread and systematic torture, in combination with the duty of States to prosecute and punish those responsible. In addition to these general obligations, the Torture Convention contains an articulate treatment of victims' reparation, based on the central obligation of States Parties to set up domestic mechanisms to provide redress for torture victims and to ensure that victims or their dependants have an "enforceable right to fair and adequate compensation, including the means for as full rehabilitation as possible". In particular, Article 14(1) establishes that:

> Each State Party shall ensure in its legal system that the victim of an act of torture obtains redress and has an enforceable right to fair and adequate compensation, including the means for as full rehabilitation as possible. In the event of the death of the victim as a result of an act of torture, his dependants shall be entitled to compensation.[36]

The Convention sets up a supervisory body, the Committee against Torture, to receive reliable information and to institute inquiries in relation to allegations of systematic torture practices in the States Parties (Article 20), to examine regular reports from States Parties, as well as to express views on individual communications from alleged victims of treaty violations (Article

---

[36] Article 14(2) further provides that: "Nothing in this article shall affect any right of the victim or other persons to compensation which may exist under national law".

17 *et seq.*).[37] The Committee also has broad powers of examination and investigation into the Convention's violations. In its practice, the Committee has often called on States not to leave victims of torture without an appropriate remedy and to set up effective mechanisms for compensation.[38]

c. Redress in Other Human Rights Instruments

Not all human rights instruments have enshrined the principle of victims' redress in detail. In some cases, such as in the International Covenant on Economic, Social and Cultural Rights (ICESCR) 1966,[39] the right of victims to access domestic remedies for violations suffered may be read into the treaty's implementation provisions. In the ICESCR, Article 2 simply provides that States Parties to the Covenant undertake to 'take steps' to achieve the full realization of the rights recognized in the Covenant "by all appropriate means, including particularly the adoption of legislative measures". However, General Comment 3 on Article 2 encompasses judicial remedies for violations of rights considered justiciable in domestic systems among the 'appropriate measures' to achieve the 'full realization' of the rights protected in the Covenant.

Certain other multilateral human rights treaties refer only to specific forms of redress, according to general considerations or the aim and purposes of the treaty. For example, under the Convention on the Rights of the Child 1989,[40] States Parties have an obligation to take 'all appropriate measures' to

---

37 The Committee began to function on 1 January 1988. Of the one hundred and twenty-eight States that had ratified the Convention, the following States have not recognized the Committee's competence under Article 20 to undertake confidential inquiries in the light of well-founded indications that torture is being systematically practised in the territory of a State party: Belarus, Bulgaria, China, Cuba, Czech Republic, Israel, Malawi, Ukraine. As for individual complaints, only fifty States have accepted the competence of the Committee under Article 22. The Committee can deal with such complaints only once all domestic remedies available in the State accused of a violation have been exhausted, except where the application of the remedies is unreasonably prolonged or is unlikely to bring effective relief to the victim of the violation. Prior to taking a decision, the Committee may request the State Party under scrutiny to take provisional measures to avoid possible irreparable damage to the alleged victim of the violation.

38 *See O. R., H. M. and M. S. v. Argentina*, Comm. Nos. 1, 2 and 3/1988.

39 International Covenant on Economic, Social and Cultural Rights, *adopted* on 16 December 1966, *entered into force* on 3 January 1976.

40 *Adopted and opened for signature, ratification and accession* by UNGA resolution 44/25 of 20 November 1989.

promote the physical and psychological recovery and social reintegration of child victims of "any form of neglect, exploitation, or abuse; torture or any other form of cruel, inhuman or degrading treatment or punishment; or armed conflict".[41] Similarly, in the field of labour law, ILO Convention No. 169 concerning Indigenous and Tribal Peoples in Independent Countries 1989,[42] only embodies the principle of compensation for damages suffered in the course of exploitation of mineral or sub-surface resources,[43] or in cases where indigenous people cannot return to their traditional lands.[44] In the case of migrant workers, Articles 15, 16 and 18(6) of the International Convention on the Protection of the Rights of All Migrant Workers and Members of Their Families 1990,[45] provide for the right to 'fair and adequate compensation' for migrant workers or members of their families who have been arbitrarily deprived of property, even by expropriation, or who have been victims of unlawful arrest or detention, or miscarriage of justice. In this context, States Parties have also an obligation to provide assistance with a view to the prompt settlement of matters regarding compensation relating to the death of a migrant worker or a member of his or her family.[46]

Even in the field of racial discrimination, where the question of redress was first raised in the early 1960s, the scope of the victims' right to redress has not been well defined. This issue generated much acrimonious debate in various fora, including in the last World Conference Against Racism, Racial Discrimination, Xenophobia and Related Intolerance held in Durban from 31

---

41 Article 39. This Article also adds that recovery and reintegration "shall take place in an environment which fosters the health, self-respect and dignity of the child".

42 *Adopted* on 27 June 1989 by the General Conference of the International Labour Organisation at its seventy-sixth session.

43 Article 15(2) provides that: "The peoples concerned shall wherever possible participate in the benefits of such activities, and shall receive fair compensation for any damages which they may sustain as a result of such activities".

44 Article 16(4) establishes that where the return of indigenous people to their traditional lands is not possible, "these peoples shall be provided in all possible cases with lands of quality and legal status at least equal to that of the lands previously occupied by them, suitable to provide for their present needs and future development. Where the peoples concerned express a preference for compensation in money or in kind, they shall be so compensated under appropriate guarantees". Article 16(5) further provides that: "[p]ersons thus relocated shall be fully compensated for any resulting loss or injury".

45 *Adopted* by UNGA resolution 45/158 of 18 December 1990, *entered into force* on 1 July 2003.

46 Article 71(2).

August to 8 September 2001, as discussed below. The right to redress for racial discrimination is guaranteed by the Declaration on the Elimination of All Forms of Racial Discrimination 1963,[47] which in Article 7(2) states that:

> Everyone shall have the right to an effective remedy and protection against any discrimination he may suffer on the ground of race, colour or ethnic origin with respect to his fundamental rights and freedoms through independent national tribunals competent to deal with such matters.

More importantly, Article 6 of the International Convention on the Elimination of All Forms of Racial Discrimination 1965,[48] guarantees victims of racial discrimination the right to seek reparation from national tribunals and other State institutions, and introduces the principles of 'just and adequate reparation or satisfaction'. Article 6 states:

> States Parties shall assure to everyone within their jurisdiction effective protection and remedies, through the competent national tribunals and other State institutions, against any acts of racial discrimination which violate his human rights and fundamental freedoms contrary to this Convention, as well as the right to seek from such tribunals just and adequate reparation or satisfaction for any damage suffered as a result of such discrimination.

Victims of treaty violations who have exhausted domestic remedies may submit written communications to the Committee on the Elimination of Racial Discrimination for consideration of their case, when the concerned State has recognized the competence of the Committee:

> to receive and consider communications from individuals or groups of individuals within its jurisdiction claiming to be victims of a violation by that State Party of any of the rights set forth in this Convention.[49]

---

47 *Proclaimed* by UNGA resolution 1904 (XVIII) of 20 November 1963.

48 *Adopted and opened for signature and ratification* by UNGA resolution 2106 A (XX) of 21 December 1965.

49 *See* Article 14(1) of the Convention.

Along the lines of the Racial Discrimination Convention, the Declaration on Race and Racial Prejudice 1978,[50] emphasizes the need for domestic legislation to establish legal remedies to provide victims with effective redress for violations suffered. Article 6(3) provides that:

> Since laws proscribing racial discrimination are not in themselves sufficient, it is also incumbent on States to supplement them by ... a comprehensive framework of legal remedies against acts of racial discrimination.

Finally, it is regrettable that reparation provisions are completely absent from at least one fundamental human rights treaty, namely the International Convention on the Suppression and Punishment of the Crime of Apartheid 1973,[51] which establishes apartheid to constitute a crime against humanity.

2. Regional Human Rights Standards

As in other fields of international law and adjudication, recent case-law of regional human rights adjudication bodies also has been revealing patterns in the emergence of standards on the victims' right to redress as applied to violations of an especially serious character.

a. Africa

The African system for the promotion and protection of human rights is still in its early stages. The African (Banjul) Charter on Human and Peoples'

---

[50] *Adopted and proclaimed* by the General Conference of the United Nations Educational, Scientific and Cultural Organization at its twentieth session, on 27 November 1978.

[51] International Convention on the Suppression and Punishment of the Crime of Apartheid, *adopted and opened for signature and ratification* by UNGA resolution 3068 (XXVIII) of 30 November 1973, *entered into force* on 18 July 1976. Article 1(1) of the Convention reads as follows: "The States Parties to the present Convention declare that apartheid is a crime against humanity and that inhuman acts resulting from the policies and practices of apartheid and similar policies and practices of racial segregation and discrimination, as defined in [A]rticle II of the Convention, are crimes violating the principles of international law, in particular the purposes and principles of the Charter of the United Nations, and constituting a serious threat to international peace and security".

Rights 1981[52] - currently the main instrument for the promotion and protection of human rights in Africa - does not protect expressly the victims' right to redress, except for spoliation of natural resources, in which case Article 21(2) provides for a right to adequate compensation. Article 7 simply establishes the right of every individual to have his or her cause heard through an appeal to the competent national organs. Aside from this general provision, no mention is made of victims' redress in case of breach of the treaty, neither through domestic nor international channels.

A lack of specific reparation provisions in the African Charter limits Africa's regional standards on redress.[53] Even the African Commission on Human and Peoples' Rights - the only quasi-judicial regional human rights institution in Africa, established under Article 30 of the African Charter to implement Charter-protected rights - has a limited mandate of a general character, particularly as regards redress issues arising from individual communications. Broadly speaking, this is due to the fact that the African Commission was originally set up mainly to receive inter-State complaints from Governments and that, according to the Charter, communications from individuals, groups of individuals and NGOs can be considered only following strict scrutiny (Article 55).[54] Also, up to 1994, the activities of the Commis-

---

[52] African [Banjul] Charter on Human and People's Rights, *adopted* by the Assembly of Heads of States and Government of the Organization of African Unity on 27 June 1981, *entered into force* on 21 October 1986. Hereinafter referred to as the 'African Charter'. By March 2000, all fifty-three member States of the OAU had ratified the Charter.

[53] For an interesting case study, *see* Michael Garcia Bochenek, "Compensation for Human Rights Abuses in Zimbabwe", *Columbia Human Rights Law Review*, Vol. 26, No. 2, Winter 1995, pp. 483-548.

[54] Although the Commission was set up to receive mostly inter-State complaints, in practice this capacity has hardly been used. In fact, by the year 2000, the inter-State communication procedure had never been used among States Parties. Oddly enough, the African Commission received one inter-State communication by Libya against the US for the removal of Libyan soldiers from Chad in 1990, following the military *coup d'état*. *See* U. Oji Umozurike, *The African Charter on Human and Peoples' Rights*, Kluwer Law International (1997) at 81. This peculiar circumstance was due to the fact that, at the beginning of the Commission's activities, there was no precise rule as to who would be allowed to present a complaint, and against whom. As a consequence, in its early stages of operation, the Commission received a large number of communications, especially from NGOs, on a wide range of issues, directed both against States Parties as well as non-States Parties to the Charter. Later, the practice of the Commission with respect to inter-State communications was revised to allow complaints coming

sion, including those related to individual communications, had been carried out on the basis of strict confidentiality, which made it difficult to evaluate the concrete results of the Commission's work in terms of human rights protection.

As regards serious or massive human rights violations, Article 58 of the African Charter sets up a special procedure to deal with "special cases which reveal the existence of a series of serious or massive violations of human and peoples' rights". To address the social structure in many African countries, the African Charter provides that communications may be submitted both by the alleged victim of a violation and, should the victim be unable to do so, by any other person or organization on his or her behalf. Also, the Commission has expressed the view that exhaustion of local remedies cannot be a strict requirement in case of serious and massive human rights violations.[55] However, in terms of independent scope of action, the Commission's powers remain rather weak and its ability to act ultimately depends upon prior authorization of the Assembly of Heads of State and Government. More specifically, in the event of a communication alleging serious or massive human rights violations, the Commission can only draw the attention of the Assembly of Heads of State and Government to the particular situation and, at the request of the Assembly, undertake an 'in-depth study' followed by a report with its findings and recommendations.[56]

In terms of reparations, the African Commission has recognized that the main objective of the individual complaint procedure is to redress the

---

exclusively from States Parties and directed exclusively against States Parties, for violations of the rights guaranteed by the Charter. Instead, the Commission has concentrated it efforts on individual communications, by using its competence under a broad reading of Article 55. On this matter, it has been argued that it is time the *de facto* competence of the Commission over all individual communications received proper legal support in the Charter, through an amendment procedure. *See* Christof Heyns, "The African Regional Human Rights System: in Need of Reform?", *African Human Rights Law Journal*, Vol. 1, No. 2 (2001) at 163.

55 *See Free Legal Assistance Group, Lawyers' Committee for Human Rights, Union Interafricaine des Droits de l'Homme, Les Témoins de Jehovah* vs. *Zaire*, African Comm. Hum. & Peoples' Rights, Comm. Nos. 25/89, 47/90, 56/91, 100/93.

56 It must be noted however, that, beginning from the mid-1990s, the African Commission has initiated a number of *in situ* investigations and fact-finding missions in response to individual communications, including in Mauritania, Nigeria, Sudan and Senegal. *See* Chidi Anselm Odinkalu, "The Individual Complaints Procedures of the African Commission on Human and Peoples' Rights: A Preliminary Assessment", *Transnational Law and Contemporary Problems*, Vol. 8, No. 359 (1998) at 365.

violation suffered by the victim.[57] In practice, however, the African Commission has rarely ordered a State to pay compensation or provide other forms of reparation. The *Mauritania Cases* are perhaps the only instances in which the Commission requested the State to provide remedies such as investigations into the violations (extra-judicial executions and torture), prosecution of the perpetrators, compensation to the victims and the 'eradication of slavery'.[58] More often, the Commission's role has been limited to negotiating so-called 'friendly settlements' between the State concerned with the allegations and the individual complainant. Unfortunately, the terms of the settlements often have not been very clear as concerns the duties of the State *vis-à-vis* the victim. In addition, so far the Commission has been unable to verify properly State compliance to the settlement. Therefore, final implementation and ultimately the full enjoyment of the victim's right to redress, have been dependent mainly upon the good faith of the concerned State.[59]

So far, the relatively low level of activity on the part of the African Commission in terms of human rights protection supports the view of those who argue that the Commission is under-utilized.[60] The same holds true in relation to the Commission's role in ensuring the victims' right to redress, which so far has been virtually non-existent. This is particularly regrettable,

---

57 *See Free Legal Assistance Group Case*, *supra* note 55, in which the Commission stated that the communication procedure should initiate a 'positive dialogue' between the complainant and the State concerned, with the aim of reaching an 'amicable resolution' which "remedies the prejudice complained of".

58 *See* the *Mauritania Cases*: *Malawi African Association*, Comm. No. 54/91; *Amnesty International*, Comm. No. 61/91; *Ms. Sarr Diop*, Comm. No. 98/93; *Union Interafricaine des Droits de l'Homme and RADDHO*, Comm. No. 164/97; and *Collectif des Veuves and Ayant-droit and Association Mauritanienne del Droits de l'Homme* v. *Mauritania* Comm. No. 210/98 at paras. 159-160.

59 However, where it is not possible to reach an amicable solution because the Government concerned refuses to acknowledge or take action with respect to the allegations, the Commission may take a decision on the merits of the case.

60 *See* Odinkalu, *supra* note 56, noting that by 1997 the Commission had received 200 communications since it begun its operation, with an average of 25 communications per year, or one communication for every two States Parties in a year. In "The Role of Case and Complaints Procedures in the Reform of the African Regional Human Rights System", *African Human Rights Law Journal*, Vol. 1, No. 2 (2001) at 244, Odinkalu also argues that the shortcomings of the African regional human rights system are "mostly practical and political matters to which treaties are ... irrelevant". Such shortcomings include matters such as poor funding, lack of political will and support, unskilled management and administration, etc.

if one considers that the African continent has been the theatre of some of the worst human rights violations of our times. More generally, to date the protective mechanisms of the African Commission have failed not only to prevent or halt crimes under international law in the region, but also to have provided effective redress to the victims.[61]

This situation reinforces the urgent need for the African Court on Human Rights, as established in the Protocol to the African Charter, to become fully operational.[62] Under the new system, States Parties, the Commission,

---

[61] One may wish to consider that in both 1991 and in 1994, the African Commission drew the attention of the Assembly of Heads of State and Government to massive and serious human rights violations in Rwanda and Burundi, but no measure was ever taken to halt the violations or to prevent their worsening. Also, in the case of *Krishna Achuthan* vs. *Malawi*, African Comm. Hum. & Peoples' Rights, Comm. Nos. 64/92 (10 October 1991), 68/92 (2 March 1992) and 78/92 (6 October 1992), the African Commission decided that Malawi was in breach of Articles 4, 5 and 7 of the African Charter on Human and Peoples' Rights and referred the situation to the Assembly of Heads of State and Government under Article 58(1) of the African Charter on Human and Peoples' Rights. However, no action was taken to halt the violations. *See further Free Legal Assistance Group*, *supra* note 55 and *Organisation Mondiale Contre La Torture* vs. *Rwanda*, African Comm. Hum. & Peoples' Rights, Comm. Nos. 27/89, 46/91, 49/91, 99/93 (not dated).

[62] The establishment of an African Court on Human Rights is foreseen in the Protocol to the African Charter on Human and Peoples' Rights on the Establishment of an African Court on Human and Peoples' Rights, *adopted* by the 34th Ordinary Session of the Assembly of Heads of State and of Government of the Organization of African Unity (OAU) on 9 June 1998, in Ouagandougou (Burkina Faso). The Protocol requires 15 ratifications to enter into force. At the time of writing, five countries had ratified the Protocol: Burkina-Faso, Gambia, Senegal, Mali and Uganda. On the functions and scope of the future African Court *see* Vincent O. Orlu Nmehielle, "Towards an African Court of Human Rights: Structuring the Court", *Annual Survey of International & Comparative Law Golden Gate University School of Law*, Vol. 6, No. 27, Spring 2000. On the need for Africa to have a human rights court *see* Umozurike, *supra* note 54 at 92. *See also* Nsongurua J. Udombana, "Toward the African Court on Human and Peoples' Rights: Better Late Than Never", *Yale Human Rights & Development Law Journal*, Vol. 3, No. 45 (2000); *see further* Mohamed A. Abdelsalam, "Individual and NGO Participation in Human Rights Litigation Before the African Court of Human and Peoples' Rights: Lessons From the European and Inter-American Courts of Human Rights", *Michigan State University - DCL Journal of International Law*, Vol. 8, No. 377, Summer 1999. For a critical view of the new Court *see* Andreas O'Shea, "A Critical Reflection on the Proposed African Court on Human and Peoples' Rights", *African Human Rights Law Journal*, Vol. 1, No. 2 (2001) at 285-298.

African intergovernmental organizations as well as individuals and NGOs can access the contentious jurisdiction of the Court.[63] Unlike the African Human Rights Charter, the Protocol establishing the African Court contains specific redress provisions modelled after those of the Inter-American Court of Human Rights. As in the Inter-American system, the African Court will have broad powers to order directly victims' redress in various forms in its adjudication on breaches of the Convention. As concerns reparations, Article 27 of the African Court's Protocol provides that:

> If the Court finds that there has been violation of a human or peoples' right, it shall make appropriate orders to remedy the violation, including the payment of fair compensation or reparation.

In grave and urgent cases, the African Court will be also empowered to adopt provisional measures necessary to avoid irreparable harm to persons. Finally, under Article 30, States Parties to the Protocol undertake "to comply with the judgment in any case to which they are parties ... and to guarantee its execution".

Despite some shortcomings relating to the restrictive approach of the Protocol to individual complaints as per Articles 5 and 34, the proposed African Court represents a good advance in the treatment of victims' redress at the regional level. Once the Court becomes operational, it will be up to the Commission to play an active role in engaging the jurisdiction of the Court, and up to the victims, relevant NGOs and civil society to find adequate and organized ways to access the Court for the purposes of redress. Unfortunately, with ten ratifications still needed, the prospects of the Protocol entering into force still seem a ways off.

b. The Americas

The Inter-American system of human rights promotion and protection dates back to May 1948, when the ninth Inter-American Conference held in Bogotá, both established the Organization of American States (OAS) and

---

[63] However, Article 5 provides the Court with the discretionary power to entitle individuals and NGOs to access its jurisdiction. In addition, individuals and NGOs can only access the Court's jurisdiction where the State Party has made a special declaration under Article 34(6) to this effect.

adopted the American Declaration of Rights and Duties of Man.[64] The American Declaration was the first regional human rights instrument ever to have been adopted, preceding even the adoption of the Universal Declaration of Human Rights. Just over a decade later, in 1959, the OAS established the Inter-American Commission on Human Rights[65] to document and collect information on gross and systematic human rights violations covered in the American Declaration of the Rights and Duties of Man[66] and simultaneously, it began to draft an Inter-American human rights treaty. A decade later, in 1969, the American Convention on Human Rights[67] was adopted as the regional human rights framework for the Americas, with the Inter-American Commission and the Inter-American Court of Human Rights[68] as supervisory

---

64 American Declaration of Rights and Duties of Man, *adopted* by the ninth Inter-American Conference in Bogotà, May 1948.

65 Hereinafter referred to as 'Inter-American Commission'

66 The Inter-American Commission could express its opinion on particular situations and recommend to concerned States that they adopt measures to address the situation.

67 The American Convention on Human rights, *signed* on 22 November 1969, *entered into force* on 18 July 1978. Hereinafter referred to as the 'American Convention'. The principles expressed in the American Convention are widely accepted throughout the region. At the time of writing, the American Convention had been *signed* by twenty-six States and *ratified* by twenty-five States. Among the States Parties, only five had not yet accepted the jurisdiction of the Inter-American Court. Of the twenty-six signatories, only the United States had not ratified the Convention nor had it recognized the jurisdiction of the Inter-American Court. Another four States had not recognized the jurisdiction of the Inter-American Court, namely: Jamaica, Grenada, Dominica and Peru. In July 1999, Peru withdrew from the jurisdiction of the Inter-American Court due to a divergence of opinion over the *Ivcher Bronstein Case.* On this episode *see* the commentary of Karen C. Sokol, Vinson & Elkins LLP, Ed. by Bernard H. Oxman in *The American Journal of International Law*, Vol. 95, No. 178, January 2001. The following States have accepted the competence of the Inter-American Court with regard to inter-State communications: Argentina, Chile, Colombia, Costa Rica, Ecuador, Jamaica, Uruguay and Venezuela.

68 Hereinafter referred to as the 'Inter-American Court'. The Inter-American Court sits permanently in San José, Costa Rica, and has both contentious and advisory jurisdiction. According to Article 64, the advisory jurisdiction of the Court may be triggered by member States of the OAS, whether or not they are parties to the American Convention, and by OAS organs listed in Chapter X of the Charter of the OAS, including the Commission. As for contentious jurisdiction, the Court may consider cases brought before it either by State parties to the Convention which have accepted the Court's jurisdiction, or by the Commission. In the latter case, Article 44 provides

organs vested with competence over matters relating to the 'fulfilment of the commitments' undertaken by States Parties under the Convention. By 1965, the Inter-American Commission was given formal competence to 'take cognition' of individual communications. As we shall see, following the adoption of the American Convention, the Commission's competence over individual communications concerning serious and systematic human rights violations of the American Convention grew well beyond its original documenting and reporting functions.[69] By the year 2000, the Inter-American Commission had examined over 10,000 communications, while the Inter-American Court had exercised its competence over 35 cases and had delivered 61 judgments.[70]

The current Inter-American system for the promotion and protection of human rights also comprises the Inter-American Convention to Prevent and Punish Torture 1985,[71] which codifies basic principles of victims' compensa

---

that "any person or group of persons, or any non governmental entity legally recognized in one of more member states" of the OAS may lodge a petition with the Commission concerning alleged violations of the Convention. Therefore, the complainant does not have to be necessarily the victim of the alleged violation. Following an individual petition, the Commission may request the concerned State to submit information on the alleged violation and, if necessary, it may also carry out an investigation on the facts with the prior consent of the State (Article 48), with a view to reaching a friendly settlement of the matter on the basis of respect for the human rights recognized in the Convention. If a friendly settlement cannot be reached, the Commission draws up a report with its conclusions for the consideration of the State party, after which, if the matter still has not been settled and the State party has accepted the jurisdiction of the Court, the Commission may bring the case before the Court. In any event, the Commission must be present in all cases brought before the Court (Article 57).

69 The adoption of the American Convention did not change the status of the Inter-American Commission as an organ of the OAS, and in this capacity the Commission continues to be responsible for the promotion and protection of human rights in the territories of OAS members. On the evolution of the Commission's powers and functions *see* Cecilia Medina, "The Inter-American Commission on Human Rights and the Inter-American Court of Human Rights: Reflections on a Joint Venture", *Human Rights Quarterly*, Vol. 12, No. 439 (1990) at 440.

70 *See* Antonio Augusto Cançado Trindade, "The Consolidation of the Procedural Capacity of Individuals in the Evolution of the International Protection of Human Rights: Present State and Perspectives at the Turn of the Century", *Columbia Human Rights Law Review*, Vol. 30, No. 1, Fall 1998 at 3.

71 Inter-American Convention to Prevent and Punish Torture, *signed* at Cartagena de Indias, Colombia, on 9 December 1985, *entered into force* on 28 February 1987. In Article 9, the Convention establishes an obligation for States Parties to incorporate into

tion, and the Inter-American Convention on the Forced Disappearance of Persons 1994.[72]

i. The Legal Basis for the Victims' Right to Redress in the American Convention

The American Convention affords victims of statutory violations double protection in terms of redress. First, Article 25 lays down the basic principle that everyone shall have an effective recourse to the domestic judicial system for violations of human rights guaranteed in the American Convention.[73] Second, Article 63 establishes perhaps one of the most far-reaching provisions in terms of redress for victims of human rights violations.[74] In case of a treaty violation:

1. The Inter-American Court may rule that the injured party is to be ensured "the enjoyment of his right or freedom that was violated";
2. Where appropriate, the Inter-American Court may rule that: "the consequences of the measure or situation that constituted the breach of such right or freedom be remedied and that fair compensation be paid

their national laws "regulations guaranteeing suitable compensation for victims of torture". Article 9 also contains a general clause preserving the right of victims to receive compensation by virtue of domestic legislation.

[72] Inter-American Convention on Forced Disappearance of Persons, *adopted* at Belém do Pará, on 9 June 1994, *entered into force* on 28 March 1996. In its preamble, the Convention reaffirms that "the systematic practice of the forced disappearance of persons constitutes a crime against humanity".

[73] To give effect to this and other provisions of the American Convention, States Parties have undertaken to adopt domestic legislation (Article 2). An enforceable right to compensation is envisaged in Article 10 for miscarriage of justice. On human rights reparation procedures in the region *see generally* Victor M. Rodriguez Rescia, "Reparations in the Inter-American System for the Protection of Human Rights", *ILSA Journal of International & Comparative Law,* Vol. 5, No. 583, Summer 1999.

[74] For a most useful, comprehensive and in-depth analysis of victims' reparation in the inter-American human rights system, *see* Jo M. Pasqualucci, "Victim Reparations in the Inter-American Human Rights System: A Critical Assessment of Current Practice and Procedure", *Michigan Journal of International Law,* Vol 18, No. 1, Fall 1996. On the procedure of the Inter-American Court *see* Dinah Shelton, "The Jurisprudence of the Inter American Court of Human Rights", *American University Journal of International Law & Policy*, Vol. 10, No. 333, Fall 1994. *See further* Richard J. Wilson and Jan Perlin, "The Inter-American Human Rights System: Activities During 1999 through October 2000", *American University International Law Review*, Vol. 16, No. 315 (2001).

to the injured party". Based on this provision, the Court may award a variety of remedies other than pecuniary compensation, including legislative measures, restitution and rehabilitation, etc.;

3. If the situation generated by the violation is of "extreme gravity and urgency, and when necessary to avoid irreparable damage to persons", the Inter-American Court may also adopt provisional measures.

In the landmark case of *Velásquez Rodriguez* which concerned the disappearance of Mr. Angel Manfredo Velásquez Rodriguez during political violence and repression in Honduras, the Court found that Article 63(1):

> does not refer to or limit the ability to ensure the effectiveness of the means of reparation available under the internal law of the State Party responsible for the violation, so it is not limited by the defects, imperfections or deficiencies of national law, but functions independently of it. This implies that, in order to fix the corresponding indemnity, the Court must rely upon the American Convention and the applicable principles of international law.[75]

Significantly, on a number of occasions the Inter-American Court reiterated that Article 63(1) of the American Convention, on reparation, codifies one of the fundamental principles of general international law, namely that when a wrongful act occurs that is imputable to a State, the State incurs international responsibility for the violation of international law, and it thus incurs a duty to make reparation.[76] This view was clearly expressed in *Velásquez Rodriguez*, in which the Court stated that:

> It is a principle of international law, which jurisprudence has considered 'even a general concept of law', that every violation of an international obligation which results in harm creates a duty to make adequate reparation.[77]

---

75 *Velásquez Rodriguez*, Compensatory Damages, Judgment of 21 July 1989, Inter-Am. Ct. H.R., Ser. C, No. 7 at paras. 30-31.

76 *See, inter alia, Velásquez Rodriguez, ibid.* at para. 25; *Godínez Cruz Case*, Compensatory Damages, Judgment of 21 July 1989, Inter-Am. Ct. H.R., Ser. C, No. 8 at paras. 23 to 26; *Aloeboetoe et al. Case*, Reparations, Judgment of 10 September 1993, Inter-Am. Ct. H.R., Ser. C, No. 15 at para. 44 *et sub.*

77 *Velásquez Rodriguez, ibid.*

In the *Aloeboetoe Case*, the Court clarified the implications of this principle for the reparation regime of the American Convention under Article 63(1), as follows:

> The obligation contained in Article 63(1) of the Convention is governed by international law in all of its aspects, such as, for example, its scope, characteristics, beneficiaries, etc. Consequently, this judgment must be understood to impose international legal obligations, compliance with which shall not be subject to modification or suspension by the respondent State through invocation of provisions of its own domestic law.[78]

As for the scope of the State duty of reparation, in *Velásquez Rodriguez*, the Court determined that:

> Reparation of harm brought about by the violation of an international obligation consists in full restitution (*restitutio in integrum*), which includes the restoration of the prior situation, the reparation of the consequences of the violation, and indemnification for patrimonial and non-patrimonial damages, including emotional harm.[79]

In the same Judgment, the Court also ruled that, under international law, indemnity based upon the principles of equity may be awarded for emotional harm, particularly in cases of human rights violations.[80]

---

78 *Aloeboetoe et al. Case*, *supra* note 76 at para. 44. *See also* the *Blake Case*, Reparations, Judgment of 22 January 1999, Inter-Am. Ct. H.R., Ser. C, No. 48 at para. 32, in which the Court, in a noteworthy *obiter dictum*, reiterated that the obligation to provide reparation in case of breach of an international obligation has been "universally accepted by international law in all its aspects: scope, nature, forms, and determination of beneficiaries, none of which the respondent State may alter by invoking its domestic law".

79 *Velásquez Rodriguez*, *supra* note 75 at para. 26

80 *Ibid.* at para. 27. The Court supported its decision by citing numerous human rights instruments both of universal and regional character which embody the principle of compensation for victims of treaty violations, as well as relevant jurisprudence. In its judgment on the merits of 29 July 1988, the Court ordered Honduras to pay fair compensation to the next-of-kin of the victim. However, the parties failed to reach a complete agreement within six months, by which time they had agreed only upon the recognition of the beneficiaries of compensation. It therefore fell to the Court to define the scope and content of 'fair compensation' to be paid by the Government to the family of Velásquez Rodríguez according to Article 63(1). In undertaking this exercise, the

ii. The Extent of the Victims' Right to Redress

The activities of Inter-American institutions devoted to the promotion and protection of human rights in the region remain particularly relevant to the determination of victims' redress standards for crimes under international law. The Inter-American human rights system has dealt frequently with human rights violations of a serious and systematic character that often amount to crimes under international law, such as disappearances, extra-judicial executions or torture. In contrast, the European human rights system has been confronted mainly with individual violations of a lesser magnitude, although its jurisprudence on serious human rights violations continues to develop rapidly, while the African system is still at an early stage and has yet to make a significant contribution to the development of redress standards.

The Inter-American Court has adjudicated on a wide range of reparation matters and has contributed greatly to the gradual expansion of the traditional notion of reparation - based primarily on compensation - to include further elements of redress in case of serious human rights violations, as set out in detail below.

The duty to prevent, investigate and punish violations. In its jurisprudence concerning serious human rights violations, which has involved mainly torture and disappearances during military dictatorships in Central and Latin America, the Inter-American Court has consistently ruled that the right to reparation encompasses the duty upon the State to prevent, investigate and punish violations of the American Convention, to restore the rights violated and to provide compensation to victims. Moreover, the Inter-American Court has linked the general obligation to provide adequate victims' redress to the duty of States to ensure the free and full enjoyment of human rights, as provided for in Article 1 of the American Convention, in effect strengthening the right to

Court interpreted the expression 'fair compensation' as referring only to compensatory damages for both material and moral injuries, and not including punitive damages. The Court argued that the principle of punitive damages as adopted by some domestic courts, particularly the Anglo-American courts, "is not applicable in international law at this time". *See* para. 38. As a result, the Court awarded seven hundred and fifty thousand Lempiras in compensatory damages to be paid to the family of Angel Manfredo Velásquez Rodríguez by the State of Honduras, of which one hundred and eighty-seven thousand five hundred Lempiras were assigned to the wife of the victim and five hundred and sixty-two thousand Lempiras to his children.

Court pointed out that it is a specific duty of the State to investigate cases of disappearance when the fate of a disappeared person is unknown. The Court stated that the purpose of such investigations was to prevent further disappearances and to punish those responsible,[88] and stressed that redress for victims of gross human rights violations must include elements such as the amendment of domestic law and the conduct of exhaustive investigations into the violation.[89] In order to fulfill Bolivia's obligations under Article 1 of the American Convention, the Inter-American Commission submitted that the Inter-American Court should order that Bolivia conduct a "complete, effective and impartial investigation" in order to "identify, criminally prosecute, and punish, the State agents responsible for the detention, torture and subsequent forced disappearance" of the victim, to locate and identify his remains and to deliver them to his family. In addition, the Inter-American Commission urged the Court to order Bolivia to 'adopt urgent measures' to incorporate the crime of forced disappearance of persons into its Criminal Code. Finally, with respect to compensation, the Inter-American Commission submitted that the Court should order Bolivia to:

> adopt the measures necessary to ensure that the victim's next-of-kin receive an adequate and timely reparation that includes full satisfaction for the corresponding human rights violations, and also payment of a fair compensation for patrimonial and extra-patrimonial damages, including moral damages.

During the proceedings, Bolivia acknowledged responsibility for the violations and expressed the wish to reach a friendly settlement with the victim's next-of-kin. Reparation proceedings were pending before the Court at the time of writing.

---

88 *Velásquez Rodriguez Case*, Judgment of 29 July 1988, Inter-Am. Ct. H.R., Ser. C, No. 4 at paras. 174 and 181.

89 *See also* the following cases the Court cites in the *Trujillo Oroza Case*, *supra* note 87; *Neira Alegría Case, Reparations,* Judgment of 19 September 1996, Inter-Am. Ct. H.R., Ser. C, No. 29 at para. 36; *Caballero-Delgado and Santana* v. *Colombia, Reparations*, Judgment of 29 January 1997, Inter-Am. Ct. H.R., Ser. C, No. 31 at para. 15; *Garrido and Baigorria Case, Reparations*, Judgment of 27 August 1998, Inter-Am. Ct. H.R., Ser. C, No. 39 at para. 40; *Loayza Tamayo Case, Reparations*, Judgment of 27 November 1998, Inter-Am. Ct. H.R., Ser. C, No. 42 at para. 84; and *Castillo Páez Case, Reparations,* Judgment of 27 November 1998, Inter-Am. Ct. H.R., Ser. C, No. 43 at para. 50.

The self-evidence of moral damages. In the *Suárez Rosero Case*,[90] in which the victim suffered physical and psychological injuries as a consequence of the cruel, inhuman, and degrading treatment to which he had been subjected during imprisonment, the Inter-American Court awarded the victim both material and moral damages.[91] Interestingly, the Court decided that there was no need to provide evidence on the existence of a moral damage, because "it is characteristic of human nature that anyone subjected to the kind of aggression and abuse that have been proved, experiences moral suffering".[92] Consistent with its earlier jurisprudence, the Court reiterated that a State's obligation to provide reparation for gross human rights violations included the duty to take domestic measures aimed at the prosecution and punishment of those responsible and the duty to ensure that such violations never again occur within the State's jurisdiction.[93] The Inter-American Court added that the obligation to take these domestic measures "must be discharged seriously and not as a mere formality" and it must be carried on until complete fulfilment.[94]

In the *Blake Case*[95] brought against Guatemala, the Inter-American Court ordered Guatemala to make reparations to the relatives of Mr. Nicholas Chapman Blake for violations of the right to a fair trial (Article 8(1)) in relation to Article 1(1)), and of the right to humane treatment (Article 5 in relation to Article 1(1)).[96] The Court ordered Guatemala to use all means at its disposal

---

90 *Suárez Rosero Case*, Reparations, Judgment of 20 January 1999, Inter-Am. Ct. H.R., Ser. C, No. 44.

91 With respect to material damages, the Inter-American Court stated that in the case of survivors, the calculation of compensation should cover, among other factors, the time that the victim remained unemployed. In support of this decision, the Court cited *El Amparo Case*, Reparations, Judgment of 14 September 1996, Inter-Am. Ct. H.R., Ser. C, No. 28 at para. 28.

92 *See also Loayza Tamayo Case supra* note 89 at para. 138 and the *Aloeboetoe et al. Case*, Reparations, at para. 50, reproduced in *Human Rights Law Journal*, Vol. 14 (1993) at 413-418, in which the Inter-American Court tried to ensure the award of reparations was appropriate having regard to the social context and cultural practices of the Saramacas (Maroons) community in Suriname.

93 *Suárez Rosero Case*, *supra* note 90 at para. 79.

94 *Ibid.*

95 *Blake Case*, Judgment of 24 January 1998, Inter. Am. Ct. H.R., Ser. C, No. 36.

96 Although the case was brought before the Court for the alleged disappearance and death of the victim, the Court could only rule on violations of Articles 8(1) and 5 in combination with Article 1(1) of the American Convention because of a limitation *ratione temporis* on its competence. In its Judgment, the Court limited its temporal competence only to "the effects and acts that occurred after the date on which

to investigate the facts, to identify and punish those responsible and to adopt the necessary measures in its internal law to ensure compliance with these obligations.[97] The Court also awarded moral damages to the victim's relatives, finding that, in cases of particularly grave violations such as the forced disappearance of a person, the State's failure to investigate the violation generates "suffering and anguish, in addition to a sense of insecurity, frustration and impotence in the face of the public authorities".[98]

iii. The Execution of Judicial Awards

Through its judicial interpretation of the American Convention, the Inter-American Court has contributed much to raising the profile of victims of serious human rights violations and to developing the substantive law on the right to redress. Over the years, the Inter-American Court has awarded victims of serious human rights violations some extraordinarily high amounts of compensation.[99] As practice has shown, States under judicial scrutiny at the

---

Guatemala accepted the competence of the Court", namely 9 March 1987, because the disappearance and death of the victim, which occurred in March 1985, could not be considered to be of a continuing nature, therefore the Court was incompetent to decide on the State's responsibility for those acts. *See ibid.* at para. 3. However, the Court also pointed out that, "although some of the acts had been completed, their effects could be deemed to be continuing until such time as the victim's fate or whereabouts were determined". Therefore, because Mr. Blake's fate or whereabouts were not known until 14 June 1992, after the date on which Guatemala accepted the Court's contentious jurisdiction, the Court declared itself competent to hear the case with regard to possible violations in connection with continuing actions and effects subsequent to the date on which Guatemala accepted the competence of the Court. *Ibid.* at paras. 54 and 67. In its judgment, the Court ordered the payment of US$151,000 for material damages to the family of the victim, US$30,000 for moral damages to each one of the four members of the victim's family, US$15,000 for medical fees awarded to Mr. Samuel Blake; US$16,000 for extrajudicial expenses and US$10,000 as compensation for the expenditures incurred for the various petitions before the Inter-American System of Human Rights. The Court also ordered that all reparation payments be exempt from taxes, both present and future.

97 *Ibid.* at para. 3.

98 *Blake Case*, Reparations, *supra* note 78 at para. 56.

99 For example, the Inter-American Court awarded US$89,500 in *Caballero-Delgado and Santana* v. *Colombia*; US$722,322 in *El Amparo Case*; and US$453,102 in *Aloeboetoe et al. Case.* On these and other considerations concerning the effectiveness of the reparation regime in the inter-American human rights system, *see generally*, Jo M. Pasqualucci, "The Inter-American Human Rights System: Establishing Precedents and Procedure in Human Rights Law", *The University of Miami Inter-*

Inter-American Court have often acknowledged their involvement and responsibility, even in cases of serious or systematic human rights violations. Despite this, States have frequently failed to comply fully with the redress obligations laid down in the Inter-American Court's judgments.[100] Generally, one must consider that situations of non-compliance on the part of States with the Inter-American Court's judgments are treated exclusively at the political level, mostly through mechanisms that do not extend beyond diplomatic pressure.[101]

It is difficult to see how the remedies awarded by the Inter-American Court could be truly effective given that the victims' chance of having a judgment executed at the domestic level, is in practice very limited. Given this situation, perhaps victims of serious human rights violations would benefit more from the establishment of a regional trust fund for the compensation of victims, than from a purely domestic approach to compensation. In this connection, the extra-judicial activities of the Inter-American Commission for the friendly settlement of disputes between individuals and States for violations of the American Convention must also be mentioned.[102] The Commission has accumulated valuable experience in this area, which has often helped victims obtain satisfactory reparation, including compensation, rehabilitation and measures of non-repetition, in cases that could not be solved domestically. When the State is willing to cooperate, friendly settlements represent a viable alternative to judicial proceedings, and one that deserves to be encouraged.

American Law Review, Vol. 26, No. 297, Winter 1995; *see further* Antonio Augusto Cançado Trindade, "State and Perspectives of the Inter-American System of Human Rights Protection at the Dawn of the New Century", *Tulane Journal of International and Comparative Law*, Vol. 8, No. 5, Spring 2000.

[100] Article 68(2) of the American Convention provides for reparation judgments to be executed in the State concerned, "in accordance with the domestic procedure governing the execution of judgments against the State". The Inter-American Court has been long concerned with the problem of the domestic execution of international judgments to the point that, in the final *Velásquez* judgment on compensation, the Inter-American Court decided not to close the file until compensation had been paid, and to follow up on the implementation of the order for compensation. *See Velásquez Rodriguez Case*, *supra* note 75.

[101] In case of non-compliance of a State Party, the Court may inform and make recommendations to the General Assembly of the OAS which, as a political body, may take appropriate action to redress the situation.

[102] On the Inter-American Commission's friendly settlements *see* Dinah Shelton, *Remedies in International Human Rights Law*, Oxford University Press (1999) at 167-169.

c. Europe

On 21 November 1990, in Paris, the Conference on Security and Cooperation in Europe adopted the Charter of Paris for a New Europe, under the motto 'A New Era of Democracy, Peace and Unity', with full respect for human rights representing "the bedrock on which we will seek to construct the new Europe".[103] One of the fundamental human rights enshrined in the Charter is recourse for everyone to "effective remedies, national or international, against any violation of his rights".

Based upon the fundamental right to a remedy as expressed in various European human rights instruments, human rights jurisprudence at the European level has clarified to a certain extent the scope of application of the right to redress for victims of serious human rights violations, particularly as regards torture, thus providing important input on the evolution of the right to redress for crimes under international law.

The scope of the right to a remedy for torture victims as expressed in recent jurisprudence of the European Court of Human Rights, is generally in line with the practice of the UN Human Rights Committee and of the Inter-American human rights system in similar cases, thus revealing a strong convergence in principles and standards applicable to victims of human rights violations that may qualify also as crimes under international law.[104] This is of particular value, considering that thus far there has been little institutional cooperation and exchange among various international bodies dealing with similar compensation matters. As we shall see, however, the European Court has lagged behind other institutional mechanisms for redress in terms of reparation measures, mainly because its awards have been limited exclusively to monetary compensation.

---

103 Charter of Paris for a New Europe: A New Era of Democracy, Peace, and Unity, *done* at Paris on 21 November 1990, Conference of Security and Cooperation in Europe.

104 On the dialogue between institutions of the ICCPR and the European Convention on Human Rights *see* Manfred Nowak, "The Inter-Relationship between the Covenant on Civil and Political Rights and the European Convention on Human Rights", in Stavroula Vassilouni (ed.), *Aspects of the Protection of Individual and Social Rights* (1995).

i. The Extent of the Right to a Remedy under Article 13 of the European Convention

Under Article 13 of the European Convention on Human Rights 1950,[105] every victim of a Convention violation is entitled to a remedy before national authorities, irrespective as to whether the violation was committed by persons acting in an official capacity - a clause specifically introduced to void doctrines of immunity of State organs.[106] As in many other human rights instruments, the manner in which the Convention's redress provisions are implemented, including the choice of remedies and related procedures, is left to the national authorities of States Parties[107] and individual access to the European Court of Human Rights has been made conditional upon the general international law principle of exhaustion of local remedies, as expressed in Article 35. Unfortunately, the notion of 'local remedy' in the sense of Article 13 remains far from clear.[108] In the past, whenever seized with the question of

---

105 European Convention for the Protection of Human Rights and Fundamental Freedoms, *signed* in Rome on 4 November 1950, *entered into force* on 3 September 1953.

106 *See* the Report of the European Commission on Human Rights in *Young, James and Webster Case*, 14 December 1979, B. 39 (1984) at 49.

107 *See Vilvarajah and Others* v. *the United Kingdom*, Judgment of 30 October 1991 at para. 102.

108 On this question, Nowak *supra* note 11 at 205 argues that: "[t]he language and objective of Article 13 are ... far from clear and the European Court of Human Rights has traditionally been inconsistent in applying this provision and reluctant to find a violation". Nowak remarks that the Court found a violation of Article 13 only in exceptional circumstances. Similarly, Judges Matscher and Pinheiro Farinha, in a dissenting opinion in the 1984 *Malone Case,* concluded that: "Article 13 constitutes one of the most obscure clauses in the Convention and its application raises extremely complicated problems of interpretation. This is probably the reason why, for approximately two decades, the Convention institutions avoided analysing this provision, for the most part advancing barely convincing reasons". As cited in Pieter van Dijk and Fried van Hoof, *Theory and Practice of the European Convention on Human Rights*, 3rd Ed., Kluwer Law International (1998) at 697. To give one example, there has been considerable discussion as to whether the absence of a civil remedy in national courts for victims of human rights violations contravenes not only Article 13, but also Article 6(1) of the Convention, which protects, *inter alia*, the right to access to court for the determination of civil rights and obligations. Recently, this issue was raised on the occasion of an application filed by a human rights NGO with the Court, in which it was alleged that the UK Home Secretary's decision not to extradite Senator Pinochet to Spain violated Articles 6(1) and 13 of the Convention. *See* Andrew Clapham, "Revisiting *Human Rights in the Private Sphere*, Postscript: Developments Related to Pinochet as of January 2001", in Craig Scott (ed.), *Torture and Tort:*

remedies, both the Commission and the European Court of Human Rights have provided little guidance on the matter, aside from reiterating basic criteria of effectiveness, fairness and adequacy of redress.[109] For many years, the general tendency of the European Court has been to read Article 13 as not binding States on the choice of redress, but rather to afford States a wide margin of discretion in the determination of remedies. However, over the last ten years or so, the European Court's jurisprudence has added greater precision to the notion of domestic remedy under Article 13, especially concerning instances of serious human rights violations, such as torture.

As in other human rights adjudication mechanisms, one of the main principles emerging from recent case law of the European Court is that domestic remedies for victims of serious human rights violations such as torture, must go beyond mere compensation, regardless of whether compensation is awarded by judicial bodies, domestic compensation schemes, or other compensation plans. In a number of recent cases involving torture, the European Court of Human Rights acknowledged that the victim's right to a remedy before national authorities can involve measures additional to compensation, such as the conduct of investigations on the part of the State aimed at the prosecution and punishment of those responsible for the violations. This constitutes a significant departure from the ordinary interpretation of Article 13, which normally has been read to encompass "every remedy available under national law which may lead to a decision that is

---

Comparative Perspectives on the Development of Transnational Human Rights Litigation, Hart Publishing (2001), pp. 717-724. In Chapter 19 of the same book, Clapham takes a broad interpretation of Article 6(1) and argues that since the absence of a civil remedy in domestic law entails a violation of Article 6(1) on fair trial, under the same provision, victims may have a right to bring a case against alleged perpetrators of torture in domestic courts, possibly even in the courts of State Parties which are not involved in the alleged violation. *See* Andrew Clapham, "Revisiting *Human Rights in the Private Sphere*: Using the European Convention on Human Rights to Protect the Right of Access to the Civil Courts", *ibid.* at 523-531. However, *see* the European Court of Human Rights in *Al-Adsani* v. *the United Kingdom,* Judgment of 21 November 2001, in which the Court found no violation of Article 6(1) in a case of torture brought before it by an individual of dual British and Kuwaiti nationality, whose claims for redress against Kuwait were dismissed by UK courts, as discussed *supra* at 88.

[109] On the principle of effectiveness of a remedy *see inter alia Klass and Others* v. *Germany*, Judgment of 6 September 1978, and the *Leander Case*, Judgment of 26 March 1987 at 31.

binding on the authorities".[110] Instead, in *Aksoy* v. *Turkey*[111] the Court argued that:

> The nature of the right safeguarded under Article 3 of the Convention has implications for Article 13. Given the fundamental importance of the prohibition of torture and the especially vulnerable position of torture victims, Article 13 imposes, without prejudice to any other remedy available under the domestic system, an obligation on States to carry out a thorough and effective investigation of incidents of torture. Accordingly, as regards Article 13, where an individual has an arguable claim that he has been tortured by agents of the State, the notion of an 'effective remedy' entails, in addition to the payment of compensation where appropriate, a thorough and effective investigation capable of leading to the identification and punishment of those responsible and including effective access for the complainant to the investigatory procedure.[112]

In the same judgment, the Court recognized that the requirement that States perform effective investigations into incidents of torture "is implicit in the notion of an 'effective remedy' under Article 13",[113] whereas the Torture

---

110 *See Lawless* v. *Ireland*, Yearbook II (1958-1959) at 308. This may include, for example, the award of any compensation from compensation commissions, administrative tribunals, or domestic compensation schemes, etc. *See Yarrow P.L.C. and Others* v. *the United Kingdom*, Appl. No. 9266/81, D&R 30 (1983) at 155; *Frederiksen and Others* v. *Denmark*, Appl. No. 12719/87, D&R 56 (1998) at 237; *Sygounis, Kotsis and 'Union of Police Officers'* v. *Greece*, Appl. No. 18598/91, D&R 78-B (1994) at 71.

111 *Aksoy* v. *Turkey*, Judgment of 18 December 1996. Mr. Zeki Aksoy - a Turkish citizen born in 1963 - was a metal worker in Mardin, Kiziltepe, South-East Turkey. On 16 April 1994, he was shot and killed in unclear circumstances. His father brought a claim before the Court to pursue allegations of Articles 3, 5, 6, 13 and 25 of the Convention, and argued that the fact that the measures complained of formed part of an administrative practice constituted an aggravating circumstance. The victim's father requested just satisfaction pursuant to Article 41 (formerly Article 50) of the Convention and was awarded compensation for pecuniary and non-pecuniary damage of just over four million Turkish Liras (approximately US$3,000), in addition to the payment of trial costs and expenses.

112 *Ibid.* at para. 98.

113 *Ibid. See also Mentes* v. *Turkey*, Judgment of 28 November 1997, concerning deliberate destruction of houses and possessions, in which the Court ruled that the right to an effective remedy "entails, in addition to the payment of compensation where appropriate, a thorough and effective investigation capable of leading to the identifica-

Convention 1984, imposes upon States only a duty to proceed to a 'prompt and impartial' investigation whenever there is a reasonable ground to believe that an act of torture has been committed. In *Aydin* v. *Turkey*,[114] which concerned allegations of rape and ill-treatment during detention, as well as the failure of the Turkish authorities to conduct an effective investigation into the complaint, the Court reaffirmed that in cases involving alleged torture by agents of the State:

> the notion of an effective remedy entails, in addition to payment of compensation where appropriate, the conduct of a thorough and effective investigation capable of leading to identification and punishment of culprits.[115]

In *Aydin* v. *Turkey,* the Court further stated that in cases involving allegations of rape in custody, a thorough and effective investigation as part of an effective domestic remedy under Article 13: "implies also that the victim be examined by competent, independent medical professionals".[116]

---

tion and punishment of those responsible and including effective access for the complainant to the investigative procedure".

114 *Aydin* v. *Turkey*, Judgment of 25 September 1997.

115 *Ibid.* The Court found that in the case under consideration: "authorities only carried out an incomplete inquiry - no meaningful measures taken to establish veracity of allegations - corroborating evidence not sought - medical reports perfunctory and not focussed on whether the applicant had in fact been raped". The Court concluded (sixteen votes to five) that Turkey was in breach of Article 13. Along the same lines, *see also Kurt* v. *Turkey*, Judgment of 25 May 1998; *Tanli* v. *Turkey*, Judgment of 10 April 2001; and *Selmouni* v. *France*, Judgment of 28 July 1999.

116 *Aydin* v. *Turkey*, *supra* note 114. On the use of professional medical examination in case of rape for the purposes of international criminal prosecution *see Prosecutor* v. *Anto Furundzija,* ICTY Case No. IT-95-17/1-T 10 of 10 December 1998 at paras. 21 *et seq.* Interestingly, in at least one case the Court found that the investigation and criminal trial were rendered ineffective by the inadequacy of the forensic investigations. *See Salman* v. *Turkey*, Judgment of 27 June 2000 at para. 73, in which the complainant made, *inter alia*, allegations of death under torture and lack of effective remedy. To establish the inadequacy of the Government's forensic investigation, the Court referred to the 1991 United Nations "Manual on the Effective Prevention and Investigation of Extra-legal, Arbitrary and Summary Executions" which includes a Model Autopsy Protocol aimed at providing authoritative guidelines for the conduct of autopsies by public prosecutors and medical personnel.

In subsequent cases, the Court added other important elements to the scope of the right to a remedy under national procedures for victims of torture, especially where torture involved also the violation of the right to life. In particular, the Court stated that the obligation of States under Article 13 to carry out a 'thorough and effective investigation' aimed at the prosecution and punishment of those responsible, must include the possibility of the complainant having effective access to the investigation procedure.[117]

In determining the admissibility of torture cases under Article 35, both the Commission and the Court considered whether or not the remedies were effective. In the *Donnelly Case*, in which the petitions were declared inadmissible on the basis that they were 'abstract complaints',[118] the Commission expressed the view that the local remedy rule does not apply in *prima facie* torture cases where the victim has filed a petition in person, if it is clear in advance that local remedies will not be effective or adequate.[119] The *prima facie* ineffectiveness of the local remedy may be declared for example, where

---

117 *See Çakici* v. *Turkey*, Judgment of 8 July 1999 and *Yasa* v. *Turkey*, Judgment of 2 September 1998 at para. 114. *See further Tanrikulu* v. *Turkey*, Judgment of 8 July 1999 and *Salman* v. *Turkey*, *supra* note 116 at para. 121.

118 As discussed below, the Court has consistently accepted individual petitions only from the direct victim of the violations, with a few exceptions regarding 'potential victims'. Therefore, in principle, the victim of the alleged violations must be also the person who has exhausted all domestic remedies prior to the filing of a petition with the Court. However, the Commission has excused individual applicants from the requirement of exhaustion of local remedies, in the following exceptional circumstances: doubt on the part of the applicant as to the effectiveness of the relevant remedy; lack of knowledge on the part of the applicant as to the existence of a particular remedy; non-admittance of an appeal because of a procedural mistake by the applicant; poor health, or advanced age, or poor financial position of the applicant; lack of free legal aid or high costs of the procedure; fear of repercussions; errors or wrong advice by a counsel or the authorities; and finally, two applicants filing the same complaint when only one has exhausted domestic remedies. *See* van Dijk an van Hoof, *supra* note 108 at 152, also citing the corresponding case law.

119 *Donnelly Case*, Appl. Nos. 5577-5583/72, Yearbook XVI (1973) at 212. *See also Handyside* v. *the United Kingdom*, Appl. No. 5493/72, Yearbook XVII (1974) at 228. On this principle as applied to inter-State procedure *see Greece* v. *the United Kingdom*, Appl. No. 299/57, Yearbook II (1958-59) at 186, cited in van Dijk and van Hoof, *supra* note 108 at 132.

there existed an administrative practice of tolerating human rights violations, such as torture in police custody and detention.[120]

ii. 'Just Satisfaction' under Article 41 of the European Convention: A 'Safety Net' for Victims

Although States Parties have a primary responsibility to provide victims of human rights violations under the Convention with adequate remedies within their domestic systems of justice administration, in practice, not all States may be willing or able to offer victims full and satisfactory compensation or other effective remedies for the violations suffered. To avoid the risk that victims of human rights violations would go uncompensated, the European Convention of Human Rights establishes a supervisory mechanism intended to provide a 'safety net' for victims who have been denied their right to a domestic remedy. Article 41 (formerly Article 50) on 'Just Satisfaction'[121] vests the European Court of Human Rights with the power to afford 'just satisfaction' to an injured party directly in cases where:

> there has been a violation of the Convention or the protocols thereto, and ... the internal law of the High Contracting Party concerned allows only partial reparation to be made.

Unfortunately, the range of redress the Court can award is rather limited. So far, the Court has held that the only possible form of reparation under Article 41 is monetary compensation both for pecuniary damages and for non-pecuniary damages related, for example, to the psychological suffering of the victim in case of serious human rights violations.

Until recently, victims could access the supervisory mechanism of Article 41 on reparations only by filing a petition with the European Commission on Human Rights[122] under Article 25 of the Convention. This procedure was not an easy one: the State against which the petition was filed had to be a

---

120 This has been the practice of the Court in a number of cases involving torture and other human rights violations in the Kurdish area of South-East Turkey, such as in *Aksoy* v. *Turkey*, Appl. No. 21987/93, D&R 79-A (1994) at 60; *Hazar and Acik* v. *Turkey*, Appl. Nos. 16311/90 and 16313/90, D&R 72 (1992) at 200; and the *Akdivar Case*, Judgment of 16 September 1996 at para. 77.

121 Article 41 of the European Convention as amended by Protocol No. 11, replacing Article 50 of the original Convention.

122 Article 20 of the Convention originally set up both the European Commission on Human Rights and the European Court of Human Rights to ensure that States would observe their engagements under the Convention.

party to the Convention, had to accept the competence of the Commission on the matter and the jurisdiction of the European Court of Human Rights. In 1998, the entry into force of Protocol No. 11[123] inaugurated the so-called 'single Court' system, which brought about far-reaching changes in both the manner in which victims can access the supervisory mechanisms of the Convention and in the award of redress. The jurisdiction of the Court in relation to both individual and inter-State applications has become *de jure* mandatory for all Contracting Parties. Alleged victims of the Convention's violations (individuals, but also non-governmental organizations and groups of individuals) can bring their cases directly before the European Court of Human Rights under the procedure set forth in Articles 35 *et seq.* of the Convention as amended by Protocol No. 11.[124] The Secretary General of the Council of Europe maintains a supervisory function over the domestic implementation of the Convention (Article 52) and may request States Parties to explain the means and methods adopted domestically to ensure victims of violations with a satisfactory redress.[125]

Normally, for an individual petition to be admissible before the European Court of Human Rights, the author must be the alleged victim of the

---

123 Protocol No. 11 to the Convention for the Protection of Human Rights and Fundamental Freedoms, restructuring the control machinery established thereby, *opened for signature* on 11 May 1994, *entered into force* on 1 November 1998. By 4 February 2002, the Protocol had been ratified by 41 countries, thus providing a wide scope of application for individuals wishing to access directly the European Court's jurisdiction - a procedure possible only provided that the State against which the application is filed is a party to the Protocol. On the background preparation work and preliminary discussions on the 'merger' of the European Commission of Human Rights and of the European Court of Human Rights into a single body it is useful to consult the Council of Europe's "Explanatory Report to Protocol No. 11 to the Convention for the Protection of Human Rights and Fundamental Freedoms", http://conventions.coe.int/Treaty/en/Reports/Html/155.htm. *See also* Andrew Drzemczewski, "The European Human Rights Convention: Protocol No. 11 - Entry into Force and First Year of Application" *Human Rights Law Journal*, Vol. 21, No. 1-3, 18 September 2000, pp. 1-17.

124 According to the jurisprudence of the Commission, groups must be established as such under the law of the Contracting party and NGOs must be private in nature. *See* van Dijk and van Hoof, *supra* note 108 at 46.

125 However, the Secretary General of the Council of Europe has performed this function only in a few occasions.

violation.[126] This requirement - which effectively rules out the possibility of *actio popularis*[127] - does not exclude *in toto* the possibility of the Court to accept petitions filed by so-called 'potential victims', as for example in the case of a systematic pattern of violations, or by 'indirect victims', being individuals who have not suffered from the alleged violation in person, but who can demonstrate sufficiently close links to the victim that they can also be considered to be victims.[128] With respect to 'potential' victims, in *Klass and Others* v. *Germany* and subsequent jurisprudence, the Court has determined that the notion of 'victim' may include individuals at risk of being directly affected by the particular matter they are seeking to bring before the Court.[129]

---

126 In contrast, under Article 33, States are allowed to file, *inter alia*, so-called applications '*in abstracto*', meaning that they do not need to refer to any specific individual case, such as, for example, in the case of a State alleging that the existence of specific national legislation or administrative practices in another State is in breach of the Convention. *See Ireland* v. *the United Kingdom* (a case concerning allegations of Articles 1, 2, 3, 5, 6 and 14 of the Convention) Judgment of 18 January 1978 at para. 240. In the same paragraph the Court also established that, as a general rule, an individual applicant should claim to have been actually affected by the violation alleged. This view is reiterated in *Klass and Others* v. *Germany*, *supra* note 109 at para. 33, in which the Court stated that "Article 25 does not institute for individuals a kind of *actio popularis* for the interpretation of the Convention; it does not permit individuals to complain against a law *in abstracto* simply because they feel that it contravenes the Convention. In principle, it does not suffice for an individual applicant to claim that the mere existence of a law violates his rights under the Convention; it is necessary that the law should have been applied to his detriment".

127 However, *see* Carol Harlow, "Access to Justice as a Human Right: The European Convention and the European Union" in P. Alston (ed.) *The EU and Human Rights*, Oxford University Press (1999) at 193, remarking how the petition brought about by potential victims of an injunction barring abortion information in Ireland in *Open Door and Dublin Well Woman* v. *Ireland*, (1992) 15 EHRR 244, is very close to an *actio popularis*.

128 The Court has often accepted petitions by 'indirect victims' as for example in the case of petitions filed by the 'next-of-kin' to the victim. On this practice, *see* some interesting examples in van Dijk and van Hoof, *supra* note 108 at 56, such as the mother filing a complaint for the son in detention, or a spouse filing a complaint for the material suffering derived from violations committed against her husband.

129 *See Klass and Others* v. *Germany*, *supra* note 109 at para. 34, in which the applicants alleged that German legislation on the monitoring of private mail and telecommunications potentially violated their right to privacy. In this case, the Court addressed the question of whether an individual who could not point out any concrete measures specifically affecting him or her (in the present case because of the secrecy of

The Court has applied a strict test when determining whether or not individuals were 'indirect victims' in cases of compensation claims, where the tendency of the Court has been to reject claims that are not filed by the person who suffered directly from the alleged violation.[130] To ensure consistency and continuity, claims for compensation have been normally considered by the judges in deciding on the merits of the case,[131] while follow-up actions on the implementation of compensation awards have been left to the Committee of Ministers pursuant to Article 54.

As victims of human rights violations increasingly enjoy easier access to the European Court of Human Rights, one of the crucial questions for victims has become the meaning of 'just satisfaction', particularly with respect to the willingness of the Court to award remedies other than mere compensation. To date, the Court has limited its awards under Article 41 to compensatory damages, costs and expenses, as well as declarations that a State had violated the applicant's rights.[132] In its practice, the Court has issued

---

the measures objected to) could still lodge a complaint with the Commission (under the old system). The Court expressed the view that, to preserve the principle of effectiveness (*l'effet utile*) of the Convention's machinery of individual complaints, under certain circumstances, these kinds of complaints may be accepted on a case-by-case basis. *See* subsequent *Campbell and Cosans*, Report of 16 May 1980, B. 42 at 36, in which the Commission reiterated the principle of effectiveness and expressed the view that individuals may file a complaint even when they are under the risk of being affected by the matter in question. However, in *Forty Mothers* v. *Sweden*, Yearbook XX (1977) at 214, in which forty mothers alleged that a Swedish legislation on pre-school education violated their potential right to send their children to a school of their choice, the Commission abstained from examining the application of those mothers whose children did not reach pre-school age and therefore considered themselves 'future victims'. *See also Costello-Roberts* v. *the United Kingdom*, (1991) at 216, in which the Commission dismissed the claim of two mothers applying on behalf of their children as potential victims of a violation of Article 3, resulting from the adoption of a system of corporal punishment in the children's school in Scotland.

130 However, *see Salman* v. *Turkey*, *supra* note 116, in which the Court established that there was a "direct causal link" between the death of Agit Salman in violation of Article 2 and the loss by his widow and children of the financial support which he provided for them. As a consequence, the Court awarded pecuniary damages for loss of income in the sum of GBP39,320.64, as well as non-pecuniary damage for the "severity and number of violations" in the sum of GBP60,000 in respect of Mr. Salman and GBP10,000 in respect of his spouse, the claimant.

131 *See Ringeisen Case*, Judgment of 22 June 1972 and *Vagrancy Case*, Judgment of 10 March 1972.

132 *See* Shelton, *supra* note 102 at 154.

compensatory awards for loss of earnings or opportunities, repayment of fines and costs unjustly awarded against the applicant, reimbursement of travel and other expenses, as well as moral damages for uncertainty, feelings of unequal treatment or frustration and unjust imprisonment.[133] In contrast to the practice of the Inter-American system, or to the views of the UN Human Rights Committee, the European Court has not, to date, ordered reparation in forms other than compensation, for example, rehabilitation, clearance of the victims' names, initiation of investigations, award of pensions, etc. Even more importantly, the Court has not ordered States to amend or nullify measures violating the Convention, and in this sense, very little has been done to prevent future violations.

On the question of reparations other than compensation, the Court has argued that, should the violation call for *restitutio in integrum*, it is up to the respondent States to give it effect, as a part of the State's:

> legal obligation to put an end to the breach and make reparation for its consequence in such a way as to restore as far as possible the situation existing before the breach.[134]

In this connection, the Court has stated that it had "neither the power nor the practical possibility of doing so itself".[135]

While the Court has so far interpreted the scope of Article 41 as limited to compensatory measures, some commentators have argued that the words 'just satisfaction' do not create an absolute limitation upon the Court on the choice of reparation measures and therefore, the Court is not prevented from extending the range of its reparation awards to measures others than compensation.[136] If the Court were to adopt a broader interpretation of Article 41, this would enhance the value of the reparation regime within the European human rights system, in particular for cases involving serious human rights violations, such as torture, disappearances or rape. In such cases, a Court's direct order to nullify or amend particular measures which have contributed to the violation in the first place, could be a key element in victims' redress, in addition to monetary compensation and effective investigations into the violations. Without a Court order to amend or nullify laws and practices contrary to basic

---

133 The cases are listed in van Dijk and van Hoof, *supra* note 108 at 255.

134 *See Papamichalopoulos and Others* v. *Greece*, 330-B (Ser. A.) 1995 at para. 34.

135 *Ibid.*

136 *See* Shelton, *supra* note 102 at 148-151.

human rights, Governments may not feel compelled to address violations by adopting laws and practice aimed at prevention and redress. More often, the circle of injustice is likely to remain unbroken, with reparation being provided only to those few victims who have had their cases examined before the Court. In contrast, an order by the Court to prevent a repetition of practices contrary to human rights would reach a much larger number of victims.

More generally, it seems that the victims' right to redress would benefit from the Court adopting a more progressive approach with respect to situations involving patterns of serious human rights violations. Despite the fact that often both the victims and, in the past the Commission, presented the Court with evidence demonstrating patterns of violations, the Court has always limited its judgment to the specific case under consideration, without attempting to determine the existence of patterns of violations which could be attributed to the State.[137] So far, this has been the approach of the Court even in cases where the consistent nature of the violation of the victims' right to a remedy strongly suggested the existence of a systematic State practice in this sense, such as in *Çakici* v. *Turkey*.[138] In its judgment, the Court remarked that:

> [t]he Delegate of the Commission sought to place this case in the context of the previous fifteen judgments rendered by the Court in which allegations of failure to protect life, disappearance, ill-treatment and destruction of homes in south-east Turkey were associated with failures to provide an effective remedy, in particular a reluctance to pursue investigations into allegations of wrongdoing by the security forces and a readiness to accept the unsubstantiated assertions of the security forces at face value. Findings had been made concerning inadequate investigative procedures in all of those cases, save the Aytekin case, which differed in that there was an

---

[137] In many of the cases brought before the European Court of Human Rights for instances of torture, rape and other serious human rights violations, the applicants maintained that the alleged violations, including the violation of the right to a remedy, were conducted as a part of systematic practices, which should be considered as 'aggravating circumstances' of the violations. *See* for example, *Salman* v. *Turkey*, *supra* note 116, in which the applicant maintained that there existed in South-East Turkey an officially tolerated practice of violations of Articles 2, 3 and 13 of the Convention, that revealed a pattern of denial of serious human rights violations by the authorities, as well as a denial of remedies.

[138] *See Çakici* v. *Turkey*, *supra* note 117.

> identified perpetrator of the lethal shooting of the applicant's husband from the outset of the incident.[139]

Nevertheless, in the same case the Court came to the conclusion that:

> the scope of examination of the evidence undertaken in this case and the material on the case file are not sufficient to enable it to determine whether the authorities have adopted a practice of violating Article 13 of the Convention.[140]

Stricto sensu, the restrictive approach of the European Court of Human Rights *vis-à-vis* the determination of systematic patterns of violation of the right to a remedy does not alter the status of the victims' claims for reparation under the European Convention. Normally, wherever the Court found a violation of Article 13, victims were awarded compensatory damages as a result of their claim for 'just satisfaction' under Article 41. More broadly however, recognition by the European Court of the 'systematic element' of serious human rights violations such as torture could be of crucial importance to the victims' pursuit of justice through law, at least for the following reasons. First, should the Court recognize a systematic pattern of violations, it could award reparation measures which may be more suitable than monetary compensation, such as orders to modify or nullify laws or policies that may be contributing to the violation, or the adoption of broad rehabilitation programmes for the victims. Second, from a political point of view, charging the State only with individual violations instead of recognizing the existence of possible patterns of violations, could send the wrong signal that systematic human rights violations will not be addressed as such, but only treated in individual instances, or even be tolerated. Third, at a more practical level, recognition by the European Court of the systematic character of serious human rights violations such as torture could itself become an important element in the eventual prosecution and punishment of individuals responsible for crimes against humanity before the International Criminal Court. One could imagine for example, that certain judgments by the European Court recognizing the systematic character of torture in a particular situation could be used as a

---

139 *Çakici* v. *Turkey*, *ibid.*

140 *Ibid.* at para. 121. *See also Mahmut Kaya* v. *Turkey*, Judgment of 28 March 2000, in which the Court adopted its classical formula stating that: "It did not find it necessary to determine whether the violations are part of a practice adopted by the authorities".

reliable source of information to assist the ICC Prosecutor to decide whether to initiate an investigation on a situation involving alleged crimes against humanity.[141]

In the interest of more effective international criminal law and justice, it would be valuable if the European Court were to consider whether such patterns or systematic elements can be established.

d. Asian National Standards

Asia has been the scene of some of the more atrocious human rights violations historically. Myanmar, Indonesia, Sri Lanka, Afghanistan, India, Pakistan, Kashmir, Nepal and East Timor are only some examples of countries where serious and systematic human rights violations have been perpetrated in recent years, or continue to be perpetrated.[142] The rise of extreme nationalism, authoritarianism and religious fundamentalism have increasingly spurred violence and intolerance against dissenting voices, and the lack of independent judiciaries, combined with poor standards of justice administration, have contributed to the climate of impunity for serious crimes.[143]

---

141 *See* Article 15 of the ICC Statute on the Prosecutor's powers to initiate an investigation *proprio motu* in combination with Article 7(1)(f) of the ICC Statute, as well as the Finalized Draft Text of the Elements of Crimes, Article 7(1)(f) 'Crime against humanity of torture', UN Doc. PNICC/2000/1/Add.2 of 2 November 2000. Similarly, the findings of human rights courts or other adjudicatory bodies may be useful in helping the ICC to establish the level of 'gravity' of a given situation under consideration.

142 For a study on the legal and political issues behind population displacement in armed conflict situations in Asia, *see* Ilaria Bottigliero, "Displaced Persons Caught Between War and Peace in Asia", *Indian Yearbook of International Humanitarian and Refugee Law*, Vol. 2 (2002).

143 On the issue of unsatisfactory standards of justice administration, one may recall that in mid-February 2002, the UN decided not to cooperate with Cambodia in efforts to establish a tribunal for the prosecution and punishment of those responsible for crimes under international law during the 1975-79 Khmer Rouge rule, because the UN considered that the proposed tribunal fell far short of international standards of justice. In particular, the UN concluded that Cambodian amnesty laws provided a high number of former Khmer Rouge leaders with easy escape from justice, relegating the new tribunal to an empty formality. Over the last several years, Cambodian leaders have refused to collaborate with the UN on the establishment of an international tribunal. Instead, the Government insisted that domestic Courts would provide a better solution for the prosecutions of the regime's leaders. Finally, Cambodia agreed on the establishment of an international adjudicating body, but the UN found itself unable to

i. *'Asian Values'*

Despite the obvious need for human rights promotion and protection, Asia is the only region of the world where there is no regional system of human rights protection. Asian countries continue to reject the idea of establishing regional mechanisms to monitor human rights situations. Under the leadership of the Governments of Indonesia, Malaysia and Singapore, a number of Asian

---

agree on the standard of justice that it was supposed to apply. There was much adverse reaction to the UN's decision to withdraw cooperation with the Government of Cambodia on the Khmer Rouge Tribunal. On the occasion of the presentation of his report on the human rights situation in Cambodia to the Commission on Human Rights, Mr. Peter Leuprecht, Special Representative of the Secretary-General on human rights in Cambodia, expressed his profound regret over the interruption of negotiations between the United Nations and the Cambodian Government regarding the Khmer Rouge Tribunal. He expressed hope that the negotiations would be resumed and brought to a positive conclusion. Mr. Leuprecht further noted that Cambodia was undoubtedly making progress on the road to democracy and greater respect for human rights. However, he remarked that much remained to be done and that further progress would be achieved through combined efforts of Cambodian society and the international community. *See* Press Release, Commission on Human Rights 58th session, 22 April 2002. On this matter, the UN Commission on Human Rights recognized the need for the Government of Cambodia and the United Nations to cooperate on the question of the prosecution and punishment of senior leaders of Democratic Kampuchea responsible for crimes under international law, according to international standards of justice, fairness and due process of law. The Commission appealed to both the Government of Cambodia and the UN "to resume discussions on the establishment of a tribunal for such a purpose" and it also appealed to the international community to provide assistance in this regard. *See* 'Situation of Human Rights in Cambodia', Commission on Human Rights resolution 2002/89 at para. 18. The establishment of a tribunal for the prosecution and punishment of former Khmer Rouge leaders must remain a priority both for Cambodia and for the international community as a whole. It is therefore to be hoped that Cambodia and the UN enter a new phase of negotiations on this matter. In this connection, it remains essential that 1) negotiations are conducted in good faith and for the common purpose to bring perpetrators to justice; and 2) the envisaged Tribunal reflects acceptable standards of justice administration. Should the Tribunal fall short of minimum standards of justice administration, justice cannot be genuine and the trials risk being an exercise of political discretion or window dressing, rather than a tool to fight impunity and to provide victims with fair redress. On 2 July 2002, Cambodian Prime Minister Hun Sen declared that his Government was prepared to seek a compromise with the UN to put formed Khmer Rouge leaders on trial for genocide, and that it was prepared to amend domestic law, if needed. *See* the South China Morning Post of 3 July 2002. These negotiations have taken many years and it remains to be seen whether agreement can be reached.

Governments have voiced scepticism about the whole concept of human rights as a Western dominated idea that does not conform well with so-called 'Asian values'.[144] In very general terms, the idea of 'Asian Values' as put forward by Indonesian former President Suharto, Malaysian Prime Minister Mahathir and Singaporean Senior Minister of State Lee Kuan Yew, has been based mainly upon the following premises:[145]

- Asian countries have cultural traditions and customs which are very much distinct, and sometimes opposed, to those of the West. In particular, Asian political traditions focus on the well being of the community as a whole, rather than of individual needs and rights;
- Asian values and traditions are more 'authentic' and 'pure' than those of western societies, which overemphasize individual liberty at the expense of social cohesion;
- Asian countries have a right to interpret universal human rights standards such as those developed in the Universal Declaration of Human Rights according to their own cultures and traditions;
- The economic and political development of Asian countries is still in its early stages, therefore, unlike in Western countries, social, economic and cultural rights must prevail over civil and political rights. Having a strong government with broad powers to ensure law and order is a better approach for achieving full economic develop-

---

144 For an excellent contribution on the debate on 'Asian Values' and on Asian views on human rights, democracy and governance, *see* Yash Ghai, "Human Rights and Governance: The Asia Debate", *The Australian Yearbook of International Law 1994*, Vol. 15. By the same author *see also* "Universalism and Relativism: Human Rights as a Framework for Negotiating Interethnic Claims", *Cardozo Law Review*, Vol. 21, No. 4, February 2000.

145 *See* Anthony J. Langlois, *The Politics of Justice and Human Rights: Southeast Asia and Universalist Theory*, Cambridge University Press (2001) at 24-25.

ment.[146] Also, a strong government will provide better control over conflicts based on ethnic, religious, or racial grounds.

Another element behind the Asian values argument has been the idea that 'universal' human rights have been used by Western powers as a way of reaching foreign markets and spreading their influence over other countries. Along the same lines, proponents of Asian values have often regarded Western critics of Asian human rights standards as applying double standards to Asia. One must bear in mind, however, that the Asian values argument has been put forward mainly by Asian Governments, rather than civil society, and that these arguments often serve to justify or excuse a diverse range of systematic human rights violations. Moreover, Asia exhibits a very wide range of political, legal and cultural systems, which makes the concept of a single set of 'Asian values' rather implausible.

In practice, some Asian Governments have chosen to 'deal with' human rights within their domestic jurisdictions, for example with the support of national human rights commissions.[147] This approach has produced mixed results. In India, victims of police torture received compensation through the national human rights commission,[148] whereas in some States, such as South Korea, national human rights commissions are still in their early stages, or they

---

146 The following quote from Malaysian Prime Minister Mahathir is significant: "Let us not be slaves to democracy... if by practising certain aspects of democracy we run the risk of causing chaos in our party and country, we have to choose our party and country above democracy". As cited in Langlois, *ibid.* at 13. For a very interesting and critical view of Singapore's approach to political debate *see* James Gomez, *Self-Censorship: Singapore's Shame*, THINK Centre, Singapore (2000), in which the author argues that Singapore's society lives in a climate of fear and self-censorship, where the concept of 'democracy' is often misrepresented, misunderstood, treated as a dirty word, or considered as 'pure paranoia'.

147 On national human rights commissions *see* the 'Principles Relating to the Status and Functioning of National Institutions for Protection and Promotion of Human Rights' (Paris Principles). The Paris Principles comprise a set of recommendations on the role, composition, status and functions of national human rights instruments, drawn up by representatives of national institutions, States, the United Nations and its specialized agencies, intergovernmental and non-governmental organization, which met at a workshop in Paris in October 1991 to review and update information on existing national human rights institutions. The Paris Principles have been endorsed by the Commission on Human Rights in resolution 1992/54 of March 1992 and by the UNGA in resolution A/RES/48/134 of 20 December 1993.

148 Human Rights Watch, *World Report 2000* at 161.

are not clearly independent of the executive, as in Indonesia, the Philippines and Mongolia. Other countries seem to lack any coherent human rights policies at all.

In general, the difficult political situation in many Asian countries makes the region a particularly challenging arena for the development and implementation of effective human rights standards, as the UN Secretary-General noted in his 1998 report to the UN Commission on Human Rights on regional human rights arrangements in Asia.[149] So far, the Association of South East Asian Nations (ASEAN) has concentrated its efforts on strengthening State sovereignty rather than addressing human rights violations. To date, few serious attempts have been made to develop common human rights principles for Asia, and the emphasis has been primarily on the role of individual States and domestic implementation, rather than on the development of common regional human rights standards.

In this context, the Bangkok Declaration 1993, drafted during the Asian intergovernmental meeting in preparation for the Vienna World Conference on Human Rights, shows the mixed attitude of Asian Governments towards unified regional human rights.[150] In paragraph 5, Asian States emphasized one the main principles of the Declaration, namely:

> the respect for national sovereignty and territorial integrity as well as non-interference in the internal affairs of States (and the non-use of human rights as an instrument of political pressure).

As for the development and implementation of universal human rights standards, paragraph 7 of the Declaration stresses:

> the universality, objectivity and non-selectivity of all human rights and the need to avoid the application of double standards in the implementation of human rights and its politicization

---

[149] *See* the Report of the Secretary-General submitted in accordance with paragraph 27 of Commission on Human Rights resolution 1997/45, entitled 'Further Promotion and Encouragement of Human Rights and Fundamental Freedoms, Including the Question of the Programme and Methods of Work of the Commission: Regional Arrangements for the Promotion and Protection of Human Rights in the Asian and Pacific Region', UN Doc. E/CN.4/1998/50 of 12 March 1998.

[150] *See however*, the Bangkok NGO Declaration which in para. 1 stresses the concept of universality of fundamental human rights and reiterates the need not to derogate universally accepted human rights for the sake of cultural pluralism or State sovereignty.

with particular emphasis on the interdependence and indivisibility of economic, social, cultural, civil and political rights (paragraph 10). In paragraph 8, Asian Governments also reiterated that, although universal in nature, human rights:

> must be considered in the context of a dynamic and evolving process of international norm-setting, bearing in mind the significance of national and regional particularities and various historical, cultural and religious backgrounds.

The strong reliance on State sovereignty and local cultural values expressed by Asian Governments in Bangkok is clearly reflected in paragraph 9 on remedies, which provides that: "States have the primary responsibility for the promotion and protection of human rights through appropriate infrastructure and mechanisms" and that "remedies must be sought and provided primarily through such mechanisms and procedures".

In the political context of Asian countries, implementation of the victims' rights to seek and obtain redress as expressed in international human rights instruments has proven particularly difficult. Many Asian Governments have been intolerant of human rights NGOs or other organized forms of victims' representation and this has resulted in victims of human rights violations being placed in a more difficult position when attempting to raise credible claims for redress.[151] As a result, although many Asian constitutions protect fundamental human rights and freedoms, the implementation of these rights and of the right to redress in cases of violation has often proved extremely difficult.[152] At the international level, the indifferent or sometimes negative attitude of many Asian countries towards the ICC demonstrates the overall lack of priority attached to values such as the fight against impunity, international criminal justice and victims' redress, among others.[153]

On the other hand, civil society in Asian countries has begun to take a lead in raising awareness on human rights issues, promoting better implementation of human rights standards both at domestic and regional levels, putting

---

151 On the NGOs efforts to support a regional human rights system *see* Ralph Wilde, "NGO Proposals for an Asia-Pacific Human Rights System", *Yale Human Rights & Development Law Journal*, Vol. 1, No. 137 (1998).

152 For a comparative study of the coverage of human rights in Asian constitutions *see* Imtiaz Omar, *Rights, Emergencies and Judicial Review*, Kluwer Law International (1996).

153 On the position of Asian countries towards the ICC *see* Lyal S. Sunga, "The Attitude of Asian Countries Towards the International Criminal Court", *Indian Yearbook of International Humanitarian and Refugee Law*, Vol. 2 (2002).

forward issues of special concern for public discussion and trying to advance the development of human rights standards common to Asia.[154] In a region that is home to more than half of the world's population, grass-root efforts at promoting human rights may be the key to better observance and implementation of fundamental rights and freedoms, including the right to receive adequate reparation in cases of violations. For the moment, victims have to rely on domestic mechanisms to enforce their right to seek and obtain redress, with the result that the implementation of this basic right has been very uneven and mostly dependent upon the development of domestic systems of justice administration. It remains therefore difficult to identify common redress principles and standards which may apply to the Asian region, or the emergence of a regional custom on redress. Rather, the right to redress has been implemented in a variety of fashions, according to domestic procedures and standards. The following case study looks at the example of India, where the victims' right to redress has been explicitly guaranteed in the Constitution and implemented directly at a high judicial level.

ii. Domestic Implementation of the Victims' Right to Redress in Asia: The Example of India

Many Asian legal systems grant constitutional status to fundamental human rights and freedoms. However, it is unusual for the right to a remedy for violations of individual rights to feature among constitutional provisions. Among Asian countries, India offers an interesting example of constitutional expression of the right to a remedy for victims of fundamental rights and freedoms. Article 32(1) of the Indian Constitution not only includes remedial rights among fundamental rights, but requires that the Supreme Court of India grant relief to victims wherever a fundamental right or freedom protected by the Constitution has been breached or infringed.[155]

---

154 *See* the efforts to draft an instrument for the protection and promotion of human rights in Asia, carried out by a large group of highly regarded academics, NGOs, international organizations and individuals, which resulted in the draft of the 'Asian Human Rights Charter: A Peoples' Charter', published on the occasion of the 50th Anniversary of the Universal Declaration of Human Rights by the Asian Human Rights Commission, Hong Kong, China. The 'Asian Human Rights Charter' can be obtained from the Asian Human Rights Commission at www.ahrchk.net. Also, in the context of the ICC, one must commend the important work of the Asia Forum for Human Rights and Development in encouraging Asian Governments to ratify the ICC Statute.

155 Article 32, Part III on Fundamental Rights of The Constitution of India, *adopted* on 26 November 1949. For supporting case law *see, inter alia, Tata Iron & Steel Co.* v. *Sarkar*, A. (1961) S.C. 65 at 68; *Kochunni* v. *State of Madras*, A. (1959)

The powers of the Indian Supreme Court to provide redress for violations of fundamental rights are remarkably broad. The Court can issue writs of *habeas corpus*, *mandamus*, prohibition, *quo warranto* and *certiorari*; it can issue orders of revision under the High Court's supervisory jurisdiction and of orders of inquiry and investigation; it can issue directions of any nature to address the alleged violation; and it can hear appeals and award compensation.[156] Perhaps most importantly, the Supreme Court and the High Court of India can directly provide redress for fundamental rights' violations by awarding compensation to individual petitioners in higher proceedings, in other words, without referring the petitioners to a lower forum for the recovery of civil damages.[157] However, the jurisprudence of the Supreme Court clarifies that it is not for every breach of fundamental rights that the Court will award compensation pursuant to a petition under Article 32. The power to grant compensation directly to the petitioner may be used only in 'appropriate cases', more specifically when the violation of a fundamental right protected by the Constitution is:

> gross and patent, that is, incontrovertible and *ex facie* glaring and either such infringement should be on a large scale affecting the fundamental rights of a large number of persons or it should appear unjust or unduly harsh or oppressive on account of their poverty or disability or socially or economically disadvantaged position to

---

S.C. 752 at 729 and *Bishan Das* v. *State of Punjab*, A. (1961) S.C. 1570 at 1575, as cited in a very comprehensive study on remedies for the enforcement of constitutional rights in India by Durga Das Basu, *Constitutional Remedies and Writs*, Kamal Law House, Calcutta (1994) at 4.

156 *See* Durga Das Basu, *ibid.* at 5-6.

157 *Ibid.* at 26. The Supreme Court of India has awarded compensation to individual victims in a number of cases. In *Peoples Union for Democratic Rights* v. *Police Commissioner*, 1989 (4) SCC 730, the Supreme Court awarded compensation of Rp. 75,000 (approximately US$1,500) to the family of a man who was beaten to death by a police officer for having demanded to be paid for his work at a police station. In *Arvinder Singh Bagga* v. *State of Uttar Pradesh*, A. (1995) S.C. 117, the Court awarded compensation in the amount of Rp. 10,000 (approximately US$200) to the victim of mental and physical torture committed by a police officer against a woman who was forced to testify against her husband. In a similar case, the Court awarded compensation and reimbursement of court fees to the mother of a young man who died in police custody due to torture, *Nilabati Behere* v. *State of Orissa*, 1993 (2) SCC 746. In *Chiranjit Kaur* v. *Union of India*, 1994 (2) SCC 1, the Court granted a pension to the family of an army major who died under unknown circumstances, for negligence of the authorities to investigate the death.

> require the persons or persons affected by such infringement to initiate and pursue action in the civil Courts.[158]

Therefore, for the victim to receive direct compensation from a higher Court, the infringement must be 'patent and incontrovertible', the violation must be 'gross', and its magnitude must be such as:

> to shock the conscience of the Court and it would have been gravely unjust to the person whose fundamental right was violated, to require him to go to the civil Court for claiming compensation.[159]

In case of petitions concerning violations of a fundamental right protected by the Constitution, in addition to individual compensation, the Supreme Court and the High Court may also award exemplary damages against the State for violating fundamental rights, or against a person acting in a public capacity for breach of a public law duty.[160]

Finally, it is interesting to note that the Supreme Court of India recalled the rationale for the direct award of compensation to victims of human rights violations in the relevant provisions of the ICCPR reviewed above. In this sense, the Supreme Court ruled that the Court is bound to award compensation for human rights violations because that is:

> the only remedy in public law for violation of such rights and that such remedy is in addition to other remedies which may be available under the private law.[161]

3. UN Standards

The channelling of international concern on redress issues through the United Nations dates back to 1948, when the basic right to a 'remedy' for victims of human rights violations was enshrined in the Universal Declaration of Human Rights. Since that time, the UN has taken steps to elaborate the

---

158 *See* Durga Das Basu, *supra* note 155. *See also Saheli* v. *C.P.*, A. (1990) S.C. 513; *Padmini* v. *State of T. N.,* (1993) Cr. L.J. 2964; *Rudul Shah* v. *State of Bihar*, A. (1983) S.C. 1086 - 1089; and *D. K. Basu* v. *State of West Bengal*, A. (1997) S.C. 416.

159 *M.C. Mehta* v. *Union of India* (Shriram Foods Case), A. (1987) S.C. 1086 at para. 7.

160 *See* Durga Das Basu, *supra* note 155 at 106.

161 *See Saheli* v. *C.P.*; *Padmini* v. *State of T. N.;* and *Rudul Shah* v. *State of Bihar*, all *supra* note 158.

principle of redress, to promote its codification both in international human rights instruments and domestic law as a distinct human right and not only as a procedural right resulting from a particular violation,[162] and to assist States to establish redress mechanisms for victims of human rights violations.[163]

The UN Declaration of Basic Principles of Justice for Victims of Crime and Abuse of Power 1985,[164] represents one of the earlier UN efforts to address the question of victims' justice in a comprehensive way. The Declaration establishes that victims of crime are entitled to have access to justice to obtain prompt redress and that the related formal or informal procedures should be expeditious, fair, inexpensive and accessible. Victims should also receive material, medical, psychological and social assistance as a part of their right to redress. In cases where public officials or other agents acting in an official or quasi-official capacity have violated domestic criminal law, the Declaration provides that victims should receive restitution from the State whose officials or agents were responsible for the harm inflicted.[165]

The Declaration does not cover specifically victims of crimes under international law and in fact this category had been removed from earlier drafts. This gap has been partially filled by Part B of the Declaration, which is dedicated to 'victims of abuse of power', where the definition of 'victims' includes:

> persons who, individually or collectively, have suffered harm, including physical or mental injury, emotional suffering, economic

---

162 In this sense, Professor Theo van Boven distinguishes between the right to reparation as a substantive right and the right to a remedy as a procedural right. *See* UN Doc. E/CN.4/Sub.2/1993/8 of 2 July 1993; E/CN.4/Sub.2/1996/17 of 24 May 1996 and E/CN.4/1997/104 of 16 January 1997.

163 Early on, ECOSOC addressed the question of reparation for crimes under international law in resolution 353 (XII) of 19 March 1951. ECOSOC resolution 353 requested Germany to consider making the fullest possible reparation to persons in respect of injuries suffered in the course of 'scientific experiments' conducted in concentration camps during the Nazi regime. Germany replied that it could afford 'practical assistance' to the victims should they not be eligible for reparation under Germany's compensation laws. *See* van Boven final report 1993 at para. 19.

164 *Adopted* in UNGA resolution 40/34 of 29 November 1985. For a good review of the drafting process of the Victims' Declaration *see* Roger S. Clark, *The United Nations Crime Prevention and Criminal Justice Program: Formulation of Standards and Efforts at Their Implementation*, University of Pennsylvania Press, Philadelphia (1994), Chapter 7 at 180-198.

165 Principle 11.

> loss or substantial impairment of their fundamental rights, through acts or omissions that do not yet constitute violations of national criminal laws but of internationally recognized norms relating to human rights.

In cases coming within this definition, the Declaration encourages States to "consider incorporating into the national law norms proscribing abuses of power and providing remedies to victims of such abuses". The Declaration also encourages States to establish national or other funds for the compensation of crime victims, especially where full compensation is not available from the offender. In an effort to ensure better participation of victims in criminal proceedings and greater coherence and simplicity in judicial procedures, the Declaration invites States to review their laws and procedures to include restitution as one of the sentencing options in criminal cases. The standards set forth in the Declaration have encouraged many countries to improve their legislation with respect to victims' assistance, protection and compensation and to harmonize norms on the treatment of crime victims.[166]

Under the umbrella of United Nations instruments, provisions on the right to redress in various forms have also appeared as follows: Article 11 of the UN Declaration on the Protection of all Persons from Being Subjected to Torture and Other Cruel, Inhuman or Degrading Treatment or Punishment 1975;[167] Article 6(3) of the UN Declaration on Race and Racial Prejudice 1978; Articles 11 and 18 of the UN Standard Minimum Rules for the Administration of Juvenile Justice (the 'Beijing Rules') 1985;[168] Principle 35 of the Body of Principles for the Protection of All Persons under Any Form of Detention or Imprisonment 1988;[169] Principle 20 of the Principles on the Effective Prevention and Investigation of Extra-legal, Arbitrary and Summary Executions

---

166 To assist States in implementing victims' redress standards as expressed in the Declaration, the UN Commission on Crime Prevention and Criminal Justice prepared a *Guide for Policy Makers in the Implementation of the UN Declaration of Basic Principles of Justice for Victims of Crime and Abuse of Power*, UN Doc. E/CN.15/1998/CRP.4 of 17 April 1998.

167 *Adopted* by UNGA resolution 3452 (XXX) of 9 December 1975. The Declaration provides that: "Where it is proved that an act of torture or other cruel, inhuman or degrading treatment or punishment has been committed by or at the instigation of a public official, the victim shall be afforded redress and compensation in accordance with national law".

168 *Adopted* by UNGA resolution 40/33 of 29 November 1985.

169 *Adopted* by UNGA resolution 43/173 of 9 December 1988.

1989;[170] and Article 19 of the UN Declaration on the Protection of All Persons from Enforced Disappearance 1992.[171]

As for the implementation of the right to redress, the Declaration on the Right and Responsibility of Individuals, Groups and Organs of Society to Promote and Protect Universally Recognized Human Rights and Fundamental Freedoms 1998, envisages the right to benefit from an effective remedy and indicates ways for victims to access such remedies before appropriate fora.[172] With respect to women's rights, Article 4 of the Declaration on the Elimination of Violence against Women 1993, establishes that women who are subjected to violence:

> should be provided with access to the mechanisms of justice and, as provided for by national legislation, to just and effective remedies for the harm that they have suffered.

---

170 *Recommended* by ECOSOC resolution 1989/65 of 24 May 1989. In para. 1, ECOSOC recommended that the Principles should be taken into account and respected by Governments within the framework of their national legislation and practices and that "families and dependants of victims of extra-legal, arbitrary or summary executions shall be entitled to fair and adequate compensation within a reasonable time".

171 *Adopted* by UNGA resolution 47/133 of 18 December 1992, providing in Article 19 that victims of acts of enforced disappearance and their families shall obtain redress and shall have the right to adequate compensation, including the means for as complete a rehabilitation as possible.

172 UN Declaration on the Right and Responsibility of Individuals, Groups and Organs of Society to Promote and Protect Universally Recognized Human Rights and Fundamental Freedoms, *adopted* by UNGA resolution 53/144 of 9 December 1998. In particular, Article 9(1) states that: "In the exercise of human rights and fundamental freedoms, including the promotion and protection of human rights as referred to in the present Declaration, everyone has the right, individually and in association with others, to benefit from an effective remedy and to be protected in the event of the violation of those rights". Article 9(2) adds that: "to this end, everyone whose rights or freedoms are allegedly violated has the right, either in person or through legally authorized representation, to complain to and have that complaint promptly reviewed in a public hearing before an independent, impartial and competent judicial or other authority established by law and to obtain from such an authority a decision, in accordance with law, providing redress, including any compensation due, where there has been a violation of that person's rights or freedoms, as well as enforcement of the eventual decision and award, all without undue delay".

To this end, States should inform women of their rights in seeking redress through these mechanisms.[173]

The United Nations Draft Declaration on the Rights of Indigenous Peoples 1994,[174] also contains special provisions on the right to restitution of property and provides for an alternative right to compensation should restitution not be possible. Article 12 establishes that:

> Indigenous peoples have the right to the restitution of cultural, intellectual, religious and spiritual property taken without their free and informed consent or in violation of their laws, traditions and customs.

Article 27 also states that:

> Indigenous peoples have the right to the restitution of the lands, territories and resources which they have traditionally owned or otherwise occupied or used, and which have been confiscated, occupied, used or damaged without their free and informed consent. Where this is not possible, they have the right to just and fair compensation. Unless otherwise freely agreed upon by the peoples concerned, compensation shall take the form of lands, territories and resources equal in quality, size and legal status.

In 1993, the World Conference on Human Rights stressed the need to provide a remedy for victims of human rights violations and reaffirmed the link between the enjoyment of the right to a remedy in the administration of justice and the "full and non-discriminatory realization of human rights". On this point, the World Conference on Human Rights expressed 'grave concern' about the lack of sufficient and effective remedies for victims of human rights violations and urged that "every State should provide an effective framework of remedies to redress human rights grievances or violations".[175] The World

---

173 On female victims of crime, *see generally Women in the Criminal Justice System*, Background paper for the workshop on women in the criminal justice system, Tenth UN Congress on the Prevention of Crime and the Treatment of Offenders, Vienna 10-17 April 2000, UN Doc. A/CONF.187/12 of 2 March 2000.

174 UN Draft Declaration on the Rights of Indigenous Peoples, UN Doc. E/CN.4/Sub.2/1994/2/Add.1 (1994).

175 Vienna Declaration and Programme of Action 1993, para. 27, section I. The World Conference on Human Rights emphasises the role of national institutions in regard to the implementation of the right to redress.

Conference also made specific reference to remedies with respect to 'ethnic cleansing' (paragraph 24 of section II(B)(1)) and torture (paragraph 59 of section II(B)(5)) and envisaged that further action would be undertaken by the United Nations Voluntary Fund for the Victims of Torture with a view to "providing assistance to victims of torture and ensuring more effective remedies for their physical, psychological and social rehabilitation".

Finally, on the occasion of the Tenth UN Congress on the Prevention of Crime and the Treatment of Offenders, held in Vienna on 10-17 April 2000, the participants affirmed that victims of crime must enjoy a number of internationally recognized 'basic elements of fairness', as expressed in the Declaration of Basic Principles of Justice discussed above, including the right to compensation from both the offender and the State.[176]

a. The Durban Declaration and Programme of Action

The World Conference Against Racism, Racial Discrimination, Xenophobia and Related Intolerance, held in Durban from 31 August to 8 September 2001, became heavily embroiled in the question of victims' reparations for historical injustice, mainly in connection with the slave trade in the sixteenth, seventeenth, eighteenth and nineteenth centuries.[177] Both during preparatory meetings and expert seminars leading to the World Conference, many delegations argued that the question of victims' compensation should be granted priority at the Conference. In particular, the Regional Conference for Africa in preparation to the World Conference, held in Dakar from 22 to 24 January 2001, discussed in detail the issue of victims' reparation with regard to the slave trade, colonialism and apartheid. In its Report, the

---

[176] *See Offenders and Victims: Accountability and Fairness in the Criminal Justice Process*, Working Paper prepared by the Secretariat of the Tenth UN Congress on the Prevention of Crime and the Treatment of Offenders, Vienna 10-17 April 2000, UN Doc. A/CONF.187/8 of 15 December 1999 at para. 14.

[177] This particularly delicate question was raised, *inter alia*, by UN Special Rapporteur van Boven in his final report. He suggested the adoption of affirmative action as a moral duty, in addition to "an accurate record of the history of slavery, including an account of the acts and the activities of the perpetrators and their accomplices and of the sufferings of the victims ... through the media, in history books and in educational materials". *See* van Boven final report 1993 at para. 24. Today, this issue is in the centre of a very contentious debate, especially in the United States. For a thought-provoking reading, *see* Katherine Stapp, "That'll Be 10 Trillion Dollars in Back Wages, Please", *Terraviva* (2000).

Regional Conference urged former colonial Powers to issue an explicit apology as part of the final outcome of the World Conference,[178] and declared that:

> States which pursued racist policies or acts of racial discrimination such as slavery and colonialism should assume their moral, economic, political and legal responsibilities within their national jurisdiction and before other appropriate international mechanisms or jurisdictions and provide adequate reparation to those communities or individuals who, individually or collectively, are victims of such racist policies or acts, regardless of when or by whom they were committed.[179]

The question of statutory limitations with respect to historical crimes emerged as one of the more troubling issues both during regional conferences and in the Durban Conference. The Convention on the Non-Applicability of Statutory Limitations to War Crimes and Crimes against Humanity 1968[180] clearly prohibits the application of statutes of limitation to war crimes and crimes against humanity. However, States have often questioned the value of this prohibition under general international law, since only forty-three States have ratified the UN Convention to date and only two States have ratified the European Convention.[181] As a result, neither the Durban Declaration nor the

---

178 Report of the Regional Conference for Africa (Dakar, 22-24 January 2001), UN Doc. A/CONF.189/PC.2/8 of 27 March 2001, at para. 18 of the Declaration.

179 *Ibid.* at para. 20 of the Declaration. In this context, the Conference also noted that: "other groups which were subjected to other scourges and injustices have received repeated apologies from different countries, as well as ample reparations, on a bilateral basis, from both public and private sources and lately through certain international organizations". *Ibid.* at para. 29 of the Declaration.

180 Convention on the Non-Applicability of Statutory Limitations to War Crimes and Crimes against Humanity, *adopted* on 26 November 1968, *entered* into force on 11 November 1970.

181 European Convention on the Non-Applicability of Statutory Limitations to Crimes against Humanity and War Crimes, *signed* on 25 January 1974, *not yet entered into force*. The Convention needs three ratifications to enter into force. To date, only the Netherlands and Romania have ratified the Convention. The hesitancy of States to embrace fully a prohibition on the application of statutory limitation seems to be confirmed by domestic judicial practice, especially as regards Japanese courts where a number of compensation cases against multinational corporations allegedly involved in slave labour during World War II have been dismissed on grounds of the applicability of statutes of limitations, *inter alia*. It is worth recalling however, that Principle 15 of the van Boven 1993 'Proposed Basic Principles and Guidelines' states that: "Statutes

Programme of Action contains any reference to the non-applicability of statutory limitations for certain crimes under international law.

The Regional Conference also reiterated the victims' right to seek and obtain redress for damages resulting from violations of human rights standards on racism, racial discrimination, xenophobia and related intolerance, and stressed the importance of ensuring that victims of racial discrimination can enjoy their right to access to justice.[182] In addition, the Regional Conference recommended that, to fulfill the victims' right to compensation, an International Compensation Scheme be set up for victims of the slave trade and of other transnational racist policies and acts, in addition to national funds and other domestic compensation mechanisms.[183] As for the financing of the proposed compensation scheme, the Regional Conference mentioned governmental sources and private contributions from those sectors who benefited from transnational racial policies and acts.[184]

Prior to the Dakar Regional Conference, a number of other regional conferences and expert meetings in preparation for the World Conference discussed the question of victims' compensation for racial discrimination. In February 2000, a group of experts, meeting in Geneva, issued a number of recommendations that reiterated the right of victims to reparation in its different forms, including restitution, compensation, rehabilitation, satisfaction

---

of limitations shall not apply in respect to periods during which no effective remedies exist for human rights violations. Claims relating to reparations for gross violations of human rights shall not be subject to a statute of limitations". Significantly, Professor van Boven noted that: "it is well established that for many victims of gross violations of human rights, the passage of time has no attenuating effect; on the contrary, there is an increase in post-traumatic stress, requiring all necessary material, medical, psychological and social assistance and support over a long period of time". *See* van Boven's final report, UN Doc. E/CN.4/Sub.2/1993/8 of 2 July 1993.

182 Report of the Regional Conference for Africa, *supra* note 178 at paras. 21 and 28 of the Declaration.

183 *Ibid.* at para. 2 of the Recommendations for a Programme of Action. Also, the Regional Conference recommended the setting up of a Development Reparation Fund to provide resources for the development process in countries affected by colonialism. *Ibid.* at para. 3.

184 *Ibid.* at para. 6. The Conference also recommended that reparations take the form of "enhanced policies, programmes and measures to be adopted by States which benefit materially from these practices in order to rectify, through affirmative action, the economic, cultural and political damage which has been inflicted on the affected communities and peoples in the full implementation of their right to development". *Ibid.* at para. 5.

and guarantees of non-repetition.[185] The recommendations also urged States to address the lack of effective domestic and international remedies for victims of persistent discrimination. During the seminar, Professor van Boven contributed substantially to the discussion on victims' compensation by stressing, *inter alia*, the importance of having international cooperation and monitoring procedures to ensure that domestic mechanisms for redress adhere to international standards.[186]

The question of compensation was a central theme of discussion also in the Seminar of Experts on the Prevention of Ethnic and Racial Conflicts in Africa, held in Addis Ababa, from 4 to 6 October 2000, in preparation for the World Conference. In Addis Ababa it was recommended that the World Conference adopt as an item in its agenda the question of 'Measures for reparation, restoration and compensation for nations, groups and individuals affected by slavery and the slave trade, colonialism, and economic and political exclusion'.[187] During the same seminar, the experts agreed on the value of policies relating to restorative justice and programmes "that are respectful of the needs of victims, offenders, communities and any other parties" and encouraged the World Conference to call for action plans in support of mechanisms for mediation and restorative justice.[188] Similarly, the preparatory Asia-Pacific Regional Seminar of Experts, held in Bangkok from 5 to 7 September 2000, debated the question of compensation pertaining to migrants and trafficking in persons, especially women and children. In this context, the seminar reiterated the need for States to ensure that victims of racial discrimination and racial violence are granted their right "to seek from tribunals just and adequate reparation or satisfaction for any damage suffered as a result of such discrimination".[189]

---

185 Report of the Expert Seminar on Remedies Available to the Victims of Racial Discrimination, Xenophobia and Related Intolerance and on Good National Practices, UN Doc. A/CONF.189/PC.1/8 of 26 April 2000, at para. 43.

186 *See* paper by Professor Theodor van Boven, presented on 17 February 2000 to the Expert Seminar on Remedies Available to the Victims of Racial Discrimination, Xenophobia and Related Intolerance and on Good National Practices, HR/GVA/WCR/SEM.1/2000/BP.5.

187 Report of the Seminar of Experts on the Prevention of Ethnic and Racial Conflicts in Africa, UN Doc. A/CONF.189/PC.2/4 of 14 March 2001 at para. 34.

188 *Ibid.* at para. 35.

189 Report of the Asia-Pacific regional seminar of experts on migrants and trafficking in persons with particular reference to women and children, UN Doc. A/CONF.189/PC.2/3 of 26 April 2001 at para. 30.

Also in October 2000, a regional seminar of experts on economic, social and legal measures to combat racism was held in Santiago de Chile in preparation for the World Conference. The experts recommended to the World Conference that Governments needed to enact legislation which provided for adequate civil compensation of victims of racial discrimination as a measure to combat racism. The experts also affirmed the value of victims' compensation and the establishment of reparation funds, together with measures for the rehabilitation of both perpetrators and victims of racism by means of truth commissions and apologies.[190] In December 2000, also in Santiago de Chile, the Regional Conference of the Americas in preparation for the World Conference urged States to adopt measures to ensure the right of an effective judicial remedy and the right to reparation for victims of racism, and to consider the creation of a development and educational fund.[191]

Similar conclusions on the question of reparations were reached also at the European Conference against Racism, which was held in Strasbourg in October 2000 in preparation for the World Conference,[192] at the Asian Regional Preparatory Meeting to the World Conference,[193] held in Tehran in February 2001, and at the Central and Eastern European regional seminar of experts on the protection of minorities and other vulnerable groups,[194] held in Warsaw in July 2000, in preparation for the World Conference.

During the World Conference itself, delegations could not agree on compensation or any other form of redress for past violations. In the end, only general provisions on remedies, reparations and compensation were included

---

[190] Report of the Latin American and Caribbean regional seminar of experts on economic, social and legal measures to combat racism with particular reference to vulnerable groups, held in Santiago de Chile from 25 to 27 October 2000. UN Doc. A/CONF.189/PC.2/5 of 27 April 2001 at para. 24 of the Recommendations.

[191] Report of the Regional Conference of the Americas, Santiago, Chile, 5-7 December 2000, UN Doc. A/CONF.189/PC.2/7 of 24 April 2001 at paras. 193 and 194.

[192] *See Déclaration Politique, Conclusions Générales et Rapport Général de la Conférence Européenne contre le Racisme*, UN Doc. A/CONF.189/PC.2/6 of 30 March 2001.

[193] *See* Report of the Asian Preparatory Meeting, UN Doc. A/CONF.189/PC.2/9 of 10 April 2001.

[194] *See* Report of the Central and Eastern European regional seminar of experts on the protection of minorities and other vulnerable groups and strengthening human rights capacity at the national level, UN Doc. A/CONF.189/PC.2/2 of 14 August 2000.

in the Durban Declaration and Programme of Action.[195] These provisions do not differ in substance from the general provisions on remedies contained in most human rights treaties. In particular, the Programme of Action urges States to provide victims of human rights violations with "just and adequate reparation and satisfaction" either in Court or in other national institutions, to ensure the enjoyment of the right of victims to seek just and adequate reparation and satisfaction and to "design effective measures to prevent the repetition" of acts of racism and of similar acts - all concepts that derive directly from existing international instruments. As for the Declaration, paragraphs 98 to 106 are grouped under the promising title 'Provisions of effective remedies, recourse, redress, and compensatory and other measures at the national, regional and international levels'. Unfortunately, the substance of the provisions falls short of the title. The core paragraphs are dedicated almost exclusively to victims of slavery in the past centuries and, as for the operating principles, the Declaration simply encourages States to fulfill their 'moral obligation' to take "appropriate and effective measures to halt and reverse the lasting consequences of those practices", to honour the memory of victims and to present official apologies for the acts committed.[196]

As for the victims' right to seek and obtain redress, the Declaration again reaffirms the right of victims to have access to justice and legal assistance, effective and appropriate protection and remedies,

> including the right to seek just and adequate reparation or satisfaction for any damage suffered ... as enshrined in numerous international and regional human rights instruments.[197]

As mentioned above, the question of victims' reparation was among the more prominent issues of debate both in the preparatory meetings and during the Durban Conference itself.[198] At various points in the process leading up to

---

195 Durban Declaration and Programme of Action, *adopted* by the World Conference Against Racism, Racial Discrimination, Xenophobia and Related Intolerances, meeting in Durban from 31 August to 8 September 2001.

196 Durban Declaration at para. 102.

197 *Ibid.* at para. 104.

198 At one of the preparatory meetings to the World Conference against Racism, held in Geneva on 17 February 2000, Professor van Boven introduced a study entitled "Common Problems Linked to All Remedies Available to Victims of Racial Discrimination", *see* HR/GVA/WCR/SEM.1/2000/BP.5, as summarized in UN Doc. A/CONF.189/PC.1/8 of 26 April 2000 at paras. 51-53, in which he argued that while remedies for the victims of racial discrimination are the principal responsibility of

the World Conference, negotiations almost stalled from a lack of consensus over redress issues. In particular, countries that historically had been heavily involved in the slave trade wished to avoid any reference to compensation for past violations in the Declaration, presumably to prevent opening the flood gates to countless compensation claims in their respective countries.

Ultimately, the Durban Declaration and Programme of Action reflect the lack of consensus among States on providing victims' compensation for historical violations. States could not agree on any legal obligation to compensate victims of the slave trade over the last four centuries, or victims of other past human rights violations also based on race. As a result, the Durban Declaration only provides that States have a 'moral obligation' to redress the consequences of those practices. On the other hand, the Declaration reiterates and endorses the right of victims of human rights violations based on race to seek and obtain "just and adequate reparation and satisfaction", as enshrined in most human rights instruments, thus strengthening the status of the victims' right to redress under international law and contributing strongly to its universal acceptance and implementation.

States, it is important that international cooperation and international monitoring are used as supplementary tools, especially with a view to ensuring that national measures meet the requirements of relevant international standards. Professor van Boven identified the following requirements as necessary to ensure the efficiency of recourse procedures:
(a) Easy accessibility, especially for those likely to be victims of racial discrimination, for both citizens and non-citizens, for individuals as well as groups;
(b) Initiation of complaints should be simple and flexible and should be available to victims and, as appropriate, authorized public agencies or third parties;
(c) Dissemination of information concerning the availability of remedies, including recourse procedures, should be widespread;
(d) Investigations should cover individual cases, as well as situations which indicated a pattern or practice of racial discrimination;
(e) All stages of the procedures should be expeditiously handled;
(f) Interim measures should be ordered to avert or prevent irreparable damage;
(g) Legal aid and assistance should be provided for victims of racial discrimination and, where appropriate, the services of an interpreter should be made available;
(h) Reparation should be awarded for material and moral damage and suffering; and
(i) The impartiality and independence of organs dealing with complaints should be assured.

b. The Contribution of Special Rapporteurs and Independent Experts of the UN Commission on Human Rights

In 1989, for the first time, the UN Sub-Commission on the Prevention of Discrimination and Protection of Minorities decided to address the specific question of victims' reparation for gross human rights violations. The Sub-Commission entrusted Professor Theo van Boven with the task of undertaking a study on the right to restitution, compensation and rehabilitation for victims of gross violations of human rights and fundamental freedoms.[199] Professor van Boven's study eventually resulted in the drafting of the 'Basic Principles and Guidelines on the Right to Reparation for Victims of Gross Violations of Human Rights and International Humanitarian Law'.[200] Professor M. Cherif Bassiouni then continued Professor van Boven's work for the Commission on Human Rights and prepared two revised versions of the reparation principles.

i. The van Boven 'Basic Principles and Guidelines'

Originally, Professor van Boven's mandate was to address reparations for victims of 'gross' human rights violations. His 1993 Draft Guidelines contained a non-exhaustive list of crimes giving rise to a State's obligation to provide reparations to victims, including genocide, slavery, summary executions, torture, enforced disappearance, arbitrary detention, deportation and systematic discrimination. The 1993 Draft Guidelines also stated that: "reparation for certain gross violations of human rights that amount to crimes under international law includes a duty to prosecute and punish perpetrators".[201] Eventually, both the adjective 'gross' and the corresponding list of violations were omitted from the 1997 version of the Draft Principles and Guidelines, with the intention of broadening the scope of application of the principles, and perhaps to make them conform more closely with the terms of the mandate, which envisaged the elaboration of 'principles and guidelines' of a general nature.[202] As a result, the 1997 Draft Principles and Guidelines depart almost completely from the notion of crimes under international law.

---

199 Sub-Commission resolution 1989/13 of 31 August 1989.

200 During his appointment, Professor van Boven prepared three versions of the Basic Principles. *See* UN Doc. E/CN.4/Sub.2/1993/8 of 2 July 1993, E/CN.4/Sub.2/1996/17 of 24 May 1996 and E/CN.4/1997/104 of 16 January 1997.

201 *See* UN Doc. E/CN.4/Sub.2/1993/8 of 2 July 1993, Principles 2 and 5.

202 The word 'gross' appears in square brackets in the 1997 Principles and Guidelines.

One of the pillars of the 1997 Draft Principles and Guidelines is the obligation of States, under international law, to respect and ensure respect for human rights and international humanitarian law - an obligation codified in many human rights instruments. This obligation imposes a series of duties on States, including duties: to prevent gross violations of human rights and international humanitarian law; to prosecute and punish the perpetrators of such violations; to ensure that victims are afforded adequate remedies and reparation; to provide victims with access to national and international redress procedures; and, in case of crimes under international law, to provide for universal jurisdiction.[203] The 1997 Draft Principles and Guidelines indicate that reparations may take the form of restitution, compensation, rehabilitation, satisfaction and guarantees of non repetition. The Principles and Guidelines do not encompass an obligation on States to establish redress mechanisms at the international level, but rather, leave States free to choose the means for redress within their domestic law.[204]

ii. The Bassiouni Revised 'Principles and Guidelines'

In 1998, the Commission on Human Rights, through resolution 1998/43, appointed Professor M. Cherif Bassiouni to the position of Independent Expert on the right to restitution, compensation and rehabilitation for victims of grave violations of human rights and fundamental freedoms. The Commission entrusted the Independent Expert with the responsibility of preparing a revised draft of the van Boven Draft Guidelines and Principles. Professor Bassiouni submitted his first report on 8 February 1999[205] and his final report on 18 January 2000.[206]

---

203 Principles 1, 2, 4 and 5 of the *Basic Principles and Guidelines on the Right to Reparation for Victims of [Gross] Violations of Human Rights and International Humanitarian Law*, annex to UN Doc. E/CN.4/1997/104.

204 *Ibid.* Principle 4 refers to the right to a remedy as including the right to access national and *any available* international procedures (italics in the original text), but there is no obligation for the State to ensure that such international procedures are actually established. Instead, Principle 11 states that reparations are to be provided in accordance with the law of each State.

205 Report of the Independent Expert M. Cherif Bassiouni on 'The Right to Restitution, Compensation and Rehabilitation for Victims of Grave Violations of Human Rights and Fundamental Freedoms', submitted pursuant to Commission on Human Rights resolution 1998/43, UN Doc. E/CN.4/1999/65.

206 'The Right to Restitution, Compensation and Rehabilitation for Victims of Grave Violations of Human Rights and Fundamental Freedoms', final report of the Independent Expert M. Cherif Bassiouni, submitted in accordance with Commission

In his first report, the Independent Expert clarified some questions of terminological consistency, in particular, with respect to the use of terms such as 'human rights', 'humanitarian law' and 'fundamental freedoms'. The report also analyzes some of the main redress issues which have yet to be resolved and introduces an involved discussion on "the sources of the international legal obligation to provide any or all modalities of redress for different types of human rights violations". The final report of the Independent Expert includes as an annex a revised version of the van Boven principles entitled 'Basic Principles and Guidelines on the Right to A Remedy and Reparation for Victims of Violations of International Human Rights and Humanitarian Law', covering human rights violations of all degrees. The Independent Expert identified at least two redress obligations which specifically attach to crimes under international law: first, the duty of States to prosecute and punish perpetrators of such crimes and to cooperate and assist with appropriate judicial organs in the investigation and prosecution of such violations; and second, the obligation to incorporate into domestic law appropriate provisions on universal jurisdiction as well as legislation to facilitate extradition and judicial assistance in the pursuit of international justice.[207] In the report, there seems to have been no differentiation of the components of the right to redress with respect to various kinds of human rights or humanitarian law violations.

Principle V defines 'victim' as:

> a person who, individually or collectively, suffered harm, including physical or mental injury, emotional suffering, economic loss, or impairment of fundamental legal rights as a result of acts or omissions constituting violations of international human rights or humanitarian law.

The revised principles and guidelines further expand on the definition of victim to include dependants, members of the immediate family or household and persons who suffered physical, mental, or economic harm in assisting the victim or preventing the occurrence of further violations, consistent with the UN Declaration of Basic Principles of Justice for Victims of Crimes and Abuse of Power 1985.

---

resolution 1999/33, UN Doc. E/CN.4/2000/62 of 18 January 2000.

207 *See* Section III of the final report entitled 'Violations of International Human Rights and Humanitarian Law That Constitute Crimes Under International Law'.

As in the van Boven draft, the Bassiouni guidelines conclude that the right to a remedy includes the victim's right to access to justice both under domestic and international law. Along the lines of the Joinet principles discussed below, the Independent Expert included as integral parts of the right to remedy both the reparation for harm suffered and the access to factual information concerning the violations. Reparation should be "adequate, effective and prompt" as well as "proportional to the gravity of the violations and the harm suffered". A special focus on the proper execution of restitution judgments must be welcomed as one of the more important elements of Bassiouni's revised principles. Principle IX, paragraph 19 reads as follows:

> A State shall enforce its domestic judgements for reparation against private individuals or entities responsible for the violations. States shall endeavour to enforce valid foreign judgements for reparation against private individuals or entities responsible for the violations.

Finally, Principle XII contains a special provision on 'non-discrimination among victims', ensuring that the application and interpretation of the principles remain consistent with internationally recognized human rights law and do not discriminate among victims on grounds such as "race, colour, gender, sexual orientation, age, language, religion, political or religious belief, national, ethnic or social origin, wealth, birth, family or other status, or disability".

As of 2000, the Commission's mandate on the right to restitution, compensation and rehabilitation for victims of gross violations of human rights and fundamental freedoms has been discontinued. Former Special Rapporteurs and Independent Experts however, continue to work in close cooperation for the development of reparation standards under the UN framework.

iii. Further Action on Redress of the UN Commission on Human Rights and Sub-Commission on the Promotion and Protection of Human Rights

The UN Commission on Human Rights has considered the question of victims' reparations in several resolutions. It is worth noting that the Commission adopted cautious language with respect to the holders of a right to reparation, referring mainly to victims of 'grave violations' of human rights and fundamental freedoms, thus suggesting a limited application of this right only to violations of a more serious character. For example, Commission resolution 1997/29 of 11 April 1997 states that:

> pursuant to internationally proclaimed human rights and humanitarian law principles, victims of grave violations of human rights should receive, in appropriate cases, restitution, compensation and rehabilitation.

Also, resolution 2000/41 relates only to the right to restitution, compensation and rehabilitation for victims of grave violations of human rights and fundamental freedoms,[208] and calls on the international community to "give due attention to the right to restitution, compensation and rehabilitation for victims of grave violations of human rights", both at the national and international levels.[209] More recently, resolution 2002/44 of 23 April 2002 calls upon the international community to "give due attention" to the right to reparation for victims of grave violations of human rights and fundamental freedoms "in a systematic and thorough way at the national and international levels". States were also asked to provide comments on the text of the 'Basic Principles and Guidelines on the Right to A Remedy and Reparation for Victims of Violations of International Human Rights and Humanitarian Law' with a view to finalizing the guidelines.

In addition to the work of the Special Rapporteur and of the Independent Expert on the right to reparation, the UN Commission on Human Rights requested a number of studies to be prepared addressing, *inter alia*, the issue of reparations for serious human rights violations. In particular, Mr. Joinet's studies on the question of the impunity of perpetrators of human rights violations contributed greatly to the development and clarification of the right to redress for victims of human rights violations.[210] Mr. Joinet identifies three main components of the victims' legal rights:

1. the right to know;
2. the right to justice; and
3. the right to reparations.

---

208 UN Doc. E/CN.4/RES/2000/41 of 20 April 2000.

209 Interestingly, resolution 2000/41 still referred to 'grave violations' of human rights, while the term 'grave' does not figure in the Independent Expert's report.

210 *See* "The Administration of Justice and the Human Rights of Detainees, Question of the Impunity of Perpetrators of Human Rights Violations (Civil and Political)", final report prepared by Mr. Joinet pursuant to Sub-Commission decision 1996/119, UN Doc. E/CN.4/Sub.2/1997/20 of 26 June 1997; and the revised final report of 2 October 1997, UN Doc. E/CN.4/Sub.2/1997/20/Rev.1.

According to Mr. Joinet, the victims' right to know gives rise to the corresponding duty of the State to establish extrajudicial commissions of inquiry into the violations. The right to justice entails the victims' right to a fair and effective remedy, including the duty of the State to investigate violations and prosecute the perpetrators. Mr. Joinet suggests that the right to reparations encompasses guarantees of non-repetition and comprises both individual and collective measures. The study refers to restitution, compensation and rehabilitation as individual measures and indicates collective measures as mainly symbolic, intended to provide moral reparation, such as apologies, State recognition of responsibility, restoration of victims' dignity, commemorative ceremonies, erection of monuments and the establishment of national days of remembrance.[211]

Finally, individual victims or groups may submit their communications under the 'ECOSOC 1503 procedure' for dealing with communications concerning human rights.[212] Under this procedure, the Working Group on Communications of the Sub-Commission for the Promotion and Protection of Human Rights examines communications from individuals and groups, as well as any Government responses, on a confidential basis,[213] in order to identify particular situations revealing a "consistent pattern of gross and reliably attested violations of human rights and fundamental freedoms". Once situations of this kind are identified, the Working Group on Communications passes the matter to the Working Group on Situations, which will decide whether or not to refer a particular situation to the Commission.

---

211 Joinet's final report, *ibid.*

212 This procedure was originally established by ECOSOC resolution 1503 (XLVIII) of 27 May 1970 and subsequently reformed by ECOSOC resolution 2000/3 of 16 June 2000. The revised procedure provides for the establishment of a Working Group on Communications to be designated on a yearly basis by the Sub-Commission on the Promotion and Protection of Human Rights, to examine communications received from individuals and groups alleging human rights violations, as well as any Government responses.

213 However, it has been established practice that the Chairperson of the Commission on Human Rights announces in a public meeting which countries have been subject to examination under the 1503 procedure, and which are no longer under the scrutiny of this procedure. The 1503 dossiers remain confidential unless a Government agrees to make them public.

c. UN Sponsored *Ad Hoc* Redress Mechanisms

In addition to research activities, studies and reports, the United Nations has promoted a series of initiatives to ensure concrete implementation of the right to redress for victims of crimes under international law. On 16 December 1981, the UN General Assembly established the UN Voluntary Fund for Victims of Torture[214] to provide humanitarian assistance to victims of torture and their families. The Fund receives voluntary contributions from Governments, NGOs and individuals, and distributes the contributions exclusively to NGOs providing medical, psychological, social, economic, legal, humanitarian or other kinds of assistance to torture victims and their families.[215] Also, in 1991 the General Assembly established the UN Voluntary Trust Fund on Contemporary Forms of Slavery[216] to assist NGOs involved in activities devoted to helping individual victims of contemporary forms of slavery and to facilitate the participation of concerned NGOs in the sessions of the Working Group on Contemporary Forms of Slavery. In addition, the fund may also consider applications from individuals whose human rights have been severely violated as a result of contemporary forms of slavery.[217] Finally, the UNDP Trust Fund for Rwanda was established in 1995 to assist the Government and the people of Rwanda to undertake development and rehabilitation activities.[218] The UNDP fund succeeded the Secretary General's Trust Fund for Rwanda, established in order to finance humanitarian relief and rehabilitation programmes.[219]

4. The Contribution of *Ad Hoc* Judicial Human Rights Bodies: The Case of the Human Rights Chamber for Bosnia and Herzegovina

The hostilities in the territory of the former Yugoslavia ended formally with the signature of the Peace Agreement for Bosnia and Herzegovina,

---

214 Established by UNGA resolution 36/151 of 16 December 1981.

215 In its activities for the years 2000/2001, the Trust Fund received about 190 grant applications for a total of US$10 million and approved 160 new grants for a total of about US$7 million to be distributed to 150 NGOs in 65 countries. *See generally* www.unhchr.ch.

216 Established by UNGA resolution 46/122 of 17 December 1991.

217 *See generally* "Report of the Secretary-General on the Status of the United Nations Voluntary Trust Fund on Contemporary Forms of Slavery", UN Doc. A/55/204 of 18 July 2000 and www.unhchr.ch.

218 *See* UNDP Trust Fund for Rwanda and other financing modalities, Progress Report No. 15 (1999).

219 *See* UN Doc. S/1994/1133.

concluded in Dayton, Ohio, on 21 November 1995, and signed in Paris on 14 December 1995.[220] The peace agreement consists of a General Framework Agreement for Peace in Bosnia and Herzegovina, supplemented by a number of annexes. With a view to maintaining respect for human rights and fundamental freedoms, the State of Bosnia-Herzegovina and its two entities, the Bosnian-Croat Federation of Bosnia Herzegovina and the Republika Srpska signed an Agreement on Human Rights, annexed to the Peace Agreement (Annex 6). As part of their obligations under the Human Rights Agreement, the parties established a Commission on Human Rights, comprising an Ombudsperson and a Human Rights Chamber which convened its first session on 27-29 March 1996.[221]

Over the last six years, the Human Rights Chamber has developed a growing body of jurisprudence which is of particular relevance to the right to reparation for victims of crimes under international law committed by the parties to the Agreement during the armed conflict in the territory of Bosnia-Herzegovina, especially as regards the restitution of houses and property taken illegally in the context of the armed conflict.[222] Pursuant to Article II of Annex 6, the Chamber's jurisdiction extends over alleged or apparent violations of human rights as provided for in the European Convention for the Protection of Human Rights and Fundamental Freedoms and the Protocols thereto, and over alleged or apparent discrimination arising from the enjoyment of the rights and freedoms provided for in the Convention and in fifteen other international agreements listed in the Appendix to Annex 6.[223] Among the violations falling

---

220 The Dayton Peace Agreement was signed by the Republic of Bosnia and Herzegovina (represented by its President, Alija Izetbegovic), the Federal Republic of Yugoslavia (represented by the President of Serbia, Slobodan Milosevic) and the Republic of Croatia (represented by its President, Franjo Tudjman), and witnessed by the European Union, France, Germany, the Russian Federation, the UK and the US. On the peace agreement, *see generally* Paola Gaeta, "The Dayton Agreements and International Law", *European Journal of International Law*, Vol. 7, No. 2 (1996).

221 The procedure of the Human Rights Chamber is modelled on that of the European Court of Human Rights. By 31 December 2000, the Human Rights Chamber had received 6,675 applications and had issued 669 decisions, resolving 846 applications. *See* the Human Rights Chamber for Bosnia and Herzegovina Annual Report 2000, http://www.gwdg.de/~ujvr/hrch/00annrep.htm.

222 Property claims are also dealt with by the Commission for Real Property Claims, also established under the Dayton Peace Agreement. The Commission's decisions are final and binding and they carry an obligation for the parties to fully implement them.

223 The human rights agreements listed in the Appendix are the following: the Convention on the Prevention and Punishment of the Crime of Genocide 1948; the four Geneva Conventions 1949, and the two Additional Protocols thereto 1977; the

within the jurisdiction of the Chamber, allegations of particularly severe or systematic violations, and violations founded on alleged discrimination on prohibited grounds take priority. Victims of alleged violations by the parties to the Agreement may submit their applications to the Human Rights Chamber either directly, through an NGO or a group of individuals. The Human Rights Ombudsman for Bosnia and Herzegovina may also submit applications to the Chamber on behalf of victims.

The competence of the Human Rights Chamber to award reparations is quite extensive. Under Article XI(1) on decisions, Annex 6, reparation matters are addressed within the Chamber's decisions on a given violation. In each decision, the Chamber determines:

> (a) whether the facts found indicate a breach by the Party concerned of its obligations under this Agreement; and if so
> (b) what steps shall be taken by the Party to remedy such breach, including orders to cease and desist, monetary relief (including pecuniary and non-pecuniary injuries), and provisional measures.[224]

The Chamber has the power to select the appropriate remedy to redress the violation in question. In this sense, although the Chamber's procedure is tailored to that of the European Court of Human Rights, its competence in terms of reparation extends well beyond the award of 'just satisfaction' typical

---

European Convention for the Protection of Human Rights and Fundamental Freedoms 1950, and the Protocols thereto; the Convention Relating to the Status of Refugees 1951, and the Protocol thereto 1966; the Convention on the Nationality of Married Women 1957; the Convention on the Reduction of Statelessness 1961; the International Convention on the Elimination of All Forms of Racial Discrimination 1965; the International Covenant on Civil and Political Rights 1966, and the Optional Protocols thereto 1966 and 1989; the International Covenant on Economic, Social and Cultural Rights 1966; the Convention on the Elimination of All Forms of Discrimination against Women 1979; the Convention against Torture and Other Cruel, Inhuman or Degrading Treatment or Punishment 1984; the European Convention on the Prevention of Torture and Inhuman or Degrading Treatment or Punishment 1987; the Convention on the Rights of the Child 1989; the Convention on the Protection of the Rights of All Migrant Workers and Members of Their Families 1990; the European Charter for Regional or Minority Languages 1992; and the Framework Convention for the Protection of National Minorities 1994.

224 Article XI(1). The decisions of the Chamber are final and binding and the respondent Parties are obligated to implement them fully. Chamber decisions on the merits are forwarded to the Office of the High Representative which monitors their compliance.

of the European system, which in practice limits the European Court to the award of monetary compensation. In contrast, the Chamber may award any form of redress, including adopting provisional measures for the preservation of the victims' rights and issuing specific orders aimed at the restoration of the *status quo ante*. However, in practice, the Chamber has rarely used its broad powers to award reparation other than monetary compensation. Apart from ordering the restitution of illegally taken property in a considerable number of cases, the Chamber has limited its reparation awards to compensation. Only in a few cases has it issued reparation orders of a different kind.[225] Even in instances of serious human rights violations, in only one case has the Chamber ordered the concerned party to take measures to initiate criminal proceedings against the offenders,[226] while the remainder of the reparation awards consisted of monetary compensation.[227] In relation to the compliance of the parties with the Chamber's decisions and the enforcement of reparation judgments, the trend has been uneven: certain parties have shown adequate compliance and cooperation with the Chamber, while others have shown more reluctance to enforce the Chamber's decisions, particularly where amendment of national law involves property matters.[228]

---

[225] In addition to a number of compensation and restitution awards, in the year 2000 the Chamber ordered only five alternative reparation measures: the amendment of the Federation's privatisation programme to achieve a fair balance "between the general interest and the protection of the property rights of the applicants as holders of old foreign currency savings accounts", *see Poropat and Others*, Case No. CH/97/48; that the respondent Party take all necessary steps to ensure that proceedings pending before its Courts are determined within a reasonable time *see e.g. Jankovic* v. *Republika Srpska*, Case No. CH/98/367; that all necessary steps be taken to grant the applicant a retrial in criminal proceedings, *see Damjanovic* v. *the Federation of Bosnia and Herzegovina*, Case No. CH/98/638; that a municipal ordinance for the closure of a Muslim cemetery be revoked, *see Islamic Community in BiH* v. *Republika Srpska*, Case No. CH/99/2177; and that an investigation be carried out into the conduct of police officers allegedly involved in the arrest and ill-treatment of an applicant, with a view to the initiation of criminal proceedings, *see Prulj* v. *the Federation of Bosnia and Herzegovina*, Case No. CH/98/1374. *See* the Human Rights Chamber for Bosnia and Herzegovina Annual Report 2000, *supra* note 221.

[226] *Prulj* v. *the Federation of Bosnia and Herzegovina*, *ibid.*

[227] For an insider's critique of the reparation practice of the Human Rights Chamber *see* Nowak, *supra* note 11 at 215-220.

[228] In its Annual Report for the year 2000, the Human Rights Chamber for Bosnia and Herzegovina commented on the uneven progress in the implementation of the Chamber's decisions throughout the country. In particular, the report points out persistent reluctance from the Republika Srpska to comply with the Chamber's

Generally, the Human Rights Chamber has been making a valuable contribution to the development of the right to redress for crimes under international law, particularly with regard to the restitution of unlawfully taken property. This is a fundamental element of the right to reparation and also a pillar of the victims' right to redress in the two *ad hoc* tribunals for the former Yugoslavia and for Rwanda. The work of the Human Rights Chamber to provide victims' redress assumes even greater importance given the absence of a functioning victims' reparation regime within the International Criminal Tribunal for the Former Yugoslavia.

However, the Chamber's contribution to the right to reparation for crimes under international law could be even greater if the Chamber were to take full advantage of its broad powers in the field of redress. In particular, when confronted with instances of serious human rights violations that amount to crimes under international law, the Chamber could use its broad powers to award reparation in a more progressive way, in line with emerging principles and standards in the law of redress for these kinds of violations. For example, in addition to providing compensation and restitution, the Chamber could order investigations and initiation of criminal proceedings against the offender, or the amendment of legislation contrary to basic human rights standards, in addition to providing compensation and restitution. This would not only make the Chamber a more valuable mechanism for the redress of victims of serious human rights violations who come within its jurisdiction, but it would more closely align the Chamber's practice with the general trend towards broader forms of reparation for crimes under international law.

---

decisions, especially with respect to the restitution of property. The report signals that often, when the applicants entered into repossession of their property, they found "the interiors of their apartments and houses looted and destroyed by previous occupants with the acquiescence of local authorities. This lack of protection clearly demonstrates ill will on the part of some public authorities to the return of refugees and displaced persons to their pre-war homes". On the other hand, the Chamber also noted that the Federation had improved its compliance and in many cases compensation was paid before the expiry of the time limit set by the Chamber in a particular case. *See* 'The Human Rights Chamber for Bosnia and Herzegovina Annual Report 2000', *supra* note 221. Article 13 of Annex 7 to the General Framework Agreement for Peace in Bosnia and Herzegovina also established a Refugees and Displaced Persons Property Fund, which has not yet been created because of a lack of funding. On the implementation and enforcement of the Human Rights Chamber's decisions, *see* the overview of Laura Palmer and Cristina Posa, "The Best-Laid Plans: Implementation of the Dayton Peace Accords in the Courtroom and on the Ground", *Harvard Human Rights Journal*, Vol. 12, Spring 1999 at 361-383.

5. Summing Up

Over the last five decades, the rapid development of international human rights law and jurisprudence at all levels has contributed enormously to the evolution of the right to redress for victims of serious human rights violations such as torture, forced disappearances, deportation, summary executions, mass rape and other violations, some of which may qualify as crimes under international law. Alongside the development of clear principles pertaining specifically to the right to redress for victims of the more serious human rights violations, the practice of judicial and quasi-judicial bodies in the implementation and monitoring of human rights has clarified the scope of the victims' right to redress for these kinds of violations.

A number of basic principles on redress that have originated from recent human rights theory and practice at all levels, apply to human rights violations of a serious character. Specifically:

- the duty of States to provide victims with appropriate reparation, including compensation for both material and moral damages, restitution, full rehabilitation and guarantees of non-repetition;
- the duty of States to carry out prompt and impartial official investigations into the allegations and to bring the perpetrators to justice;
- the duty of States to establish measures for the prevention of serious human rights violations; and
- the incompatibility between amnesty laws for perpetrators of serious human rights violations and the right to a remedy.

In addition, a number of subsidiary principles on victims' redress for serious human rights violations have found increasing support in human rights laws and practices, namely:

- the duty of States to amend domestic legislation that is incompatible with fundamental human rights guarantees;
- the effective access of complainants to investigatory procedures; and
- an expanded notion of 'victim', which may include also the victim's next-of-kin or immediate family, as well as 'indirect victims', namely individuals who are at risk of being directly affected by the particular matter they seek to bring before an adjudication body.

These principles and standards provide a solid framework for the implementation of the victims' right to redress in cases of crimes under international law and establish some basic minimum standards upon which further elements can be added through normative evolution and practical implementation. In this context, the ICC will be the next important test for victims of crimes under international law who wish to exercise their right to redress, both for the verification of the validity of common principles and standards and, more importantly, for the practical impact of these normative developments for individual victims themselves, as discussed in the next Chapter.

CHAPTER VI

Victims' Redress in International Criminal Law: Current Mechanisms and Future Prospects

As discussed in the previous Chapter, the growth of human rights law and implementation has contributed much to the development of principles and standards on the victims' right to effective redress for serious human rights violations. In cases of crimes under international law however, the exercise of victims' redress through human rights mechanisms suffers from certain inherent weaknesses. These derive mainly from the fact that the system of human rights implementation was never specifically designed to address crimes under international law. Could victims of these kinds of crimes have a better chance of realizing their right to redress in international mechanisms designed to deal with crimes under international law?

The idea of compensating victims of grave violations of human rights and humanitarian law through international mechanisms is not a new one. During the drafting of the 1864 Geneva Convention concerning the treatment of wounded in time of war,[1] Gustave Moynier proposed the insertion of a provision aimed at punishing certain particularly grave violations of the Convention.[2] A few years later, following the events of the 1870 Franco-

---

1 Convention for the Amelioration of the Condition of the Wounded in Armies in the Field, *signed* on 22 August 1864 in Geneva, *entered into force* on 22 June 1865.

2 Gustave Moynier (1864-1910) was one of the founders of the Red Cross and Red Crescent Movement together with Louis Appia, Théodore Maunoir, Henri Dunant and Guillaume Henri Dufour. In February 1863, the *Société Genevoise d'Utilité Publique* of Geneva selected a Committee of Five Swiss citizens to discuss and take action on the ideas proposed by Henri Dunant in his book *Un Souvenir de Solferino* (published in English with the title *A Memory of Solferino*, ICRC, Geneva, 1986). In October 1863, the Committee set up an international conference with the participation of sixteen Governments, which adopted various resolutions and principles, decided on an international emblem and appealed to all nations to form voluntary units to help wartime sick and wounded. These units eventually became the National Red Cross Societies, and the Committee of Five eventually formed the International Committee of the Red Cross, with Gustave Moynier as President. The following year, an international diplomatic conference held in Geneva adopted the Geneva Convention of 1864, which

Prussian war, Moynier also proposed the establishment of an international judicial body for the prevention and repression of breaches of the 1864 Geneva Convention, with competence to provide compensation for victims to be triggered by a request for damages from a State Party.[3] Article 7(1) of the Draft Convention reads as follows:

---

included, *inter alia*, provisions guaranteeing neutrality for medical personnel and equipment.

[3] Draft Convention for the Establishment of an International Judicial Body Suitable for the Prevention and Punishment of Violations of the Geneva Convention, by Gustave Moynier, Geneva, 1872. Moynier suggested that States should first determine the nature and scale of the penalties for violations of the Convention "in accordance with the principles of international criminal law" (Article 5, para. 2 of the Draft Convention), and then set up an "acceptable judicial organ" to punish the perpetrators. At the time, Moynier also argued against solving the question of the punishment of perpetrators of serious breaches of the Convention purely from the domestic angle, on grounds that: "...By leaving each State completely free to draft its own penal legislation independently - that is to say to determine the acts to be considered as infractions and the manner in which their authors are to be dealt with - we forfeit the principal advantage which an international law would have afforded - namely, the assurance that every ill-intentioned individual will know in advance the risk he is incurring by defying the Convention". However, sensing that States might be uncomfortable with the idea of establishing a purely international judicial organ, he also proposed a compromise solution envisaging the setting up of a 'model law' to be adopted by various Governments with the purpose of harmonizing domestic legislation on the matter. In Moynier's words: "[c]omplete uniformity could not be expected; but something approaching it might be attained". The idea of a 'model law' was eventually taken up in 1895 by the Cambridge Institute of International Law, which also adopted a proposal to establish an international convention under which every State would undertake to enact penal legislation for the repression of breaches of the Geneva Convention. *See* Jean Pictet (ed.), *Commentary to Geneva Convention I for the Amelioration of the Condition of the Wounded and Sick in Armed Forces in the Field of 12 August 1949*, Geneva, ICRC at 353-355. On the relationship between the ICC and Moynier's early proposal to set up an international adjudicating body *see* Christopher K. Hall, "The First Proposal for a Permanent International Criminal Court", *International Review of the Red Cross*, No. 322, 31 March 1998, pp.57-74. *See also* Toni Pfanner, "The Establishment of a Permanent International Criminal Court: ICRC Expectations of the Rome Diplomatic Conference", *International Review of the Red Cross*, No. 322, pp. 21-27, 31 March 1998.

> Where a complaint is accompanied by a request for damages and interest, the tribunal will have the competence to rule on this claim and to fix the amount of the compensation.[4]

Following the determination of the damages, the Draft Convention envisaged the delegation of enforcement of compensation awards and orders to the Government of the offender and proposed that: "the Government of the offender will be responsible for implementing the decision". Interestingly, Moynier insisted on the importance of having compensation paid directly from the perpetrator, and suggested that the State should only hold a subsidiary obligation to pay damages in case the perpetrator was unable to do so.[5]

Moynier's pioneering and far-sighted ideas did not find sufficient support at the time and remained dormant for more than a century and a half. While the notion of individual criminal responsibility for grave violations of human rights and humanitarian law developed over the years and gained legal specificity and support, States did not grant similar recognition to the ancillary idea of compensating victims of crimes under international law by way of an international mechanism. Neither the Nuremberg or Tokyo Charters, nor the Genocide Convention,[6] contemplate the compensation of victims. As discussed in Chapter IV, compensation matters were normally left to each State to

---

4 Article 7(1) of the Draft Convention.

5 *See* Hall, *supra* note 3, quoting G. Moynier, "Note sur la Création d'une Institution Judiciaire Internationale Propre à Prévenir et à Réprimer les Infractions à la Convention de Genève", *Bulletin International des Sociétés de Secours aux Militaires Blessés*, Comité International, No. 11, Avril 1872.

6 It is interesting that Article XIII of the initial draft of the Genocide Convention prepared by the Human Rights Division of the UN Secretariat contained an obligation for States Parties to provide reparation to victims of genocide as follows: "When genocide is committed in a country by the government in power or by a section of the population, and if the government fails to resist it successfully, the State shall grant to the survivors of the human group that is a victim of genocide redress of a nature and in an amount to be determined by the United Nations", *see* UN Doc. E/447. The principle of reparation in the initial draft was based upon the idea of collective responsibility of 'populations' for the conduct of their governments. The draft proposed that reparation be awarded in the form of compensation, restitution and special benefits both for individual victims and groups of victims. *Ibid.* at 47-49. On the *travaux préparatoires* of the Genocide Convention *see* William Schabas, *Genocide in International Law*, Cambridge University Press (2000) at 51-102, and more specifically on reparations, at 400-401, where the author indicates that the question of reparation was passed to the ILC for consideration within the context of the creation of a permanent international criminal court.

address according to its own requirements, even where the violations were clearly of international concern, such as in the case of crimes under international law. Only very recently have States begun to consider the idea that compensation matters for crimes under international law could be administered either directly at the international level or by States according to internationally defined standards. In this sense, the question of victims' compensation was considered during the process of establishing the two *ad hoc* tribunals for the former Yugoslavia and for Rwanda. In 1998, the drafters of the Rome Statute of the ICC included specific reparation provisions for victims of genocide, crimes against humanity, war crimes and eventually the crime of aggression, as discussed below.

In light of recent landmark developments in international criminal law, the present Chapter evaluates the victims' right to redress in current mechanisms of international criminal justice adjudication and identifies an imbalance between the fundamental principle of victims' redress and its practical implementation. The discussion then focusses on the innovations the Rome Statute of the ICC has introduced to this field and on the prospects it opens up for more effective redress for victims of crimes under international law.

1. The Victims' Right to Reparation in the International Criminal Tribunals for the Former Yugoslavia and for Rwanda

The Statutes of the International Criminal Tribunal for the Former Yugoslavia (ICTY) and of the International Criminal Tribunal for Rwanda (ICTR) cover the victims' right to redress for crimes under their jurisdiction through basically identical provisions. Essentially, both Statutes envisage only one form of redress directly applicable by the Tribunals' competent organs in the course of the proceedings, namely the restitution of unlawfully taken property. As we shall see, all compensation issues were delegated to national courts or other competent bodies, as may exist or be established.

a. The Tribunals' Restitution Scheme

The two Statutes contain identical provisions on restitution, respectively in Articles 24(3) and 23(3) on penalties. Once an individual has been found guilty of a crime within the jurisdiction of the Tribunals, the Trial Chamber shall "pronounce judgements and impose sentences and penalties on persons convicted of serious violations of international humanitarian law".[7] As

[7] Article 22 of the ICTY and ICTR. Both Statutes exercise competence *ratione materiae* over crimes under international law that undoubtedly form part of international customary law. *See Report of the Secretary-General pursuant to Paragraph 2 of Security Council Resolution 808 (1993)*, U.N. Doc. S/25704 and Add. 1 (3 May 1993). More specifically, Article 1 of the ICTY Statute on the 'Competence of the International Tribunal' determines that the ICTY "shall have the power to prosecute persons responsible for serious violations of international humanitarian law", namely grave breaches of the Geneva Conventions of 1949 (Article 2), violations of the laws or customs of war (Article 3), genocide (Article 4) and crimes against humanity (Article 5). The scope *ratione materiae* of the ICTR Statute presents some slight variations that adapt the Tribunal's competence to the armed conflict situation that occurred in the territory of Rwanda anytime during 1994. Under the chapeau of Article 1, which vests the ICTR with the competence to prosecute those responsible for "serious violations of international humanitarian law", the Statute determines that the Tribunal's jurisdiction shall cover genocide (Article 2), crimes against humanity (Article 3), and violations of Article 3 common to the Geneva Conventions and of Additional Protocol II (Article 4). Although virtually identical in most aspects, it is interesting to note the considerable difference in the Tribunals' definition of 'crimes against humanity', which is much narrower in the ICTY Statute than in the ICTR. In a much criticized reading of the state of the law on crimes against humanity, the drafters of the ICTY linked crimes against humanity to the existence of an armed conflict, thus openly restricting the Secretary-General's indications that crimes against humanity were "prohibited regardless of whether they are committed in an armed conflict". *See* Report of the Secretary-General, UN Doc. S/25704 of 3 May 1993, to which the ICTY Statute is annexed. As Tomuschat remarks on this point: "This divergence may only be explained as an implication of the general mandate of the Tribunal, which is to prosecute persons responsible for serious violations of international humanitarian law. Thus, the Security Council shows its acute awareness of the need to remain within the bounds of the function assigned to it, namely to maintain international peace and security". *See* Christian Tomuschat, "A System of International Criminal Prosecution is Taking Shape", *The ICJ Review*, Vol. 50, June 1993, at 64. In 1995, the ICTY Appeals Chamber in the Dusko Tadic Trial clarified the matter by ruling that: "It is by now a settled rule of customary international law that crimes against humanity do not require a connection to international armed conflict. Indeed, [...] customary international law may not require a connection between crimes against humanity and any conflict at all". *Prosecutor* v. *Dusko Tadic*, Decision of the Appeals Chamber on the Defense Motion of the Interlocutory Appeal concerning Jurisdiction, Case No. IT-94-1-D of 2 October 1995 at 73. As we shall see, the drafters of the Rome Statute of the International Criminal Court followed the same approach and did not require any link between the commission of a crime against humanity and the existence of an armed conflict whether of international or internal character.

regards penalties, Articles 24(1) and 23(1) of the ICTY and ICTR Statutes respectively establish that:

> In addition to imprisonment, the Trial Chambers may order the return of any property and proceeds acquired by criminal conduct, including by means of duress, to their rightful owners.

The principle of restitution has been further developed in the Rules of Procedure and Evidence of the two Tribunals.[8] Rule 98 *ter* (B) (Judgement) of Section 3 of the ICTY on 'rules of evidence' and Rule 88 (B) (Judgement) of the ICTR on 'case presentation' which, at the time of writing had not been applied, provide that:

> If the Trial Chamber finds the accused guilty of a crime and concludes from the evidence that unlawful taking of property by the accused was associated with it, it shall make a specific finding to that effect in its judgement. The Trial Chamber may order restitution as provided in Rule 105.

For the Trial Chamber to order restitution, the unlawful taking of property must be associated with a crime under the Statute and it must be the object of a specific finding in the judgment of the Trial Chamber.[9] Once these conditions are fulfilled, common Rule 105 of Section 5 on Sentencing and Penalties establishes a detailed procedure for the restitution of unlawfully taken property.[10] As common Rule 105 indicates, the Trial Chamber has ample

---

8 ICTY Rules of Procedure and Evidence, IT/32/REV.17, as amended on 17 November 1999; and ICTR Rules of Procedure and Evidence, *adopted* on 29 June 1995, as amended on 12 January 1996, 15 May 1996, 4 July 1996, 5 June 1997 and 8 June 1998.

9 On this point *see* Susanne Malmström, "Restitution of Property and Compensation to Victims", in R. May et al. (eds.), *Essays on ICTY Procedure and Evidence*, Kluwer Law International (2001) at 375, indicating that the requirement of 'association' with a crime within the jurisdiction of the Statute may be difficult to determine in such cases because of the complexity and seriousness of the crimes in question.

10 Rule 105 of the ICTY and ICTR Rules of Procedure and Evidence, as amended on 30 November 1999, IT/32/Rev. 17, provides as follows:
(a) After a judgement of conviction containing a specific finding as provided in Sub-rule 98 *ter* (b), the Trial Chamber shall, at the request of the Prosecutor, or may, *proprio motu*, hold a special hearing to determine the matter of the restitution of the property or the proceeds thereof, and may in the meantime order such provisional measures for the

power to order the restitution of property to victims where such property was unlawfully taken in connection with a crime under the Statute for which a person has been found guilty.[11] In fact, it is an exclusive prerogative of the Trial Chamber, acting either *proprio motu* or at the request of the Prosecutor, to hold a special hearing for the determination of restitution matters. In this sense, victims cannot institute civil claims directly within the criminal proceedings. With the introduction of a rather innovative procedure, the Trial Chamber is entitled to make a determination for restitution purposes not only with respect to the perpetrator's property or proceeds, but also with respect to property or proceeds in the hands of third parties not necessarily connected with the crime in question.[12] In the course of the restitution proceedings, the

---

preservation and protection of the property or proceeds as it considers appropriate.
(b) The determination may extend to such property or its proceeds, even in the hands of third parties not otherwise connected with the crime of which the convicted person has been found guilty.
(c) Such third parties shall be summoned before the Trial Chamber and be given an opportunity to justify their claim to the property or its proceeds.
(d) Should the Trial Chamber be able to determine the rightful owner on the balance of probabilities, it shall order the restitution either of the property or the proceeds or make such other order as it may deem appropriate.
(e) Should the Trial Chamber not be able to determine ownership, it shall notify the competent national authorities and request them so to determine.
(f) Upon notice from the national authorities that an affirmative determination has been made, the Trial Chamber shall order the restitution either of the property or the proceeds or make such other order as it may deem appropriate.
(g) The Registrar shall transmit to the competent national authorities any summonses, orders and requests issued by a Trial Chamber pursuant to Sub-rules (c), (d), (e) and (f).

11 Rules 98 *ter* (ICTY) and 88 (ICTR).

12 Although Sub-Rule 105(c) provides that third parties shall be summoned before the Chamber and shall be allowed to justify their claims with respect to property and proceeds affected by a restitution order, Rule 105 can still affect the rights of *bona fide* third parties, especially considering that neither of the Tribunals has an appeal procedure for third parties against restitution orders by the Trial Chamber. During the drafting of the ICC, this procedural gap was filled by Article 82(4) of the ICC Rules of Procedure and Evidence, providing for the right to appeal against an order for reparations for a "legal representative of the victims, the convicted person or a *bona fide* owner of property adversely affected by an order under article 75".

Trial Chamber can also order provisional measures "for the preservation and protection of the property or proceeds".[13]

Where the Trial Chamber is able to determine the rightful owner of the property or proceeds, Rule 105(D) authorizes it to make an order for restitution or other orders as may be appropriate.[14] Of course, this would require the competent organs - particularly the prosecution - to undertake a sufficient level of investigation during the trial stages. Where the Trial Chamber does not have sufficient information to determine the rightful owner of the property or proceeds, the request for the determination of the rightful owner must be transmitted to the 'competent national authorities' pursuant to Rule 105(E), at which point the Trial Chamber must wait for a determination to be made before it can order the restitution of property or proceeds. Considering that the domestic authorities competent for the restitution of the property might be unable or unwilling to initiate restitution procedures, the simplest, most direct way for victims to obtain restitution of unlawfully taken property seems to be through a Trial Chamber's order upon determination of the rightful owner by the Chamber itself.

b. The Tribunals' Indirect Approach to Compensation

While the Judges of the two Tribunals are vested with the independence and authority to issue restitution awards, common Rule 106, entitled 'Compensation to Victims', defers all actions for compensation to the competence of 'national courts' or 'other competent bodies', pursuant to the relevant national legislation.[15] Common Rule 106, which to date has not been applied, reads as follows:

---

[13] Rule 61(D) on 'Procedure in Case of Failure to Execute a Warrant' authorizes the Trial Chamber to "order a State or States to adopt provisional measures to freeze the assets of the accused, without prejudice to the rights of third parties" either upon request of the Prosecutor or *proprio motu* after having heard the Prosecutor.

[14] As Jones notes, the formula of Rule 105(D) and (F) "or make such other order as it may deem appropriate" was introduced in 1995 to allow the Chamber to award compensation orders in favour of third parties in case an order for restitution would be inappropriate or would not render justice to such third party. *See* John R.W.D. Jones, *The Practice of the International Criminal Tribunals for the Former Yugoslavia and Rwanda*, Second Ed., Transnational Publishers at 444-445.

[15] Para. (B) of Rule 106 of the ICTR Rules of Procedure and Evidence is slightly different from the ICTY provision. It reads as follows: "Pursuant to the relevant national legislation, a victim or persons claiming through *him* [italic added] may bring an action in a national court or other competent body to obtain compensation".

> (A) The Registrar shall transmit to the competent authorities of the States concerned the judgement finding the accused guilty of a crime which has caused injury to a victim.
> (B) Pursuant to the relevant national legislation, a victim or persons claiming through the victim may bring an action in a national court or other competent body to obtain compensation.
> (C) For the purposes of a claim made under Sub-rule (B) the judgement of the Tribunal shall be final and binding as to the criminal responsibility of the convicted person for such injury.

In resolution 827 (1993) of 25 May 1993 establishing the ICTY, the UN Security Council stated that:

> the work of the International Tribunal shall be carried out without prejudice to the right of the victims to seek, through appropriate means, compensation for damages incurred as a result of violations of international humanitarian law.

In the drafting stage of the Rules of Procedure and Evidence, States opted for an indirect approach to compensation, perhaps fearing that the Tribunals would not be able to handle a potentially very high number of compensation claims. As a result, neither the ICTY nor the ICTR provide for any direct mechanism for the monetary compensation of victims of crimes within their respective spheres of jurisdiction. Significantly, when confronted with the question as to how to improve the victims' compensation regime of the ICTY, the Tribunal's Rules Committee excluded any direct competence or responsibility of the Tribunal with respect to compensation procedures. In support of its argument, the Rules Committee cited resolution 827 which states that the Security Council created the Tribunal for the "sole purpose of prosecuting persons for serious violations of international humanitarian law".[16] Similarly, as we shall

---

[16] *See Victims' Compensation and Participation*, a report prepared by the Rules Committee in which the Committee reviewed the question of victims' compensation and participation to ICTY proceedings and recommended practical procedures to compensate victims, Appendix to a Letter dated 12 October 2000 from the President of the ICTY addressed to the Secretary-General, Annex to UN Doc. S/2000/1063 of 3 November 2000. It the Report, the Committee indicated that the ICTY Rules of Procedure and Evidence had not been drafted to implement the victims' right to compensation. To support this argument, the Report cites Morris and Scharf arguing that the Security Council excluded the possibility of the Tribunal hearing victims' claims for compensation. *See* Virginia Morris and Michael Scharf, *An Insiders Guide to the International Criminal Tribunal for the Former Yugoslavia* (1995) at 167, 286-

discuss, the Judges also dismissed the possibility of creating 'appropriate means' for compensation within the Tribunals.

As such, Rule 106, deferring all compensation matters to domestic courts, appears very difficult to implement given the specific nature of the crimes under consideration and, in particular, considering the potential difficulties victims of these violations typically experience in attempting to access domestic courts within their own countries.[17] Also, the deferral of compensation matters to domestic courts entails a strong risk of unfairness and discrimination among victims of the crimes under the jurisdiction of the Statutes with respect to the enjoyment of their right to redress. Under the current system, a person whose house, property, or art collection, to take some examples, has been unlawfully taken in connection with one of the crimes under the jurisdiction of the Statute, is entitled to the restitution of these properties through the procedure set up by the Statutes. However, a victim of torture or rape, or a survivor of genocide, is not entitled to receive direct compensation from the Tribunal and, considering the difficulties victims encounter in accessing domestic remedies, it is likely that many victims of such crimes will never obtain redress for the damage suffered. Similarly, victims of the same crime under the Statutes may obtain uneven results in seeking compensation through domestic mechanisms because of the variations among domestic law and practice.

c. Implementing ICTY and ICTR Redress Provisions: The Denial of a Right or Simply Too Difficult a Task?

As discussed, both the ICTY and the ICTR Statutes include a number of detailed provisions for the restitution of property and provide for an indirect mechanism for the compensation of victims of crimes under their jurisdiction. Of the final judgments rendered to date at the ICTY and ICTR however, none has issued a single restitution order or deferred compensation matters to domestic courts. The denial of the victims' right to redress in the ICTY is so

---

287.

[17] Although common Rule 106(A) requests the Registrar to transmit the relevant judgment "to the competent authorities of the States concerned" - thus implying that the States concerned might be more than one - compensation claims are normally processed by the State of the *locus delictum*, which is likely to be also the State of nationality of the victims. Given the nature of the crimes, this places victims in a very difficult position, because their State of nationality may be unable or unwilling to guarantee victims fair access to justice.

evident that it is difficult to ignore or justify: eight years of operation; a regular annual budget of almost US$100 million; 1,188 staff members from 77 countries; 23 accused tried; six accused sentenced; 12 accused at appeal; and not a single case of restitution to victims or deferral of a case to national courts for compensation.[18] The situation is no better in the ICTR: a regular budget of US$80 million; 810 staff members of more than 80 nationalities, and a Victim and Witnesses Unit in operation could not activate a single restitution or compensation claim.

On a number of occasions, Carla del Ponte, Prosecutor of the ICTY and ICTR, tried to stimulate action on the issue of victims' compensation. In an interview of 9 June 2000 on the situation of victims in the ICTR, del Ponte expressed concern for the structural lack of procedures providing for victims' participation in the Tribunals' proceedings:

> the fact that [victims] are not represented in this trial troubles me a lot. I feel that something is missing. Of course, the Prosecutor's role is to get defendants convicted, and that is his or her chief task. In the current system, there is little time and space left to plea in the favour of victims. I think we should take the lead from civil law here, where there is a complainant and a lawyer who represents him or her. ... A system of criminal law that does not take into account the victims of crimes is fundamentally lacking.[19]

---

[18] Figures from 'Fact Sheet on ICTY Proceedings', http://www.un.org/icty/glance/procfact-e.htm. However, the two tribunals considered the issue of property restitution in at least two cases, with no results in terms of actual restitution. In the *Aleksovski Case* the Trial Chamber determined that the accused, in his capacity as prison warden, had unlawfully stolen various objects and belongings from the victims during body-searches of detainees. Nonetheless, the issue of restitution was dropped on appeal. *See Prosecutor* v. *Aleksovski*, Judgment, Case No. IT-95-14/1/T of 25 June 1999 at para. 87. In *Prosecutor* v. *Théoneste Bagosora*, Case No. ICTR-96-7, the Rwandan Government requested to appear as *amicus curiae* and asked the Tribunal to order the restitution of property and proceeds illegally taken by the accused. *See* Malmström, *supra* note 9 at 377. The decision on this matter was pending at the time of writing.

[19] *Compensating Victims with Guilty Money*, interview with Carla del Ponte, Chief Prosecutor of the two international tribunals, in *Judicial Diplomacy: Chronicles and Reports on International Criminal Justice*, The Hague, 9 June 2000, http://www.diplomatiejudiciaire.com. In the same interview, the Prosecutor also argued in favour of providing victims with compensation directly from the defendant's frozen assets in case of a conviction.

Unfortunately, there does not appear to be a solution to the lack of proper victims' representation in the Tribunals since, in contrast to the ICC, neither of the Tribunals were created to allow victims to participate in the proceedings, either directly or through a legal representative.

Nevertheless, the Prosecutor's call for a more efficient system of victims' compensation, as expressed in the passage cited below, assumes a completely different significance in light of the fact that both the Statutes and Rules of Procedure and Evidence contain specific provisions for the direct restitution of illegally taken property and for the compensation of victims through deferral to national judicial systems. Undeniably, some gaps remain in the Rules of Procedure in relation to the eventual restitution of property, for example as regards access to frozen or confiscated funds or the eventual distribution of such funds after conviction. However, these gaps could quite easily be addressed if there were the political will to implement restitution and compensation procedures as provided for in the Statutes. In this sense, it is difficult not to agree with the Prosecutor's invitation to the Security Council to consider ways to better implement the reparation and compensation procedures already included in the ICTY and ICTR Statutes. The Prosecutor argued as follows:

> It is regrettable that the Tribunal's statute makes no provision for victim participation during the trial, and makes only a minimum of provision for compensation and restitution to people whose lives have been destroyed. And yet my office is having considerable success in tracing and freezing large amounts of money in the personal accounts of the accused.[20] Money that could very properly be applied by the courts to the compensation of the citizens who deserve it. We should therefore give victims the right to express themselves, and allow their voice to be heard during the proceedings. In the event of a conviction, that would then create a legal basis for the Judges to decide upon the confiscation of monies sequestrated from the accused. The money might also go towards defraying the costs of the prosecution. I would therefore respectfully suggest to the Council that the present system falls short of delivering justice to the people of Rwanda and the former Yugoslavia, and I would invite you to give serious and

---

[20] On 18 September 2001, the Government of Greece responded to the Prosecutor's request to probe Mr. Slobodan Milosevic's financial accounts [author's footnote].

> urgent consideration to any change that would remove this lacuna in our process.[21]

Despite the strong words of the Prosecutor, the position of the Judges of both Tribunals concerning possible amendments to the current regime of victims' redress seems to have remained negative. To date, neither the ICTY nor the ICTR have indicated their readiness to improve victims' access to redress.

i. The Response of the ICTY to the Question of Victims' Redress

On the initiative of the Office of the Prosecutor, in September 2000, the Judges of the ICTY acknowledged the right of victims of crimes committed in the former Yugoslavia to seek compensation.[22] At the same time, they also approved the Rules Committee's report reviewing the question of victims' compensation and participation in ICTY proceedings, which concluded that:

> victims of crimes within the Tribunal's jurisdiction have a legal right to seek compensation for their injuries' and suggested that 'methods of compensating victims of crimes in the former Yugoslavia, ... be considered by the appropriate organs of the United Nations.[23]

Soon after, in a letter dated 12 October 2000 from the President of the ICTY to the UN Secretary-General,[24] the Judges of the ICTY expressed their opinion on the question of victims' compensation and commented on how the ICTY should deal with the issue. On that occasion, the Judges argued strongly against any amendment of the Statute creating direct compensation mechanisms for victims, similar to those envisaged by the Rome Statute of the ICC, but at least they did not question the existence of a right to compensation for victims under international law. To the contrary, the letter cites the Rules Committee's report on 'Victims' Compensation and Participation' as it "takes note of a

---

21 Address to the UN Security Council by Carla del Ponte, Prosecutor of the International Criminal Tribunals for the former Yugoslavia and Rwanda, 21 November 2000. ICTY Doc. JL/P.I.S./542-e of 24 November 2000.

22 ICTY Press Release of 14 September 2000, JL/P.I.S./528-e.

23 *Victims' Compensation and Participation*, *supra* note 16 at paras. 46 and 48.

24 Letter dated 12 October 2000 from the President of the International Tribunal for the Former Yugoslavia addressed to the Secretary-General, annex to a Letter dated 2 November 2000 from the Secretary-General addressed to the President of the Security Council, UN doc. S/2000/1063 of 3 November 2000.

general trend towards recognizing a right to compensation in international law" and concludes that "the victims of the crimes over which the Tribunal has jurisdiction are entitled to benefit from a right to compensation".[25] Instead, the Judges expressed a negative view on the incorporation of compensation procedures in the proceedings of the Tribunals, based on the argument that the additional workload resulting from such a move would have a "significant impact on the conduct of the proceedings and the length of the trials", and that the implementation of a new system "would counter all the efforts of the last few years to minimize the length of preventive detention, which is a fundamental right of the accused, by shortening trials".[26] The Judges cite the Report on a number of other practical questions running against the creation of direct mechanisms for victims' compensation. These include financial matters such as where to obtain the funds for compensation, given the fact that, in the words of the report: "the accused do not have any resources"; the lack of procedures for victims' participation in the proceedings; the fact that such procedures have never been applied in practice at the international level; and again the negative consequences for the accused's right to an expeditious trial due to an inevitable lengthening of proceedings and an increase in the workload of the Chambers. This last point in particular was perhaps the one which weighed most heavily on the Judges as they decided to oppose the establishment of direct victims' compensation mechanisms[27] - almost leaving the impression that the rights of the victims and of the accused are somehow incompatible and that, ultimately, the victims' right to compensation under the ICTY had been traded off in favour of the accused's right to a fair and expeditious trial.[28]

---

25 *Victims' Compensation and Participation*, *supra* note 16. More explicitly, the Report states that "there is a clear trend in international law to recognize a right of compensation in the victim to recover from the individual who caused his or her injury". The Report goes on to say that: "there does appear to be a right to compensation for victims under international law. Although there is an emerging right of compensation, the law is much less developed on the mechanism by which that right can be exercised".

26 *Ibid.* at para. 32.

27 *Ibid.* at paras. 33 to 36.

28 The right of the accused to a fair and expeditious trial is a fundamental human right embodied in Articles 9(3), 9(4), 14(1) and 14(3)(c) of the ICCPR. However, it must be recalled that Articles 2(3)(a), 2(3)(b) and 2(3)(c) of the ICCPR also protect the victims' right to an effective remedy. To ensure speedy proceedings while preserving the victims' right to participation and redress, the Rome Statute grants the Chamber the power to ask groups of victims of the same crime to choose a common legal representative. This avoids multiple claims, which inevitably lengthen the proceedings, and preserves the accused's right to a fair and expeditious trial as well as the possibility

Consequently, the ICTY Judges unanimously took up the Rules Committee's suggestion to set up a mechanism "modelled on that of an international compensation commission" and turned the question over to the Security Council and other competent UN organs to find appropriate solutions.[29]

ii. *The Response of the ICTR to the Question of Victims' Redress*

The President of the ICTR, Judge Navanethem Pillay, addressed the issue of compensation for victims in a comprehensive letter of 9 November 2000 to the UN Secretary-General,[30] where she declared that:

> the judges wholeheartedly empathize with the principle of compensation for victims, but ... believe that the responsibility for processing and assessing claims for such compensation should not rest with the Tribunal.

In line with the view of the ICTY Judges, the ICTR Judges also rejected any proposals to amend the Statute with a view to providing direct compensation to victims, by arguing that any such proposal: "would not be efficacious, would severely hamper the everyday work of the Tribunal and would be highly destructive to the principal mandate of the Tribunal".[31] Judge Pillay 'liquidated' the issue by declaring that:

> the calendar of the Tribunal is full for the foreseeable future. All three Trial Chambers are fully committed and will remain so for the life of the Tribunal. ... If the Tribunal adds to its responsibilities a whole new area of law relating to compensation, then the Tribunal will not only have to develop a new jurisprudence; it will also have

---

for victims to be represented in the proceedings for reparation purposes.

29 On this point, the report states that to give effect to the right of victims of crimes in the former Yugoslavia to compensation "a far better approach would be for an international claims commission to be established" and suggests the establishment of such a body be considered by the appropriate organs of the UN. *See Victims' Compensation and Participation*, *supra* note 16 at para. 48.

30 Letter of the President of the ICTR to the UN Secretary-General, annex to a letter of 14 December 2000 by the UN Secretary-General, Kofi Annan, to the UN Security Council, UN Doc. S/2000/1198 of 15 December 2000.

31 The Judges refer to a possible amendment of the Statute reflecting Article 75 of the ICC Statute on reparations. *Ibid.*

> to expand its staffing considerably and establish new rules and procedures for assessing claims.[32]

The letter further explains that some of the reasons why compensation claims should not be handled directly by the Tribunal involve the fact that:

> victim satisfaction with compensation programmes appears to be quite low. Victims usually express considerable frustration with the complexity of compensation documentation procedures. It seems likely that if the Tribunal embarks upon the processing of claims for compensation, then, in addition to any dissatisfaction with its present progress, it can expect to add to this the frustration and disappointment of those attempting to establish claims.[33]

As the ICTR Judges have argued, compensation procedures are often complex and time consuming for the victims. Yet, one wonders whether victims and survivors of genocide, torture, rape and other serious human rights violations in Rwanda would prefer more the Judges' "wholehearted empathy with the principle of compensation for victims", or whether they would be willing to put up with a measure of "disappointment and frustration" in connection with claim procedures. To solve the question, the ICTR Judges suggested that "there are other, quicker and simpler methods which will ensure that the victims of criminal acts in Rwanda receive just compensation".[34] The Judges proposed the following options:

---

[32] *Ibid.* Here the Judges also seem to have rejected a previous proposal by the Prosecutor, suggesting that there was no need to make recourse to the Security Council to change the compensation provisions of the Statutes, since the Statutes themselves grant the Judges the power to rule "on sentences and sanctions". On this basis, the Prosecutor argued that the Judges could confiscate the defendant's assets to compensate victims as a part of a 'sanction'. *See Compensating Victims with Guilty Money*, *supra* note 19.

[33] Letter of the President of the ICTR to the UN Secretary-General, *supra* note 30. To support their argument, the Judges inserted a footnote to the letter, quoting R. Elias, *The Politics of Victimization: Victims, Victimology and Human Rights* (1986) at 162, 212 and 238, in an attempt to acknowledge the frustration of victims in accessing compensation.

[34] Letter of the President of the ICTR to the UN Secretary-General, *supra* note 30.

a. a specialized agency set up by the United Nations to administer a compensation scheme or trust fund that can be based upon individual application, or community need or some group-based qualification;
b. a scheme administered by some other agency or governmental entity on similar lines to (a);
c. an arrangement which could operate in tandem with options (a) and (b) and which would allow the Tribunal to exercise a limited power to order payments from a trust fund for victims actually appearing before it as witnesses in a case.[35]

However, the proposals of the Judges seem to lack detail and specificity and appear difficult to implement in the short to medium term. In addition, proposal (c) seems openly unfair and would discriminate against victims who do not have a witness role in particular proceedings.[36]

d. What Role for the Victims Aside From Being Witnesses?

The limited attention of the Tribunals to victims is reflected in the approach both Statutes take to victims who are not involved directly in the tribunals' proceedings as witnesses. Based upon Articles 15 and 14 of the ICTY and ICTR Statutes respectively,[37] as well as common Article 22,[38] Rule 34 sets up a Victim and Witnesses Section under the authority of the Registrar to recommend protective measures for victims and witnesses and to provide counselling and support for them, particularly in cases of rape or sexual assault.

---

35 *Ibid.*

36 In its Report, the Rules Committee concluded that limiting direct compensation claims to victims who actually testify would be 'clearly unfair'. *See Victims' Compensation and Participation*, *supra* note 16 at para. 27.

37 Articles 15 and 14 set out a general obligation for the Judges to adopt Rules of Procedure and Evidence on, *inter alia*, the protection of victims and witnesses and other appropriate matters.

38 Article 22 on 'Protection of victims and witnesses', assigns the Tribunals with the task of elaborating Rules of Procedure and Evidence for the protection of victims and witnesses, including for the conduct of *in camera* proceedings and the protection of the victim's identity. In a different context, Article 20 states that, in the trial proceedings, the Trial Chambers shall ensure "full respect for the rights of the accused and due regard for the protection of victims and witnesses" (Article 20). On witness protection *see* Yvonne O. M. Featherstone, "The International Criminal Tribunal for the Former Yugoslavia: Recent Developments in Witness Protection", *Leiden Journal of International Law*, Vol. 10, No. 1 (1997).

During consultations for the setting up of the Victim and Witnesses Section, some experts had advanced the idea of placing the Section under the authority of the Prosecutor, rather than of the Registrar. Finally, however, the view that the Victim and Witnesses Section should do more than provide assistance to prosecution witnesses prevailed and the Section was therefore placed under the more 'neutral' wing of the Registry. It was considered that this approach could provide the Section with more flexibility to extend its protection to both witnesses and to victims in general.[39] However, despite its broad competence, so far the Victim and Witnesses Section of the ICTY has provided practical assistance and protection only to witnesses, mainly to further the prosecutorial effort, rather than to assist victims *per se*, for example as regards restitution claims. While the jurisprudence of the ICTY and ICTR on witness protection is abundant, there are no cases mentioning victims beyond their role as witnesses.[40] Similarly, witnesses have been the only recipients of protection under Rule 69 on 'Protection of Victims and Witnesses' and Rule 75 on 'Measures for the Protection of Victims and Witnesses' which concentrate on

---

[39] *See The Victims and Witnesses Unit (Article 43.6 of the Rome Statute): A Discussion Paper*, by Thordis Ingadottir, F. Ngendahayo and P. V. Sellers, PICT, March 2000 at 11.

[40] One can mention, *inter alia*, the *Prosecutor* v. *Dusko Tadic,* Decision on the Prosecutor's Motion Requesting Protective Measures for Victims and Witnesses, rendered with a majority vote on 10 August 1995, in which the Judges of Trial Chamber II enumerated a number of measures to fulfill the obligation of Article 22 on protection of victims and witnesses, all of which mainly target witnesses protection. Specifically, these are: "the submission of evidence by way of deposition, i.e., testimony given by a witness who is unable or unwilling to testify in open court (Rule 71)"; the setting up of arrangements not to disclose the identity of witnesses who may be at risk for a certain period of time (Rule 69); the taking of "appropriate measures for the privacy and protection of victims and witnesses" (Rule 75); and particular provisions drafted to cover cases of sexual assault. In *Prosecutor* v. *Tadic,* Decision on the Prosecutor's Motion Requesting Protective Measures for Witness L., rendered on 14 November 1995, Trial Chamber II raised issues concerning the applicability of protective measures to a witness with a criminal record. Also, Trial Chamber I ruled extensively on the question of witnesses' anonymity in *Delalic et al.*, Decision on the Defence Motion to Compel the Discovery of Identity and Location of Witnesses, decision rendered on 18 March 1997. The same issue was raised in *Blaskic*, Decision on the Application of the Prosecutor, requesting Protective Measures for Victims and Witnesses, decision rendered on 5 November 1996. As for the ICTR, *see, inter alia, Prosecutor* v. *Jean-Paul Akayesu*, Decision on the Preliminary Motion Submitted by the Prosecutor for Protective Measures for Witnesses, 27 September 1996, Trial Chamber I, Case No. ICTR-96-4-T.

protective measures specifically applicable to witnesses, such as the "non-disclosure of the identity of a victim or witness who may be in danger or at risk until such person is brought under the protection of the Tribunal" (Rule 69(A)).[41]

e. Enjoying the Right to Redress in the ICTY and ICTR: A Lost Cause for Victims?

As the ICTY and ICTR Judges have argued, the *ad hoc* tribunals were created along retributivist lines and, as such, their activities should remain focussed on the prosecution and punishment of the perpetrator rather than on the compensation or rehabilitation of the victim. It is also true that, since they became operational, both Tribunals have had to face an increasingly heavy workload. Arguably, the Tribunals have had little time to go beyond strictly necessary tasks such as the prosecution and punishment of the accused. Be that as it may, both Tribunals clearly have failed in their task of implementing statutory provisions granting victims some form of redress. As discussed above, there have not been any restitution awards made by either Tribunal nor a single deferral to domestic courts to order compensation. Since it is the exclusive prerogative of the Tribunals' designated organs, and not of individual victims, to trigger restitution and compensation mechanisms under the Statutes, it is certainly regrettable that a better solution could not have been found.

What can reasonably be expected is perhaps the full implementation of the reparation and compensation procedures already established by the Statutes for the enjoyment of the victims' basic right to redress, despite all the faults these procedures may have, rather than the establishment of completely new compensation schemes. Somehow, the debate over possible amendments to the Statutes aimed at direct victims' compensation has given rise to the notion that victims' reparations within the Tribunals is simply too difficult to implement and is therefore practically unfeasible. As a result, the discussions on victims' redress in the ICTY and ICTR seem to have reached an impasse and the redress mechanisms in each Statute seem unlikely to be implemented in practice.

---

[41] Other measures include expunging names and identifying information from the Tribunal's public records; the non-disclosure to the public of any records identifying the victim; the giving of testimony through image or voice-altering devices or closed circuit television; the assignment of a pseudonym; closed trial sessions; and the adoption of appropriate measures to facilitate the testimony of vulnerable victims and witnesses, such as one-way closed circuit television.

2. The Role of Victims and Their Right to Redress in the International Criminal Court

On 17 July 1998, after five weeks of intense negotiations in Rome, Italy, the UN Diplomatic Conference of Plenipotentiaries adopted the Statute of the International Criminal Court.[42] Under the ICC Statute - a milestone in international criminal law - individuals shall be held responsible for crimes under international law, in particular, genocide, crimes against humanity, war crimes, and eventually the crime of aggression,[43] irrespective of their rank or

---

42 Following the adoption of the Rome Statute creating the ICC, many authors have clarified difficult issues relating to the ICC. Among the most useful sources, *see* Roy S. Lee (ed.), *The International Criminal Court: The Making of the Rome Statute, Issues, Negotiations, Results*, Kluwer Law International (1999); Kai Ambos, "General Principles of Criminal Law in the Rome Statute", *Criminal Law Forum,* No. 10 (1999); Lyal S. Sunga, "The Crimes within the Jurisdiction of the International Criminal Court (Part II, Articles 5-10)", *European Journal of Crime, Criminal Law and Criminal Justice*, Vol. 6/4 (1998); Mahnoush H. Arsanjani, "Developments in International Criminal Law: the Rome Statute of the International Criminal Court", *The American Journal International Law*, Vol. 93, No. 22, January 1999; Roger S. Clark, "Creating a Statute for the International Criminal Court: A Jurisdictional Quandary", *Suffolk Transnational Law Review,* Vol. 22, No. 461, Summer 1999; Philippe Kirsch and John T. Holmes, "Developments in International Criminal Law: the Rome Conference on An International Criminal Court: The Negotiating Process", *The American Journal International Law,* Vol. 93, No. 2, January 1999; and Timothy L. H. McCormack and Sue Robertson, "Jurisdictional Aspects of the Rome Statute for the New International Criminal Court", *Melbourne University Law Review,* Vol. 23, No. 635, December 1999.

43 As concerns the jurisdiction of the Court over the crime of aggression, Article 5(2) of the ICC Statute establishes that the Court shall exercise jurisdiction only "once a provision is adopted in accordance with Articles 121 and 123 defining the crime and setting out the conditions under which the Court shall exercise jurisdiction with respect to this crime". In Rome, States could not reach a precise definition of aggression and of its elements. Nor could they reach agreement on the procedures to follow should a crime of aggression be committed. Therefore, all discussions on these and other questions were postponed for later consideration by a Review Conference on the definition, elements and conditions under which the Court shall exercise jurisdiction with respect to aggression. Through this amendment process, States Parties can make statutory changes which will become operative seven years after the Statute enters into force. At this stage, a Working Group on Aggression has been compiling various proposals submitted by States, with the aim of sorting out the main issues and identifying areas of agreement and differences. Several States have contributed proposals on the crime of aggression, including Bahrain, Iraq, Lebanon, Libya, Oman,

official capacity. The ICC Statute not only provides for substantive norms on individual criminal responsibility for breaches of the Statute's obligations, but also requires the Court to establish rules of procedure and evidence. With the entry into force of the Rome Statute, issues such as victims reparations which have been usually consigned to domestic implementation, will find for the first time full expression at the international level.

As the Preamble to the Rome Statute indicates, one of the main reasons for the establishment of the ICC is the fact that "during this century millions of children, women and men have been victims of unimaginable atrocities that deeply shock the conscience of humanity". However, the path from the Preamble's general concern for victims of past and future atrocities to the drafting of concrete norms offering victims a place at different stages of the proceedings as well as the possibility of receiving some form of reparation for the damages suffered, was a long and difficult one.[44] A large number of very active NGOs, organized under the umbrella of the 'NGO Coalition for the ICC' (CICC), embraced the question of victims' rights and worked side-by-side with Government delegations and independent experts to make sure that the ICC would afford victims the best possible standards in terms of protection, participation and redress.[45] The role of NGOs proved critical in the negotiation and drafting process of victims' provisions in the ICC Statute. Indeed, Article 75 of the Rome Statute on reparations is only one example of fruitful cooperation between State delegations (in this case mainly France and the United Kingdom) and concerned NGOs, including Redress, Amnesty International, Juristes sans Frontières, the Women's Caucus for Gender Justice, Human Rights Watch and No Peace Without Justice, among others.

Although delegations seemed generally in favour of the idea of having some form of victims' reparation in the ICC Statute, there was a great deal of concern over the practical consequences of recognizing a specific right of

---

Sudan, Syria and Yemen. There have also been separate proposals by Russia and Germany as well as a Joint Proposal submitted by Greece and Portugal. In March 2000, Colombia also made a proposal and suggestions were made orally by Italy.

44 For an analysis of the events leading to the final drafting of victims' reparation provisions in Rome *see* Christopher Muttukumaru, "Reparation to Victims", in Lee (ed.), *supra* note 42 pp. 262-270.

45 Under the guidance of William Pace, the NGO Coalition for an International Criminal Court - a coalition composed of some one thousand member organizations - managed to accredit over 200 institutions with 450 representatives to the Rome Diplomatic Conference. For an account of the role of NGOs in the Rome negotiations, *see* William Pace and Mark Thieroff, "Participation of Non-Governmental Organizations", in Lee (ed.), *supra* note 42 pp. 391-398.

victims to seek and obtain redress. In particular, delegations referred to the risks such provisions might entail in terms of implementation, especially in relation to possible financial and legal implications for the State should the individual not be able to pay compensation, as well as to potential difficulties in the determination of damages and reparations. Also, the process was slowed down by the fact that many delegations were not familiar with the *partie civile* system typical of civil law countries that was put forward in Rome as a general framework for victims' participation and reparations. More generally, delegations and NGOs lobbying for a more restorative approach to justice in the ICC had to swim against the traditional retributive current running through criminal law. Some delegations felt that the prosecution and punishment of the offender would perhaps provide victims with sufficient redress in themselves so as to render other forms of reparation unnecessary.

In the end however, the drafters of the ICC came to the realization that an International Criminal Court with competence over some of the most heinous violations of fundamental rights and freedoms could be more meaningful and fair if some basic provisions on victims' redress were included. As a result of this more comprehensive approach to justice, the ICC Statute embodies the principle of direct participation of victims and their families in the proceedings; establishes the right of victims to obtain reparations; and creates a Trust Fund for this purpose. The ICC reparation regime represents substantial innovation in the field of victims' redress, not only in the administration of international criminal justice, but in international law in general. It marks a significant departure from traditional inter-State approaches to individual claims for a breach of an international obligation, which are based on fundamental principles of State responsibility, towards a more comprehensive regime in which individual victims have a right under international law to seek and obtain reparations for damages suffered directly from individuals responsible for genocide, war crimes, crimes against humanity and eventually the crime of aggression.[46]

Now that the ICC has begun operations and has the support of a considerable number of States, it is expected to play a central role in ensuring victims of crimes under international law enjoy fully their right to redress. It is therefore essential to explore the guiding principles and main components of the ICC reparation regime.

---

[46] During the negotiations that led to the adoption of the Rome Statute, State and corporate responsibility were dropped, although there is no rule in the Statute against possible vicarious State responsibility, for example in the case where a State has failed to prevent the violation or to respond to it with due diligence.

a. The Three Pillars of the ICC Reparation Regime

The victims' reparation regime as envisaged in the Rome Statute rests on three main pillars:

1) the active participation of the victims and their families at various stages of the proceedings;
2) the establishment of implementation procedures for the victims' right to reparation, including the creation of a Trust Fund; and
3) the institution of a Victim and Witness' Unit with broad competence over victims' related questions.

ICC provisions on victims' reparation and participation are not designed to work in a vacuum. To the contrary, they are centrally placed within the general architecture of the ICC and are effectively interlinked to other relevant provisions. This approach provides victims not only with a solid normative basis that recognizes their right to seek and obtain redress (a concept already present to a certain extent in the ICTY and ICTR, as discussed above), but with the operational tools necessary for the implementation of the right. Empowered with a much more coherent and comprehensive victims' redress structure as compared to that of the ICTY or of the ICTR, it is hoped that the ICC will be able to overcome some of the difficulties encountered by its predecessors in implementing redress mechanisms at the international level.

i. Ensuring Effective Victims' Participation in the ICC: A Question of Procedure

Participation in judicial proceedings is a well-established prerogative of victims in most civil law legal systems known as the '*partie civile*'. Based on this concept, the drafters of the Rome Statute elaborated a formula that allows victims to participate actively in the proceedings, both at the pre-trial and trial stages. Article 68(3) on 'Protection of the victims and witnesses and their participation in the proceedings' provides that:

> Where the personal interests of the victims are affected, the Court shall permit their views and concerns to be presented and considered at stages of the proceedings determined to be appropriate by the Court [...]. Such views and concerns may be presented by the legal representatives of the victims where the Court considers it appropriate [...].

Both the Statute and the Rules of Procedure and Evidence[47] expand upon this general provision and provide for the protection and participation of victims at different levels of the proceedings, from the beginning of an investigation to the sentencing stage.[48]

The interconnection among victims' provisions in the Rome Statute is such that an effective enjoyment of the victims' right to redress may depend on the initiative victims themselves take in the proceedings, whether individually or through class actions. Therefore, before exploring specific elements of the victims' right to redress, it is essential to identify what victims can do in the innovative procedural scheme of the Rome Statute. In this context:

Victims can provide information to the Prosecutor for the purpose of initiating an investigation. At the Rome Conference, States decided not to

---

47 The Rules of Procedure and Evidence related to victims' redress and participation to the ICC have been inspired greatly by the work of the Paris International Expert Seminar on Victims' Access to the International Criminal Court, set up to develop a text on reparations and compensation for victims of crimes under international law for official submission to the Preparatory Commission on the International Criminal Court. In April 1999, experts from sixty countries gathered in Paris, France, to discuss at length topical issues such as the definition of victims, their role during the proceedings according to various legal traditions, the protection of victims and witnesses and reparation in its various forms. The results of the Seminar were made public in a report which has been extensively used in the drafting stages of the Rules of Procedure and Evidence by the Preparatory Commission in New York. *See* PCNICC/1999/WGRPE/INF/2. *See also* PCNICC/1999/WGRPE/RT.5/Rev.1/Add.3 on reparations.

48 In particular, Rules 89 to 99 of Subsection 3 on 'Participation of victims in the proceedings' define the procedures for victims and their legal representatives to follow throughout the proceedings. Also, Rule 87 sets up criteria for the application of protective measures to victims and witnesses. In contrast to the ICTY and ICTR, the protective measures in Rule 87 are designed for the benefit of both victims and witnesses, not only to protect witnesses who gave testimony in a particular case. More specifically, the competent Chamber can order measures to protect "a victim, a witness or another person at risk on account of testimony given by a witness". Accordingly, the testimony of a witness can trigger the adoption of protective measures which can extend to beneficiaries other than the witness himself or herself. Rule 86 also establishes that, in ordering protective measures for victims under Article 68(1), a Chamber shall pay particular attention to the needs of children, elderly persons, persons with disabilities and victims of sexual or gender violence. This provision is further enhanced by Rule 88 on special measures which may be needed to facilitate the testimony of traumatized victims, children, the elderly or victims of sexual violence.

provide victims of the crimes under the jurisdiction of the Court with an independent power to institute proceedings.[49] As a consequence, victims have only 'indirect' access to the Court through the action of the Prosecutor. More specifically, at the very initial stages of the judicial process, victims are among those who can provide the Prosecutor with information which may trigger the initiation of an investigation into a crime falling within the jurisdiction of the Court.[50] Under Article 15, the Prosecutor can in fact "initiate investigations *proprio motu* on the basis of information on crimes within the jurisdiction of the Court". Considering that the kind of situations that will be presented to the Prosecutor to initiate an investigation are likely to involve a large number of victims, NGOs and other organizations dealing with serious human rights violations are likely to be in the front line in the process of organizing victims groups for the purpose of presenting coherent and relevant information to the Prosecutor. It is therefore crucial for victims to obtain proper representation when approaching the Court's relevant organs, so as to maximize their efforts at redress and participation in the proceedings.

In principle, the limitation of not having an independent power to initiate proceedings could prevent victims from accessing the Court should the Prosecutor fail to give proper consideration to the information provided by victims. However, the Prosecutor has an obligation to "analyse the seriousness of the information received" and, in this context, he or she may "seek additional information" and "receive written or oral testimony at the seat of the Court".[51] At this stage, it is possible for victims to be called to provide further

---

49 In his report on impunity prepared for the Sub-Commission on Human Rights, Mr. Joinet raised concerns over this general issue in the context of State responsibility and argued that: "Although the decision to prosecute [alleged perpetrators of human rights violations] is initially a State responsibility, supplementary procedural rules should allow victims to be admitted as civil plaintiffs in criminal proceedings or, if the public authorities fail to do so, to institute proceedings themselves". *See* "The Administration of Justice and the Human Rights of Detainees: Question of the Impunity of Perpetrators of Human Rights Violations (Civil and Political)", revised final report prepared by Mr. Joinet pursuant to Sub-Commission decision 1996/119, UN Doc. E/CN.4/Sub.2/1997/20/Rev.1 of 2 October 1997 at 7, hereinafter referred to as Joinet Final Report.

50 Article 15 does not list specifically who is entitled to provide information to initiate an investigation. Rather, Article 15 mentions that the Prosecutor can call upon "States, organs of the United Nations, intergovernmental or non-governmental organizations or other reliable sources" to seek additional information in assessing the seriousness of the information received.

51 Article 15.

information and testimony on a particular case under consideration. Should the Prosecutor decide that the information received is not adequate to satisfy the 'reasonable basis' requirement to proceed with an investigation, victims are allowed to submit further information on the same situation "in light of new facts or evidence" (Article 15(6)).

It is hoped that the decision to include only indirect mechanisms will not discourage victims from accessing the ICC. Broadly speaking, the ICC Statute balances the lack of independent access to the Court with a set of provisions drafted to achieve transparency in the proceedings and to grant a high priority to victims' issues. In addition, the future activities of the Court and its organs are likely to be subjected to a high level of 'public scrutiny' from the international community. Overall, the combination of these three elements - transparency, publicity and public scrutiny - is likely to enhance the fair access of victims to the Court, especially where they are well organized.

Victims shall be informed of the Prosecutor's request for authorization from the Pre-Trial Chamber to proceed to an investigation. In deciding whether to proceed with an investigation into a crime under the jurisdiction of the Court, the Prosecutor must, *inter alia*, evaluate all available information and take into account the gravity of the crime and the interest of the victims (Article 53).

In the Rome Statute, the Prosecutor has ample discretion to decide whether or not to initiate an investigation or to proceed to a prosecution upon investigation. With respect to the initiation of an investigation, Article 53(1)(c) provides that, should the Prosecutor have "substantial reasons to believe that an investigation would not serve the interests of justice", he or she may determine that there is no reasonable basis to proceed to an investigation. This determination must take into account elements such as "the gravity of the crime and the interests of victims". The Prosecutor has similar powers to decide whether or not to proceed with a prosecution even following an investigation, as provided in Article 53(2)(c). More specifically, the Prosecutor may decide not to proceed because a prosecution:

> is not in the interests of justice, taking into account all the circumstances, including the gravity of the crime, the interests of victims and the age or infirmity of the alleged perpetrator, and his or her role in the alleged crime.

If left unchecked, the Prosecutor's ample discretionary powers to decide on whether a particular prosecution should go ahead or not, could seriously limit the possibility of victims seeking and obtaining redress through the ICC, especially if the decision is based on rather broad or unclear grounds such as that the prosecution would not serve the 'interests of justice'. Although in his or her determination the Prosecutor must take into account the interests of victims, it seems that the Prosecutor would still have much discretion to decide the future of a particular case. To avoid politically motivated decisions on the initiation of cases or the abuse of the Prosecutor's power, the Rome Statute provides for a series of checks and balances aimed at 'supervising' the Prosecutor's broad powers in key moments of the proceedings. For example, should the Prosecutor decide not to proceed with an investigation or with a prosecution following an investigation, he or she must notify the Trial Chamber and those who referred the case to the Prosecutor, namely either a State Party or the Security Council.[52] In this case, the referring party may ask the Pre-Trial Chamber to review the Prosecutor's decision not to proceed and request him or her to reconsider the decision. In addition, if the Prosecutor's decision not to proceed is based solely on the lack of 'interests of justice', the decision shall be effective "only if confirmed by the Pre-Trial Chamber", as provided in Article 53(3)(b). The Pre-Trial Chamber also retains the independent power to review the decision.

Should the Prosecutor decide that there is a 'reasonable basis' to proceed with an investigation, under Article 13(3) he or she must obtain authorization from the Pre-Trial Chamber and must submit "any supporting material collected". At this point, according to Rule 50 of the Rules of Procedure and Evidence, the Prosecutor must also inform the victims or their legal representatives that he or she is seeking authorization from the Pre-Trial Chamber to commence an investigation.[53] Rule 50 allows only one derogation to this obligation: where the Prosecutor at his or her discretion decides that to inform the victims "would pose a danger to the integrity of the investigation or the life or well-being of victims and witnesses".

To inform victims of the intention to initiate an investigation, the Prosecutor can either inform "victims, known to him or her or to the Victims and Witnesses Unit, or their legal representatives",[54] or the Prosecutor may

---

52 The Prosecutor also has an obligation to notify the victims, is they were the persons who had informed the Prosecutor of the situation in question.

53 Similarly, Rule 92 establishes that victims shall be informed of the Prosecutor's decision not to initiate an investigation or not to prosecute.

54 Under Rule 16(3) the Registrar will be responsible for keeping a "special register for victims who have expressed their intention to participate in relation to a specific case". The organization and updating of this register will be essential for identifying and informing victims in relation to particular cases. As for the legal

"give notice by general means in order to reach groups of victims" (Rule 50). The Prosecutor may choose the second option only if, in the particular circumstances of the case, a general public notice directed to groups of victims would not pose "a danger to the integrity and effective conduct of the investigation or to the security and well-being of victims and witnesses".

Victims can make representations to the Pre-Trial Chamber. Once the Prosecutor has decided to proceed with an investigation of a situation under the jurisdiction of the Court, the matter goes to the Pre-trial Chamber for a judicial review of the decision. At this stage, victims can make representations to the Pre-Trial Chamber (Article 15(3)), in writing and within a defined time limit in accordance with Rule 50(3). Interestingly, victims are the only ones who can make representation at the pre-trial stage, since neither States Parties nor individual suspects can challenge the admissibility of the Prosecutor's request for authorization of an investigation.[55] Thus, the pre-trial phase of judicial review is likely to become one of the more critical moments for victims. At this stage, victims can provide the Pre-Trial Chamber with information which can prove essential at trial. In this connection, the Pre-Trial Chamber may decide to hold a hearing with "any of the victims who have made representation" to collect additional information. Indeed, during the pre-trial stage victims can also trigger the power of the Pre-Trial Chamber to take protective measures for the purpose of forfeiture, which is often an essential step in ensuring proper financial coverage of an eventual reparation award.[56] Finally, the Pre-Trial Chamber has a duty to notify victims who have made

---

representation of victims to the proceedings, Rule 90 provides that, *inter alia*, victims shall be free to choose a legal representative. Since it is foreseeable that the crimes under the jurisdiction of the Court will involve large numbers of victims related to the same case, Rule 90 also states that the Chamber may ask a group of victims to choose a common legal representative with the assistance of the Registry - a procedure which would ensure both the effectiveness of the proceedings and better representation for victims. Victims lacking financial means to cover the expenses of a common legal representative may receive financial assistance from the Registry.

55 Concerned States and individuals can only challenge the admissibility of a case or the jurisdiction of the Court in a subsequent phase of the proceedings (Article 19). Similarly, victims can also submit observations to the Court in case the Prosecutor seeks a ruling from the Court regarding a question of jurisdiction or admissibility (Article 19(3)).

56 *See* Rule 99 together with Article 57(3)(e). Victims can exercise the same triggering function at the Trial phase with respect to the Trial Chamber power to seek measures under Article 93(1) for the purposes of victims' reparation.

representations of its decision on the authorization to proceed with an investigation.

Full participation of victims at the pre-trial stage is an essential prerequisite both for the preparation of an eventual trial and for the purposes of reparation. In order to play a significant role in the pre-trial proceedings, it is essential that victims find coherent and organized ways to make proper representation.[57] Now that the Victims and Witnesses Unit has been set up, it is likely that victims will be among the first to test the functioning of the ICC.

Victims can make representation to the competent Chamber in case of a question or challenge of jurisdiction or admissibility of a specific case of concern. In case the Prosecutor seeks a ruling on a question of jurisdiction or on the admissibility of a case, victims or their representatives can make representations to the Court to submit their observations.[58] However, only victims who have already communicated with the Court in relation to the specific case under consideration are allowed to submit observations. Similarly, the Registrar has an obligation to provide information on any question or challenge of jurisdiction or admissibility arising with respect to a particular case only to victims who had previous communications with the Court on the case under consideration.[59]

Victims can make opening and closing statements and participate in hearings. In order to 'present their views and concerns' as expressed in Article 68(1), victims must file a written application to the Registrar, who will then pass it to the Chamber for consideration. Should the Chamber accept the application, the Chamber must also specify appropriate ways for victims to participate in the proceedings, including the making of opening and closing statements (Rule 89). Under this broad approach, the Chamber has wide discretion to determine ways in which victims can participate effectively in the proceedings. However, the ICC Statute indicates at least one way in which victims may participate in the proceedings. According to Rule 91, the victims'

---

57 *See* Rule 16 on the 'Responsibilities of the Registrar relating to victims and witnesses', stating that the Registrar will be responsible, *inter alia*, for assisting victims "in obtaining legal advice and organizing their legal representation, and providing their legal representatives with adequate support, assistance and information, [...] for the purpose of protecting their rights during all stages of the proceedings in accordance with rules 89 to 91".

58 Article 19(3) in combination with Rule 59.

59 Rule 59.

legal representatives may participate in a hearing and pose questions to witnesses, experts or the accused, subject to the Chamber's prior approval. Should the Chamber consider it inappropriate for the victims' legal representative to participate directly in the hearing, he or she may be allowed to present written observations or submissions. In the case of a hearing for reparations, Rule 91 establishes that the victims' legal representative must not be subject to any restriction on the questioning of witnesses, experts or the accused prior to the approval of the Chamber. Both the Statute and the Rules clarify that victims' participation in the proceedings will be allowed only if it is "not prejudicial to or inconsistent with the rights of the accused and a fair and impartial trial" (Article 68(3)) or, to use the language of Rule 91, if it does not hinder the "need for a fair, impartial and expeditious trial". In the light of these broad preconditions to the participation of victims in judicial proceedings, it is hoped that the Chamber will be responsive to the requirements of the Statute on victims' access to the proceedings and that proper ways to ensure victims' participation will be identified and implemented. Bearing in mind the main reasons for the failure of the ICTY and ICTR to implement redress provisions, it is incumbent upon the Chamber to find ways to cope with the inevitable time pressures surrounding the criminal proceedings, while preserving the victims' right to participate in the proceedings.

Victims are to receive notification of the Court's relevant decisions. Finally, victims must be informed of the proceedings of decisions concerning their claims at all stages, from the Prosecutor's decision whether to investigate or prosecute, to the Court's decision to hold a hearing to confirm charges, to the agenda and results of the proceedings, etc. As a general rule, the responsibility for the prompt notification of victims rests with the Registrar.

ii. ICC Reparation Mechanisms and the Establishment of a Trust Fund

Perhaps the most far-reaching innovation of the ICC Statute on victims' redress will prove to be the extent of powers conferred upon the Court in relation to the victims' right to seek and obtain reparation for the damages suffered. The Court's power to award reparations directly to the victims was among the more controversial issues debated both prior to and during the Rome Diplomatic Conference. Delegations expressed concern that a direct reparation system would be difficult to manage and would not be compatible with the

Court's main activities of prosecution and punishment of the offender.[60] However, delegations finally agreed on a rather innovative formula providing the Court with the power to determine the scope and extent of damages, losses and injuries suffered by victims once an individual is found guilty of one of the crimes under the jurisdiction of the ICC. According to Article 75:

> The Court shall establish principles relating to reparations to, or in respect of, victims, including restitution, compensation and rehabilitation. On this basis, in its decision the Court may, either upon request or on its own motion in exceptional circumstances, determine the scope and extent of any damage, loss and injury to, or in respect of, victims and will state the principles on which it is acting.

Article 75(1) adopts non-exhaustive language, and at the same time lists specific reparation elements such as restitution, compensation and rehabilitation, thus resolving what had been a lengthy debate over redress terminology.[61]

---

60 Prior to the Diplomatic Conference, the French delegation proposed an indirect approach according to which the Trial Chamber would determine the scope and extent of the damages "in order to allow victims to rely on that judgment for the pursuit of civil remedies ... either in national courts or through their governments". UN Doc. A/AC.249/1997/WG.4/DP.3, quoted in Muttukumaru, *supra* note 44. Finally, delegations agreed on a text drafted upon a joint proposal by the UK and France. The French delegation also proposed that the ICC should be able to make orders to pay reparations not only against individuals, but also against States. These proposals were subsequently dropped in Rome. However, the possibility of vicarious State liability remains open where the individual in question was a State actor.

61 The principle of victims' reparation is further articulated in Rules of Procedure and Evidence 94 to 99. As discussed in Chapter V, special rapporteurs and independent experts of the UN Commission on Human Rights have long discussed the constituent elements of the right to reparation for victims of human rights violations. Experts generally agree on a three-fold composition of the right to reparation, which should include at least restitution, compensation and rehabilitation. *See* the 'Joinet Final Report' *supra* note 49, where Mr. Joinet lists restitution, compensation and rehabilitation among individual measures that should be available for all victims of human rights violations. *See also* the 'Basic Principles and Guidelines on the Right to Reparation for Victims of Gross Violations of Human Rights and Humanitarian Law' prepared by Professor Theo van Boven, Special Rapporteur of the Sub-Commission on Human Rights, UN Doc. E/CN.4/1997/104. *See further* the Final Report of Professor M. Cherif Bassiouni, Special Rapporteur of the Commission on Human Rights on the right to restitution, compensation and rehabilitation for victims of gross violations of human rights and fundamental freedoms, UN Doc. E/CN.4/2000/62 of 18 January 2000.

The Court has an obligation to establish principles relating to victims' reparation in its various forms and it is likely that the early establishment of good reparation principles could influence positively the Court's determination of damages, losses or injuries suffered by victims.

Although the Court may determine damages, losses or injuries either upon request or *proprio motu*, the reparation procedure is designed to be accessible mainly upon the request of victims. Therefore the Court will act on its own initiative only "in exceptional circumstances".[62] Victims may request reparations under Article 75 following the procedure of Rule 94. A victim's request for reparation must be made in writing and filed with the Registrar, and must contain certain specific information such as the "identity and address of the claimant"; a "description of the injury, loss or harm"; the location and date of the incident; the identity of the person the victim believes to be responsible for the violation, if possible; a description of the objects for which restitution is claimed; a claim for monetary compensation, rehabilitation and other forms of remedy; and any other relevant supporting documentation.[63] The Registrar has a duty to notify interested persons or States Parties, and other persons identified in the victim's request. In this regard, Article 75(3) establishes that prior to making a reparation order, the Court may invite representations from the convicted person, the victims, other interested persons or interested States, with the aim of protecting the interests of *bona fide* third parties which may be affected by the reparation order. Article 75(5) further protects the rights of *bona fide* third parties who may be affected by the domestic enforcement of fines and forfeitures for the purposes of reparation.

In general, the drafters of the Rome Statute envisaged the reparation regime and relevant proceedings to be a widely publicized process. Under Rule 96, the Registrar has an obligation to give publicity "as widely as possible and by all possible means" to the reparation proceedings before the Court "to other

---

[62] Should the Court decide to proceed on its own motion with the determination of damages, the Registrar has a duty to inform those against whom the Court intends to make a determination, as well as victims and other interested persons and States. Those who have been notified can file a representation with the Registry (Rule 95). Rule 95 also establishes that if a victim who has been notified of the Court's initiative to determine damages decides to file a separate reparation claim, such claim will be handled as if it had been triggered directly by the victim and not by the Prosecutor. Conversely, should a victim request the Court not to make an order for reparation in his or her specific case, the Court is under the obligation not to proceed with that individual order.

[63] The Rules of Procedure and Evidence do not set a range in the amount that victims can claim for compensation.

victims, interested persons and interested States". To this end, the Registrar may seek the cooperation of relevant States Parties and the assistance of NGOs. Finally, Article 75(6) reproduces a standard formula found in many human rights treaties safeguarding the rights of victims as follows: "nothing in this article shall be interpreted as prejudicing the rights of victims under national or international law".

Following the determination of the scope and extent of damages, losses and injuries suffered by the victims, the Court can expedite payment in one of two ways. It could:

1) make an order directly against the convicted person "specifying appropriate reparations to, or in respect of, victims, including restitution, compensation and rehabilitation";[64] or
2) where appropriate, order that "the award for reparations be made through the Trust Fund" established under Article 79 of the Statute.[65]

The Court has the authority to exercise its full discretion in the choice of the reparation awards. Reparation may be awarded in the form of restitution of property, compensation or rehabilitation, but also in forms other than those specifically listed in the Rome Statute, such as orders for apologies, satisfaction or guarantees of non-repetition. Although the Rome Statute does not contemplate expressly the possibility of awarding punitive damages in addition to compensatory damages, it seems that this option may be left to the discretion of the Court.[66] Interestingly, the Court must give consideration "to the extent of the damage caused, in particular the harm caused to the victims and their families" in determining a sentence under Article 78. Conversely, where appropriate the Court must also consider efforts by the convicted person to compensate the victims as a mitigating circumstance (Rule 145).

The Trust Fund. The Victims' Trust Fund will be one of the ICC's main tools for implementing the victims' right to redress. In light of the difficulties the Court and domestic legal systems may encounter in enforcing individual reparation orders, the Trust Fund might become the primary source

---

64 Article 75(2).

65 *Ibid.*

66 On the question of punitive damages, the ICC will have to reconcile the different approaches of the common law and civil law systems, since civil law legal systems do not have a specific concept of 'punitive damage'. However, the award of 'moral damages' in civil law judicial systems can convey the sense of punitive damages.

of victims' reparations in the ICC. Therefore, it is essential that States contribute to the Trust Fund in order to ensure its effectiveness.

Article 79 provides that the Trust Fund shall be established "by decision of the Assembly of States Parties for the benefit of victims of crimes within the jurisdiction of the Court, and of the families of such victims". Aside from this basic provision, the Statute assigns most operational matters for future elaboration to the Assembly of States Parties, including the definition of criteria for the management of the Trust Fund, its financial structure and sources, and the identification of beneficiaries. This open approach provides considerable flexibility in determining the future operation of the Trust Fund and it avoids States having to go through the Statute's complicated amendment procedure, should they consider it necessary to modify the operational criteria of the Fund. However, the lack of specific indications on the future operation of the Trust Fund leaves many questions unanswered. These questions have mainly to do with the extent of powers and functions of the Trust Fund beyond the reparation regime and with its managerial structure and financial support. Indeed, it is likely that the approach of States to these very issues will shape the structure of the Fund and its eventual success in redressing the sufferings of victims.[67]

---

[67] As Ingadottir remarks, "the Trust Fund is by and large an entity on its own, [it] does not have any direct link with any organs of the Court, and no provision in the Rome Statute gives the Court power to manage or utilize the Trust Fund", *see The Trust Fund for Victims (Article 79 of the Rome Statute): A Discussion Paper*, Project on International Courts and Tribunals (PICT), ICC Discussion Paper No. 3, February 2001 at 5. During the negotiations in Rome, States felt that technical and operational matters concerning the Trust Fund would be better developed by the Assembly of States Parties, rather than being included in the body of the Rome Statute. As a consequence, many issues related to the functioning of the Trust Fund remain under discussion. In particular, States have been considering whether the Fund should be managed by an independent body created by the Assembly of States Parties, by the Assembly of States Parties itself, or by the UN, along the lines of the UN Voluntary Fund for Victims of Torture (established by UNGA resolution 36/151 of 16 December 1981) and of the UN Voluntary Trust Fund on Contemporary Forms of Slavery (established by UNGA resolution 46/122 of 17 December 1991). One of the main issues under discussion is the maintenance of the Fund's independence. Some commentators have argued that a Trust Fund under UN management could lose its independence and flexibility and become subject to unnecessary bureaucratic restrictions that could threaten its effectiveness. *See* Amnesty International, *International Criminal Court: Ensuring an Effective Trust Fund for Victims*, IOR 40/005/2001 of 1 September 2001 at 3. Others have supported a UN managed Fund by arguing that placing the Trust Fund under the

Essentially, the ICC Statute sets some very basic guidelines for the financial structure of the Fund and its sources of income. More specifically, the Statute identifies the following two sources of income for the Trust Fund:

1) reparation awards against a convicted person ordered by the Court to be made through the Trust Fund (Article 75(2)); and
2) money or other property collected through fines or forfeiture under Article 77, ordered by the Court to be transferred to the Trust Fund for the benefit of the victims and their families (Article 79(2)).

The choice of the language in Articles 75 and 79 reflects the different scope of application of the two provisions with respect to the Trust Fund. Article 75(2) establishes that "the Court may order a reparation award against a convicted person to be made *through* the Trust Fund", thus suggesting that the Trust Fund will be bound to use the proceeds of a specific reparation award exclusively for the benefit of the victims in that particular case, as specified in the Court's order. In this situation, the Trust Fund would function more as an intermediary for the transfer of individual awards. In this connection, Rule 98(2) indicates that the Court could order an award for reparation against a convicted person to be deposited with the Trust Fund only in cases where, at the time of the order, "it is impossible or impracticable to make individual awards directly to each victim". This particular award will remain separate from other resources of the Trust Fund and will be distributed to each victim "as soon as possible". However, Rule 98(3) also specifies that "where the number of victims and the scope, forms and modalities of reparations makes a collective award more appropriate", the Court can order such award to be made through the Trust Fund. Indeed, collective awards resulting from class actions appear to be the most likely form of reparation to be distributed by the ICC, as compared to individual awards, which can be narrowly targeted and administratively onerous.

In contrast, Article 79(2) indicates broadly that the Court may order "the transfer of money or other property collected through fines or forfeiture to the Trust Fund".[68] This suggests that the Trust Fund is not bound by the

administration of the Court might unnecessarily burden the Court, it might become 'politically awkward' or it might even restrain the Fund's activities. *See* Ingadottir, *ibid.* at 29-31.

[68] Rule 146 sets out the criteria for the imposition of a fine under Article 77 as a supplementary penalty against a convicted person, should the Court determine that imprisonment is not a sufficient penalty. In determining the amount of the fine, the

Statute with respect to the use of money or property collected from fines or forfeiture, as long as the funds are used "for the benefit of victims of crimes within the jurisdiction of the Court, and of the families of such victims" as per Article 79(1). Rule 85(a) defines 'victims' as: "natural persons who have suffered harm as a result of the commission of any crime within the jurisdiction of the Court", but also:

> organizations or institutions that have sustained direct harm to any of their property which is dedicated to religion, education, art or science or charitable purposes, and to their historic monuments, hospitals and other places and objects for humanitarian purposes.[69]

Court must consider the financial capacity of the convicted person, the existence of standing orders for forfeiture or reparations, whether and to what degree the crime was motivated by personal financial gain, the damage and injuries caused to victims, as well as the proportionate gains of the perpetrator. Also, Rule 146(2) determines that a fine cannot exceed 75% of the total value of the convicted person's "identifiable assets, liquid or realizable, and property", after deduction of an "appropriate amount" for the needs of the convicted person and his or her dependants. The payment may be made as a lump sum or by way of instalments over a period of time specified by the Court. In case of continued and wilful non-payment, as a last resort, the Court can extend the term of imprisonment for a period not exceeding "a quarter of such term or five years, whichever is less". As for forfeitures, Rule 147 establishes that the Chamber may issue an order of forfeiture of specific proceeds, property or assets which have been derived "directly or indirectly" from the crime.

69 At the Rome Conference, States had the chance not only to define 'victims' for the purposes of the ICC Statute, but also to finally codify a definition which had been previously developed in various soft law instruments, in particular in the UN Declaration of Basic Principles of Justice for Victims of Crime and Abuse of Power, *adopted* by UNGA resolution 40/34 of 29 November 1985. During the 1999 Paris seminar on the role of victims in the ICC, NGOs proposed the adoption of a definition consistent with existing international standards, in particular, the 1985 UN Declaration. However, both in Paris and in the subsequent Preparatory Commission of March 2000, it was difficult to find agreement on a definition of 'victim' along the lines of the UN Declaration. As a result, the definition finally adopted in Rule 85 appears comparatively more restrictive with respect to the UN definition of 'victims of crime and abuse of power' as embodied in the 1985 Declaration. More specifically, the UN Declaration is broader in the sense that it defines victims of crime as "persons who, individually or collectively, have suffered harm, including physical or mental injury, emotional suffering, economic loss or substantial impairment of their fundamental rights, through acts or omissions that are in violation of criminal law operative within Member States, including those laws proscribing criminal abuse of power". Also, under the UN Declaration, a person can be considered to be a victim "regardless of the

Accordingly, intergovernmental, international or national organizations approved by the Trust Fund may become beneficiaries of reparation awards directed through the Fund.[70]

The ICC Statute establishes that the Court and the Victims' Trust Fund will have different budgets and financing schemes. Because the Trust Fund will not be funded directly from the budget of the Court, it is likely that it will require supplementary funding in addition to fines and forfeitures collected during the proceedings, in order to provide fair redress.[71] In particular, voluntary contributions to the Trust Fund will prove indispensable for achieving adequate compensation of victims. The ICC Statute does not prevent in any way States voluntarily contributing to the Trust Fund. In principle, such contributions could come even from States that are not parties to the Statute. It will be up to the Assembly of States Parties to decide upon the modalities of these contributions which, as some have suggested, could follow the lines of Article 116, which provides that the Court as an institution may receive additional funds and voluntary contributions from Governments, international organizations, individuals, corporations and other entities.[72] In this context, States are currently discussing a number of critical issues relating to the financing of the Trust Fund, including the central question as to whether the Trust Fund should have independent competence to negotiate with Governments and corporations willing to make voluntary contributions in particular

---

familial relationship between the perpetrator and the victim". Finally, the term 'victim' under the UN Declaration includes, where appropriate, "the immediate family or dependants of the direct victim and persons who have suffered harm in intervening to assist victims in distress or to prevent victimization". For a survey of the negotiations leading to the adoption of Rule 85, *see* Roy S. Lee (ed.), *The International Criminal Court: Elements of Crimes and Rules of Procedure and Evidence*, Transnational Publishers Inc. (2001) at 427-433.

70 Rule 98(5), also providing that the Court must consult with interested States and the Trust Fund prior to ordering the award.

71 On the financing of the Court, *see generally* S. Rama Rao, "Financing of the Court, Assembly of States Parties and the Preparatory Commission", in Lee (ed.) *supra* note 42 at 399-420.

72 At various stages during the drafting of the Rules of Procedure and Evidence, both the French and the Italian Governments proposed that voluntary contributions may be received from Governments, NGOs, individuals, international organizations, corporations and from the Court's financial resources. *See* UN Docs. PCNICC/1999/WGRPE(7)/DP.1 of 19 November 1999, PCNICC/2000/WGFIRR/DP.33 of 30 November 2000, PCNICC/2000/WGFIRR/L.1 and PCNICC/2000/WGFIRR/DP.35 of 1 December 2000. *See generally* PICT, *The Trust Fund for Victims*, *supra* note 67.

cases under the jurisdiction of the Court.[73] The possible negotiating function of the Trust Fund could assume special relevance if the Assembly of States Parties decides to grant the Fund a broader scope to provide redress even beyond cases under the jurisdiction of the Court, as discussed below.

At present, it is still unclear what the precise role and extent of the powers of the Trust Fund will be within the ICC framework. It is mainly up to the Assembly of States Parties to elaborate clear rules and criteria for an effective and fair allocation of the funds collected, and to interpret the statutory obligation to use available funds only in ways that benefit the victims and their families.[74] In addition to financial matters, many other pivotal questions for the future direction of the whole ICC reparation regime need to be resolved before the Fund becomes fully operational.

Who should be considered a 'victim' for the purposes of the Trust Fund? One of the core issues currently under discussion is the determination of who should qualify as a 'victim' for the purposes of the Trust Fund, since the Statute's only indication is that the Trust Fund is established for "victims of crimes within the jurisdiction of the court" (Article 79(1)). This is a fundamental question that will shape the future operation, fairness and possibly the effectiveness of the Trust Fund. Some commentators have interpreted the provision of Article 79(1) as conferring 'victim's status' for the purpose of the Trust Fund exclusively on family members and victims of violations under consideration in ICC proceedings, thus aligning the scope of application

---

[73] Although the Court has competence exclusively over individuals, this scenario may occur where a Government involved in any way in a crime under consideration by the Court feels an obligation, even a moral one, to provide victims with some form of reparation, and decides to provide redress through the ICC Trust Fund. In this case, the Fund may act as an intermediary, as in the event of reparations awarded under Article 75 of the Statute through the Trust Fund.

[74] In a paper by Dinah L. Shelton and Thordis Ingadottir entitled *The International Criminal Court - Reparations to Victims of Crimes (Article 75 of the Rome Statute) and the Trust Fund (Article 79)*, Part II at 22, Ingadottir postulates that the power to decide how to allocate funds from fines and forfeitures should rest with the Court, as in Article 75 on reparations. He argues that the Trust Fund should only be granted a subsidiary power over the allocation of funds in case the Court declines to exercise such power. *See a contrario* Amnesty International, *supra* note 67 at 7, suggesting that the Fund's Manager should have discretionary power to make an 'interim award' in special circumstances, such as in support of special measures taken by the Court.

ratione personae of the Trust Fund to that of the Victims and Witnesses Unit.[75] Others have suggested that the Trust Fund's scope of action should cover also victims of violations who are not under consideration in the Court's proceedings.[76]

This latter proposal is based on the argument that, contrary to the Victims and Witnesses Unit which is to be established for the sole assistance of victims who appear before the Court (Article 43(6)), Article 79 creates the Trust Fund for the benefit of victims of "crimes within the jurisdiction of the Court" in general, without specifically mentioning their participation in the proceedings. Based on this proposal, the resources of the Trust Fund could be accessed by any victim of the crimes falling under the jurisdiction of the Court, irrespective of the victim's participation in the proceedings, either as a witness or for reparation purposes. In this sense, while the Trust Fund's scope of application and operational coverage would become much broader, its 'affiliation' to the ICC would be much weaker. In principle, the extension of the Fund's competence to all victims of genocide, crimes against humanity, war crimes and the crime of aggression, even in the absence of any link with the ICC, could help address the lack of adequate compensation mechanisms currently available at the international level for victims of these crimes. Arguably, a Trust Fund which provides support only to victims having a particular role in the Court's proceedings might discriminate among victims of the same crime who, instead, have to access domestic reparation systems to obtain redress even where they may be wholly inadequate for such purpose. After all, according to the principle of complementarity expressed in Article 1 of the ICC Statute, the ICC is supposed to exercise jurisdiction only in the presumably rare cases in which domestic jurisdictions are unwilling or unable to prosecute. As a result, it is possible that the victims accessing the ICC and its Trust Fund would be in the minority compared to those who could seek redress before domestic courts which, in many cases, may not have the proper funds to compensate victims. In this context, does it make sense to have a Trust Fund fully supported institutionally and financially for the sole benefit of victims who are 'lucky' to make it to the ICC?

On the other hand, the extension of the Fund's coverage to victims who have no connection with the ICC proceedings may not be consistent with the requirements of Article 79(1), which provides that the Trust Fund is established for "victims of crimes within the jurisdiction of the Court" and for their families. In order to establish that a person has been the victim of a crime

---

75 *See* the proposal of Amnesty International, *supra* note 67 at 5-6.

76 *See The Trust Fund for Victims*, *supra* note 67 at 9.

within the jurisdiction of the Court, a determination or at least some form of recognition by the Court's competent organs to this effect would seem necessary. It has been proposed that, as regards the question of maintaining a threshold for the access of victims to the Trust Fund, the Fund's coverage should only be extended once the Pre-Trial Chamber has made a ruling under Article 15 to authorize the Prosecutor to commence an investigation.[77] This way, victims known to the Registrar either for the purposes of participation in the proceedings or for reparation purposes could benefit from the assistance of the Trust Fund very early in the proceedings, immediately following the judicial review and decision of the Pre-Trial Chamber. Generally speaking, this solution would provide an acceptable compromise between completely independent action on the part of the Trust Fund, and total inaction until final judgment is reached. On the other hand, this approach would have its own shortcomings.

First, the early involvement of the Trust Fund in the assistance of 'alleged victims' is likely to result in the distribution of 'support funds' to a potentially very high number of 'alleged victims' of a crime for which there has not yet been a conviction. These preliminary funds for the interim support of 'alleged victims' would not be reparations *strictu sensu*, since the reparation regime can be activated only at the end of the trial phase, once an individual has been convicted for a crime under the jurisdiction of the Court. In this case, the Trust Fund must ensure that sufficient funds are pre-allocated exclusively for the purpose of reparation to victims following the conviction of an offender. In this context, an early distribution of funds prior to the sentencing stage could be taken into account in the eventual determination of a reparation award.

Second, if the Trust Fund were to develop broad discretionary powers, the Assembly of States Parties will have to exercise particular care to define the extent of such powers *vis-à-vis* the activities of the Victims and Witnesses Unit. On this last point, Rules 16(1)(b) and 16(1)(c) state that the Registrar, through the Victims and Witnesses Unit, will be responsible for providing victims with adequate support, assistance and information "for the purpose of protecting their rights during all stages of the proceedings" and for assisting them "in participating in the different phases of the proceedings". Since the Victims and Witnesses Unit is an organ of the Court with regular budget funding, the competence of the Unit and of the Fund would have to be clearly defined to avoid overlap, dispersion of funds and resources, or even interference. Similarly, the proposal to have a Trust Fund Manager with full discretion to assess awards and determine beneficiaries outside the restitution

---

77 *See* Amnesty International, *supra* note 67 at 5-6.

procedure of Article 75 raises serious concerns over the legitimacy of such powers, granted outside specific provisions of the Rome Statute and Rules of Procedure and Evidence.[78]

Regardless of whether States opt for a Trust Fund with a broader or narrower scope for action, it is essential that the functions and powers of the Fund respect the general parameters of the Rome Statute and remain within its spirit and operating principles. With this in mind, questions such as budget, fundraising, management of the Fund and determination of potential beneficiaries can be addressed with precision in the early stages of the ICC's operation, together with the creation of necessary procedures for future amendments.

iii. The Role and Functions of the Victims and Witnesses Unit

The Victims and Witnesses Unit is envisaged to be a permanent statutory organ of the ICC. In contrast with the ICTY and ICTR, where similar units were established through the Rules of Procedure and Evidence to deal with cases on an *ad hoc* basis, Article 43(6) of the Rome Statute establishes the Victims and Witnesses Unit as part of the Registry. In consultation with the Office of the Prosecutor, the Unit is intended to provide:

> protective measures and security arrangements, counselling and other appropriate assistance for witnesses, victims who appear before the Court, and others who are at risk on account of testimony given by such witnesses.

Although the Unit was placed in the Registry to ensure its independence, Article 43(6) provides that all activities of the Unit must be undertaken "in consultation with the office of the Prosecutor", thus establishing a close link between the Unit and the Prosecutor's office.[79] Accordingly, it remains to be seen whether and to what extent the Unit will be able to maintain its independence from the Prosecutor's office. In particular, the Unit will have to exercise great care not to favour Prosecution witnesses over Defence witnesses. Similarly, witnesses should not be given preference over victims who might not

---

78 According to this proposal, assessment should follow guidelines on the determination of loss, damage and injury incurred by victims to be set up under Article 79(3). *Ibid.* at 8.

79 At the Rome Conference, this provision resulted from a compromise among delegations who supported an independent Unit under the Registry and those who preferred a Unit under the supervision of the Prosecutor, with a view to facilitating investigations through the protection of witnesses. *See The Victims and Witnesses Unit*, *supra* note 39 at 12-13.

appear as witnesses. In this context, it must be remarked that Rule 16 establishes that the services of the Unit are intended for the benefit of both witnesses and victims who may not be witnesses.

Article 68(4) of the ICC Statute on 'Protection of the victims and witnesses and their participation in the proceedings' grants the Victims and Witnesses Unit the independent power to "advise the Prosecutor and the Court on appropriate protective measures, security arrangements, counselling and assistance as referred to in Article 43, paragraph 6". The Rules of Procedure and Evidence further develop the responsibilities of the Registrar relating to victims and witnesses in Rule 16, the functions and responsibilities of the Unit in Rules 17 and 18, and the expertise in the Unit in Rule 19.[80] Rules 16(1)(b) and 16(1)(c) expressly state that the Registrar is responsible for providing victims with adequate support, assistance and information "for the purpose of protecting their rights during all stages of the proceedings" and for assisting them "in participating in the different phases of the proceedings". In this context, the Registrar may enter into negotiations with States to draft confidential relocation agreements and to provide support services for traumatized or threatened victims. Full State cooperation on this matter will be critical to effective victims' protection. Ultimately, the effective functioning of a victims and witnesses' protection scheme within the ICC will depend on the cooperation of States Parties in implementing protective schemes and in granting protection to victims and witnesses within their respective territories.[81]

---

80 According to Rule 16, the Registrar will be responsible for handing out notices or notifications to victims; for assisting victims in obtaining legal advice and organizing legal representation; for providing "adequate support, assistance and information" to legal representatives of victims at all stages of the proceedings; for taking gender-sensitive measures to help victims of sexual violence in the proceedings; for informing victims of their rights under the Statute and Rules; for ensuring that victims are aware of the relevant decisions of the Court; and for keeping a special register for victims who intend to participate in a given proceeding.

81 The drafting of cooperation agreements with concerned countries for victims and witnesses' assistance and relocation will not necessarily be easy. The ICTY and ICTR faced enormous difficulties trying conclude such agreements. In that context, most witnesses were able to receive effective protection only on the premises of the tribunals and on the territory of the host country. *See The Victims and Witnesses Unit*, *supra* note 39 at 24-27. *See also* the issues raised by Amnesty International on the need to have functional immunities for witnesses and victims in case the trial is conducted elsewhere than at the seat of the Court in the host State. Amnesty International, *The ICC: Concerns at the Eighth Session of the Preparatory Commission (24 September to 5 October 2001)*, IOR 40/006/2001 of September 2001 at 25.

Finally, as an organ of the Court, the Unit will be financed by regular budget funding and could be provided with a special account.[82]

b. The Principle of Complementarity *vis-à-vis* Victims' Redress: What Happens If Domestic Courts Are Unable or Unwilling to Provide Redress?

The complementarity of the ICC's jurisdiction with national criminal jurisdiction forms one of the fundamental principles of the Rome Statute. Both the preamble of the Rome Statute and Article 1 clearly indicate that the Court shall be complementary to domestic criminal jurisdiction and shall have jurisdiction only where domestic courts are unwilling or unable to prosecute and punish individuals responsible for genocide, crimes against humanity, war crimes and eventually the crime of aggression. Domestic courts will continue to hold the primary responsibility for exercising jurisdiction over crimes under international law and ensuring that victims receive fair and adequate redress. Against this background, could the jurisdiction of the Court be invoked in cases where a country fails to provide an adequate remedy to victims of genocide, crimes against humanity or war crimes? Further, can victims who did not receive adequate redress at the domestic level for crimes also falling under the jurisdiction of the Court later access the ICC victims' Trust Fund for the purposes of compensation?

Article 17 of the Rome Statute sets out the rules governing the 'interplay' between the ICC and domestic jurisdictions and enumerates four instances in which a case brought before the ICC shall be found inadmissible. In particular, the Court cannot exercise its jurisdiction over a case where:

---

82 At the eighth session of the Preparatory Committee, Amnesty International argued in favour of having a separate account for the Victims and Witnesses Unit and of including in the Financial Regulations and Rules for the Court provisions allowing the Unit to make cash payments and confidential transfers of funds in certain situations. *See* Amnesty International, *ibid.* at 18. The draft budget for the first financial year of the Court places the Unit under the new 'Court Management and Support Section', responsible for: "managing courtroom operations, providing legal aid through the assignment of defence counsel, recommending protective measures and providing counselling and support to victims and witnesses". *See* Draft budget for the first financial year of the Court, Working Group on a Draft Budget for the First Financial Year of the Court, New York 24 September - 5 October 2001, PCNICC/2001/WGFYB/L.1 of 8 August 2001 at paras. 92 and 94.

a. a State which has jurisdiction over the case is already investigating or prosecuting it, unless the State under question is "unwilling or unable genuinely to carry out the investigation or prosecution";
b. a State which has jurisdiction over the case has decided not to prosecute the person concerned, unless the decision not to prosecute "resulted from the unwillingness or inability of the State genuinely to prosecute";
c. the person concerned in the particular case has been tried for the same crime (*ne bis in idem*); or
d. the case is not of sufficient gravity.

Difficult questions relating to the admissibility of a case are likely to arise, mainly with respect to the unwillingness or inability of domestic courts to deal with crimes under international law (points 'a' and 'b') and in relation to the meaning of the words 'sufficient gravity' of a particular case (point 'd'). To guide the Judges in the difficult process of determining the admissibility of a given case, Article 17 establishes that in determining the *unwillingness* of a State in a particular case, the Court shall have regard to "the principles of due process recognized by international law" and shall consider whether the proceedings or the decision:

a. were undertaken "for the purpose of shielding the person concerned from criminal responsibility for crimes within the jurisdiction of the Court";
b. were subject to "unjustified delay which in the circumstances is inconsistent with an intent to bring the person concerned to justice"; or
c. "[w]ere not or are not being conducted independently or impartially, and ... in a manner which, in the circumstances, is inconsistent with an intent to bring the person concerned to justice".

Article 17(3) further indicates that, in order to determine the *inability* of domestic courts in a particular case, the Court shall consider whether:

> due to a total or substantial collapse or unavailability of its national judicial system, the State is unable to obtain the accused or the necessary evidence and testimony or [is] otherwise unable to carry out its proceedings.

During the Rome negotiations, delegations agreed to link the criteria for 'inability' to the partial or total collapse of a country's judicial system.[83] However, delegations did not consider it necessary to provide a detailed definition of 'total or substantial collapse or unavailability' of a judicial system and opted for a more concise provision instead. As a result, Article 17(3) only refers to the inability of a State to acquire custody over the accused, to gather relevant evidence and to carry out judicial proceedings arising from the collapse of its judicial system.[84]

While the 'total or substantial collapse' of a national judicial system remains the core element in the determination of a country's inability to prosecute crimes under the jurisdiction of the Statute, it seems that the Court will have some flexibility in determining factors that make a country "unable to carry out its proceedings" following a collapse of its judicial system. One could imagine a situation where the judiciary has been eliminated as part of a genocidal policy, as in Rwanda in 1994, or where a country does not have the proper skills and training to set up prosecutions following a military regime, dictatorship or armed conflict, as in Cambodia.

Along the same lines, one could argue also that, where the judicial system has collapsed, the inability of a State to provide adequate redress for victims of genocide, war crimes or crimes against humanity, should be considered to qualify as the "inability of a State to carry out its proceedings", thereby allowing the Court to exercise jurisdiction in a particular case. Keeping in mind the special focus that the Rome Statute attributes to victims' reparations, the Court could consider a serious and structural lack of adequate and effective domestic redress mechanisms among the criteria to determine the inability of a State to administer justice in a situation falling within the jurisdiction of the ICC. In such a case, so as not to frustrate the victims' right to seek and obtain redress, it would be advisable that the Court either:

- take over the case and exercise jurisdiction directly; or,
- allow the victims of the crime under consideration to have access to the ICC Victims' Trust Fund where the country's inability is associated exclusively with the absence of domestic reparation procedures.

By following this approach, the Court would limit the potential for discrimination between victims of the same category of crimes accessing the

---

83 *See* John T. Holmes, "The Principle of Complementarity", in Lee (ed.), *supra* note 42 at 48-51.

84 *Ibid.*

ICC and its comprehensive reparation framework and victims seeking redress domestically in countries that might not be able to provide adequate redress.

c. Implementation and Support Provisions of the ICC Reparation Regime

To work effectively for the benefit of victims, the ICC reparation regime requires the full cooperation of States Parties, non-States Parties and all others concerned. The Rome Statute contains a number of provisions aimed at supporting and implementing the reparation regime. Cooperation provisions come under the general umbrella of Articles 86, 87 and 88 in Part 9 of the Rome Statute. Article 86 imposes a general obligation on States to "cooperate fully with the Court in its investigation and prosecution of crimes within the jurisdiction of the Court". Article 87 grants the Court the power to request State cooperation and sets out some basic procedures to seek the assistance of victims, potential witnesses and their families.[85] Finally, under Article 88, States parties have an obligation to ensure that "there are procedures available under their domestic law for all forms of cooperation" specified under Part 9.

State cooperation is required from the early stages of the proceedings, for example, where the Pre-Trial Chamber, acting under Article 58, issues a warrant of arrest or a summons to appear before it and decides to take 'protective measures' for the purpose of forfeiture, in particular for the ultimate benefit of victims' under Article 57(3)(e).[86] In its preliminary work, the Pre-Trial Chamber can request the cooperation of States under Article 93, which is likely to include the identification and freezing of the defendant's assets. It can also request cooperation at subsequent stages of the enforcement of ICC reparation orders. States cooperation will be essential, particularly in the early stages of identification, tracing and freezing of assets which might later become the object of a reparation order. In particular, prompt State action at the request of the Court's competent organs could effectively prevent the alleged

---

85 *See* Article 87(4) on assistance and the Court's power to take protective measures.

86 Prior notification to the person against whom a request is made is not required by the Rules of Procedure and Evidence, unless the Court so decides. Under Rule 99 however, notification to the concerned person as well as to any interested persons or State becomes necessary "as soon as is consistent with the effectiveness of the measures requested". Rule 99 also establishes that the Pre-Trial Chamber may determine whether measures should be requested on its own motion, at the request of the Prosecutor, or at the request of the victims or of their legal representatives.

offender from relocating his or her assets to countries not willing to enforce a Court's reparation order.

As mentioned, victims or their legal representatives can request the Trial Chamber to determine whether measures should be requested, which might include the "identification, tracing and freezing or seizure of proceeds, property and assets and instrumentalities of crimes" and "the execution of searches and seizures". Once the Trial Chamber has decided to take measures, States Parties have a duty under Article 93(1) to cooperate with the Court in relation to investigations or prosecutions, both according to the provisions of the Statute and to their procedures under domestic law. Finally, Article 109 on 'Enforcement of fines and forfeiture measures' obliges States Parties to "give effect to fines or forfeitures ordered by the Court"; to "take measures to recover the value of the proceeds, property or assets ordered by the Court to be forfeited" in case the State in question is "unable to give effect to an order for forfeiture"; and to transfer to the Court "property, or the proceeds of the sale of real property or, where appropriate, the sale of other property, which is obtained by a State Party as a result of its enforcement of a judgement of the Court". To this end, States may be requested, for example, to transfer to the Court properties, assets or proceeds related to a crime under consideration.[87] All these obligations must be carried out without prejudice to the rights of *bona fide* third parties.

d. ICC Reparation Awards in Practice: Where International Law Meets Private Law

The practical questions related to the implementation of the reparation provisions of the Rome Statute are numerous and are not always easy to address, in particular with respect to compensation claims. It should not be forgotten that in the ICTY and ICTR, it was mainly due to practical concerns over compensation questions such as the determination of damages, losses and injuries suffered by victims, or the tracing and freezing of the defendant's assets, that proposals to amend the Statutes to include direct victims' compensation were finally abandoned by the Security Council - perhaps prematurely - following the recommendation of the Judges to this effect.

In principle, the implementation of reparation provisions in the ICC should be considerably easier than in the two *ad hoc* tribunals, mainly because the Rome Statute and Rules of Procedure and Evidence establish a special framework for restitution and compensation. Unless the two tribunals

---

87 Articles 77(2)(a) and (b) on 'Applicable Penalties'.

unexpectedly decide to change their procedure, the ICC will be the first international judicial mechanism to address directly the question of victims' compensation for crimes under international law. Consequently, the Judges will be presented with the challenging task of implementing completely new procedures - a situation that carries inevitable risks. Also, both the Statute and the Rules of Procedure and Evidence are virtually silent on the question of assessment of reparations: Rule 97 simply provides that the Court can award reparations "on an individualized basis or, where it deems it appropriate, on a collective basis or both" and offers the Court a graceful 'way out' of the problem by authorizing the appointment of:

> appropriate experts to assist [the Court] in determining the scope, extent of any damage, loss and injury ... and to suggest various options concerning the appropriate types and modalities of reparations.[88]

This does not solve the question of how to assess reparations, however. One of the main challenges will be the application of procedures substantially pertaining to private law such as, *inter alia*, the determination of victims' damages, losses and injuries, the calculation of the amount of compensation and the award of punitive damages. Will the Judges, the appointed experts or other competent organs be able to harmonize and reconcile various reparation theories of common law and civil law systems for the purpose of creating a consistent reparation regime under international law?[89] Will they be able to find common principles, to address foreseeable problems and to find practical solutions to redress questions in the interest of victims and of international

---

[88] At both the Paris International Expert Seminar on Victims' Access to the International Criminal Court and the Preparatory Commission in New York, States raised concerns over the extent and role of the experts' participation in assessing reparation claims. In particular, some delegations worried that expert opinion would influence more than necessary the decision of the Court. Consequently, Rule 99 was drafted carefully to preserve the ultimate power of decision of the Court, thus confining the experts to a limited, although essential, role of 'assistance' to the Court for the purpose of 'suggesting various options' concerning reparation. *See* PCNICC/1999/ WGRPE/RT.5/ Rev.1/Add.3.

[89] At the domestic private level there has been much discussion on reparation issues. In particular, in the common law system there is an ongoing debate on whether judges should merge common law and equity in remedies. *See generally* A. Burrows, *Fusing Common Law and Equity: Remedies, Restitution and Reform*, Sweet & Maxwell Asia (2001).

criminal justice? Ultimately, the fairness and effectiveness of the ICC reparation regime will depend much on the extent to which the Court will be able to translate into international practice concepts originally developed in the context of domestic legal procedure.

The ICC will be expected to award reparations in various forms to both individuals and groups of victims. In principle, the Court has full discretion to decide whether to make a reparation order and to determine the kind of reparation to award in each specific case. In practice, however, it is likely that a large proportion of claims will involve monetary compensation, thus requiring the Court to assess the amount of reparation commensurate with the level of damages, injuries and losses suffered. This will be a crucial and difficult task. As Lord Donaldson of Lymington remarks:

> Paradoxically as it may seem, one of the commonest tasks of a judge sitting in a civil court is also one of the most difficult. This is the assessment of general damages for pain, suffering or loss of the amenities of life. Since no monetary award can compensate in any real sense, these damages cannot be assessed by a process of calculation. Yet whilst no two cases are ever precisely the same, justice requires that there be consistency between awards.[90]

As mentioned above, neither the Rome Statute nor the Rules of Procedure and Evidence establish principles for the assessment of damages. It is therefore likely that the Court will act on the basis of reparation principles determined under Article 75. It is only on the basis of clearly stated principles that the Court will be able to set up and implement a reparation system that is consistent, effective, fair and in conformity with relevant international standards. As reparation issues have usually been left to the competence of domestic courts, it is essential that the Assembly of States Parties develop coherent rules suitable for the ICC, in line with UN standards on redress as discussed in Chapter V. In this way, the truly international character of the

---

90 Foreword of Lord Donaldson of Lymington to the First Edition of *Guidelines for the Assessment of General Damages in Personal Injury Cases*, Judicial Studies Board, Fifth Ed., Blackstone Press Ltd., London (1992) at ix. In the future practice of the ICC, it will be important also that the Judges follow consistent rules in assessing damages for psychological and psychiatric injury, mental distress, nervous shock, post-traumatic stress disorder and similar situations, since many of the victims who file claims for reparation will likely have suffered from both physical and psychiatric injuries. On this crucial question, *see* M. Napier and K. Wheat, *Recovering Damages for Psychiatric Injury*, Blackstone Press Ltd., London (1995).

ICC and its proceedings will be respected and victims will become better protected from inconsistent or unfair treatment.[91]

3. The 'Value Added' of the ICC

From many points of view, the ICC represents the ideal solution for victims of crimes under international law: it codifies the more progressive principles and standards on redress; it allows victims to participate at various stages of the proceedings; it offers them ample possibilities to initiate an investigation through the Prosecutor's action; it makes perpetrators directly responsible for both the crimes committed and for the payment of reparation; and it establishes a trust fund to ensure that victims are not left uncompensated. Also, the high number of States Parties to the Rome Statute testifies to the broad support for redress principles as codified in the ICC as well as to the readiness of the international community to make the new reparation regime work for the benefit of future victims of crimes under international law.

In practice, only time will tell whether the ICC will provide effective redress for victims. At this stage, and in current political circumstances, it is difficult to foresee how many cases will actually reach the ICC and how many victims will ultimately be able to access its redress mechanisms. After all, as an institution, the ICC has been established to operate only in exceptional circumstances and on a complementary basis, where domestic courts are unable or unwilling to bring to justice perpetrators of the most serious violations of human dignity. In practice, will this mean that it will be only in exceptional cases that victims of crimes will be able to benefit from the ICC's high redress standards and implementation mechanisms? Most probably, the answer is yes.

This does not mean however that the international community's tremendous efforts to establish a modern and coherent regime for victims' redress have been in vain, or that the creation of the ICC will be seen as a great exercise of codification with little practical use. The ICC has already positively affected domestic standards on human rights and justice administration. Each State wishing to be a party to the ICC must amend its domestic legislation to make it consistent with ICC standards. As a consequence, since the adoption of the Rome Statute, any legal process having to do with genocide, crimes against humanity, war crimes or, in the future, the crime of aggression,

---

91 *See* Christoph J. M. Safferling, *Towards an International Criminal Procedure*, Oxford University Press (2001) at 2, arguing that the future ICC should have its own truly international criminal procedure and not be a medley of common law and civil law procedural traditions.

will no longer be considered legitimate if it does not meet minimum redress standards. In this context, it is expected that broad State participation in the ICC will bring domestic legislation on victims' redress for crimes under international law in an increasing number of countries into closer conformity with current international standards as codified in the Rome Statute.

In this context, a considerable number of States Parties or signatories to the ICC are in the process of enacting domestic legislation for the implementation of the Rome Statute's provisions on various matters, in particular cooperation and elements of crime. To date, eight countries have drafted legislation on ICC implementation,[92] while ten countries have enacted legislation either of a general character or on specific aspects of cooperation.[93] As for victims' redress, many countries have introduced into their domestic legislation specific clauses to implement the victims' right to reparation as expressed in the Rome Statute and to ensure proper cooperation with the ICC in the enforcement both of reparation orders under Article 75 and of fines and forfeiture measures ordered as part of a sentence under Article 77(2).

---

92 The following countries have drafted implementing legislation: Democratic Republic of the Congo, *see* Draft Legislation - Implementation of the Statute of the International Criminal Court; Argentina, *see* Second Draft Law on Crimes under the Jurisdiction of the International Criminal Court; Belgium, *see* Belgian Provisional Draft Law on Cooperation with the ICC and the International Criminal Tribunals, *see also* Belgian Interpretive Law: Proposition De Loi Interpretative De La Loi Du 16 Juin 1993; France, *see* French Senate Draft Cooperation Bill with the ICC, presented by Senator Robert Badinter; Germany, *see* Draft Legislation to Implement the Rome Statute; Italy, *see* Draft ICC Legislation; Liechtenstein, *see* First Draft Implementing Legislation, 22 September 2000; Slovenia, *see* Implementing Law: Predlog Zakona O Sodelovanju Med Republiko Slovenijo In Mednarodnim Kazenskim Sodiščem.

93 The following legislation has been enacted already: the International Criminal Court Bill of South Africa; Canada's Crimes Against Humanity and War Crimes Act 2000; Loi no. 2002-268 du 26 Février 2002 relative à la Coopération avec la Cour Pénale Internationale, of France; Act to Introduce The Code of Crimes against International Law of 26 June 2002 of Germany; Dutch Bill on International Crimes (Rules concerning serious violations of international humanitarian law) 2001; Norwegian Act on Implementation of the Rome Statute, 15 June 2001; Slovenian Law on Nomination of Judges to International Tribunals/Courts; Swiss Federal Law on Cooperation with the ICC; United Kingdom ICC (Scotland) Bill; United Kingdom International Criminal Court Act 2001; United Kingdom Magistrates' Courts (International Criminal Court) Rules 2001; Australian International Criminal Court (Consequential Amendments) Act 2002 (inserting the relevant crimes into the Criminal Code); Australian International Criminal Court Act 2002 (cooperation provisions).

The extent of State legislation on victims' redress varies from country to country. Perhaps the most progressive ICC implementation legislation with respect to victims' redress is Canada's Crimes Against Humanity and War Crimes Act 2000. Canadian implementation legislation not only provides for detailed cooperation provisions for the enforcement of the ICC's reparation and fines and forfeitures orders, but it establishes a 'Crimes Against Humanity Fund' for the benefit of the victims of crimes covered under the Act.[94] Canada's Crimes Against Humanity Fund will be funded by:

> (a) all money obtained through enforcement in Canada of orders of the International Criminal Court for reparation or forfeiture or orders of that Court imposing a fine;
> (b) all money obtained from the disposition of any property referred to in the *Seized Property Management Act* if the property was derived as the result of the commission of an offence under this Act; amounts paid or recovered as a fine imposed under the *Criminal Code* in relation to proceedings for an offence under this Act; and
> (c) any money otherwise received as a donation to the Crimes Against Humanity Fund.

In turn, the Attorney General of Canada has the discretionary power to make payments out of the Crimes Against Humanity Fund to the ICC, the Trust Fund established under Article 79 of the Rome Statute, victims of offences under the Crimes Against Humanity and War Crimes Act, or of offences within the jurisdiction of the ICC, and to the families of those victims. Unfortunately, for the moment this kind of forward-looking legislation remains the exception rather than the rule. States are generally implementing legislation for the enforcement of ICC reparation orders, rather than for the development of independent victims' funds for domestic prosecution purposes according to the principle of complementarity, as the following examples indicate.

In the United Kingdom, Part Four of the United Kingdom International Criminal Court Act 2001 (Enforcement of Fines, Forfeiture and Reparation Orders) and Regulations 2001, entrusts the Secretary of State with the power

---

94 In this sense, Canada falls squarely within Amnesty International's guidelines for ICC implementation legislation, advising that States: "should ensure that national law and procedures permit victims to exercise all their rights under national and international law. States should not only contribute to the Trust Fund established pursuant to Article 79, but should also establish similar trust funds at the national level." *See* Amnesty International, the International Criminal Court: Summary Checklist for Effective Implementation, AI Index: IOR 40/15/00 1/8/2000.

to make provision for enforcement of ICC fines or forfeitures and orders by the ICC against convicted persons specifying reparations to, or in respect of, victims. The act also authorizes the Secretary of State to "appoint a person to act on behalf of the ICC for the purposes of enforcing the order". As a precondition of enforcement however, an ICC order must be registered by a court in England and Wales or Northern Ireland, and such order "shall not be so registered unless the court is satisfied that the order is in force and not subject to appeal". Once the order is registered, "proceedings for its enforcement may be taken in the same way as if the order were an order of a court in England and Wales or Northern Ireland". As for orders involving the rights of *bona fide* third parties, the Act provides that the order shall not be enforced unless the court is:

> satisfied that a reasonable opportunity has been given for persons holding any interest in the property to make representations to the court, and that the exercise of the powers will not prejudice the rights of *bona fide* third parties.

Chapter II of French Law No. 2002-268 of 26 February 2002 on ICC cooperation deals with the question of enforcement of ICC reparation orders and authorizes the 'Tribunal Correctionnel de Paris' upon request of the Republic's Prosecutor to enforce all orders concerning victims' reparations. The Tribunal is bound by the decision of the ICC, including on matters concerning rights of third parties.[95] All proceeds from fines and forfeitures will be transferred directly to the Court, to the Trust Fund, or directly to the victims, if the Court so decides.

In Australia, Clauses 151 and 152 of Part 10 of the International Criminal Court Bill 2002 cover the domestic enforcement of ICC reparation orders and fines. More specifically, if the ICC orders a convicted person to make reparations to the victims or to pay a fine, and requests Australia to give effect to this order as a fine or forfeiture order, then the Attorney-General shall authorise the Department of Public Prosecutions (DPP) to register the fine or order for reparations, unless the conviction or the penalty are being appealed.[96] Once registered, according to Clause 154 on the effect of an order, an order for reparation to victims can be enforced "as an order for the payment of money

---

95 However, on this particular matter, Article 627-16 provides for an exception aimed at protecting the rights of *bona fide* third parties.

96 *See* The Parliament of the Commonwealth of Australia, House of Representatives, International Criminal Court Bill 2002 Explanatory Memorandum.

into court and an order for a fine can be enforced as an order by the court imposing that fine".[97] A similar provision was drafted for the enforcement of forfeiture orders under Clause 155, providing that if the ICC requests Australia to give effect to an order

> for a person to forfeit property that is believed to be in Australia, and the Attorney-General is satisfied that the person has been convicted of the relevant crime by the ICC, then the Attorney-General shall authorise the DPP to apply to register the order

with due regard to the rights of *bona fide* third parties, as in Subclauses (2) and (3). Under Clause 159, a forfeiture may be treated as a pecuniary penalty order, for example when the person has disposed of the property that was to be forfeited.

At the time of writing, a number of countries were in the process of drafting implementing provisions of the victims' right to redress, including the Democratic Republic of the Congo (DRC), Argentina and Italy. Article 64 of the draft implementation law of the DRC provides that:

> the execution of penalties or fines and confiscation or decisions concerning reparations ordered by the International Criminal Court are authorized by the *Tribunal de Grande Instance* of Kinshasa/ Gombe, then seized by the Office of the Public Prosecutor of the Republic

and that "the execution is in conformity with procedure set forth by national legislation in good will and without prejudice of the rights of *bona fide* third parties". The draft law makes clear that although the tribunal is bound by the decision of the ICC, it can take:

> all the necessary measures allowing for the recuperation of the value of the products or goods ordered for confiscation by the Court, once it appears that the order of confiscation cannot be carried out.

According to draft Article 65, proceeds of fines and forfeitures will be either transferred to the Court or given directly to the designated victims, if the Court so decides.

In the case of Argentina, Article 79 of the draft ICC implementation law provides that the competent authorities will give effect to ICC reparations

---

97 *Ibid.*

and other orders without prejudice to *bona fide* third parties. Finally, Article 13 of the draft ICC implementation law of Italy provides that wherever a Judge is seized with restitution matters, he or she shall give priority to the victims' right to restitution, compensation, restoration and return to the place of origin. The draft law ensures the restoration, reconstruction or recuperation of goods to be returned to their lawful owner. Also, Article 114 sets up cooperation procedures for victims' and witnesses protection programmes.

This ongoing process of harmonization, together with efforts at broadening the victims' access to the ICC Trust Fund, will hopefully minimize the chance of discrimination among victims of similar crimes, and help to ensure that all victims of crimes under international law can eventually enjoy the same treatment in terms of redress no matter where their case is heard.

CHAPTER VII

Towards a Comprehensive Redress Regime for Victims of Crimes Under International Law

Victims of the most heinous crimes typically face great difficulty in obtaining even the most basic forms of redress, as we have discussed in earlier chapters. The well-known *Pinochet Case* shows how thoroughly politicized the issue of redress can become and how frustrating it can be for victims and survivors to surmount basic preliminary legal hurdles to obtain justice. Even where a legal process culminates in a clear award in favour of the victims, and where funds held in foreign bank accounts are finally released and transferred to the victims' country, as in the Marcos Case, access to funds for compensation can remain substantially blocked for years until obstacles at the domestic level are overcome.

As discussed in Chapter IV, severe difficulties can arise not only in cases involving large sums of money, but even where victims request 'only' an official State apology. This has been true for the struggle of the 'comfort women' of south-east Asia, of the families of the victims of the 1950 No Gun Ri killing of some 400 South Korean refugees by the US army, of the families of the 'desaparecidos' of Central and Latin America and of many other victims of serious violations in other countries that could be cited.

Victims' issues are receiving more attention today than they ever have been previously, however. There have been many encouraging developments at domestic, regional and international levels in the field of victims' redress, including: the rise of organized victims' groups; the contribution of truth commissions and quasi-judicial mechanisms; the contribution of regional human rights jurisprudence and the practice of the UN Human Rights Committee which, at the time of writing, was in the process of drafting a general comment on the right to a remedy; the whole ICC reparation regime; the work of the UN Commission on Human Rights and Sub-commission on the Promotion and Protection of Human Rights mandates on restitution; recent advances in domestic litigation, including with respect to corporate liability; interesting developments in out-of-court settlements and negotiations; and in general a greater willingness on the part of Governments to incorporate restorative principles into their justice systems.

As examined in earlier chapters, the victims' right to redress has evolved in the context of various domestic, regional and international regimes, including human rights and humanitarian law, international criminal law, the practice of domestic courts and Governments, as well as in intergovernmental frameworks such as the UN and the European, Inter-American and African systems. Each of these fora has contributed in some way to guiding the evolution of the victims' right to redress. In particular, the victims' right to redress for crimes under international law, in its various manifestations and contexts, must be adequate, fair and effective, just and equitable as well as prompt and proportional to the damage suffered, and must include at least the following basic elements:

- compensation, restitution, satisfaction, rehabilitation and guarantees of non-repetition;
- a duty upon the State involved in these kinds of violations to prevent and investigate the crime and to prosecute, punish or extradite the responsible individuals; and
- reparation for both material and moral damages.

Additional elements also have been emerging as essential components of the right to redress for victims of crimes under international law, such as:

- a State duty to amend legislation incompatible with fundamental human rights guarantees;
- the effective access of complainants to investigatory procedures; and
- the access of the victims' families and of 'indirect victims' to redress mechanisms.

At this juncture, the challenge for the future is to consolidate the achievements in victims' redress thus far and to move towards a more comprehensive and coherent redress regime to address adequately, fairly and promptly the needs of victims of crimes under international law.

How should such a consolidated victims' redress regime look? Above all, it should accord victims the recognition and respect they deserve by granting them a central place in norm-setting and implementation. Ideally, a comprehensive victims' redress regime will be unencumbered by excessive formalities, procedural and technical requirements, and will instead focus on recognizing the dignity of all victims, as well as on their rehabilitation and reintegration into community life. A comprehensive victims' redress regime must extend beyond pure monetary forms of redress to embrace avenues to facilitate State apologies, reconciliation and mediation frameworks that allow direct contact between perpetrator and victim, wherever this is desired and appropriate.

It is to this end that the victims' right to redress must continue to develop to meet the needs of individual victims and to address their suffering effectively. However, solutions for victims' redress in cases of crimes under international law cannot be developed in an institutional vacuum. To work effectively and promptly, a comprehensive redress regime for victims of major crimes needs more than to be based on the principles enunciated above. It requires the active participation and positive will of all actors and players in the international community at all levels. Although domestic avenues are often blocked or ineffective in situations involving crimes under international law, reparations provided in the victims' country must remain an essential element of the process of reconciliation, national peace-building, confidence-building and restoration of a dialogue between offender and victim. In this context, it is necessary that States:

- comply with redress principles and standards as they are developed at the UN level, in domestic and international jurisprudence, in the practice of UN treaty bodies and in other fora;
- ensure that reparation judgments are duly enforced in a fair and prompt manner and in a spirit of international cooperation and friendly relations among nations, whether those judgments are foreign or domestic; and
- establish domestic compensation funds for victims of crimes under international law.

In short, States should have clear rules and clear enforcement procedures consistent with international standards, and they should make adequate funds available for redress.

At the international level, a comprehensive redress regime would greatly benefit from the following:

- the establishment of a broadened thematic mandate of the UN Commission on Human Rights on the question of reparations - a mandate that should build upon the excellent work that has been done in the course of the last ten years or so. A broadened Commission mandate could grant the Special Rapporteur on the Right to Reparation the power to investigate concrete situations involving serious and systematic breaches of the victims' right to a remedy for gross human rights violations;

- a more comprehensive and systematic treatment of the question of victims' redress by relevant UN human rights treaty bodies and special procedures wherever appropriate, with a view to maintaining the international community's focus on redress in situations of gross human rights violations;
- the adoption of the 'Basic Principles and Guidelines' on the right to reparation by the Commission on Human Rights and eventually by the General Assembly as well, in the form of a Declaration of Victims' Rights or a Bill of Victims' Rights;
- the establishment of an international mediation commission - an independent body that could meet whenever necessary to consider situations of serious and systematic breaches of the victims' right to a remedy for gross human rights violations or crimes under international law. The international mediation commission could work on principles of restorative justice and could act as an intermediary between victims and offenders, whether they are individuals, States or corporations, with a view to facilitating apologies, collective reparations, satisfaction, acknowledgment of guilt, expressions of regret, and other forms of redress. In practical terms, UN Commission on Human Rights Special Rapporteurs could, for example, refer some of the more serious situations they come across that involve breaches of the victims' right to a remedy, to such mediation commission in order to facilitate dialogue on reparation issues. Such an institution could provide States and other entities involved in redress-related disputes with a neutral and independent forum for negotiation, discussion and problem-solving. Unlike an international compensation or claims commission,[98] an international mediation commission could be designed to respond to redress issues in a broader sense, using restorative and alternative justice techniques to encourage dialogue and national reconciliation and to facilitate apologies as well as rehabilitation of both victims and offenders.
- the establishment of a trust fund for victims of crimes under international law, equipped with adequate means to provide victims with prompt reparations. The fund could work on a subsidiary and complementary basis to other available redress mechanisms, almost as a sort of 'social security system', based on equity and social solidarity.

---

98 *See* the proposal of the ICTY Judges at 207.

It could be a system in which the international community intervenes to provide reparations wherever victims of crimes under international law have not received adequate redress in other fora. In principle, nothing would prevent the international community from using the ICC Trust Fund for this purpose. In this way, the ICC Trust Fund could provide reparations both to victims who participate in ICC proceedings and to those who have no connection to ICC prosecutions.

The world has become a smaller place for all of us. Today, the voices of millions of women, men and children from all over the globe whose basic human rights and freedoms have been violated, even those in remote areas, travel fast over national boundaries, making their concerns our concerns also. No one is immune from serious human rights violations. Just as some innocent people are today's victims, we may be tomorrow's victims. Just as their basic, universal human rights have been violated today, our same basic, universal human rights may be violated tomorrow. With other pieces of the international legal order falling into place, it is now time for the international community to develop a comprehensive redress regime for today's victims of the most basic violations of human dignity, and for those of tomorrow.

* * *

BIBLIOGRAPHY

A. UNITED NATIONS DOCUMENTS (chronological order)

GENERAL ASSEMBLY

i. Draft resolutions

Situation of human rights in Bosnia and Herzegovina, Croatia and the Federal Republic of Yugoslavia (Serbia and Montenegro): draft resolution, A/C.3/48/L.74 of 30 November 1993.

Situation of human rights in Bosnia and Herzegovina, Croatia and the Federal Republic of Yugoslavia (Serbia and Montenegro): revised draft resolution, A/C.3/48/L.74/REV.1 of 3 December 1993.

ii. Resolutions

Resolution 94(I) of 1946 on Draft Code of Offences against the Peace and Security of Mankind.

Resolutions 174 (A/180) and 177(II) of 21 November 1947 on Draft Code of Offences against the Peace and Security of Mankind.

Resolution 96(I) of 1947 on genocide.

Resolution 217 A (III) of 10 December 1948, adopting the Universal Declaration of Human Rights.

Resolution 1904 (XVIII) of 20 November 1963, proclaiming the Declaration on the Elimination of All Forms of Racial Discrimination.

Resolution 2106 A (XX) of 21 December 1965, adopting the International Convention on the Elimination of All Forms of Racial Discrimination.

Resolution 2200 A (XXI) of 16 December 1966, adopting the International Covenant on Civil and Political Rights.

Resolution 3068 (XXVIII) of 30 November 1973, adopting the International Convention on the Suppression and Punishment of the Crime of Apartheid.

Resolution 3074 (XXVIII) of 3 December 1973, adopting the Principles of International Cooperation in the Detection, Arrest, Extradition and Punishment of Persons Guilty of War Crimes and Crimes against Humanity.

Resolution 3452 (XXX) of 9 December 1975, adopting the UN Declaration on the Protection of all Persons from Being Subjected to Torture and Other Cruel, Inhuman or Degrading Treatment or Punishment.

Resolution 36/151 of 16 December 1981, establishing the UN Voluntary Fund for Victims of Torture.

Resolution 39/46 of 10 December 1984, adopting the UN Convention against Torture and Other Cruel, Inhuman or Degrading Treatment or Punishment.

Resolution 40/33 of 29 November 1985, adopting the UN Standard Minimum Rules for the Administration of Juvenile Justice (the 'Beijing Rules').

Resolution 40/34 of 29 November 1985, adopting the UN Declaration of Basic Principles of Justice for Victims of Crime and Abuse of Power.

Resolution 43/173 of 9 December 1988, adopting the Body of Principles for the Protection of All Persons under Any Form of Detention or Imprisonment.

Resolution 44/25 of 20 November 1989, adopting the UN Convention on the Rights of the Child.

Resolution 45/158 of 18 December 1990, adopting the International Convention on the Protection of the Rights of All Migrant Workers and Members of Their Families.

Resolution 46/122 of 17 December 1991, establishing the UN Voluntary Trust Fund on Contemporary Forms of Slavery.

Resolution 47/133 of 18 December 1992, adopting the UN Declaration on the Protection of All Persons from Enforced Disappearance.

Resolution A/RES/48/134 of 20 December 1993, endorsing the 'Principles Relating to the Status and Functioning of National Institutions for Protection and Promotion of Human Rights' (Paris Principles).

Resolution 48/153 of 7 February 1994, on the situation of human rights in the territory of the former Yugoslavia: violations of human rights in the Republic of Bosnia and Herzegovina, the Republic of Croatia and the Federal Republic of Yugoslavia (Serbia and Montenegro).

Resolution 53/144 of 9 December 1998, adopting the UN Declaration on the Right and Responsibility of Individuals, Groups and Organs of Society to Promote and Protect Universally Recognized Human Rights and Fundamental Freedoms.

SECURITY COUNCIL

Statute of the International Tribunal for the Prosecution of Persons Responsible for Serious Violations of International Humanitarian Law Committed in the Territory of the Former Yugoslavia Since 1991, *approved* by Security Council resolution 827 (1993), *adopted* on 25

May 1993, and ICTY Rules of Procedure and Evidence, IT/32/REV.17, *as amended* on 17 November 1999.

Statute of the International Criminal Tribunal for the Prosecution of Persons Responsible for Genocide and Other Serious Violations of International Humanitarian Law Committed in the Territory of Rwanda and Rwandan citizens responsible for genocide and other such violations committed in the territory of neighbouring States, between 1 January 1994 and 31 December 1994, *decided* by Security Council res. 955 of 8 November 1994 and ICTR Rules of Procedure and Evidence, *adopted* on 29 June 1995, *as amended* on 12 January 1996, 15 May 1996, 4 July 1996, 5 June 1997 and 8 June 1998.

COMMISSION ON HUMAN RIGHTS

i. Draft resolutions

The right to restitution, compensation and rehabilitation for victims of gross violations of human rights and fundamental freedoms: draft resolution, E/CN.4/1994/L.50 of 28 February 1994.

The right to restitution, compensation and rehabilitation for victims of grave violations of human rights and fundamental freedoms: draft resolution, E/CN.4/1995/L.44 of 27 February 1995.

The right to restitution, compensation and rehabilitation for victims of grave violations of human rights and fundamental freedoms: draft resolution, E/CN.4/1996/L.76 of 16 April 1996.

The right to restitution, compensation and rehabilitation for victims of grave violations of human rights and fundamental freedoms: draft resolution, E/CN.4/1997/L.58 of 8 April 1997.

ii. Resolutions

Compensation for victims of gross violations of human rights, E/CN.4/RES/1990/35 (1990).

The right to restitution, compensation and rehabilitation for victims of gross violations of human rights and fundamental freedoms, E/CN.4/RES/1994/35 (1994).

The right to restitution, compensation and rehabilitation for victims of grave violations of human rights and fundamental freedoms, E/CN.4/RES/1995/34 (1995).

The right to restitution, compensation and rehabilitation for victims of grave violations of human rights and fundamental freedoms, E/CN.4/RES/1996/35 (1996).

The right to restitution, compensation and rehabilitation for victims of grave violations of human rights and fundamental freedoms, E.CN.4/RES/ 1997/29 (1997).

The right to restitution, compensation and rehabilitation for victims of grave violations of human rights and fundamental freedoms, E/CN.4/RES/ 1998/43 (1998).

The right to restitution, compensation and rehabilitation for victims of grave violations of human rights and fundamental freedoms, E/CN.4/RES/ 1999/33 (1999).

The right to restitution, compensation and rehabilitation for victims of grave violations of human rights and fundamental freedoms, E/CN.4/RES/ 2000/41 (2000).

The right to restitution, compensation and rehabilitation for victims of grave violations of human rights and fundamental freedoms, E/CN.4/RES/ 2002/44 (2002).

Situation of human rights in Cambodia, E/CN.4/RES/2002/89 (2002).

iii. Reports and others

Report on the situation of human rights in El Salvador prepared by the Independent Expert of the Commission on Human rights, E/CN.4/1994/11 of 3 February 1994.

The right to restitution, compensation and rehabilitation for victims of grave violations of human rights and fundamental freedoms: report of the Secretary-General prepared pursuant to Commission resolution 1995/34, E/CN.4/1996/29 of 27 November 1995.

The right to restitution, compensation and rehabilitation for victims of grave violations of human rights: report of the Secretary-General prepared pursuant to Commission resolution 1995/34, E/CN.4/1996/29/Add.1 of 4 January 1996.

The right to restitution, compensation and rehabilitation for victims of grave violations of human rights and fundamental freedoms: report of the Secretary-General prepared pursuant to Commission resolution 1995/34, E/CN.4/1996/29/Add.2 of 18 January 1996.

The right to restitution, compensation and rehabilitation for victims of grave violations of human rights and fundamental freedoms: report of the Secretary-General prepared pursuant to Commission resolution 1995/34, E/CN.4/1996/29/Add.3 of 25 March 1996.

The right to restitution, compensation and rehabilitation for victims of gross violations of human rights and fundamental freedoms: report of the Secretary-General, E/CN.4/1997/29 of 23 January 1997.

The right to restitution, compensation and rehabilitation for victims of grave violations of human rights and fundamental freedoms: report of the Secretary-General, E/CN.4/1997/29/Add.1 of 19 February 1997.

Question of the human rights of all persons subjected to any form of detention or imprisonment: note, E/CN.4/1997/104 of 16 January 1997.

Report of the independent expert on the right to restitution, compensation and rehabilitation for victims of grave violations of human rights and fundamental freedoms, submitted pursuant to Commission on Human Rights resolution 1998/43, E/CN.4/1999/65 of 8 February 1999.

Final report of the Independent Expert on the right to restitution, compensation and rehabilitation for victims of grave violations of human rights and fundamental freedoms, submitted pursuant to Commission Resolution 1999/33, UN Doc. E/CN.4/2000/62 of 18 January 2000.

SUB-COMMISSION ON THE PROMOTION AND PROTECTION OF HUMAN RIGHTS

i. Draft resolutions

Compensation for victims of gross violations of human rights: draft resolution, E/CN.4/SUB.2/1988/L.27 of 24 August 1988.

Compensation for victims of gross violations of human rights: draft resolution, E/CN.4/SUB. 2/1989/L.9 of 17 August 1989.

Compensation for victims of gross violations of human rights: draft resolution, E/CN.4/SUB.2/1990/L.26 of 23 August 1990.

The right to restitution, compensation and rehabilitation for victims of gross violations of human rights and fundamental freedoms: draft resolution, E/CN.4/SUB.2/1991/L.33 of 22 August 1991.

The right to restitution, compensation and rehabilitation for victims of gross violations of human rights and fundamental freedoms: draft resolution, E/CN.4/SUB.2/RES/1991/25 of 24 October 1991.

The right to restitution, compensation and rehabilitation for victims of gross violations of human rights and fundamental freedoms: draft resolution, E/CN.4/SUB.2/1992/L.25 of 24 August 1992.

Study concerning the right to restitution, compensation and rehabilitation for victims of gross violations of human rights and fundamental freedoms: draft resolution, E/CN.4/SUB.2/1993/L.32 of 18 August 1993.

The situation in Bosnia Herzegovina: draft resolution, E.CN.4/SUB.2/1993/ SR.21 of 5 July 1994.

The right to restitution, compensation and rehabilitation for victims of gross violations of human rights and fundamental freedoms: draft resolution, E/CN.4/SUB.2/1994/L.16 of 17 August 1994.

Situation in the former Yugoslavia: draft resolution, E/CN.4/SUB.2/1995/L.24 of 15 August 1995.

The right to restitution, compensation and rehabilitation for victims of gross violations of human rights and fundamental freedoms: draft resolution, E/CN.4/SUB.2/1996/L.19 of 19 August 1996.

ii. Resolutions

Compensation for victims of gross violations of human rights, E/CN.4/SUB.2/RES/1988/11 of 25 October 1988.

Compensation for victims of gross violations of human rights, E/CN.4/SUB.2/RES/1989/13 of 31 August 1989.

The right to restitution, compensation and rehabilitation for victims of gross violations of human rights and fundamental freedoms, E/CN.4/SUB.2/RES/1992/32 of 14 October 1992.

Situation in Bosnia and Herzegovina, E/CN.4/SUB.2/RES/1993/17 of 25 October 1993.

Study concerning the right to restitution, compensation and rehabilitation for victims of gross violations of human rights and fundamental freedoms, E/CN.4/SUB.2/RES/1993/29 of 25 October 1993.

The right to restitution, compensation and rehabilitation for victims of gross violations of human rights and fundamental freedoms, E/CN.4/SUB.2/RES/1994/33 of 28 October 1994.

Situation in the territory of the former Yugoslavia, E/CN.4/SUB.2/RES/1995/8 of 23 October 1995.

The right to restitution, compensation and rehabilitation for victims of gross violations of human rights and fundamental freedoms, E/CN.4/SUB.2/RES/1996/28 of 25 September 1996.

iii. Reports

Study concerning the right to restitution, compensation and rehabilitation for victims of gross violations of human rights and fundamental freedoms: preliminary report, E/CN.4/SUB.2/1990/10 of 26 July 1990.

Study concerning the right to restitution, compensation and rehabilitation for victims of gross violations of human rights and fundamental freedoms: progress report, E/CN.4/SUB.2/1991/7 of 25 July 1991.

Study concerning the right to restitution, compensation and rehabilitation for victims of gross violations of human rights and fundamental freedoms: 2nd progress report, E/CN.4/SUB.2/1992/8 of 29 July 1992.

Study concerning the right to restitution, compensation and rehabilitation for victims of gross violations of human rights and fundamental freedoms: final report, E/CN.4/SUB.2/1993/8 of 2 July 1993.

Review of further developments in fields with which the Sub-Commission has been concerned: Commission on Human Rights, Sub-Commission on Prevention of Discrimination and Protection of Minorities: report of the Secretary-General prepared pursuant to Sub-Commission resolution 1993/29, E/CN.4/SUB.2/1994/7 of 9 June 1994.

Report of the Sessional Working Group on the Administration of Justice and the Question of Compensation, E/CN.4/SUB.2/1994/22 of 15 August 1994.

The administration of justice and the human rights of detainees: report of the Secretary-General prepared pursuant to Sub-commission resolution 1994/33, E/CN.4/SUB.2/1995/17/ADD.1 of 13 June 1995.

Progress report on the question of the impunity of perpetrators of violations of human rights (civil and political rights) E/CN.4/SUB.2/1995/18 of 28 June 1995.

Report of the Sessional Working Group on the Administration of Justice and the Question of Compensation, E/CN.4/SUB.2/1995/16 of 11 August 1995.

Basic principles and guidelines on the right to reparation for victims of gross violations of human rights and international law, E/CN.4/Sub.2/1996/17 of 24 May 1996.

Preliminary report of the Special Rapporteur on the situation of systematic rape, sexual slavery and slavery-like practices during periods of armed conflict, E/CN.4/SUB.2/1996/26 of 16 July 1996.

Report of the sessional Working Group on the Administration of Justice and the Question of Compensation, E/CN.4/Sub.2/1996/16 of 13 August 1996.

Final Report on the question of the impunity of perpetrators of human rights violations (civil and political), UN Doc. E/CN.4/Sub.2/1997/20 of 26 June 1997.

Revised Final Report on the question of the impunity of perpetrators of human rights violations (civil and political), UN Doc. E/CN.4/Sub.2/20/1997/Rev.1 of 2 October 1997.

Basic principles and guidelines on the rights to reparation for victims of gross violations of human rights and international law, annex to E/CN.4/1997/104 of 16 January 1997.

iv. Others

Administrative and programme budget implications of the draft resolution contained in document E/CN.4/SUB.2/1990/L.26: statement, 31 August 1990.

Administrative and programme budget implications of the draft resolution contained in document E/CN.4/SUB.2/1991/L.33: statement, 2 September 1991.

Summary record of the 26th meeting, held at the Palais des Nations, Geneva, on Friday, 21 August 1992: Commission on Human Rights, Sub-Commission on Prevention of Discrimination and Protection of Minorities, 44th session, E./CN.4/SUB.2/1992/SR.26 of 16 February 1993.

Letter from the Special Rapporteur on the Right to Restitution, Compensation and Rehabilitation for Victims of Gross Violations of Human Rights and Fundamental Freedoms addressed to the Working Group on Contemporary Forms of Slavery pursuant to Sub-Commission resolution 1992/2, E/CN.4/SUB.2/AC.2/1993/9 of 22 April 1993.

The right to restitution, compensation and rehabilitation for victims of gross violations of human rights and fundamental freedoms, E/CN.4/DEC/1993/107 (1993).

The right to restitution, compensation and rehabilitation for victims of gross violations of human rights and fundamental freedoms, E/CN.4/DEC/1993/291 of 7 September 1993.

Summary record of the 25th meeting, held at the Palais des Nations, Geneva, on Thursday, 19 August 1993: Commission on Human Rights, Sub-Commission on Prevention of Discrimination and Protection of Minorities, 45th session, E/CN.4/SUB.2/1993/SR.5 of 29 August 1994.

The right to restitution, compensation and rehabilitation for victims of gross violations of human rights and fundamental freedoms, E/CN.4/SUB.2/DEC/1995/117 of 23 October 1995.

Summary record of the 35th meeting, held at the Palais des Nations, Geneva, on Thursday, 29 August 1996: Commission on Human rights, Sub-Commission on Prevention of Discrimination and Protection of Minorities, 48th session, E/CN.4/SUB.2/1996/SR.35 of 9 September 1996.

Revised Set of Basic Principles and Guidelines on the Right to Reparation for Victims of Gross Violations of Human Rights and Humanitarian Law, pursuant to Sub-Commission decision 1995/117, E/CN.4/SUB.2/1996/17 of 24 May 1996.

Revised Set of Basic Principles and Guidelines on the Right to Reparation for Victims of Gross Violations of Human Rights and Humanitarian Law, pursuant to Sub-Commission decision 1997/27 of 11 April 1997.

ICC RELATED DOCUMENTS

Report of the Preparatory Commission for the International Criminal Court, Second Session, New York, PCNICC/1999/L.4/Rev.1.

Report on the international seminar on victims' access to the International Criminal Court, PCNICC/1999/WGRPE/INF/2 and PCNICC/1999/WGRPE/RT.5/Rev.1/Add.3

Draft budget for the first financial year of the Court, Working Group on a Draft Budget for the First Financial Year of the Court, New York 24 September-5 October 2001, PCNICC/2001/WGFYB/L.1 of 8 August 2001.

ICTY AND ICTR RELATED DOCUMENTS

Victims' compensation and participation, Report prepared by the ICTY Rules Committee, Appendix to a Letter dated 12 October 2000 from the President of the ICTY addressed to the Secretary-General, Annex to UN doc. S/2000/1063 of 3 November 2000.

Letter dated 12 October 2000 from the President of the International Tribunal for the Former Yugoslavia addressed to the Secretary-General, annex to a Letter dated 2 November 2000 from the Secretary-General addressed to the President of the Security Council, UN doc. S/2000/1063 of 3 November 2000.

Letter dated 14 December 2000 from the UN Secretary-General Kofi Annan to the UN Security Council, UN Doc. S/2000/1198 of 15 December 2000.

Address to the UN Security Council by Carla del Ponte, Prosecutor of the International Criminal Tribunals for the former Yugoslavia and Rwanda, 21 November 2000. ICTY Doc. JL/P.I.S./542-e of 24 November 2000.

Address by the Registrar of the ICTR Adama Dieng to the Preparatory Commission for the International Criminal Court during its Eighth Session, New York, 1 October 2001 at http://www.iccnow.org/htlm/ICTR.html.

OTHERS

ILC Draft Articles on State Responsibility, 1976, UN Doc. A/CN.4/Ser.A/1976/Add.1.

Compensation for victims of gross violations of human rights, E/RES/1990/36 of 16 July 1990.

Situation of human rights in the territory of the former Yugoslavia: written statement, E/CN.4/1993/NGO/35 of 18 February 1993.

Report of the Commission on the Truth for El Salvador, annex to a Letter dated 29 March 1993 from the Secretary-General to the President of the Security Council, UN Doc. S/25500 of 1 April 1993.

Report of the Secretary-General pursuant to Paragraph 2 of Security Council Resolution 808 (1993), U.N. Doc. S/25704 and Add. 1 of 3 May 1993.

Letter dated 10 August 1993 from the Permanent Representative of the United Republic of Tanzania to the United Nations addressed to the Secretary-General, A/48/322 of 19 August 1993.

Report of the Secretary-General on the implementation of the recommendations of the Commission of the Truth, UN Doc. S/26581 of 14 October 1993.

Summary record of the 20th meeting: 6th Committee, held on Friday, 20 October 1995, New York, General Assembly, 50th session, A/C.6/50/SR.20 of 31 October 1995.

Report of the International Law Commission on the work of its forty-eight session, 6 May-26 July 1996 General Assembly Official Records, Fifty-first Session, Supp. No. 10 (A/51/10).

The situation in Central America: procedures for the establishment of a firm and lasting peace and progress in fashioning a region of peace, freedom, democracy and development: note by the Secretary-General, A/51/790 of 31 January 1997.

Report of the Secretary-General, "Further Promotion and Encouragement of Human Rights and Fundamental Freedoms, Including the Question of the Programme and Methods of Work of the Commission: Regional arrangements for the promotion and protection of human rights in the Asian and Pacific region", UN Doc. E/CN.4/1998/50 of 12 March 1998.

Guide for Policy Makers in the Implementation of the UN Declaration of Basic Principles of Justice for Victims of Crime and Abuse of Power, UN Commission on Crime Prevention and Criminal Justice, UN Doc. E/CN.15/1998/CRP.4 of 17 April 1998.

Offenders and victims: accountability and fairness in the criminal justice process, working paper prepared by the Secretariat of the Tenth UN Congress on the Prevention of Crime and the Treatment of Offenders, Vienna 10-17 April 2000, UN Doc. A/CONF.187/8 of 15 December 1999.

Women in the criminal justice system, Background paper for the workshop on women in the criminal justice system, Tenth UN Congress on the Prevention of Crime and the Treatment of Offenders, Vienna 10-17 April 2000, UN Doc. A/CONF.187/12 of 2 March 2000.

Report of the Expert Seminar on Remedies Available to the Victims of Racial Discrimination, Xenophobia and Related Intolerance and on Good National Practices, UN Doc. A/CONF.189/PC.1/8 of 26 April 2000.

ILC Articles on State responsibility as adopted at the fifty-third session of the ILC (2001), Official Records of the General Assembly, Fifty-sixth Session, Supplement No. 10 (A/56/10).

Report of the Regional Conference for Africa in preparation for the Durban Conference (Dakar, 22-24 January 2001), UN Doc. A/CONF.189/PC.2/8 of 27 March 2001.

Report of the Seminar of Experts on the Prevention of Ethnic and Racial Conflicts in Africa, UN Doc. A/CONF.189/PC.2/4 of 14 March 2001.

Report of the Asian-Pacific regional seminar of experts on migrants and trafficking in persons with particular reference to women and children, UN Doc. A/CONF.189/PC.2/3 of 26 April 2001.

B. TREATIES / CONVENTIONS / AGREEMENTS (chronological order)

Convention for the Amelioration of the Condition of the Wounded in Armies in the Field, *signed* on 22 August 1864 in Geneva, *entered into force* on 22 June 1865.

Convention Respecting the Laws and Customs of War on Land (Hague Convention No. IV), *adopted* on 18 October 1907.

Convention Relative to the Creation of an International Prize Court (Hague Convention No. XII), *adopted* on 18 October 1907.

Treaty of Versailles of 28 June 1919.

Convention for the Protection of Minorities of 15 May 1922.

Protocol for the Prohibition of the Use in War of Asphyxiating, Poisonous or Other Gases, and of Bacteriological Methods of Warfare, *adopted* on 17 June 1925, *entered into force* on 8 February 1928.

London Agreement of 8 August 1945 Concerning the Prosecution and Trial of the Major War Criminals of the Axis Powers, with Annexed the Nuremberg Charter Creating the International Military Tribunal at Nuremberg.

The Four Geneva Conventions of 12 August 1949.

UN Convention on the Prevention and Punishment of the Crime of Genocide, *adopted unanimously* 9 Dec. 1948, *entered into force* 12 January 1951.

European Convention for the Protection of Human Rights and Fundamental Freedoms, *signed* in Rome on 4 November 1950, *entered into force* on 3 September 1953.

Treaty of Peace with Japan, *signed* at San Francisco on 8 September 1951, *entered into force* on 28 April 1952.

Convention relating to the Status of Refugees, *adopted* on 28 July 1951, *entered into force* on 22 April 1954.

Convention on the Nationality of Married Women, *opened for signature and ratification* by General Assembly resolution 1040 (XI) of 29 January 1957, *entered into force* on 11 August 1958.

Treaty of Rome establishing the European Economic Community, *adopted* on 25 March 1957, *entered into force* on 1 January 1958.

Convention on the Reduction of Statelessness, *adopted* on 30 August 1961, *entered into force* on 13 December 1975.

Vienna Convention on Consular Relations, *done* at Vienna on 24 April 1963, *entered into force* on 19 March 1967.

International Convention on the Elimination of All Forms of Racial Discrimination, *adopted and opened for signature and ratification* by General Assembly resolution 2106 A (XX) of 21 December 1965.

International Covenant on Civil and Political Rights, *adopted and opened for signature, ratification and accession* by General Assembly resolution 2200 A (XXI) of 16 December 1966.

Optional Protocol to the International Covenant on Civil and Political Rights, *adopted and opened for signature, ratification and accession* by General Assembly resolution 2200 A (XXI) of 16 December 1966, *entered into force* on 23 March 1976.

International Covenant on Economic, Social and Cultural Rights, *adopted* 16 December 1966, *entered into force* 3 January 1976.

Brussels Convention of 27 September 1968, as *amended* by the 1989 Accession Convention.

Hague Convention for the Suppression of Unlawful Seizure of Aircraft, 1970.

International Convention on the Suppression and Punishment of the Crime of Apartheid, *adopted and opened for signature and ratification* by General Assembly resolution 3068 (XXVIII) of 30 November 1973, *entered into force* on 18 July 1976.

Protocols Additional to the Geneva Conventions of 12 August 1949, *adopted* on 8 June 1977.

American Convention on Human Rights, *signed* on 22 November 1969, *entered into force* on 18 July 1978.

African [Banjul] Charter on Human and People's Rights, *adopted* on 27 June 1981, *entered into force* on 21 October 1986.

Convention against Torture and Other Cruel, Inhuman or Degrading Treatment or Punishment *adopted and opened for signature, ratification and accession* by General Assembly resolution 39/46 of 10 December 1984, *entered into force* 26 June 1987.

Inter-American Convention to Prevent and Punish Torture, *signed* at Cartagena de Indias, Colombia, on December 9, 1985, *entered into force* on 28 February 1987.

European Convention on the Compensation of Victims of Violent Crimes, *adopted* by the Committee of Ministers in June 1983, *opened for signature* on 24 November 1983, *entered into force* on 1 February 1988.

European Convention for the Prevention of Torture and Inhuman or Degrading Treatment or Punishment, *opened for signature* on 26 November 1987, *entered into force* on 1 February 1989.

UN Convention against Illicit Traffic in Narcotic Drugs and Psychotropic Substances, 1988.

Lugano Convention of 16 September 1988.

Convention on the Rights of the Child, *adopted and opened for signature, ratification and accession* by General Assembly resolution 44/25 of 20 November 1989.

ILO Convention (No. 169) concerning Indigenous and Tribal Peoples in Independent Countries, *adopted* on 27 June 1989.

International Convention on the Protection of the Rights of All Migrant Workers and Members of Their Families, *adopted* by General Assembly resolution 45/158 of 18 December 1990.

Mexico agreements of 27 April 1991.

European Charter for Regional or Minority Languages, *opened for signature* on 5 November 1992, *entered into force* on 1 March 1998.

Protocol No. 11 to the Convention for the Protection of Human Rights and Fundamental Freedoms, restructuring the control machinery established thereby, *opened for signature* on 11 May 1994, *entered into force* on 1 November 1998.

Inter-American Convention on Forced Disappearance of Persons, *adopted* at Belém do Pará, on 9 June 1994, *entered into force* on 28 March 1996.

Framework Convention for the Protection for National Minorities, *adopted* on 10 November 1994, *opened for signature* on 1 February 1995, *entered into force* on 1 February 1998.

Convention on the Safety of United Nations and Associated Personnel, *adopted unanimously* on 17 February 1995.

Peace Agreement for Bosnia and Herzegovina, *concluded* in Dayton, Ohio, on 21 November 1995, and *signed* in Paris on 14 December 1995.

Protocol to the African Charter on Human and Peoples' Rights on the Establishment of an African Court on Human and Peoples' Rights, *adopted* by the 34th Ordinary Session of the Assembly of Heads of State and of Government of the Organization of African Unity (OAU) on 9 June 1998.

Statute of the International Criminal Court, *adopted in Rome in a non-recorded vote*, 120 *in favour*, 7 *against* and 21 *abstaining*, on 17 July 1998 (A/CONF.183/9).

C. DECLARATIONS / PRINCIPLES / DRAFT CONVENTIONS (chronological order)

Draft Convention for the Establishment of an International Judicial Body Suitable for the Prevention and Punishment of Violations of the Geneva Convention, Geneva, 1872.

Harvard Research Draft Convention on Jurisdiction with Respect to Crime, 1935, *American Journal of International Law*, Vol. 29, No. 443 Supp. (1935).

American Declaration of Rights and Duties of Man, *adopted* by the ninth Inter-American Conference in Bogotà, May 1948.

Universal Declaration of Human Rights, *adopted* and *proclaimed* by General Assembly resolution 217 A (III) of 10 December 1948.

Declaration on the Elimination of All Forms of Racial Discrimination, *proclaimed* by General Assembly resolution 1904 (XVIII) of 20 November 1963.

Principles of International Cooperation in the Detection, Arrest, Extradition and Punishment of Persons Guilty of War Crimes and Crimes against Humanity, *adopted* by General Assembly resolution 3074 (XXVIII) of 3 December 1973.

UN Declaration on the Protection of all Persons from Being Subjected to Torture and Other Cruel, Inhuman or Degrading Treatment or Punishment, *adopted* by General Assembly resolution 3452 (XXX) of 9 December 1975.

Declaration on Race and Racial Prejudice, *adopted and proclaimed* by the General Conference of the United Nations Educational, Scientific and Cultural Organization at its twentieth session, on 27 November 1978.

UN Standard Minimum Rules for the Administration of Juvenile Justice ('The Beijing Rules'), *adopted* by General Assembly resolution 40/33 of 29 November 1985.

Principles on the Effective Prevention and Investigation of Extra-legal, Arbitrary and Summary Executions, *recommended* by Economic and Social Council resolution 1989/65 of 24 May 1989.

Declaration of Basic Principles of Justice for Victims of Crime and Abuse of Power, *adopted* by General Assembly resolution 40/34 of 29 November 1985.

Body of Principles for the Protection of All Persons under Any Form of Detention or Imprisonment, *adopted* by General Assembly resolution 43/173 of 9 December 1988.

Principles on the Effective Prevention and Investigation of Extra-legal, Arbitrary and Summary Executions, *recommended* by Economic and Social Council resolution 1989/65 of 24 May 1989.

Charter of Paris for a New Europe: A New Era of Democracy, Peace, and Unity, *done* at Paris on 21 November 1990

UN Declaration on the Protection of All Persons from Enforced Disappearance, *adopted* by General Assembly resolution 47/133 of 18 December 1992.

Bangkok Declaration, *adopted* by the Asian Intergovernmental Meeting, Bangkok, 29 March to 2 April 1993.

Principles Relating to the Status and Functioning of National Institutions for Protection and Promotion of Human Rights (Paris Principles), endorsed by the Commission on Human Rights with resolution 1992/54 of March 1992 and by the General Assembly in resolution A/RES/48/134 of 20 December 1993.

Declaration on the Elimination of Violence against Women, *proclaimed* by UN General Assembly resolution 48/104 of 20 December 1993.

Draft Declaration on the Rights of Indigenous Peoples, UN Doc. E/CN.4/Sub.2/1994/2/Add.1 (1994).
Draft Code of Crimes against the Peace and Security of Mankind, *adopted* by the Drafting Committee on Second Reading at its 47th and 48th sessions, UN Doc. A/CN.4/L.522 of 31 May 1996.
UN Declaration on the Right and Responsibility of Individuals, Groups and Organs of Society to promote and Protect Universally Recognized Human Rights and Fundamental Freedoms, *adopted* by General Assembly Resolution 53/144 of 9 December 1998.
Preliminary Draft Convention on Jurisdiction and Foreign Judgments in Civil and Commercial Matters, *provisionally adopted* on 30 October 1999 by the Special Commission of the Hague Conference on private international law.
Durban Declaration and Programme of Action, *adopted* by the World Conference against Racism, Racial Discrimination, Xenophobia and Related Intolerances, meeting in Durban from 31 August to 8 September 2001.

D. DOMESTIC LEGISLATION (chronological order)

Code of Hammurabi, c. 1750 BC.
Hittite Laws, c. 1600-717 BC.
Assyrian Code, c. 1450-1250 BC.
Law of the XII Tables c. 451-450 BC.
Alien Tort Claims Act, 1789.
Austrian General Civil Code, 1811
UK Offences Against the Person Act, 1861.
German Civil Code (BGB), 1896
Italian Civil Code (Codice Civile Italiano), R.D. 16 Marzo 1942, n. 262.
Greek Civil Code, 1946.
Ordinance No. 120 of the French Commander, 10 November 1947.
US Military Government Law No. 59, 20 November 1947.
UK Military Government Law No. 59, 12 May 1949.
Austrian Government Liability Act, 1949.
Israeli Nazi and Nazi Collaborators Law, 1951.
German Final Federal Compensation Law (*Bundesentschadigungsschlussgesetz*, or BEG), 1965.
Portuguese Civil Code (Codigo Civil Português), Decreto-Lei no. 47 344, de 25 de Novembro de 1966.

Austrian Act for the Grant of Assistance to Victims of Crime, 1 September 1972.
Finnish Criminal Injuries Compensation Act, 1973.
Irish General Scheme of Compensation for Personal Injuries Criminally Inflicted, 1974.
Dutch State Compensation Scheme, Criminal Injuries Compensation Fund Act, 1975.
Austrian Penal Code, 1975.
Norwegian scheme on Compensation from the State for Personal Injury Caused by a Criminal Act, 1976.
US Foreign Sovereign Immunities Act, 1976.
German Victim Compensation Act, 11 May 1976.
Amnesty decree law of Chile, 1978.
Swedish Criminal Injuries Compensation Act, 1978.
Danish damages liability act, 1984.
Belgian Victims Compensation Act, 1985.
Peruvian Law No. 23.506, 1985.
Ley Organica del Poder Judicial, 6/1985 del 1 de Julio.
Danish Compensation from the State for Victims of Crimes (Consolidation) Act, 1985.
US Omnibus Diplomatic Security and Anti-Terrorism Act, 1986.
US Civil Liberties Act, 1988.
UK extradition act, 1989.
French General Compensation Scheme, 6 July 1990.
Argentinian Acts No. 23.852 and 24.043, September 1990.
Portuguese Law No. 423/91 on Protection of Victims of Violent Crimes, 30 October 1991.
US Torture Victim Protection Act, 1991.
Chilean Law 19.123 establishing a National Corporation for Reparation and Reconciliation, 8 February 1992.
US Principles of supplemental jurisdiction, 1993.
Colombian Law No. 288, 1996.
US General Federal Question Jurisdictional Statute, 1998.

E. INTERNATIONAL CASES (chronological order)

The Cutting Case, 1886.
Russian Indemnity Case, 1912.
Mavrommatis Palestine Concession Case (Jurisdiction), PCIJ 1924.
Spanish Zones of Morocco Claims, PCIJ 1925.

The Lotus Case, PCIJ 1927.
Chorzów Factory Case, PCIJ 1928.
Martini Case, PCIJ 1930.
Palmagero Gold Fields Case, PCIJ 1931.
The I'm Alone, Interim and Final Reports of a Joint Commission, 1933 and 1935.
Greece v. *the United Kingdom*, Application 299/57, Yearbook II ECHR, 1958-59.
Temple Case, ICJ 1962.
Barcelona Light and Power Co. v. *Spain*, ICJ 1970.
Ringeisen Case, ECHR Judgment of 22 June 1972.
Vagrancy Case, ECHR Judgment of 10 March 1972.
Donnelly Case, Applications 5577-5583/72, Yearbook XVI ECHR, 1973.
Handyside v. *the United Kingdom*, Application 5493/72, Yearbook XVII ECHR, 1974.
Klass v. *Federal Republic of Germany*, Yearbook XVII ECHR, 1974.
40 Mothers v. *Sweden*, ECHR Yearbook XX, 1977.
United States Diplomatic and Consular Staff in Tehran Case, ICJ 1980.
Yarrow P.L.C. and Others v. *the United Kingdom*, Application 9266/81, ECHR, 1983.
Rainbow Warrior, 1986.
Leander Case, ECHR Judgment of 26 March 1987.
Velásquez Rodriguez v. *Honduras*, Inter-Am. Ct. H.R. Judgment of 29 July 1988.
Ian Cowan v. *Le Tresor Public*, ECJ Case 186/87 of 2 February 1989.
Velásquez Rodriguez Case, Compensatory Damages, Inter-Am. Ct. H.R. Judgment of 21 July 1989.
Vilvarajah and Others v. *the United Kingdom*, ECHR Judgment of 30 October 1991.
Open Door and Dublin Well Woman v. *Ireland*, ECHR, 1992.
Hazar and Acik v. *Turkey*, Applications 16311/90 and 16313/90, ECHR, 1992.
Aloeboetoe Case, Reparations, Inter-Am. Ct. H.R., 1993.
Sygounis, Kotsis and 'Union of Police Officers' v. *Greece*, Application 18598/91, ECHR, 1994.
Prosecutor v. *Dusko Tadic*, Decision of the Appeals Chamber on the Defense Motion of the Interlocutory Appeal Concerning Jurisdiction, ICTY Case No. IT-94-1-D, 2 October 1995.
Prosecutor v. *Dusko Tadic*, Decision on the Prosecutor's Motion Requesting Protective Measures for Victims and Witnesses, ICTY, 10 August 1995.

Prosecutor v. *Dusko Tadic,* Decision on the Prosecutor's Motion Requesting Protective Measures for Witness L., ICTY, 14 November 1995.

Suleiman Al-Adsani v. *Kuwait* (Engcas C.A.) (Evans L.J.), March 1996.

Suleiman Al-Adsani v. *Kuwait*, (Engcas C.A.) (Smith L.J.), November 1996.

Aksoy v. *Turkey*, ECHR Judgment of 18 December 1996.

Akdivar Case, ECHR Judgment of 16 September 1996.

Prosecutor v. *Jean-Paul Akayesu,* Decision on the Preliminary Motion Submitted by the Prosecutor for Protective Measures for Witnesses, Case No. ICTR-96-4-T, 27 September 1996.

Prosecutor v. *Blaskic,* Decision on the Application of the Prosecutor, dated 17 October 1996 Requesting Protective Measures for Victims and Witnesses, ICTY, 5 November 1996.

Neira Alegría Case, Reparations, Inter-Am. Ct. H.R. Judgment of 19 September 1996.

El Amparo Case, Reparations, Inter-Am. Ct. H.R. Judgment of 14 September 1996.

Prosecutor v. *Théoneste Bagosora*, Case No. ICTR-96-7, 1996.

Delalic et al., Decision on the Defence Motion to Compel the Discovery of Identity and Location of Witnesses, ICTY, 18 March 1997.

Mentes v. *Turkey*, ECHR Judgment of 28 November 1997.

Aydin v. *Turkey*, ECHR Judgment of 25 September 1997.

Caballero Delgado and Santana Case, Reparations, Inter-Am. Ct. H.R. Judgment of 29 January 1997.

Yasa v. *Turkey*, ECHR Judgment of 2 September 1998.

Kurt v. *Turkey*, ECHR Judgment of 25 May 1998.

Frederiksen and Others v. *Denmark*, ECHR, Application 12719/87, 1998.

Jankovic v. *Republika Srpska*, Human Rights Chamber for Bosnia-Herzegovina, CH/98/367.

Damjanovic v. *the Federation of Bosnia and Herzegovina*, Human Rights Chamber for Bosnia-Herzegovina, CH/98/638.

Prulj v. *the Federation of Bosnia and Herzegovina,* Human Rights Chamber for Bosnia-Herzegovina, CH/98/1374.

Paraguay v. *US Case*, Provisional Measures, 1998.

Garrido and Baigorria Case, Reparations, Inter-Am. Ct. H.R. Judgment of 27 August 1998.

Loayza Tamayo Case, Reparations, Inter-Am. Ct. H.R. Judgment of 27 November 1998.

Castillo Páez Case, Reparations, Inter-Am. Ct. H.R. Judgment of 27 November 1998.

Prosecutor v. *Anto Furundzija,* ICTY Case No. IT-95-17/1-T 10 of 10 December 1998.
Paniagua Morales et al. Case, Inter-Am. Ct. H.R. Judgment of 8 March 1998.
Islamic Community in BiH v. *Republika Srpska*, Human Rights Chamber for Bosnia-Herzegovina, CH/99/2177.
Prosecutor v. *Aleksovski*, ICTY Case No. IT-95-14/1/T of 25 June 1999.
Villagrán Morales et al. Case (the 'Street Children' Case), Inter-Am. Ct. H.R. Judgment of 19 November 1999.
Suárez Rosero Case, Reparations, Inter-Am. Ct. H.R. Judgment of 20 January 1999.
Blake Case, Reparations, Inter-Am. Ct. H.R. Judgment of 22 January 1999.
Selmouni v. *France*, ECHR Judgment of 28 July 1999.
Çakici v. *Turkey,* ECHR Judgment of 8 July 1999.
Tanrikulu v. *Turkey*, ECHR Judgment of 8 July 1999.
Case Concerning the Vienna Convention on Consular Relations (La Grand Case), ICJ 2001.
Trujillo Oroza Case, Inter-Am. Ct. H.R. Judgment of 26 January 2000.
Mahmut Kaya v. *Turkey,* ECHR Judgment of 28 March 2000.
Salman v. *Turkey*, ECHR Judgment of 27 June 2000.
Tanli v. *Turkey*, ECHR Judgment of 10 April 2001.
Al-Adsani v. the United Kingdom, ECHR Judgment of 21 November 2001
Arrest Warrant of 11 April 2000: Democratic Republic of the Congo v. *Belgium*, ICJ 2002.

F. DOMESTIC CASES (chronological order)

Kochunni v. *State of Madras* A. (1959) S.C. India, 752.
Bishan Das v. *State of Punjab*, A. (1961) S.C. India, 1570.
Tata Iron & Steel Co. v. Sarkar, A. (1961) S.C. India, 65.
Attorney-General of the Government of Israel v. *Eichmann* (D. Ct. Jerusalem) 1961.
Filartiga v. *Peña-Irala*, 630 F.2d 876 (2nd Cir. 1980).
Piper Aircraft v. *Reyno*, 454 U.S. 235 (1981).
Rudul Shah v. *State of Bihar* A. (1983) S.C. India 1086 - 1089.
Tel-Oren v. *Libyan Arab Republic Case*, 726 F.2d 774, 824 (D.C.Cir. 1984).
Demjanjuk v. *Petrovsky*, 776 F.2d 571, 584 (6th Cir. 1985).
Fédération Nationale des Déportés et Internés Résistants et Patriotes et al. v. *Barbie*, 1985.
M.C. Mehta v. *Union of India* (Shriram Foods Case), A. (1987) S.C. India, 1086.

Forti and another v. *Suarez-Mason*, 672 F. Supp. (1987, 1988).

US v. *Yunis (no.2)*, 681 F. Supp. 896 (1988).

Argentine Republic v. *Amerada Hess Shipping Corporation*, 488 U.S. 429 (1989).

Peoples Union for Democratic Rights v. *Police Commissioner* A. (1989) S.C. India, 730.

Saheli v. *C.P.*, A. (1990) S.C. India, 513.

Siderman de Blake v. *Republic of Argentina*, 965 F.2d 699 (9th Cir. 1992).

In re *Estate of Ferdinand E. Marcos Litigation*, 978 F.2d 493 (9th Cir. 1992).

Padmini v. *State of T. N.* (1993) Cr. L.J., 2964.

Paul (et al.) v. *Avril*, 812 F. Supp. (1993).

Nilabati Behere v. *State of Orissa*, (1993) S.C. India, 746.

Todd v. *Panjaitan*, D.C. Mass., No. 92-122255 (1994).

Lafontant v. *Aristide*, 844 F. Supp. 128 (E.D.N.Y. 1994).

Doe v. *Karadzic*, 866 F. Supp. 734 (S.D.N.Y. 1994).

In re *Estate of Marcos*, 25 F.3d 1467, 1994 W.L. 262053 (9th Cir. 1994).

In re *Estate of Ferdinand E. Marcos Litigation*, D. Hawaii 1994.

Chiranjit Kaur v. *Union of India*, (19940 S.C. India, 1.

Arvinder Singh Bagga v. *State of Uttar Pradesh*, A. (1995) S.C. India, 117.

X et al v. the State, Tokyo District Court, Judgment of 27 July 1995.

Kadic v. *Karadzic*, 70 F.3d 232 (2nd Cir. 1995).

Mushikiwabo v. *Barayagwiza* No.94, Civ. 3627 (JSM), 1996 WL 164496 (S.D.N.Y. 1996).

Cabiri v. Assasie-Gyimah 921 F. Supp. 1189 (S.D.N.Y. 1996).

D.K.Basu v. *State of West Bengal* A. (1997) S.C. India, 416.

Public Prosecutor v. *Djajic*, Supreme Court of Bavaria, 3rd Strafsenat, Case No. 20/96 of 23 May 1997.

In Re G., Military Tribunal Division 1, Lausanne, 18 April 1997.

Auszug aus dem Urteil der I. öffentlichrechtlichen Abteilung i.S. BAP gegen Aguamina Corporation, Arrêt du Tribunal Federal 123 II 595, 10 December 1997.

The Matter of an Application for a Writ of Habeas Corpus ad Subjicendum. Re: Augusto Pinochet Duarte, The High court of Justice, Queen's Bench Division, Divisional Court, 28 October 1998.

Regina v. Bartle and the Commissioner of Police for the Metropolis and Others (Appellants) EX Parte Pinochet (Respondent) (on appeal from a Divisional Court of the Queen's Bench Division), Regina v. *Evans and Another and the Commissioner of Police for the Metropolis and Others (Appellants) EX Parte Pinochet (Respondent) (on appeal from a Divisional Court of the Queen's Bench Division)*, 25 November 1998.

The Queen v. *Clotworthy*, Appeal Court of New Zealand 114/98, Wellington, 1998.

F. INDIVIDUAL COMMUNICATIONS TO THE UN HUMAN RIGHTS COMMITTEE (chronological order)

Irene Bleier Lewenhoff and Rosa Valiño de Bleier v. Uruguay, Comm. No. 30/1978.
Antonio Vianna Acosta v. *Uruguay*, Comm. No. 110/1981.
Tshitenge Muteba v. *Zaire*, Comm. No. 124/1982.
Tshitenge Muteba v. *Zaire*, Comm. No. 124/1982.
Guillermo Ignacio Dermit Barbato and Hugo Haroldo Dermig Barbato v. *Uruguay*, Comm. No. 84/1981.
John Khemraadi Baboeram et al. v. *Suriname*, Comm. Nos. 146/1983 and 148-154/1983.
H.C.M.A. v. *the Netherlands*, Comm. No. 213/1986 of 30 March 1989.
S.E. v. Argentina, Comm. No. 275/1988 of 26 March 1990.
R.A., V.N. et al. v. *Argentina* Comm. No. 343-345/1988 of 26 March 1990.
Rodriguez v. *Uruguay*, Comm. No. 322/1988, CCPR/C/51/D/322/1988 of 9 August 1994.
Zelaya v. *Nicaragua*, Comm. No. 328/1988, CCPR/C/51/D/328/1988 of 18 August 1994.
Bautista v. *Colombia*, Comm. No. 563/1993, CCPR/C/55/D/563/1993 of 13 November 1995.
Laureano v. *Peru*, Comm. No.540/1993, CCPR/C/56/D/540/1993 of 16 April 1996.

G. INDIVIDUAL COMMUNICATIONS TO THE AFRICAN COMMISSION ON HUMAN AND PEOPLES' RIGHTS (chronological order)

Krishna Achuthan vs. *Malawi*, Comm. No. 64/92 (October 10,1991), 68/92 (March 2, 1992), 78/92, (October 6, 1992).
Free Legal Assistance Group, Lawyers' Committee for Human Rights, Union Interafricaine des Droits de l'Homme, Les Témoins de Jehovah vs. *Zaire*, Comm. No. 25/89, 47/90, 56/91, 100/93 (not dated).
Organisation Mondiale Contre La Torture vs. *Rwanda*, Comm. No. 27/89, 46/91, 49/91, 99/93 (not dated).

Mauritania Cases: *Malawi African Association*, Comm. No. 54/91; *Amnesty International* Comm. No. 61/91; *Ms. Sarr Diop* Comm. No. 98/93; *Union Interafricaine des Droits de l'Homme and RADDHO* Comm. No. 164/97; and *Collectif des Veuves and Ayant-droit and Association Mauritanienne des Droits de l'Homme* v. *Mauritania* Comm. No. 210/98.

H. BOOKS / EDITED BOOKS / COMMENTARIES (alphabetical order)

ALFREDSSON, Gudmundur, EIDE, Asbjørn (eds.), *The Universal Declaration of Human Rights: A Common Standard of Achievement*, Martinus Nijhoff, Dordrecht, 1999.

ALSTON, Philip (ed.), *The EU and Human Rights*, Oxford University Press, 1999.

ALSTON, Philip, CRAWFORD, James (eds.), *The Future of UN Human Rights Treaty Monitoring*, Cambridge University Press, 2000.

BARKAN, Elazar, *The Guilt of Nations: Restitution and Negotiating Historical Injustices,* Johns Hopkins University Press, 2001.

BASSIOUNI, M. Cherif, *The Statute of the International Criminal Court: A Documentary History*, Transnational Publishers, Ardsley, New York, 1998.

BASSIOUNI, M. Cherif, WISE, Edward, *Aut Dedere Aut Judicare: The Duty to Extradite or Prosecute in International Law*, Martinus Nijhoff, The Hague, 1995.

BASU, Durga Das, *Constitutional Remedies and Writs*, Kamal Law House, Calcutta, 1994.

BEDJAOUI, Mohammed (ed.), *International Law: Achievements and Prospects*, Martinus Nijhoff, Dordrecht, 1991.

BEHRENDT, Larissa, *Aboriginal Dispute Resolution: A Step Towards Self-Determination and Community Autonomy*, Australia Federation Press, 1995.

BOTHE, Michael (ed.), *National Implementation of International Humanitarian Law*, Martinus Nijhoff, Dordrecht, 1990.

BROWER, Charles N., BRUESCHKE, Jason D., *The Iran-United States Claims Tribunal*, Martinus Nijhoff, Dordrecht, 1998.

BROWNLIE, Ian, *Principles of Public International Law*, Fourth Edition, Clarendon Press, Oxford, 1990.

BURROWS, Andrew, *Fusing Common Law and Equity: Remedies, Restitution and Reform*, Sweet & Maxwell Asia, 2001.

CAMERON, Iain, *The Protective Principle of International Criminal Jurisdiction*, Dartmouth Publishing Company, 1994.

CASSESE, Antonio, *International Law*, Oxford University Press, 2001.

CICERO, (Ciceronis) Marcus Tullius, *De Oratore* Book I, 44, Loeb Classical Library, Translated by E.W. Sutton & H. Rackham, Harvard University Press, Cambridge, 1996.

CONFORTI, Benedetto, *International Law and the Role of Domestic Legal Systems*, Kluwer Academic Publishers, The Hague, 1993.

CONFORTI, Benedetto, FRANCIONI, Francesco (eds.), *Enforcing International Human Rights in Domestic Courts*, Kluwer Law International, The Hague, 1997.

CLARK, Roger S., *The United Nations Crime Prevention and Criminal Justice Programme*, University of Pennsylvania Press, 1994.

CRAWFORD, James, *The ILC's Articles on State Responsibility: Introduction, Text, and Commentaries*, Cambridge University Press, 2002.

DUNANT, Henri, *Un Souvenir de Solferino*, 1862, published in English under the title *A Memory of Solferino*, ICRC, Geneva, 1986.

ESER, Albin, WALTHER, Susanne (eds.), *Reparation in Criminal Law: International Perspectives,* Vol. I and II, Ed. Iuscrim, Max-Planck Inst. Für Ausländisches und International Strafrecht, 1996.

FRIGESSI di RATTALMA, Marco, TREVES, Tullio (eds.), *The United Nations Compensation Commission: A Handbook*, Kluwer Law International, The Hague, 1999.

GILBERT, Geoff, *Aspects of Extradition Law*, Martinus Nijhoff, Dordrecht, 1991.

GOMEZ, James, *Self-Censorship: Singapore's Shame*, THINK Centre, Singapore, 2000.

GREEN, Ross, *Justice in Aboriginal Communities: Sentencing Alternatives*, Purich Publishing, Saskatoon, Saskatchewan, 1998.

GREER, Desmond (ed.), *Compensating Crime Victims: A European Survey*, Ed. Iuscrim, Max-Planck Inst. Für Ausländisches und International Strafrecht, 1996.

HENZELIN, Marc, *Le Principe de l'Universalité en Droit Pénal International: Droit et Obligation pour les États de Poursuivre et Juger Selon le Principe de l'Universalité,* Helbing & Lichtenhahn, Genève, 2000.

HICKS, George, *The Comfort Women*, W. W. Norton & Co., New York (1995).

IMTIAZ, Omar, *Rights, Emergencies and Judicial Review*, Kluwer Law International, The Hague, 1996.

IOVANE, Massimo, *La Riparazione nella Teoria e nella Prassi dell'Illecito Internazionale*, Giuffrè, Milano, 1990.
JONES, John R. W. D., *The Practice of the International Criminal Tribunals for the Former Yugoslavia and Rwanda*, Second Edition, Transnational Publishers, Ardsley, New York.
KÄLIN, Walter (ed.), *Human Rights in Times of Occupation: The Case of Kuwait*, Law Books in Europe, Berne, 1994.
KAMMINGA, Menno T., *Inter-State Accountability for Violations of Human Rights*, Philadelphia, University of Pennsylvania Press, 1992.
KEEN, Maurice Hugh, *The Laws of War in the Late Middle Ages*, 1965.
KELSEN, Hans, *What is Justice? Justice, Law and Politics in the Mirror of Science*, Collected Essays, University of California Press, Berkeley and Los Angeles, 1957.
LANGLOIS, Anthony J., *The Politics of Justice and Human Rights: Southeast Asia and Universalist Theory*, Cambridge University Press, 2001.
LAUTERPACHT, Hersch, *The Development of International Law by the International Court*, Stevens, London, 1958.
LEBIGRE, Arlette, *Quelques Aspects de la Responsabilité Pénale en Droit Romain Classique*, Presses Universitaires de France, Paris, 1967.
LEE, Roy S. (ed.), *The International Criminal Court: The Making of the Rome Statute*, Kluwer Law International, The Hague, 1999.
LEE, Roy S. (ed.), *The International Criminal Court: Elements of Crimes and Rules of Procedure and Evidence*, Transnational Publishers, Ardsley, New York, 2001.
LILLICH, Richard B., *International Claims; Their Settlement by Lump Sums Agreements*, Charlottesville, 1975.
LILLICH, Richard B., MAGRAW, Daniel B. (eds.), *The Iran-United States Claims Tribunal: Its Contribution to the Law of State Responsibility*, Transnational Publishers, Ardsley, New York, 1998.
LAWSON, Edward, *Encyclopaedia of Human Rights*, Second Edition, Taylor & Francis (1996).
MERRILLS, John G., *The Development of International Law by the European Court of Human Rights*, Manchester University Press, 1993.
MIERS, David, *State Compensation for Criminal Injuries*, Blackstone Press Ltd., London 1997.
MOORE, John Bassett, *Digest of International Law*, Vol. II, Washington, D.C., Government Printing Office, 1906.
MORRIS, Virginia, SCHARF, Michael, *An Insiders Guide to the International Criminal Tribunal for the Former Yugoslavia*, 1995.

NAPIER, Michael; WHEAT, Kay, *Recovering Damages for Psychiatric Injury*, Blackstone Press Ltd., London, 1995.

NOWAK, Manfred, *UN Covenant on Civil and Political Rights: CCPR Commentary*, N. P. Engel Publisher, Kehl, 1993.

PICTET, Jean (ed.), *Commentary to the I Geneva Convention for the Amelioration of the Condition of the Wounded and Sick in Armed Forces in the Field. Geneva, 12 August 1949*, Geneva, ICRC.

RANDELZHOFER, Albrecht, TOMUSCHAT, Christian (eds.), *State Responsibility and the Individual: Reparation in Instances of Grave Violations of Human Rights*, Kluwer Law International, The Hague, 1999.

RATNER, Steven R., ABRAMS, Jason S., *Accountability for Human Rights Atrocities in International Law: Beyond the Nuremberg Legacy*, Clarendon Press, Oxford, 1997.

ROHT-ARRIAZA, Naomi, *Impunity and Human Rights in International Law and Practice*, Oxford University Press, New York and London, 1995.

ROUNER, Leroy S. (ed.), *Human Rights and the World's Religions*, University of Notre Dame Press, Notre Dame, Indiana, 1988.

SAFFERLING, Christoph J. M., *Towards an International Criminal Procedure*, Oxford University Press, 2001.

SCHABAS, William A., *Genocide in International Law*, Cambridge University Press, 2000.

SCHACHTER, Oscar, *International Law in Theory and Practice*, Martinus Nijhoff, Dordrecht, 1991.

SCHMIDLIN, Bruno, CANNATA, Carlo Augusto, *Droit Privé Romain: Obligations - Successions - Procédure*, Vol. II, Payot, Lausanne, 1991.

SHAW, Malcom N., *International Law*, Fourth Edition, Cambridge University Press, 1997.

SHELTON, Dinah, *Remedies in International Human Rights Law*, Oxford University Press, 1999.

SIEGHART, Paul, *The International Law of Human Rights*, Clarendon Press, Oxford, 1983.

STEINER, Henry J., ALSTON Philip, *International Human Rights in Context: Law, Politics, Morals*, Second Edition, Clarendon Press, Oxford, 2000.

STEPHENS, Beth, RATNER, Michael, *International Human Rights Litigation in U.S. Courts*, Transnational Publishers, Ardsley, New York, 1996.

STRANG, Heather, BRAITHWAITE, John, *Restorative Justice: Philosophy to Practice*, Ashgate Dartmouth, Sydney, 2000.

SUNGA, Lyal S., *Individual Responsibility in International Law for Serious Human Rights Violations*. Martinus Nijhoff, Dordrecht, 1992.

SUNGA, Lyal S., *The Emerging System of International Criminal Law: Developments in Codification and Implementation*, Kluwer Law International, The Hague, 1997.
UMOZURIKE, Oji U., *The African Charter on Human and Peoples' Rights*, Kluwer Law International, The Hague, 1997.
VAN DIJK Pieter, VAN HOOF Fried, *Theory and Practice of the European Convention on Human Rights*, Third Edition, Kluwer Law International, The Hague, 1998.
VASSILOUNI, Stavroula (ed.), *Aspects of the Protection of Individual and Social Rights*, Marangopoulos Foundation for Human Rights and Hestia Publishers & Booksellers, Athens, 1995.
WALKER, Nigel, *Why Punish? Theories of punishment reassessed*, Oxford University Press, 1991.
WILSON, Richard A., *The Politics of Truth and Reconciliation in South Africa: Legitimizing the Post-Apartheid Regime*, Cambridge University Press, 2001.
WINIGER, Bénédict, *La Responsabilité Aquilienne Romaine: Damnum Iniuria Datum*, Helbing & Lichtenhahn, Bâle et Francfort-sur-le-Main, 1997.
WRIGHT Cecil A., LINDEN Allen M., *Canadian Tort Law: Cases, Notes & Materials*, Seventh Edition, Butterworths, Toronto, 1980.
WRIGHT, Martin, *Justice for Victims and Offenders, A Restorative Approach to Crime*, Second Edition, Waterside Press, Winchester, 1996.

I. ARTICLES / BOOK SECTIONS

ABDELSALAM, Mohamed A., "Individual and NGO Participation in Human Rights Litigation before the African Court of Human and Peoples' Rights: Lessons From the European and Inter-American Courts of Human Rights", *Michigan State University-DCL Journal of International Law*, Vol. 8, No. 377, Summer 1999.
ALDRICH, George H., CHINKIN, Christine M., "Symposium: the Hague Peace Conferences: A Century of Achievement and Unfinished Work", *The American Journal of International Law*, Vol. 94, No. 90, January 2000.
AMBOS, Kai, "General Principles of Criminal Law in the Rome Statute", *Criminal Law Forum*, No. 10, 1999.
ARSANJANI, Mahnoush H., "Developments in International Criminal Law: The Rome Statute of the International Criminal Court", *The American Journal International Law*, Vol. 93, No. 22, January 1999.

BARTON, Charles, "Empowerment and Retribution in Criminal Justice", in *Restorative Justice: Philosophy to Practice*, Ashgate Dartmouth, Sidney, 2000.

BEDERMAN, David J., "The United Nations Compensation Commission and the Tradition of International Claims Settlement", *New York University Journal of International Law and Politics*, Vol. 27, No. 1, Fall 1994.

BIANCHI, Andrea, "Immunity versus Human Rights: The Pinochet Case", *European Journal of International Law*, Vol. 10, No. 2, 1999.

BIRKS, Peter, "Inconsistency Between Compensation and Restitution", *Law Quarterly Review*, Vol. 112, July 1996.

BOED, Roman, "The Effect of a Domestic Amnesty on the Ability of Foreign States to Prosecute Alleged Perpetrators of Serious Human Rights Violations", *Cornell International Law Journal,* Vol. 33, No. 297, 2000.

BOCHENEK, Michael Garcia, "Compensation for Human Rights Abuses in Zimbabwe", *Columbia Human Rights Law Review*, Vol. 26, No. 2, Winter 1995.

BOTTIGLIERO, Ilaria, "Displaced Persons Caught Between War and Peace in Asia", *Indian Yearbook of International Humanitarian and Refugee Law*, Vol. 2, 2002.

BOTTIGLIERO, Ilaria, "The International Criminal Court - Hope for the Victims", 32 *SGI Quarterly*, April 2003, pp. 13-15.

BROWN, B. F., "Equity in the Law of the United States of America", in *Equity in the World's Legal Systems: A Comparative Study*, R. A. Newman (ed.) Etablissement Emile Bruylant, Brussels, 1973.

BROWN, Jeffrey J., "The Jurisprudence of the Foreign Claims Settlement Commission: Vietnam Claims", *Virginia Journal of International Law*, Vol. 27, No. 1, Fall 1986.

CANCADO TRINDADE, Antonio Augusto, "The Consolidation of the Procedural Capacity of Individuals in the Evolution of the International Protection of Human Rights: Present State and Perspectives at the Turn of the Century", *Columbia Human Rights Law Review*, Vol. 30, No. 1, Fall 1998.

CANÇADO TRINDADE, Antonio Augusto, "State and Perspectives of the Inter-American System of Human Rights Protection at the Dawn of the New Century", *Tulane Journal of International and Comparative Law,* Vol. 8, No. 5, Spring 2000.

CARMICHAEL, Keith, McKAY, Fiona, DISHINGTON, William, "The Need for Redress", *Torture*, Vol. 6, No. 1, 1996.

CARON, David D., "The Nature of the Iran-United States Claims Tribunal and the Evolving Structure of International Dispute Resolution", *American Journal of International Law,* Vol. 84.

CHUNGHEE, Sarah Soh, "The Korean 'Comfort Women': Movement for Redress", *Asian Survey*, Vol. 36, No. 12, December 1996.

CLAGETT, Brice M., "The Expropriation Issue Before the Iran-United States Claims Tribunal: Is 'Just Compensation' Required by International Law or Not?", *Law and Policy in International Business*, Vol. 16, No. 3, 1984.

CLAPHAM, Andrew, "UN Human Rights Reporting Procedures: An NGO Perspective" in P. Alston and J. Crawford (eds.), *The Future of UN Human Rights Treaty Monitoring*, Cambridge University Press, 2000.

CLAPHAM, Andrew, "Revisiting *Human Rights in the Private Sphere*, Postscript: Developments Related to Pinochet as of January 2001", in Craig Scott (ed.), *Torture and Tort: Comparative Perspectives on the Development of Transnational Human Rights Litigation*, Hart Publishing, 2001.

CLAPHAM, Andrew, "Revisiting *Human Rights in the Private Sphere*: Using the European Convention on Human Rights to Protect the Right of Access to the Civil Courts", in Craig Scott (ed.), *Torture and Tort: Comparative Perspectives on the Development of Transnational Human Rights Litigation* Hart Publishing, 2001.

CLARK, Roger S., "Creating a Statute for the International Criminal Court: A Jurisdictional Quandary", *Suffolk Transnational Law Review,* Vol. 22 No. 461, Summer 1999.

COHEN-JONATHAN, Gerard, "Responsabilité pour l'Atteinte aux Droits de l'Homme", in *La Responsabilité dans le Système International*, Paris, Pedone, 1991.

COTTEREAU, Gilles, "Responsabilité de l'Iraq: Aperçu sur les Indemnisations Urgentes des Personnes Physiques", *Annuaire Français de Droit International*, Vol. 41, 1995.

CROOK, John R., "Current Development: The United Nations Compensation Commission - a New Structure to Enforce State Responsibility", *The American Journal International Law*, Vol. 87, No. 144, January 1993.

DAVIDSON, Scott, "Remedies for Violations of the American Convention on Human Rights", *International and Comparative Law Quarterly*, Vol. 44, No. 2, April 1995.

DE SENA, Pasquale, "Immunity of State Organs and Defence of Superior Orders as an Obstacle to the Domestic Enforcement of International Human Rights", in B. Conforti and F. Francioni (eds.), *Enforcing International Human Rights in Domestic Courts*, Kluwer Law International, 1997.

DE ZAYAS, Alfred, "The Examination of Individual Complaints by the UN Human Rights Committee under the Optional Protocol to the International Covenant on Civil and Political Rights", in G. Alfredsson, J. Grimheden, B. G. Ramcharan and A. de Zayas (eds.), *International Human Rights Monitoring Mechanisms*, Kluwer Law International, 2001.

DRINAN, Robert F., KUO, Teresa T., "Putting the World's Oppressor on Trial: The Torture Victim Protection Act", *Human Rights Quarterly*, Vol. 15, No. 3, August 1993.

DRZEMCZEWSKI, Andrew, "The European Human Rights Convention: Protocol No. 11 - Entry Into Force and First Year of Application", *Human Rights Law Journal*, Vol. 21, No. 1-3, 18 September 2000.

ENSALACO, Mark, "Truth Commissions for Chile and El Salvador: A Report and Assessment", *Human Rights Quarterly*, Vol. 16, 1994.

ENSLEN, Alan Frederick, "*Filartiga*'s Offspring: The Second Circuit Significantly Expands the Scope of the Alien Tort Claim Act with its Decision in *Kadic* v. *Karadzic*", *Alabama Law Review*, Vol. 48, No. 2, Winter 1997.

FEATHERSTONE, Yvonne O. M., "The International Criminal Tribunal for the Former Yugoslavia: Recent Developments in Witness Protection", *Leiden Journal of International Law*, Vol. 10, No. 1, 1997.

FISHBANE, Michael, "The Image of the Human and the Rights of the Individual in Jewish Tradition" in Leroy S. Rouner (ed.), *Human Rights and the World's Religions*, University of Notre Dame Press, Notre Dame, Indiana, 1988.

FERENCZ, Benjamin B., "Compensating Victims of the Crimes of War", *Virginia Journal of International Law*, Vol. 12, No. 3, April 1972.

FLETCHER, George P., "The Place of Victims in the Theory of Retribution", *Buffalo Criminal Law Review,* No. 3, 1999.

FRANCIONI, Francesco, "The Jurisprudence of International Human Rights Enforcement: Reflections on the Italian Experience", in B. Conforti and F. Francioni (eds.), *Enforcing International Human Rights in Domestic Courts*, Kluwer Law International, 1997.

GAETA, Paola, "The Dayton Agreements and International Law", *European Journal of International Law*, Vol. 7, No. 2, 1996.

GAJA, Giorgio, "New Instruments and Institutions?" in P. Alston (ed.), *The EU and Human Rights*, Oxford University Press, 1999.

GHAI, Yash, "Human Rights and Governance: The Asia Debate", *The Australian Yearbook of International Law 1994*, Vol. 15.

GHAI, Yash, "Universalism and Relativism: Human Rights as a Framework for Negotiating Interethnic Claims", *Cardozo Law Review*, Vol. 21, No. 4, February 2000.

GIBNEY, Mark, "Compensation for Civilians Harmed in the Pursuit of Foreign Policy Goals: Recent Litigation in Us Courts", *California Western International Law Journal*, Vol. 22, No. 1, 1991/1992.

GIBNEY, Mark, ROXSTROM, Erik, "The Status of State Apologies", *Human Rights Quarterly*, Vol. 23, No. 4, November 2001.

GOWLLAND-DEBBAS, Vera, "Security Council Enforcement Action and Issues of State Responsibility", *International and Comparative Law Quarterly*, No. 43, 1994.

GRAEFRATH, Bernhard, "Iraq: Reparations and the Security Council", *Zeitschrift für Ausländisches öffentliches Recht und Völkerrecht*, 1995.

GRAEFRATH, Bernhard, "Universal Criminal Jurisdiction and an International Criminal Court", *European Journal of International Law*, Vol. 1, No. 1-2, 1990.

GRAY, Catherine, "The Choice between Restitution and Compensation", *European Journal of International Law*, Vol. 10, No. 2, 1999.

GUEST, James J. R., "Aboriginal Legal Theory and Restorative Justice", *Justice as Healing: A Newsletter on Aboriginal Concepts of Justice*, Vol. 3, No. 4, Winter 1998.

HAASDIJK, S., "The Lack of Uniformity in the Terminology of the International Law of Remedies", *Leiden Journal of International Law*, Vol. 5, No. 2, October 1992.

HALL, Christopher K., "The First Proposal for a Permanent International Criminal Court", *International Review of the Red Cross*, No. 322, 31 March 1998.

HARVARD LAW REVIEW ASSOCIATION, "Corporate Liability for Violations of International Human Rights", *Harvard Law Review*, May 2001.

HARLOW, Carol, "Access to Justice as a Human Right: The European Convention and the European Union", in P. Alston (ed.), *The EU and Human Rights*, Oxford University Press, 1999.

HAYNER, Priscilla B., "Fifteen Truth Commissions - 1974 to 1994: A Comparative Study", *Human Rights Quarterly*, Vol. 16, No. 4, November 1994.

HENDERSON, Lynne N., "The Wrongs of Victims' Rights", *Stanford Law Review*, Vol. 37, April 1985.

HENKIN, Louis, "International Human Rights Standards in National Law: The Jurisprudence of the United States", in Conforti and Francioni (eds.), *Enforcing International Human Rights in Domestic Courts*, Kluwer Law International, 1997.

HENRARD, Kristin, "The Viability of National Amnesties in View of the Increasing Recognition of Individual Criminal Responsibility in International Law", *Michigan State University - DCL Journal of International Law,* Vol. 8, No. 595, Fall 1999.

HEYNS, Christof, "The African Regional Human Rights System: In Need of Reform?", *African Human Rights Law Journal*, Vol. 1, No. 2, 2001.

HUCULAK, Bria, "From the Power to Punish to the Power to Heal", *Justice as Healing: A Newsletter on Aboriginal Concepts of Justice,* Fall 1995.

JOHNSON, Eric, "*Kadic* v. *Karadzic* and *Doe I and II* v. *Karadzic*: The Latest Stage in Alien Tort Act Jurisprudence", *German Yearbook of International Law*, Vol. 39, 1996.

KIRSCH, Philippe, HOLMES, John T., "Developments in International Criminal Law: The Rome Conference on an International Criminal Court: The Negotiating Process", *The American Journal of International Law,* Vol. 93, No. 2, January 1999.

KAISER, Michael, KILCHLING, Michael, "Germany", in D. Greer (Ed.), *Compensating Crimes Victims - A European Survey*, Ed. Iuscrim, Max-Planck Inst. Für Ausländisches und International Strafrecht, 1996.

KAZUKO, Watanabe, "Militarism, Colonialism, and the Trafficking of Women: "Comfort Women" Forced into Sexual Labour for Japanese Soldiers", *Bulletin of Concerned Asian Scholars*, Vol. 26, No. 4, October - December 1994.

KLERK, Yvonne, "The Character of the Views of the Human Rights Committee", in F. Coomans *et al.* (eds.), *Rendering Justice to the Vulnerable,* Kluwer Law International, The Hague, 2000.

LAPPI-SEPPALA, Tapio, "Finland", in A. Eser and S. Walther, *Reparation in Criminal Law: International Perspectives,* Max-Planck Inst. Für Ausländisches und International Strafrecht, 1996.

LEANZA, Umberto, SICO, Luigi, "Compensation for Victims of Maritime Terrorism", *Maritime Terrorism and International Law*, Dordrecht, Martinus Nijhoff, 1990.

LEE, Luke T., "The Right to Compensation: Refugees and Countries of Asylum", *American Journal of International Law*, Vol. 80, No. 3, July 1986.

LEE, Luke T., "The Right of Victims of War to Compensation", *Essays in Honour of Wang Tieya*, Dordrecht, Martinus Nijhoff, 1994.

LIBERA, Rosemary E., "Divide, Conquer, and Pay: Civil Compensation for Wartime Damages", *Boston College International & Comparative Law Review*, Vol. 24.

MALANCZUK, Peter, "International Business and New Rules of State Responsibility? - The Law Applied by the United Nations (Security Council) Compensation Commission for Claims Against Iraq", in K. - H. Böckstiegel (ed.), *Perspectives of Air Law, Space Law and International Business Law for the Next Century*, Carl Heymanns Verlag KG, 1996.

MALMSTRÖM, Susanne, "Restitution of Property and Compensation to Victims", in Richard May *et al.* (eds.), *Essays on ICTY Procedure and Evidence*, Kluwer Law International, 2001.

MARZOUK, M. S., "Iraqi Reparation After the Gulf War: How Much, How Likely?", *Rivista Internazionale di Scienze Economiche e Commerciali*, Vol. 42, Nos. 7/8, Luglio/Agosto 1995.

MATHESON, Michael J., "The Twelfth Waldemar A. Solf Lecture in International Law", *Military Law Review*, Vol 161, No. 181, September 1999.

MCCORMACK, Timothy L. H., ROBERTSON Sue, "Jurisdictional Aspects of the Rome Statute for the New International Criminal Court", *Melbourne University Law Review,* Vol. 23, No. 635, December 1999.

MEDINA, Cecilia, "The Inter-American Commission on Human Rights and the Inter-American Court of Human Rights: Reflections on a Joint Venture", *Human Rights Quarterly*, Vol. 12, No. 439, 1990.

MENDELSON, Maurice, "The United Kingdom Nationalization Cases and the European Convention on Human Rights", *British Yearbook of International Law*, Vol. 57, 1986.

MENDEZ, Juan E., "Accountability for Past Abuses", *Human Rights Quarterly*, Vol. 19, No. 2, May 1992.

MINOW, Martha, "Between Vengeance and Forgiveness: Feminist Responses to Violent Injustice", *New England Law Review*, Vol. 32, Summer 1998.

MOYNIER, Gustave, "Note sur la Création d'une Institution Judiciaire Internationale Propre à Prévenir et à Réprimer les Infractions à la Convention de Genève", *Bulletin International des Sociétés de Secours aux Militaires Blessés*, Comité International, No. 11, Avril 1872.

MULLER-RAPPARD, Ekkehart, "Perspectives on the Council of Europe's Approach to the Issue of Basic Principles of Justice for Victims of Crime", *Human Rights Quarterly*, Vol. 12, No. 2, May 1990.

MURPHY, Sean D., "Contemporary Practice of the United States Relating to International Law", *The American Journal of International Law*, Vol. 93, No. 628, July 1999.

MUTTUKUMARU, Christopher, "Reparation to Victims", in *The International Criminal Court: The Making of the Rome Statute*, Roy S. Lee (ed.), Kluwer Law International, 1999.

NMEHIELLE, Vincent O. Orlu, "Towards an African Court of Human Rights: Structuring the Court", *Annual Survey of International & Comparative Law Golden Gate University School of Law*, Vol. 6, No. 27, Spring 2000.

NOWAK, Manfred, "The Inter-Relationship between the Covenant on Civil and Political Rights and the European Convention on Human Rights", in S. Vassilouni (ed.), *Aspects of the Protection of Individual and Social Rights*, 1995.

NOWAK, Manfred "The right of victims of gross human rights violations to reparation" in F. Coomans *et al.* (eds.) *Rendering Justice to the Vulnerable,* Kluwer Law International, The Hague (2000) at 203-225.

ODINKALU, Chidi Anselm, "The Role of Case and Complaints Procedures in the Reform of the African Regional Human Rights System", *African Human Rights Law Journal*, Vol. 1, No. 2, 2001.

OLIVER, Covey T., "The Jurisdiction (Competence) of States", in M. Bedjaoui (ed.), *International Law: Achievements and Prospects*, Martinus Nijhoff, 1991.

PACE, William, THIEROFF, Mark, "Participation of Non-Governmental Organizations", in Roy S. Lee (ed.), *The International Criminal Court: The Making of the Rome Statute*, Kluwer Law International, 1999.

PALMER, Laura, POSA, Cristina, "The Best-Laid Plans: Implementation of the Dayton Peace Accords in the Courtroom and on the Ground", *Harvard Human Rights Journal*, Vol. 12, Spring 1999.

PAUST, Jordan J., "Suing Karadzic", *Leiden Journal of International Law*, Vol. 10, 1997.

PASQUALUCCI, Jo M., "The Whole Truth and Nothing but the Truth: Truth Commissions, Impunity and the Inter-American Human Rights System", *Boston University International Law Journal,* Vol. 12, No. 321, Fall 1994.

PASQUALUCCI, Jo M., "The Inter-American Human Rights System: Establishing Precedents and Procedure in Human Rights Law", *The University of Miami Inter-American Law Review*, Vol. 26, No. 297, Winter 1995.

PASQUALUCCI, Jo M., "Victim Reparations in the Inter-American Human Rights System: A Critical Assessment of Current Practice and Procedure", *Michigan Journal of International Law*, Vol. 18, No. 1, Fall 1996.
PETERSON, Michael R., "Developing a Restorative Justice Programme", *Justice as Healing: A Newsletter on Aboriginal Concepts of Justice*, Vol. 5, No. 3, Fall 2000.
PFANNER, Toni, "The Establishment of a Permanent International Criminal Court: ICRC Expectations of the Rome Diplomatic Conference", *International Review of the Red Cross*, No. 322, 31 March 1998.
RASCHKA, Wolfgang, "National Reports on Crime Victim Compensation in Various Member States of the Council of Europe: Austria", in D. Greer (Ed.), *Compensating Crime Victims: A European Survey*, Ed. Iuscrim, Max-Planck Inst. Für Ausländisches und International Strafrecht, 1996.
REISMAN Michael, "Compensation for Human Rights Violations", in Randelzhofer and Tomuschat (eds.), *State Responsibility and the Individual: Reparation in Instances of Grave Violations of Human Rights*, Kluwer Law International, The Hague, 1999.
REISS, Rena H., "The Extradition of John Demjanjuk: War Crimes, Universality Jurisdiction, and the Political Offense Doctrine", *Cornell International Law Journal*, Vol. 20, No. 2, 1987.
RENDTORFF, Trutz, "Christian Concepts of the Responsible Self", in Leroy S. Rouner (ed.), *Human Rights and the World's Religions*, University of Notre Dame Press, Notre Dame, Indiana, 1988.
RESCIA, Victor M. Rodriguez, "Reparations in the Inter-American System for the Protection of Human Rights", *ILSA Journal of International & Comparative Law,* Vol. 5, No. 583, Summer 1999.
ROHT-ARRIAZA, Naomi, "State Responsibility to Investigate and Prosecute Grave Human Rights Violations in International Law", *California Law Review*, Vol. 78, No. 451, March 1990.
ROSENNE, Shabtai, "War Crimes and State Responsibility", *Israel Yearbook on Human Rights*, Vol. 24.
ROSS, Rubert, "Aboriginal Community Healing in Action: the Hollow Water", *Justice as Healing: A Newsletter on Aboriginal Concepts of Justice*, Native Law Centre at the University of Saskatchewan, Spring 1995.
SAITO, Taylor Natsu, "Symbolism Under Siege: Japanese American Redress and the 'Racing' of Arab Americans as 'Terrorists'", *Asian Law Journal*, Vol. 8, No. 1, May 2001.

SCALESE, Giancarlo, "Un Nuovo Passo Verso l'Ampliamento del Catalogo dei Diritti Umani: La Convenzione Europea sul Risarcimento delle Vittime di Crimini Violenti", *Comunità Internazionale*, Vol. 51, No. 3, 1996.

SCHACHTER, Oscar, "Compensation for Expropriation", *American Journal of International Law*, Vol. 78, No. 1, January 1984.

SHELTON, Dinah, "The Jurisprudence of the Inter American Court of Human Rights", *American University Journal of International Law & Policy*, Vol. 10, No. 333, Fall 1994.

SCHMIDT, Marcus G., "Follow-up Procedures to Individual Complaints and Periodic State Reporting Mechanisms", in G. Alfredsson, J. Grimheden, B. G. Ramcharan and A. de Zayas (eds.) *International Human Rights Monitoring Mechanisms*, The Raoul Wallenberg Institute Human Rights Library, Vol. 7, 2001.

SCHMIDT, Petra, "Japan's Wartime Compensation: Forced Labour", *Asia-Pacific Journal on Human Rights and the Law*, Vol. 2, 2000.

SCHRIML, Ron, "State, the Community and Restorative Justice", *Justice as Healing: A Newsletter on Aboriginal Concepts of Justice,* Vol. 1, No. 1, Spring 1996.

SCOVAZZI, Tullio, "The Application by Italian Courts of Human Rights Treaty Law", in B. Conforti and F. Francioni (eds.), *Enforcing International Human Rights in Domestic Courts*, Kluwer Law International, The Hague, 1997.

SNYDER, R. Neil, "Natural Law and Equity", in R. A. Newman (ed.), *Equity in the World's Legal Systems: A Comparative Study*, Etablissement Emile Bruylant, Brussels 1973.

SOKOL, Karen C., VINSON & ELKINS LLP, "Commentary on the Ivcher Bronstein Case", by Bernard H. Oxman (ed.), *The American Journal of International Law*, Vol. 95, No. 178, January 2001.

STAPP, Katherine, "That'll Be 10 Trillion Dollars in Back Wages, Please", *Terraviva*, 2000.

STEIN, Peter, "Equitable Principles in Roman Law", in R. A. Newman (ed.), *Equity in the World's Legal Systems: A Comparative Study*, Etablissement Emile Bruylant, Brussels, 1973.

SUNGA, Lyal S., "The First Indictments of the International Criminal Tribunal for Rwanda", *Human Rights Law Journal,* Vol. 18, No. 9-12, 1997.

SUNGA, Lyal S., "The Crimes within the Jurisdiction of the International Criminal Court (Part II, Articles 5-10)", *European Journal of Crime, Criminal Law and Criminal Justice,* Vol. 6/4, 1998.

SUNGA, Lyal S., "The Attitude of Asian Countries Towards the International Criminal Court", *Indian Yearbook of International Humanitarian and Refugee Law*, Vol. 2, 2002.

SUNGA, Lyal S., "Full Respect for the Rights of Suspect, Accused and Convict: from Nuremberg and Tokyo to the ICC", in Henzelin et al. (eds.), *Le Droit Pénal à l'Épreuve de l'Internationalisation*, University of Geneva, 2002.

TARDU, Maxime E., "The United Nations Convention against Torture and Other Cruel and Inhuman or Degrading Treatment or Punishment", *Nordic Journal of International Law*, Vol. 56, No. 4, 1987.

TOMUSCHAT, Christian, "A System of International Criminal Prosecution is Taking Shape", in *The ICJ Review*, Vol. 50, June 1993.

TONG, Yu, "Reparations for Former Comfort Women of World War II", *Harvard International Law Journal*, Vol. 36, No. 2, Spring 1995.

UDOMBANA, Nsongurua J., "Toward the African Court on Human and Peoples' Rights: Better Late Than Never", *Yale Human Rights & Development Law Journal*, Vol. 3, No. 45, 2000.

VAN DEN WYNGAERT, Christine, "National Reports on Crime Victim Compensation in Various Member States of the Council of Europe: Belgium", in D. Greer (ed.), *Compensating Crime Victims: A European Survey*, Ed. Iuscrim, Max-Planck Inst. Für Ausländisches und International Strafrecht, 1996.

VAN DYKE, Jon M., "The Fundamental Human Right to Prosecution and Compensation", *Denver Journal of International Law and Policy*, Vol. 9, No. 2, Spring 2001.

VAN SCHAACK, Beth, "In Defense of Civil Redress: The Domestic Enforcement of Human Rights Norms in the Context of the Proposed Hague Judgments Convention", *Harvard International Law Journal*, Vol. 42, No. 1, Winter 2001.

VON HEBEL, Herman, ROBINSON, Darryl, "Crimes Within the Jurisdiction of the Court", in Roy S. Lee (ed.), *The International Criminal Court: The Making of the Rome Statute, Issues, Negotiations, Results*, Kluwer Law International, 1999.

WILDE, Ralph, "NGO Proposals for an Asia-Pacific Human Rights System", *Yale Human Rights & Development Law Journal*, Vol. 1, No. 137, 1998.

WILLIAMS, Glanville, "The Aims of the Law of Tort", *Current Legal Problems*, Vol. 137, 1951.

WILSON, Richard J., PERLIN, Jan, "The Inter-American Human Rights System: Activities During 1999 through October 2000", *American University International Law Review*, Vol. 16, No. 315, 2001.

WOLFRUM, Rüdiger, "The Decentralized Prosecution of International Offences Through National Courts", *Israel Yearbook on Human Rights*, Vol. 24.

YAZZIE, Robert, "The Navajo Response to Crime", *Justice as Healing: A Newsletter on Aboriginal Concepts of Justice*, Vol. 3, No. 2, Summer 1998.

YAZZIE, Robert, "Healing as Justice: the American Experience", *Justice as Healing: A Newsletter on Aboriginal Concepts of Justice*, Spring 1995.

ZEDNER, Lucia, "England", in Eser and Walther (eds.), *Reparation in Criminal Law: International Perspectives,* Ed. Iuscrim Max-Planck Inst. Für Ausländisches und International Strafrecht, 1996.

ZOGLIN, Kathryn, "United Nations Action Against Slavery: A Critical Evaluation", *Human Rights Quarterly*, Vol. 8, No. 2, 1986.

J. REPORTS / STUDIES / SEMINARS / CONFERENCES / SYMPOSIA / OTHERS (chronological order)

Report of the Interregional Preparatory Meeting for the Seventh United Nations Congress on the Prevention of Crime and the Treatment of Offenders on Topic 3: Victims of Crime, Ottawa, 9-13 July 1984, A/CONF.121/IPM/4 of 10 September 1984.

Seminar on the Right to Restitution, Compensation and Rehabilitation for Victims of Gross Violations of Human Rights and Fundamental Freedoms, Maastricht, 1992, Special No. 12, 264 p.

Guidelines for the Assessment of General Damages in Personal Injury Cases, Judicial Studies Board, Fifth Ed., Blackstone press Ltd., London (1992).

Report No. 6 of the Community Law Reform Committee of the Australian Capital Territory, June 1993, Internet at http://actg.canberra.edu.au/actag/Reports/CLRC.R6.Report6c2.html.

The United Nations and El Salvador, 1990-1995, The United Nations Blue Books Series, Vol. IV, UN Department of Public Information, New York (1995).

International Responses to Traumatic Stress: Humanitarian, Human Rights, Justice, Peace and Development Contributions, Collaborative Actions and Future Initiatives, Unsymbolled (1996).

Report No. 36/96, Case No. 10.843, Inter-American Commission on Human Rights, 15 October 1996.

Proposals of the Hague Conference and their Effect on Efforts to Enforce International Human Rights Through Adjudication, Working Document No. 17 of the Hague Conference on Private International Law, Special Commission on International Jurisdiction and the Effects of Foreign Judgments in Civil and Commercial Matters.

Multilateral Instruments - Justice for Victims: Ensuring Effective Enforcement Abroad of Court Decisions Concerning Reparations, Amnesty International Report, IOR 53/02/99, June 1999.

The International Criminal Court - Reparations to Victims of Crimes (Article 75 of the Rome Statute) and the Trust Fund (Article 79), Dinah L. Shelton and Thordis Ingadottir, Centre on International Cooperation, New York University (1999).

The International Criminal Court: Ensuring an Effective Role for Victims - Memorandum for the Paris seminar, April 1999, Amnesty International Report, IOR 40/06/99, April 1999.

Asian Human Rights Charter: A Peoples' Charter, published on the occasion of the 50th Anniversary of the Universal Declaration of Human, Asian Human Rights Commission, Hong Kong, China.

Indigenous Systems and Tribal Society, paper by A. Pecos Melton, the American Indian Development Associates, Internet at http://www.opj.usdoj.gob/nij/rest-just/ch1/indigenous.htm.

The Victims and Witnesses Unit (Article 43(6) of the Rome Statute): A Discussion Paper, Thordis Ingadottir, Françoise Ngendahayo and Patricia V. Sellers, PICT, March 2000.

Compensating Victims with Guilty Money, interview with Carla del Ponte, chief Prosecutor of the two international tribunals, in *Judicial Diplomacy: Chronicles and Reports on International Criminal Justice*, The Hague, 9 June 2000.

Human Rights Watch World Report 2000.

The Human Rights Chamber for Bosnia and Herzegovina Annual Report 2000, internet at http://www.gwdg.de/~ujvr/hrch/00annrep.htm.

The Associated Press Special Report Bridge at No Gun Ri (2000).

Paper by Theodor van Boven, presented on 17 February 2000 to the Expert Seminar on Remedies Available to the Victims of Racial Discrimination, Xenophobia and Related Intolerance and on Good National Practices, HR/GVA/WCR/SEM.1/2000/BP.5.

The Trust fund for Victims (Art. 79 of the Rome Statute): A Discussion Paper, Project on International Courts and Tribunals (PICT), ICC Discussion Paper No. 3, February 2001.

International Criminal Court: Ensuring an Effective Trust Fund for Victims, Amnesty International Report, IOR 40/005/2001 of 1 September 2001.

The ICC: Concerns at the eight session of the Preparatory Commission (24 September to 5 October 2001), Amnesty International Report, IOR 40/006/2001 of September 2001.

US Department of the Army Inspector General, No Gun Ri Review, January 2001.

Council of Europe's Explanatory Report to Protocol No. 11 to the Convention for the Protection of Human Rights and Fundamental Freedoms, internet at http://conventions.coe.int/Treaty/en/Reports/ Html/155.htm

Report of the Special Commission on the Draft Hague Convention, internet at ftp://hcch.net/doc/jdgmpd11.doc.

INDEX

A

Aboriginal people . 1, 33, 34, 103
Abuse of justice 20
Abuse of power 6, 89, 168
169, 219, 228
Access to court 88, 147
Achille Lauro 43
Actio popularis 154
Affirmative action 172, 174
Afghanistan 65, 159
Africa . . 128, 129, 132, 172-175
African Commission on Human
and Peoples' Rights . . . 129-132
African Court on Human
and Peoples' Rights . . . 132, 133
Aggression 7, 8, 10, 20, 143
196, 212, 214
231, 235, 242
al Qaeda 65
Alfonsín, Raúl 104, 105
Amendment of domestic
legislation 88, 142, 188, 189
Amnesties . . . 104, 105, 108, 118
120, 121, 159, 190
Apartheid 1, 9, 48, 75, 107
108, 128, 172
Apologies . . 1, 4, 33, 37, 97-103
172, 173, 176, 177
184, 225, 249, 251-252
Appia, Louis 193
Aquilian Law 22
Arbitral tribunals 80, 81, 83
84, 90, 91, 95
Arbitrary detention 58, 65
75, 179
Argentina 51, 56, 103-105
122, 134
ASEAN 163
Asian values 160-162
Asian Woman's Fund 100
Australia 1, 48, 103
243, 245, 246
Aut dedere aut judicare . . 40, 41
48, 57
Authoritarianism 159
Avril, Prosper 58
Aylwin, Patricio 105

B

Bahrain 212
Bangladesh 1, 102
Belarus 125
Belgium 27, 30, 49
Biblical law 17
Brazil 97
Bulgaria 125
Burundi 132

C

Cambodia 159, 160, 237
Canada 33, 81, 243, 244
Cardozo, Fernando Henrique . 97
CAT 124
Catholic Church 97
CEDAW 89
Central American
Court of Justice 83
CERD 127
Chad 103, 129

Chiang Kai-Shek 86
Chile 43-45, 103, 105, 120, 134, 176
China . 48, 85, 86, 100, 101, 125
Christianity 17
CICC 213
Cicero 19
Circle of justice 32, 34
Civil law 5, 19, 21, 22, 39, 54, 55, 67, 114, 203, 214, 215, 225, 240, 242
Class actions . 57, 58, 60, 63-65, 96, 101, 216, 227
Colombia 118-120, 122, 134, 135, 213
Colonial domination . . 10, 75, 98, 101, 173
Comfort women 1, 100, 101, 249
Common law . . . 30, 31, 34, 114, 225, 240, 242
Compensation
- compensation by the community . . . 16
- domestic compensation schemes . . 27, 31, 68, 98, 100, 104, 148, 149, 169
- double compensation 21
- monetary compensation 2, 17, 20, 21, 25, 28, 35, 62, 63, 77, 88, 90, 96, 103, 104, 111, 113, 116, 122, 146, 152, 156, 158, 187, 188, 201, 224, 241, 250
- State compensation . . 23, 26-32, 68, 81-88, 105, 117-119, 121-123, 131, 138, 172, 190
- subsidiary compensation 28, 30, 31

Corporations 69, 78, 92-94, 173, 229, 252
Costa Rica 83, 134
Council of Europe 26, 28, 30, 153
Counterfeiting of monetary currency 10
Crimes against humanity . . . 1, 2, 7-9, 37, 39, 40, 46-48, 51, 52, 60, 61, 73-75, 77, 96, 99, 105, 109, 158, 159, 173, 196, 197, 212, 214, 231, 235, 237, 242-244
Crimes against internationally protected persons 10
Crimes against the King's peace 23
Crimes under international law . . . 3, 4, 6-11, 13, 26, 35, 37, 39-43, 46-53, 56, 57, 60-69, 73, 74-78, 84, 87, 91, 95, 96, 103, 104, 109, 111, 115, 116, 123, 124, 132, 139, 146, 159, 160, 168, 174, 179-181, 185, 186, 189-191, 193, 195-197, 212, 214, 216, 235, 236, 240, 242, 243, 247, 249-253
Cuba 125
Culpa 21, 22
Cultural traditions 13, 143, 161, 164
Czech Republic 97, 125

D

Damages
material damages . 21, 23
29, 94, 138, 139
142-144, 149
152, 155, 158
178, 190, 250
moral damages .. 21, 29
94, 138, 139
142-144, 149
152, 155, 156
178, 190, 224, 250
punitive damages ... 54
58-60, 63-65
76, 139, 225, 240
Death penalty . 14-17, 24, 52, 57
del Ponte, Carla 203, 205
Delict 20-22, 37, 70
Democratic Republic
of the Congo 49, 243, 246
Denial of justice 74, 75
Deportation . 9, 84, 90, 179, 190
Diplomatic protection 79, 91, 92
Disappearances 1, 9, 58, 65
75, 90, 104-106
111, 116, 118-120
136, 137, 139, 140
142-144, 156, 157
170, 179, 190
Divine Law 15
Dolus 21, 22
Double criminality 44
Drug trafficking 10, 48, 75
Dufour, Guillaume Henri ... 193
Dunant, Henri 193
Duress 22, 198
Duty to investigate 116, 117
120, 121, 139, 140, 142
144, 166, 184, 250

E

East Timor 58, 83, 159
Ecuador 122, 134
EFTA 67
Egyptian civilization 15
El Salvador ... 83, 103, 106, 107
Enforced prostitution 9, 100
Enforced sterilization 9
Enforcement of judgments ... 11
55, 59, 62-64, 66-68
71, 72, 74, 76, 77
78, 170, 182, 188
195, 238, 239, 245
England 23, 245
Enlai, Zhou 86
Equity 22, 27, 138, 240
Ethiopia 103
Ethnic cleansing 71, 172
Europe 23, 25, 26-31
51, 68, 146
European Court of
Human Rights . 57, 88, 146-148
152, 153, 155-159, 186-188
Exhaustion of local remedies . 53
83, 92, 117, 130, 147, 151
Expropriation 126
Extermination 9
Extradition 41, 43-45
48, 77, 181
Extrajudicial killing 54, 57
58, 60
Extraterritorial jurisdiction 44, 70

F

Fact-finding commissions .. 103
109, 111, 130
Fair trial 62, 77, 143, 148

Fines 23, 156, 224, 227-230, 239, 243-246
Forced labour 96, 101
Forced pregnancy 9, 65
Forfeiture ... 220, 224, 227-230, 238, 239, 243-246
Forgiveness 33, 35, 37
Forum non conveniens ... 56, 76
France 81, 96, 186, 213, 216, 223, 243
Franco-Prussian War .. 193, 194
Fraud 22
Friendly settlements 77, 101, 122, 131, 135, 142, 145, 251
Furtum manifestum 20

G

Garzon, Baltasar 43
Genocide .. 1, 2, 8, 9, 37, 39-41, 43-48, 52, 60-62, 71, 73-75, 99, 109, 160, 179, 195-197, 202, 208, 212, 214, 231, 235, 237, 242
Germ Warfare Unit 731 1, 85, 86
Germany 29, 52, 83, 84, 87, 96, 97, 168, 186, 213, 243
Grave breaches of the Geneva Conventions 8, 9, 41, 48, 52, 82, 197
Greece 42, 204, 213
Guarantees of non-repetition . 76, 113, 145, 157, 184, 190, 225, 250
Guatemala ... 83, 140, 143, 144

H

Habitual residence principle . 68, 69, 71
Haiti 57, 58, 103
Henry I 23
Henry II 23
Hijacking 10, 75
Historical crimes 173
Hittite Laws 15
Holy Scriptures 17
Homicide 17, 24, 43, 96
Honduras 83, 103, 137, 138
Hostage-taking ... 10, 44, 57, 90
Howard, John 103
Human Rights Chamber for Bosnia and Herzegovina 185-189
Human Rights Committee ... 98, 104, 113-125, 146, 156, 249
Human trafficking 9, 175
Hun Sen 160

I

ICRC 193
ICTR 3, 8, 62, 95, 196-205, 207-211, 215, 216, 222, 233, 234, 239
ICTY 3, 8, 95, 150, 196, 197-207, 209-211, 215, 216, 222, 233, 234, 239, 252
ILC ... 7, 76, 80, 86, 87, 99, 195
Immunity 45, 49, 57, 58, 61, 62, 86, 88, 147
Impunity 35, 49, 51, 88, 107, 121, 141, 159, 160, 164, 183, 217
India 159, 162, 165-167

Indigenous people . . 32, 33, 103
126, 171
Indonesia 58, 100, 159-161, 163
Iniuria 20, 22
Injury
Material injury . 29, 139
Mental injury . . . 6, 9, 93
168, 181, 228, 241
Moral injury 29, 62
119, 139, 143
Physical injury . . 6, 7, 9
62, 74, 75, 143
168, 181, 228
Inter-American Commission
on Human Rights . 134, 135, 141
142, 145
Inter-American
Conference 133, 134
Inter-American Court
of Human Rights 133-145
International compensation
commission 207, 252
International Criminal Court
Admissibility 220
221, 236
Complementarity 73
230, 234, 243
Hearing for
reparations 220
Investigation . . 216-221
232, 233, 236
238, 239, 242
Pre-Trial
Chamber 218-220
232, 238
Prosecutor 159
216-222, 224
232-234, 238, 242
Trust Fund 89, 214, 215
222, 225-227
229-235, 242
244, 253
Victim and Witness'
Unit . 215, 221, 231-235
victims'
representation . 204, 217
220, 221, 224, 234
International Military
Tribunal at Nuremberg . . . 7, 195
International Military
Tribunal at Tokyo . . . 7, 86, 100
International Prize Court 83
Iran 65, 80, 81
Iran-US Claims Tribunal 80
Iraq 65, 89-91, 93-95, 212
Ishii, Shiro 86
Islam 18
Israel 17, 49, 51, 52
55, 115, 116, 125
Italy 31, 212, 213, 243, 246

J

Japan 1, 2, 85, 86, 97, 98
100-102, 173
Japanese Americans 97, 98
Jewish tradition 17
Jus gentium 47

K

Karadzic, Radovan 54, 56, 60-62
Kashmir 159
Kean, William 98
Kelsen, Hans 19, 20, 37, 38
Khmer Rouge 159, 160
Kim Jong-il 98
Koizumi, Junichiro 98, 100

Korean War 98
Kuwait 88, 90-95, 148

L

Lebanon 50, 116, 212
Lee Kuan Yew 161
Lex talionis 15, 20, 22
Liaoning massacre 85
Libya 129, 212
Lis pendens 76
Locus standi 27, 83
Loss of profit 29, 94, 156
Lump sum agreements 85
97, 228

M

Macapagal-Arroyo, Gloria . . . 60
Mahathir, Mohamad . . . 161, 162
Malawi 125, 132
Malaysia 160-162
Marcos, Ferdinand 58-60
64, 249
Maunoir, Théodore 193
Mauritania 130, 131
Mediation 175, 251, 252
Mercenarism 10, 76
Mesopotamian civilizations . . 15
Mexican Claims Commission 80
Mexico 1, 106
Middle Ages 1, 23
Migrant workers . . 126, 175, 187
Miscarriage of justice 114
126, 136
Mixed claims
commissions 80, 92
Mongolia 163
Moynier, Gustave 193-195
Murder . 1, 9, 15, 17, 43-45, 140
Myanmar 159

N

National human rights
commissions 105, 162
National minorities 83, 84
176, 187
Nationality principle 42, 46
48, 50, 52, 72, 91, 92
Native North American
Indian justice system . 25, 32-34
Natural Law 18
Nazism . . 51, 52, 77, 78, 96, 168
Negligence 22, 119, 166
Nepal 159
New Testament 17
NGOs 2, 4, 62, 100, 104
114, 129, 132, 133, 147
153, 163-165, 185, 187
213-217, 225, 228, 229
Nigeria 130
No Gun Ri 98, 249
North Korea 98
Nuremberg Trials 7, 195

O

Organization of
African Unity (OAU) . . 129, 132
Organization of American
States (OAS) 133-135, 145

P

Pakistan 1, 102, 159
Palestine 49, 50, 55, 92, 115, 116
Paraguay 54, 63, 80
Pardon 104, 107
Paris Principles 162

Partie civile 30, 39, 67, 214, 215
Passive personality principle 42-46, 51
Penalty 24, 227, 245, 246
Persons with disabilities 166, 182, 216
Peru 118, 122, 134
Petitions 84, 115, 135, 141, 144, 151-154, 166
Philippine war damage commission 80
Philippines 60, 64, 103, 163
Pinochet, Augusto . . . 42-46, 49, 147, 249
Piracy 7, 47, 50, 61, 75
Pope John Paul II 97
Portugal 213
Praetorial law 21-23
Private justice 19
Protective measures 70, 71, 209-211, 216, 220, 233-235, 238
Protective principle . . 42, 43, 51
Provisional measures 70, 71, 125, 133, 137, 187, 188, 198, 200
Provisional remedies 31

R

Racial discrimination . . 126-128, 172-178
Rape 1, 7, 9, 65, 102, 150, 156, 157, 190, 202, 208, 209
Reagan, Ronald 97
Reconciliation . 2, 24, 35, 37, 95, 100, 103, 107-109, 251, 252
Recovery of damages . . . 4, 5, 54, 63, 166
Refugees 49, 98, 189, 249
Rehabilitation 1, 4, 6, 13, 25, 32, 34, 37, 59, 62, 76, 81, 89, 102, 108, 113, 121, 124, 137, 145, 156, 158, 170, 172, 174, 176, 179, 180, 182-185, 190, 211, 223-225, 250, 252
Reparations
- Inter-State reparations 79-91, 96, 111
- Partial reparations . . 152
- Post-conflict reparations 2, 102
- Private reparations . . 19
- Reparations from the offender 25, 26, 31, 32, 169
- State-based reparations . . . 11, 79, 80, 83, 95, 99, 104
- Symbolic reparations 65, 95, 105, 184

Republika Srpska 186, 188
Restitutio in integrum 5, 22, 28, 80, 81, 138, 156
Restitution 4-6, 15, 17, 22, 25, 29, 33, 62, 66, 70, 71, 76, 81, 89, 96, 97, 99, 100, 113, 118, 137, 138, 168, 169, 171, 174, 179, 180, 182-184, 186, 188-190, 195, 196, 198-200, 202-204, 210, 211, 223-225, 232, 239, 247, 249, 250
Restorative justice 5, 11, 13, 24, 25, 32-37, 95, 109, 175, 184, 214, 247, 249, 251, 252

Retaliation 15, 20
Retribution 11, 13, 14
17, 18, 22-25, 32
34-37, 63, 211, 214
Revenge 14, 17, 19, 34
Roman law 1, 18, 19, 21
Russian Federation 186, 213
Rwanda 1, 3, 39, 62
103, 132, 185, 189
196, 197, 202
204, 208, 237

S

Sabra and Shatila 50
Satisfaction . . . 14, 22, 52, 62, 76
81, 99, 101, 113, 127
142, 145, 149, 152
155, 156, 158, 174, 175
177, 178, 180, 187
208, 225, 250, 252
Senegal 130, 132
September 11 65
Sexual slavery 9, 100, 101
Sexual violence . 9, 29, 101-102
209, 210, 216, 234
Sharon, Ariel 49
Sierra Leone 120
Singapore 160-162
Slavery . . 7, 9, 15, 16, 47, 48, 75
96, 101, 131, 172-175
177-179, 185, 226
Social solidarity 27, 30, 252
South Africa 1, 103, 107
108, 243
South Korea 98, 100, 101
162, 249
Spain 43-45, 97, 147
Spanish Civil War 97
Sri Lanka 159
State responsibility 3, 4, 11
79, 80, 87, 89
90, 91, 99, 214, 217
Status quo ante 5, 23, 28
33, 35, 140, 188
Statutory limitations 55, 173, 174
Submarine cables 10
Sudan 130, 213
Suharto 161
Summary executions . 57, 58, 65
90, 150, 169, 170, 179, 190
Switzerland 52, 59
Syria 213

T

Taiwan 86, 100
Taliban 65
Territorial jurisdiction . . . 27, 28
33, 41, 48, 54, 56
Terrorism 10, 31, 43, 44, 47
48, 57, 65, 75, 76
Torture 9, 10, 44-46, 48, 49
51, 53-60, 62, 65, 75
88, 90, 105, 111, 116
117, 121, 123, 124-126
131, 135, 136, 139-142
146, 148-152, 156-158
162, 166, 169, 172
179, 185, 187, 190
202, 208, 226
Trials *in absentia* 50
Tribal courts 33
Tribal mediator 33
Truth commissions 103-106, 108
109, 176, 249
Turkey 149, 150-152, 157

U

Uganda 103, 132
Ukraine 125
UN Charter 89, 128
UN Commission on
Human Rights . . . 107, 160, 162
163, 179-184, 223, 249
251, 252
UN Security Council . . 8, 89, 90
91, 92, 94, 106, 197
201, 204, 205, 207
208, 219, 239
UN Voluntary Fund
for torture victims 172, 185, 226
UN Voluntary Trust Fund
on Slavery 185, 226
UNCC 90-95
UNDP 92, 185
UNHCR 92
United Kingdom . . 30, 31, 42-46
48, 88, 96, 147, 148
186, 213, 223, 243, 244
United States . 33, 42, 43, 52-63
65, 80, 81, 86, 96-98, 101
117, 129, 134, 172, 249
Universal jurisdiction 42-52
74, 180, 181
UNRWA 92
Uruguay 103, 116, 117, 121, 134
US-German joint trust fund . 96

V

Vichy 96
Victims
Ascendants 7, 32, 58, 149
Children victims 1, 9, 98
102, 103, 126, 139, 140
155, 175, 213, 216, 253
Definition of victim . . . 7
168, 169, 181, 216, 228
Descendants 7, 32
Future victims 155
Indirect victims . . 7, 135
154, 155, 190, 250
Next-of-kin 7, 24
138, 142, 154, 190
Potential victims . 7, 151
154, 155
Victims' dependands . . 7
124, 139, 170, 181, 228
Victims' heirs 23
Victim's family . 1, 7, 17
33, 55, 65, 77, 78
96, 98, 102, 106-108
118-120, 126, 138-142
144, 166, 170, 181
185, 190, 214, 215
225-231, 238, 244
249, 250
Vindication 5

W

War crimes . 1, 2, 7-9, 37, 39, 40
46, 47, 51, 52, 60
61, 66, 73-75, 77
99-101, 109, 173, 196
212, 214, 231, 235
237, 242-244
War damages 83
Witnesses 21, 54, 56, 203
209-211, 215, 216
219-222, 231-235
238, 247
World Conference
Against Racism . . 126, 172-178
World Conference
on Human Rights 163, 171

World War I 84
World War II 1, 7, 48, 66
85, 86, 96, 97
99-101, 173

Y

Yemen 213

Z

Zimbabwe 103

MIX
Papier aus verantwortungsvollen Quellen
Paper from responsible sources
FSC® C105338

If you have any concerns about our products,
you can contact us on
ProductSafety@springernature.com

In case Publisher is established outside the EU,
the EU authorized representative is:
Springer Nature Customer Service Center GmbH
Europaplatz 3, 69115 Heidelberg, Germany

Printed by Libri Plureos GmbH
in Hamburg, Germany